This boc

30 M.

PSYCHOTHERAPY:
AN ECLECTIC-INTEGRATIVE APPROACH
SECOND EDITION

Psychotherapy:
An Eclectic-Integrative Approach

Second Edition

Sol L. Garfield
Washington University

A WILEY-INTERSCIENCE PUBLICATION

JOHN WILEY & SONS, INC.

New York • Chichester • Brisbane • Toronto • Singapore

This text is printed on acid-free paper.

Copyright © 1995 by John Wiley & Sons, Inc.

This publication is designed to provide accurate and authoritative
information in regard to the subject matter covered. It is sold
with the understanding that the publisher is not engaged in
rendering professional services. If legal, accounting, medical,
psychological, or any other expert assistance is required, the
services of a competent professional person should be sought.

Library of Congress Cataloging-in-Publication Data:

Garfield, Sol L. (Sol Louis), 1918–
    Psychotherapy : an eclectic-integrative approach / Sol. L.
Garfield. — 2nd ed.
      p. cm. — (Wiley series on personality processes)
    Includes bibliographical references and index.
    ISBN 0-471-59556-X (cloth : alk. paper)
    1. Eclectic psychotherapy. 2. Psychotherapy. I. Series.
    [DNLM: 1. Psychotherapy. WM 420 G231p 1995]
RC489.E24G37 1995
616.89′ 14—dc20
DNLM/DLC
for Library of Congress   94-38838

Printed in the United States of America

10 9 8 7 6 5 4 3 2 1

Series Preface

This series of books is addressed to behavioral scientists interested in the nature of human personality. Its scope should prove pertinent to personality theorists and researchers as well as to clinicians concerned with applying an understanding of personality processes to the amelioration of emotional difficulties in living. To this end, the series provides a scholarly integration of theoretical formulations, empirical data, and practical recommendations.

Six major aspects of studying and learning about human personality can be designated: personality theory, personality structure and dynamics, personality development, personality assessment, personality change, and personality adjustment. In exploring these aspects of personality, the books in the series discuss a number of distinct but related subject areas: the nature and implications of various theories of personality; personality characteristics that account for consistencies and variations in human behavior; the emergence of personality processes in children and adolescents; the use of interviewing and testing procedures to evaluate individual differences in personality; efforts to modify personality styles through psychotherapy, counseling, behavior therapy, and other methods of influence; and patterns of abnormal personality functioning that impair individual competence.

IRVING B. WEINER

University of South Florida
Tampa, Florida

Preface

I was very pleased at the positive reception that the first edition of this book received and I was particularly pleased that the book was published in German and Japanese editions. An eclectic psychotherapy approach was recognized as being a meaningful and useful approach to the practice of psychotherapy, and this was personally gratifying.

In the years since the first edition was published, an eclectic approach to psychotherapy has remained popular and an increased interest in the integration of theoretical approaches to psychotherapy also has been evident. These developments will be discussed in the first chapter. It was the need to organize and integrate my own views and understanding of the psychotherapeutic process that led me to write the first edition.

The proliferation of the psychotherapies noted prior to 1980 has continued without abatement. Thus, there have been two counterbalancing developments during the same period of time—proliferation and integration. Another development that has become more pronounced in the past 15 to 20 years has been the increased emphasis on briefer forms of psychotherapy and the relative decrease in importance of long-term psychotherapy. A variety of factors that have played a role in these changes will be discussed in this book.

Changes and modifications have also taken place in the area of psychotherapy research. The research evaluating the effectiveness of psychotherapy while becoming more sophisticated has also become more time-consuming and complex. The introduction of therapy manuals for the training of the psychotherapists in research projects in order to insure treatment integrity is one example of this development. The use of meta-analysis to review a large group of research studies, introduced less than 20 years ago, has now become the accepted procedure in reviewing studies of psychotherapy.

Although there have been many developments, some features of psychotherapy have remained the same. A number of books on psychotherapy continue to be devoted to the description of just one form of psychotherapy, be it psychoanalysis or behavior therapy. At the same time, a number of introductory textbooks on psychotherapy consist of relatively brief presentations of 10 to 20 different forms of psychotherapy written by proponents or advocates of the particular approaches or orientations selected. As I stated in the preface to the first edition, "I personally have found neither type of book really adequate for instructing students who are beginning their study of psychotherapy. The first type presents only a single theoretical view; and the other emphasizes the unique features of several schools of psychotherapy without any attempt to synthesize or delineate their common factors" (p. vii).

It was this situation that also motivated me to write the 1980 book, *Psychotherapy: An Eclectic Approach,* a book that included emphases and procedures drawn from a variety of approaches. I emphasized those features that appeared to me to be common to most forms of psychotherapy, but included others as well. The bases for my selection were the empirical literature where available and relevant, and my own clinical and supervisory experience as a practitioner and teacher of psychotherapy.

The second edition retains the same orientation and emphases as the first—an eclectic and integrative approach to psychotherapy emphasizing both the factors that appear to be shared by most major therapeutic orientations as well as specific factors or procedures that have been shown to be effective in the treatment of certain specific disorders. I am happy to note also that in the years since then, there has been a greater acknowledgment of the existence and importance of the therapeutic factors common to most forms of psychotherapy.

As in the first edition, I have had recourse to a variety of empirical findings as well as to the published views of many investigators and workers in the field of psychotherapy. Where possible, I have indicated the varied sources for the statements and observations offered. Some chapters and chapter titles have been omitted or modified and others added. I have continued to use the terms "client" and "patient" interchangeably to reflect the usage of the various professions engaged in psychotherapy. I have also tried to make the actual process of psychotherapy the centerpiece of the book, and I sincerely hope that the present edition will also be useful in the training of psychotherapists and mental health counselors as well as of interest to more experienced therapists.

I am grateful to the many students who have taken psychotherapy courses and practica with me; to the graduate students, interns, and residents whom I have supervised in psychotherapy; and to those who have attended my lectures and workshops. I have learned much from these experiences, further reinforcing the fact that learning is a lifetime process.

Finally, I want to acknowledge with thanks the support of my wife, Amy, in this as well as all my professional endeavors, and the always congenial cooperation of Judith Knese who faithfully and correctly transcribed my handwritten drafts into legible type.

SOL L. GARFIELD

St. Louis, Missouri
March 1995

Contents

CHAPTER 1

Introduction

The field of psychotherapy has had an interesting development. In several respects, the development is somewhat unique. There is a large number of different forms of psychotherapy, but there is no single profession of psychotherapy. Rather there are many kinds of professionals, as well as nonprofessionals, engaged in diverse types of counseling and psychotherapy. Psychotherapy was a relatively small and obscure field when I first entered it more than 50 years ago. It was largely influenced by the views of Sigmund Freud and his followers. Initially, the only intensive training in psychotherapy was that offered in the official psychoanalytic training institutes. Carl Rogers published his *Counseling and Psychotherapy* in 1942, which offered a very different approach to psychotherapy. However, Rogers' client-centered approach, first referred to as *nondirective therapy,* appealed mainly to counselors, counseling psychologists, and some clinical psychologists.

However, in the years that followed, the number of new forms of psychotherapy increased drastically. I found this development to be both puzzling and somewhat disturbing. I began to collect and list the names of these new forms of psychotherapy as they appeared. By the mid-1960s, I had accumulated over 60 different approaches to psychotherapy. I can recall discussing these different therapeutic approaches as a surprising development in a talk I gave at the University of Colorado Medical School at that time. However, what has occurred since that time makes the earlier development look like a warm-up exercise. In the 1970s, a report from the National Institute of Mental Health made reference to the existence of over 130 different forms of psychotherapy (Report of the Research Task Force of the National Institute of Mental Health, 1975). And, this burst of unusual creative efforts in psychotherapy has continued. Just five years later, Herink (1980) published *The Psychotherapy Handbook. The A to Z Guide to More than 250 Therapies in Use Today.* A few years later, Kazdin (1986) made reference to the existence of over 400 therapeutic techniques.

In a previous publication, I commented on this development as follows:

> Needless to say, if this rate of increase continues, at some point we will have a different form of psychotherapy for every person in the United States. This

1

manifestation of the free enterprise system, perhaps, may epitomize true democracy, but whether it is an ideal situation for psychotherapy is another matter. (Garfield, 1989, p. 19)

Ford (1991) has also commented on this proliferation of the psychotherapies in a recent review in *Contemporary Psychology:*

> The growing popularity and profitability of psychotherapy has resulted in a proliferation of concepts, explanations, and methods. The popularity of different approaches appears to wax and wane as a function as much of their creator's charisma and promotional effectiveness as of the accumulation of solid evidence of each approach's effectiveness. Periodic efforts to simplify the picture through comparative analyses of different approaches have not slowed this growth industry. Students trying to find their way through the maze of proposals are often confused and overwhelmed. (Ford, 1991, p. 250)

Such diversity is confusing to people entering the field. It is equally confusing for individuals outside the field. There can be too much of a good thing. This diversity raises some basic and intriguing questions concerning what is really important in psychotherapy. In other words, what are the variables or processes that lead to positive change in psychotherapy? Does one school of thought have a more correct view of these fundamental processes, or are all approaches either viewing different parts of the elephant or characterizing similar phenomena in different ways? The theories are quite diverse with various emphases. Thus, there are psychodynamic approaches, cognitive approaches, behavioral approaches, humanistic approaches, and so on. Is one actually more beneficial than another? Are some more effective with certain types of individuals or with certain types of problems than with others, and if so, how do we tell which is which? These questions were raised in the first edition, and although we still have few definitive answers, the research findings of the past decade and a half do provide some tentative answers. Although, not everyone would agree with this latter statement.

Another aspect of psychotherapy that has influenced my own thinking about the psychotherapeutic process is the difference between what therapists say they do in therapy and what they actually do. There are frequent discrepancies between what therapists say about a particular session in psychotherapy and what appeared to have taken place on the basis of a recording of the session. Apart from the obvious occurrences of memory loss and subjective distortion on the part of the therapist, there is also the problem generated by the exclusive use of concepts and abstract words in particular schools of psychotherapy, as well as in psychotherapy generally. If the therapist uses such terms as transference, resistance, affect, defensiveness, relationship, and insight, there may be serious problems in communicating what behaviors, cognitions, and affects are actually being described and what specific interactions actually took place.

Such developments and observations have played an important part in my attempts to understand what appears to occur in the psychotherapeutic interaction. They have been manifested in one guise or another in discussions I have had about psychotherapy, in my teaching and supervision in this area, and in several post-doctoral workshops I have conducted on issues in psychotherapy and on the practice of brief psychotherapy. This book is an attempt to come to grips with these problems and to present a reasonably organized view of psychotherapy. The book's subtitle, *An Eclectic-Integrative Approach,* indicates that no particular school or system of psychotherapy is exclusive to the presentation. Beyond this, the term eclectic does not have any precise meaning (Garfield & Kurtz, 1977). What it does *not* signify for the present volume is a presentation simply of a number of different approaches or schools of psychotherapy. Rather, it represents an attempt to order what appear to be significant variables or phenomena in psychotherapy with recourse to research data wherever possible. Personal beliefs, hunches, and biases of the author will be identified as such whenever they are presented.

Although there are many different forms of psychotherapy, it is quite common to refer to psychotherapy as if it were one type of uniform process. It would be more accurate to refer to the psychological therapies. Nevertheless, in both discussions about psychotherapy per se or when discussing the relative merits of psychotherapy and pharmacotherapy, it has been commonplace to use the simple designation, psychotherapy. Kiesler (1967, 1971) has referred to this as the "uniformity myth" and includes generalized statements of "the patient" and "the therapist" as also conveying the uniformity myth. It is well for the reader to keep this in mind for there will be frequent references to the generalized terms of client, therapist, and therapy.

Although some well-known schools or orientations within psychotherapy will be discussed in Chapter 2, some initial comments can be offered here. First, while such popular orientations as psychoanalysis and its derivatives and behavior therapy have had a marked influence on the developments within the field, a majority of practitioners do not appear to follow any particular school exclusively, or to limit themselves to the theories and procedures of just one theoretical orientation. For example, in a 1970s survey of 855 clinical psychologists, over half of them indicated that they were eclectics (Garfield & Kurtz, 1976). Since that time, a number of additional surveys have been conducted, and although the percentage of individuals identifying themselves as eclectics has varied from study to study, the eclectic orientation has generally been the most popular. In a recent study of clinical psychologists, psychiatrists, social workers, and marriage and family therapists, 68% of the sample of 423 individuals indicated an eclectic preference (Jensen, Bergin, & Greaves, 1990). There were some differences between the four professions evaluated. Psychiatrists, for example, had the smallest percentage of eclectics with 59%, and 36% of that subsample indicated a preference for a psychodynamic approach. In contrast, 70% of clinical psychologists indicated an eclectic preference and only 9% preferred a psychodynamic approach. Marriage and family therapists were similar to the psychologists whereas the social workers more closely resembled the psychiatrists in terms of their preferences for these two orientations. These findings are particularly interesting since much of the published work and training in psychotherapy appear to be very much school-oriented.

Another interesting aspect is how individual therapists select the particular therapeutic approach that they tend to use. There isn't very much reliable information on this matter. It would appear that the kind of training the individual received or the institution he or she attended may have been an important factor. The personal therapy that a psychotherapist received may have also played a role in such decisions—or the individual may have had other personal reasons for selecting a specific type of psychotherapy as a preferred one. It also seems likely that therapists may modify their approach as they gain experience. This does appear to be the case for individuals eventually selecting an eclectic approach.

A designation or naming of a particular type of therapy does not necessarily tell what specific operations are used in therapy. In other words, two therapists who label themselves identically may not actually perform in therapy in identical ways. They may utilize similar descriptive terms and theoretical constructs, but they may actually interact with given clients in quite different ways. Thus, one cannot take school designations at face value if the actual operations in psychotherapy are the focus of interest.

Finally, as alluded to earlier, in spite of the different descriptions of the therapeutic process provided by the various schools of psychotherapy, we are still far from certain as to what processes or procedures actually produce either positive or negative changes in the patient or client. Each orientation tends to construe and describe what actually occurs in psychotherapy in somewhat different ways and in different theoretical terminology.

Consequently, when all of the therapies claim to be effective, it is difficult to distinguish what variables in the therapeutic approach actually produce change. Do the various psychotherapeutic approaches secure the desired changes by different means, or are they simply using different theoretical terms to describe what may be similar but unclearly understood phenomena? This is an important and complex question which will be discussed in more detail in later sections of the book.

The increase in the number of different forms or approaches to psychotherapy has also been accompanied by a general increase in the popularity and acceptance of psychotherapy. One reason appears to be related to a more benign attitude in recent years toward psychological disturbance or

"mental illness" in general. With the advent of briefer forms of psychotherapy and with an increased expansion in the availability of psychotherapeutic services, psychotherapy has been viewed as an important and accepted
form of treatment for a variety of psychological problems. Although this
positive view has been noted mainly among the middle and upper classes of
our society, progress has also been evident with other groups. Recently, attention has been focused more on culturally diverse groups in our society
and the underprivileged who have particular needs and problems (Garfield,
1994; Lorion & Felner, 1986; Sue, Zane, & Young, 1994).

Today, psychotherapy is both a popular and accepted form of treatment. It
has been featured in the popular press and on television programs, and an increasing number of popular books on psychotherapy, including self-help
books, have appeared in bookstores. As I noted in a previous article, "In the
April 1977 issue of the "St. Louisan Magazine," the midwestern alternative to
the "New Yorker" magazine, the featured article was entitled "The Therapy
Game: An Introduction to the Topic More Talked About Than Sex" (Rivero,
1977). That is real popularity, indeed!" (Garfield, 1981).

As one aspect of this popularity or acceptance, psychotherapy has been
viewed, singly or in combination with other treatments, as a potential treatment for a wide variety of problems and social ills including psychoses, alco-
hol and drug addictions, psychosomatic illnesses, eating disorders, marital
problems, delinquency, and learning disabilities. Although at times the enthusiasm has been overly exuberant, undoubtedly there are differing opinions
among psychotherapists concerning the effectiveness of psychotherapy for
various types of disorders. This probably varies to some extent with the professional identity, personality, and theoretical views of the individual practitioner. In the following section, we discuss the individuals who are the
providers of psychotherapeutic services.

THE PSYCHOTHERAPIST

At the present time there are many routes to take to become a psychotherapist. This is due to the fact that there is no specifically designated or recognized profession of psychotherapy. Rather, there are many professions that
include psychotherapy as one of their professional functions. This situation
is the more or less fortuitous result of various historical developments. In the
not too distant past when deviant behavior was linked with evil spirits and
sin, society's designated "healers" were either the state or the church. De-
viates were either incarcerated or subjected to various rituals; some, such as
being doused in water or burnt at the stake, were rather severe treatments indeed. In modern times and with various advances in the field of medicine,
deviant behavior began to be viewed as possibly organic, conceptualized as

illness. "Mental illness" thus could be viewed as a possible dysfunction of the brain and the central nervous system. In the latter part of the 19th century, largely but not solely due to the development of psychoanalysis by Freud, some of the disorders without any clearly discernable organic causes began to be viewed as psychologically caused.

Psychoanalysis provided both a theoretical explanation of neurotic disorders and a psychological means of treatment. Both the fact that such disorders were seen as illnesses and the fact that Freud was a physician tended toward the designation of psychotherapy as a form of medical therapy, even though Freud's own theoretical views were not well received by his medical colleagues. Freud (1926), himself, did not believe that psychoanalysis should be viewed as a medical form of treatment or be restricted to physicians. In fact, he believed that medical training was at times an impediment to the successful practice of psychoanalysis. However, Freud's view was not accepted by his followers in the United States, overwhelmingly psychiatrists, who stated that conditions here were very different from those in Europe, and that a great many "quacks" would be attracted to psychoanalysis if it were not restricted to physicians.

Consequently, in the first two or three decades of this century, psychotherapy, although still a modest development and dominated to some extent by psychoanalysis, was largely viewed as being within the province of medicine. Clinical psychology, for example, was primarily concerned with the application of psychological tests and psychiatric social workers were occupied with casework. While there were individuals in these latter professions who did engage in psychotherapy to some extent and there were individuals engaged in counseling of an educational and vocational nature, the total number of people involved appears to have been small. In a similar fashion, although there were some rather well-known "lay analysts," they were few and far between.

This situation, however, has changed markedly. Most of this growth has occurred since the second World War and in part was related to the large number of psychiatric casualties resulting from the war. In the United States, the Department of Veteran Affairs participated in a joint program with selected universities to train clinical and counseling psychologists. The National institute of Mental Health also provided funding for the training of psychiatrists, clinical psychologists, psychiatric social workers, and psychiatric nurses to better meet the mental health needs of our society. These training programs also included some training in psychotherapy.

In addition, a number of other specialities such as pastoral counseling, school psychology, educational counseling, and marital and family therapy, also provided some training in counseling and psychotherapy. Furthermore, a variety of new types of mental health workers with less formal training also appeared on the scene, all eager to provide psychological services of one kind or another. As a result, there are individuals with varying types and amounts of training in psychotherapy who in some fashion or other are functioning as psychotherapists.

The backgrounds and training of the more traditional mental health professions are generally known and will be described very briefly. Psychiatrists are first trained as physicians, and although they receive some instruction in interviewing and possibly psychotherapy during medical school, their main training occurs during their psychiatric residency or in specialized training after that. Training in psychotherapy, however, is not a primary or exclusive emphasis during the psychiatric residency but is only one of many types of experiences provided, and the amount of time or emphasis devoted to it varies depending upon the particular residency center. The psychiatric resident, among other things, is also instructed in pharmacotherapy, neurology, the psychiatric examination, and psychopathology. They also are given an opportunity to manage a ward of patients. Thus, psychotherapy training will only constitute a part of the psychiatrist's instruction during the three-year period of the residency. Because of this, a number of psychiatrists who are primarily interested in psychotherapy go on to take additional training in a psychoanalytic or other type of psychotherapy training institute. The psychiatrist who has completed his psychiatric residency may later go on to take his Boards in the speciality of psychiatry. However, these specialty examinations attempt to appraise the candidate's knowledge in the basic areas of psychiatry, and in no way certify competency in psychotherapy per se.

The training of the clinical psychologist in the United States, although quite different from that of the psychiatrist, has some similarities in terms of patient contact and general issues of diagnosis and treatment. The student, after completion of college, during which period he or she will have taken a sequence of basic courses in psychology, enrolls in a doctoral program in clinical psychology. Although such programs are usually described as four- or five-year programs, many students take a longer period of time to complete the program. Until about 1970, all of these graduate programs were Ph.D. programs administered through university graduate schools and departments of psychology. As such, there were certain general features common to most programs. Following general guidelines recommended at several earlier important national conferences on training (Raimy, 1950; Hoch, Ross, & Winder, 1966), these graduate programs stressed basic areas of general psychology, personality theory, psychopathology, diagnostic testing, research, and psychotherapy. Over the years, the emphasis on testing has gradually diminished while that on psychotherapy has increased. This has paralleled the increasing importance of psychotherapy as the primary activity of clinical psychologists (Garfield & Kurtz, 1976). Practicum training and a one-year internship are also important parts of the program.

The traditional university training of clinical psychologists, thus, is quite different from that of the psychiatrist although psychotherapy is included in varying degrees in the training of both disciplines. Although basic medical training and the use of medications and drugs are essential aspects in the training of the psychiatrist, the traditional graduate program of the clinical psychologist has emphasized basic psychology and research competence. The two professions thus share a common interest in psychopathology and psychotherapy, but each has its own basic traditions, values, and emphases. Although psychiatrists, as physicians, are more inclined to view psychological disorders as diseases or illnesses, psychologists have tended in the past to view them more as learned patterns of behavior or habit disorders. With the publication of the more recent official diagnostic manuals, DSM-III & DSM-III-R, (American Psychiatric Association, 1980, 1987), this appears to be changing. Much of the research in the field of psychotherapy, however, has been carried out by psychologists trained in the traditional scientist-practitioner model.

In the past 25 years or so, there have been some significant new developments in the training of clinical psychologists. One has been the growth of independent "free-standing" professional schools of psychology (Pottharst, 1970). Another has been the introduction of programs that award a Doctor of Psychology (Psy.D.) degree instead of the traditional doctorate (Ph.D.) degree (Peterson, Eaton, Levine, & Snepp, 1980). In both of these programs, there is a greater emphasis on practical training and less on research. Most of these are four-year programs. Thus, at present, there is some diversity in the training of clinical psychologists.

The training of the psychiatric social worker and the psychiatric nurse also differs noticeably from that of the psychiatrist and clinical psychologist. Most psychiatric social workers receive their training in a two-year program within a graduate school of social work, whereas the psychiatric nurse may receive a comparable period of training in a graduate program of nursing education. Again, each field has its own traditional emphases which need not be spelled out here. The total amount of training generally, and in psychotherapy specifically, will tend to be less intensive or of shorter duration than that of the two professions mentioned previously, unless it is augmented by additional specialized training. While social workers work in outpatient facilities, hospitals, and in private practice, nurses tend to work mainly in hospital settings.

In addition to the members of these traditional professions, there are many others who perform some type of psychotherapeutic function (Garfield, 1977). Doctoral programs in counseling and school psychology bear some resemblance to the programs in clinical psychology. Although counseling psychologists traditionally have emphasized working with less severe or "normal" problems of adjustment, and school psychologists have been concerned with a variety of educational, as well as adjustment problems of children in the schools, both receive some training in psychotherapy or counseling and engage in such activities. Such programs, similar to the clinical psychology programs, are accredited by the American Psychological Association.

There are many master's level programs in counseling, school psychology, and guidance, as well as in clinical psychology which provide more limited training in psychotherapeutic procedures. In addition, there are pastoral counselors, marriage counselors, growth enhancement specialists, encounter group leaders, psychodramatists, indigenous mental health workers, mental health associates, and the like (Garfield, 1969, 1983). Thus, there are many individuals with varying types of educational backgrounds and training who may be involved in some form of psychotherapy whether it be called counseling, psychotherapy, growth experience, or some other name. In the absence of legal definitions of what psychotherapy is and what training is required in order to engage in it, we have an unusual and sometimes confusing situation. Psychotherapy is not the exclusive domain of any *single* profession. Rather, in some guise or other, it is practiced by a great variety of individuals and professions. Although an individual may be licensed or certified to practice medicine, law, clinical psychology, or some other occupation, there are no current provisions for regulating the practice of psychotherapy, except as it is related to the regulation of a recognized profession. There was one serious attempt made a few years ago to consider the possibility of establishing a separate and distinctive profession of psychotherapy, but it was unsuccessful (Holt, 1971). We will say a bit more about this in Chapter 4.

WHAT IS PSYCHOTHERAPY?

Some general description or definition of psychotherapy will be useful, fully recognizing that it may be difficult to capture the diversity of views and practices of this field. Psychotherapy consists of an interaction between two individuals (although more than two can be involved) where one of the individuals, the client or patient, is seeking help for a problem which either he or she, some other individual or agency, or the therapist deem potentially helped by psychotherapeutic intervention. The other participant is obviously the therapist, who supposedly has the training and personal resources to provide the necessary therapeutic help. The interaction between the two participants is mediated primarily by verbal means although bodily gestures, movements, facial expressions, and displays of affect also are used. Psychotherapy, thus, appears to be largely a verbal interaction between two people, a therapist and a client, by means of which the former somehow attempts to help the latter overcome difficulties. Verbal interactions go on between two people in many other types of interpersonal situations, but what is unique about this particular relationship or interaction is that it is potentially capable of helping a person to surmount problems and to improve personal adjustment. The rest of this volume is devoted to how such interactions work.

Most sophisticated individuals have some conception of psychotherapy or of some forms of psychotherapy based on their reading and other experiences. However, the average person may have a somewhat hazy or even distorted view of what is involved. Some may tend to see the psychotherapist as similar to any other "doctor" and expect the therapist to diagnose what is wrong and what needs to be done. Others may expect the therapist to require only a few sessions in which to diagnose their difficulties and apply the appropriate remedy or remedial action. Some individuals may be quite skeptical of how "just talking" can in any way help them. The preconceptions or expectancies which the patient brings to the therapeutic situation, thus, may be of some importance in terms of how therapy proceeds, particularly when the preconceptions of the patient are not congruent with those of the therapist.

In many traditional forms of psychodynamic and relationship therapy, psychotherapy has been viewed as an opportunity for the individual client to explore aspects of himself which he has tended to keep from awareness and which theoretically are factors in his disturbance. Although the therapist is there as a guide and to provide support, it is the client who must be willing to engage in what is viewed as the difficult work of self-exploration and the facing up to the negative events in his past and current life which have produced his present difficulties. Although this is a somewhat oversimplified view, it does convey one view of the therapeutic process, and one which has been a dominant view in past years. Even in some more recent variants of psychotherapy, the burden of the work for improved adjustment is placed on the client. The client's subjective discomfort and her motivation for change must be such that she is willing to undertake and persevere in the sometimes arduous task of self-exploration and subsequent modification of current behaviors. While it is easy to place all of the responsibility and blame for change or lack of change on the client, there is some truth to the view that the client must be an interested and active participant in this process. Even in more directive therapies, such as behavior therapy or rational-emotive therapy, where the client is given instructions and tasks to perform by the therapist, he or she will have to be an active and cooperative participant if any change is to take place (Emmelkamp, 1986; Marks, 1978). However, in the latter instances, there will be more structure and direction provided by the therapist, and a greater emphasis on compliance by the client.

Psychotherapy, then, is an interaction between the therapist and client that utilizes verbal means but in which there are more structured roles for both participants than in many other interactions in which personal matters may be discussed. The client has to be actively involved and also be willing to discuss matters of a highly personal or confidential nature. In many instances, the topics to be discussed may be ones that are highly upsetting to him and which he is hesitant to discuss with others. The therapist has a special role to play which helps to make the interaction a somewhat unique one. She is supposedly an expert in the area of handling psychological distress and performs in the socially designated role of mental healer. Because of this, she is one to whom the client can turn to for help and to whom he can confide his difficulties. To the extent that the therapist is perceived as a knowing and trusted individual who will not judge the client as others might do, the client may more readily confide disturbing and private concerns to the therapist. As a result, a rather close relationship tends to develop between therapist and client, with the latter being able to explore himself more readily, follow the leads of the therapist and be willing to try to change.

Although this description may be most descriptive of more traditional or relationship forms of therapy, many of the general features described would also apply to some degree to other forms of psychotherapy. Regardless of the type of therapy offered, the client is usually asked to describe his difficulties, the situations in which his problems are manifested, previous attempts to deal with them, and why he seeks therapeutic help at this time. The client is asked to give a frank account of his or her problems, which may be of a highly personal nature. The therapist, regardless of orientation, must inspire some degree of trust and confidence in the client if the client is to reveal such information and to continue in therapy. Furthermore, if the client perceives the therapist as an accepting person and as promising some hope for improvement in the future, or as indicating that the client's problems are in no way unusual, the client will tend to see the therapist in a positive light and be more highly motivated to collaborate in the therapeutic enterprise. He will tend to look forward to his sessions and to place some positive value on his psychotherapy and on the new relationship with the therapist.

To some extent, therefore, the psychotherapeutic situation or relationship is a somewhat special one that may allow certain processes to occur. The highly confidential nature of the interaction, the role of the therapist as an interested and understanding expert, the discomfort or motivation of the client for possible change, and the close relationship that may develop between the two participants are all aspects that help to make this situation unique and potentially therapeutic. We will explore the complexities of the therapeutic interaction in much greater detail later.

AVAILABILITY OF PSYCHOTHERAPEUTIC SERVICES

A great variety of people, from all social strata and backgrounds, experience psychological distress of some sort or other and in various ways seek help for their difficulties. A source frequently consulted for help is the family physician or, in the case of children, the pediatrician. In many instances, the individual may have some complaints that appear to be somatic or rather vague or diffuse in nature. The family's doctor is, thus, a first source of contact. If the discussion with the physician and/or medication, plus the passing of time, appears to alleviate the individual's complaints, no further treatment usually will be required. However, if there is no improvement and the symptoms come to be viewed as primarily psychological in nature, then the patient may be referred to a mental health professional or agency, depending on the experiences, predilections, or personal contacts of the referring physician.

In the case of children who are manifesting difficulties or behavioral disturbance in school, a somewhat different pattern may be followed. In some situations, after a report from the school or conference with school officials, the parents may take their child to their pediatrician, consult the latter about a referral, or directly seek psychological help. The child may be referred by the teacher to the school counselor or psychologist. After some evaluation, the child may be seen by these school personnel for some type of psychological help or recommendations will be made to the parents for appropriate referral elsewhere. In some cases, the family's minister or priest may be consulted and some type of consultation provided. This may also lead to some type of direct pastoral counseling or to a referral elsewhere.

Although such individuals and agencies are significant sources of both service and referrals, with the increased public knowledge in recent years about psychological problems and the greater availability of resources for help with such problems, larger numbers of individuals appear to seek help on their own or on the advice of friends who have themselves received such services. This is particularly true of better educated individuals who are not only more knowledgeable about mental health problems and resources, but also appear to have a more positive attitude about seeking and receiving psychological help. Although attitudes toward "mental illness" have undergone some change in recent times, individuals in the lowest socioeconomic groups tend more frequently to associate shame with psychological symptoms and to resist receiving help for their problems until the situation becomes quite acute or severe (Hollingshead & Redlich, 1958). If they are pressured to see a mental health expert, they are quite likely to drop out of therapy (Garfield, 1994).

Another source of service and referral is made up of a variety of social and public agencies. These include social service and welfare agencies, the courts, institutions for delinquents, the aged, the physically handicapped, and other comparable agencies. Within the heterogeneous populations served by these agencies and institutions, there are manifested the usual variety of psychological disorders. Although some of these institutions may be able to provide some direct service for these problems, the individuals afflicted will often be referred to more specific mental health agencies or practitioners. Although the economic status of the individual involved may determine the type of referral made, public agencies are more likely to refer their cases to other comparable agencies, whereas private practitioners, such as the family physician, may refer more frequently to other private practitioners.

Individuals who are seen as having psychological difficulties, therefore, may go through some sort of screening process before they finally make contact with a potential psychotherapist. Some people will wind up with psychotherapists who are in private practice. These generally are those who are able to pay the rather substantial fees involved or who have health policies that cover such services. A large number of people will seek out or be referred to a variety of outpatient clinics in which the fees for service are generally more moderate or where the fee is determined by the patient's income. Some clinics are attached to hospitals, some to university psychology departments, some to medical schools, some are primarily community mental health centers, and some provide services specifically for children. Some may also specialize in providing one type of psychotherapy, or for a specified type of population. The U.S. Department of Veterans' Affairs, for example, has a network of clinics and hospitals for military veterans. Most universities also have counseling centers as well as student health services to take care of the needs of students. Psychotherapeutic services are also provided in both general and psychiatric hospitals.

The types of psychotherapeutic services that are offered in these institutions and situations may vary greatly. In some, the psychotherapy offered may consist of only a few interviews oriented around the current crisis, whereas in others, notably the private practice of psychoanalysis, the therapy will last for several years. In some situations, the focus will be on individual therapy whereas in others it will be on a couple, a group of individuals, or a family. Who provides the psychotherapy will also vary. In private practice, it is generally individuals in the more traditional mental health professions who have completed their training and have chosen this style of professional career. In clinics, hospitals, and medical schools which are involved in training, a significant amount of the psychotherapy performed will be done by those in training—clinical and counseling psychology interns, psychiatric residents, and social work trainees. In some agencies, the personnel may be made up almost exclusively of individuals of one profession, whereas in others the staff may be interdisciplinary. Psychotherapeutic services are also provided through managed health care by Health Maintenance Organizations (HMOs) and Preferred Provider Organizations (Vandenbos, Cummings, & DeLeon, 1992).

There are, thus, a variety of services at varying levels of quality in existence for those who are in need of such services. The distribution and availability of services varies with the personal resources and knowledgeability of prospective clients and with their location. Large urban centers such as New York and Los Angeles have large numbers of professional psychotherapists available while rural settings have considerably fewer such resources. Important training centers for mental health personnel also contribute to the availability of such services at relatively modest cost.

THE FOCUS OF THE BOOK

The main purpose of this edition, as in the first edition, is to present a systematic description of what is entailed in psychotherapy as understood and described by a particular participant-observer. The objective of the author is to attempt some integration of the findings and observations in this field, paying attention to empirical data wherever possible. On a comparative basis, psychotherapy is as yet a relatively young and not fully developed field and one in which research investigations have constituted a relatively recent development. As pointed out earlier, the field has been characterized by a variety of schools and theoretical viewpoints, and much of the published material has consisted of presentations of these viewpoints primarily at a theoretical and clinical level. The present volume will not duplicate such previous efforts or be a presentation of brief descriptions of selected schools of psychotherapy. Rather, an attempt will be made to provide some coherent description of the psychotherapeutic process and the roles and activities of the participants involved, as well as discussing problems of research and the gaps that exist in our current knowledge. The presentation will be eclectic in that attention will be paid to ideas and contributions from different viewpoints if they help in explaining and understanding the processes of psychotherapy. An attempt will also be made to synthesize or redefine processes and procedures that have been given somewhat different designations and explanations by the different orientations in psychotherapy.

Since the first edition of this book was published, there has been a continued interest in eclecticism in psychotherapy as well as a more recent development for integration (Norcross & Goldfried, 1992). Two journals devoted to eclectic and integrative emphases have been published—The *Journal of Integrative and Eclectic Psychotherapy* and the *Journal of Psychotherapy Integration.* This book with its emphasis on the commonalities among diverse psychotherapies reflects and supports those developments.

It is the author's hope that the present volume will give the reader a comprehensive and meaningful view of psychotherapy and of the processes involved in this particular approach to therapy. This presentation should prove useful to the student or practitioner of psychotherapy regardless of his or her particular professional identification or eventual theoretical allegiance.

REFERENCES

American Psychiatric Association (1980). *Diagnostic and statistical manual of mental disorders* (3rd ed.). Washington, DC: Author.

American Psychiatric Association (1987). *Diagnostic and statistical manual of mental disorders* (3rd ed.-revised). Washington, DC: Author.

Emmelkamp, P. M. G. (1986). Behavior therapy with adults. In S. L. Garfield & A. E. Bergin (Eds.), *Handbook of psychotherapy and behavior change* (3rd ed.) (pp. 385–442). New York: Wiley.

Ford, D. H. (1991). Guiding students through the labyrinth of psychotherapy approaches. A review of Burke, J. F., *Contemporary approaches to psychotherapy and counseling: The self-regulation and maturity model. Contemporary Psychology, 36,* 250.

Freud, S. (1927). *The question of lay analysis.* New York: Norton.

Garfield, S. L. (1969). New developments in the preparation of counselors. *Community Mental Health Journal, 5,* 240–246.

Garfield, S. L. (1977). Research on training the professional psychotherapists. In A. S. Gurman & A. M. Razin (Eds.), *Effective Psychotherapy. A Handbook of Research.* New York: Pergamon Press.

Garfield, S. L. (1981). Psychotherapy: A Forty-Year Appraisal. *American Psychologist, 36,* 174–183.

Garfield, S. L. (1989). *The practice of brief psychotherapy.* Elmsford, NY: Pergamon.

Garfield, S. L. (1994). Research on client variables in psychotherapy. In A. E. Bergin & S. L. Garfield (Eds.), *Handbook of psychotherapy and behavior change* (4th ed.) (pp. 190–228). New York: Wiley.

Garfield. S. L., & Kurtz, R. (1976). Clinical psychologists in the 1970s. *American Psychologist, 31,* 1–9.

Garfield, S. L., & Kurtz, R. (1977). A study of eclectic views. *Journal of Consulting and Clinical Psychology, 45,* 78–83.

Herink, R. (Ed.) (1980). *The psychotherapy handbook: The A to Z guide to More than 250 different therapies in use today.* New York: A Meridian Book, New American Library.

Hoch, E. L., Ross, A. O., & Winder, C. L. (Eds.) (1966). *Professional preparation of clinical psychologists.* Washington, DC: American Psychological Association.

Hollingshead, A. B. & Redlich, F. C. (1958). *Social class and mental illness: A community study.* New York: Wiley.

Holt, R. R. (Ed.) (1971). *New horizon for psychotherapy. Autonomy as a profession.* New York: International Universities Press.

Jensen, J. P., Bergin, A. E., & Greaves, D. W. (1990). The meaning of eclecticism: New survey and analysis of components. *Professional Psychology: Research and Practice, 21,* 124–130.

Kazdin, A. E. (1986). Comparative outcome studies of psychotherapy: Methodological issues and strategies. *Journal of Consulting and Clinical Psychology, 54*, 95–105.

Kiesler, D. J. (1966). Some myths of psychotherapy research and the search for a paradigm. *Psychological Bulletin, 65*, 110–136.

Kiesler, D. J. (1971). Experimental design in psychotherapy research. In A. E. Bergin & S. L. Garfield (Eds.), *Handbook of psychotherapy and behavior change.* New York: Wiley.

Lorion, R. P., & Felner, R. D. (1986). Research on psychotherapy with the disadvantaged. In S. L. Garfield & A. E. Bergin (Eds.) (pp. 739–775). New York: Wiley.

Marks, I. (1978). Behavioral psychotherapy of adult neurosis. In S. L. Garfield & A. E. Bergin (Eds.), *Handbook of psychotherapy and behavior change* (2nd ed.). New York: Wiley.

Norcross, J. C., & Goldfried, M. R. (1992). *Handbook of psychotherapy integration.* New York: Basic Books.

Peterson, D. R., Eaton, M. M., Levine, A. R., & Snepp, F. P. (1980). Development of doctor of psychology programs and experiences of graduates through 1980. *The Rutgers Professional Psychology Review, 2*, 29–39.

Pottharst, K. E. (1970). To renew vitality and provide a challenge in training—The California School of Professional Training. *Professional Psychology, 1*, 123–130.

Raimy, V. (Ed.) (1950). *Training in clinical psychology.* New York: Prentice-Hall.

Report of the Research Task Force of the National Institute of Mental Health. *Research in the Service of Mental Health.* DHEW Publication No. (ADM) 75–236. Rockville, MD.

Rivero, A. (April, 1977). The therapy game: An introduction to the topic more talked about than sex. *St. Louisan*, pp. 49–54, 67.

Rogers, C. R. (1942). *Counseling and psychotherapy.* Boston: Houghton Mifflin.

Sue, S., Zane, N., & Young, K. (1994). Research on psychotherapy with culturally diverse populations. in A. E. Bergin & S. L. Garfield (Eds.) *Handbook of psychotherapy and behavior change* (4th ed.) (pp. 783–817). New York: Wiley.

Vandenbos, G. R., Cummings, N. A., & DeLeon, P. H. (1992). A century of psychotherapy: Economic and environmental influences. In D. A. Freedheim (Ed.) *History of psychotherapy: A century of change* (pp. 65–102). Washington, DC: American Psychological Association.

CHAPTER 2

Orientations and Viewpoints
in Psychotherapy

Without going into the ancient history of healing procedures and practices, we can note that the first organized system of psychotherapy, one that has exerted considerable influence on the field, was psychoanalysis, the contribution of Sigmund Freud (1938). Since probably most readers have some acquaintance with the history and development of the psychoanalytic movement (Freud, 1938), there is little need for any detailed account here. Instead we can mention some of the major aspects of this system that have had an important influence on the development of psychotherapy, and also make some reference to more recent developments.

Freud's views of psychotherapy were influenced by the scientific and cultural trends of his time, as well as by his own clinical experience and attempts at theoretical formulations. Particularly important were his experiences with patients classified as cases of hysteria. After earlier experience using hypnosis and cathartic methods, he gradually abandoned these procedures and developed the now classic procedures of psychoanalysis. These procedures or techniques of psychoanalysis were very closely intertwined with his developing notions of human personality and abnormal behavior. Freud's views of repression, unconscious motivation, psychic determinism, and psychosexual development influenced his therapeutic approach. Neurotic symptoms were viewed as manifestations of underlying conflicts which the individual had repressed because they were painful and disturbing. Consequently, Freud believed that even seemingly successful attempts at removing the patient's symptoms would be of short duration and that substitute symptoms would subsequently appear if the repressed conflicts were not uncovered and resolved. Until this was done, no lasting improvement would result.

Because the ideas, affects, or strivings which the individual had repressed were initially very painful, it was not to be expected that they could be brought forth easily by the patient. Not only had the patient repressed the material and developed and utilized various defenses against their appearance in consciousness, but he appeared also to resist the attempts of the analyst to help him overcome his difficulties. This apparent paradox was explainable by psychoanalytic theory. Any direct attack on a patient's problems or defenses would be resisted in a number of ways because the individual experienced this as personally threatening. Any person who was utilizing psychic energy and a defensive structure to avoid facing material that was threatening to his ego would be expected to try to ward off any attempts made to expose such material and, thus, to avoid experiencing the pain that might result. Such defensive maneuvers in therapy by the patient might be manifested by being late to therapy sessions, refusing to cooperate with the analyst, dropping out of treatment, talking about trivia in the therapy sessions, and similar phenomena. Freud termed these behaviors as resistances.

As a consequence, as well as the fact that Freud believed, with some justification, that attempts to break down defenses and reveal repressed and threatening material too quickly could be traumatic for many individuals, the analytic process had to proceed slowly. The process obviously had to be geared to the particular patient in terms of his own level of adjustment and his particular problems.

The primary procedure that Freud finally devised, and which has been identified with psychoanalysis, was that of free association. In this procedure, the client is requested to lie down on a couch with the analyst sitting back of him and outside of his direct line of vision. The client is instructed to relax and to allow his thoughts to flow freely, verbalizing whatever comes to mind. It is hypothesized that in this relaxed state the client can more readily verbalize his associations and that eventually they would lead to problem areas. The analyst was to intrude as little as possible in order to facilitate the flow of material from the client, but he also was to observe hesitations, blockings, sudden changes in the associations, and the like. At appropriate times, comments and interpretations might be offered by the analyst, but the emphasis was on the production of associations by the client. The analyst's role, particularly in the early stages of therapy, was to facilitate the patient's free associations.

As therapy progressed, initially on an almost daily basis, the relationship between analyst and patient deepened and at times certain characteristic patterns of response to the therapist were manifested by the patient which Freud designated as *transference reactions*. In some instances, the client, frequently a female, would admit to being in love with the analyst, a situation which Freud at first found disconcerting and unanticipated. At other times, the client might show just the opposite reaction and accuse the analyst of being a hateful person and of not being really interested in her case. From the psychoanalytic point of view, these responses were seen as distortions on the part of the patient. The latter was not actually responding to the analyst as a real person, but instead was responding to the analyst as a substitute or father figure with patterns or affects that had never been expressed to the real person(s) in the patient's previous life experience. The patient, thus, was transferring or displacing such responses on to the analyst and perceiving him, therefore, in a personally determined or distorted manner. Although this was considered to be a regular and important phenomenon in psychoanalysis, individual analysts conceivably could influence the patient by how they responded and interacted in the therapy sessions. It was for such reasons that it was deemed important that the analyst have some understanding of his or her own personality and not intrude it unnecessarily in the analytic session.

Although a positive transference might be viewed positively as a factor that helped motivate the patient to continue in therapy, it could not continue indefinitely if progress were to be made. The same was true for instances of negative transference. At some point, the client had to understand the reality of the situation. Toward this goal, the analyst offered interpretations of what was actually occurring. This was not as simple as it sounds, for the client might resist the interpretation offered by the analyst. The latter, however, would persist in this task, pointing out associations or interactions that tended to support his interpretations. The process or techniques of interpretation has been emphasized as being of decided importance in resolving transference problems, overcoming resistances in therapy, and in providing insight and understanding to the client about his underlying problems. Although we will say a bit more about the matter of interpretation here, we will offer some more general comments about it later in the book.

The matter of the timing and accuracy of interpretation in psychoanalytic therapy have been particular topics of discussion (Hammer, 1968). Whereas an accurate and appropriately timed interpretation is viewed as facilitating the process of psychotherapy, an inaccurate or premature interpretation may possibly retard therapy or even be harmful to the patient. On the positive side, if the client accepts the interpretation offered by the analyst, it may signify that the client has enlarged his awareness of the problems producing his difficulties, that a particular impasse in therapy has been resolved, that the interpretation probably was valid, and that the client is responding positively to the activities of the therapist. On the other hand, if the interpretation is faulty or poorly timed, not only are the converse of the previous events likely, but the resistance of the patient may be increased and, in some instances, the individual may become more disturbed. That is, the premature confrontation of the patient with threatening material that he is unable to accept, may actually increase the client's level of disturbance. The client is essentially confronted with realities with which he is not yet able to cope. Interpretation, consequently, is considered an important technique of psychoanalysis and one which demands considerable skill and sensitivity on the part of the analyst if therapy is to proceed satisfactorily.

Two other aspects of psychoanalytic therapy that have been important components of the therapy are the attaining of insight on the part of the client and "the working through." Although the attainment of insight and understanding by the client of his underlying difficulties was viewed as a long and difficult process, it was considered essential for real progress. Only when the patient understood the causes of his disturbed behavior, was he able gradually to modify and improve his behavior. Instead of reacting in ways influenced by earlier misunderstood and distorted experiences, he could now react more appropriately and realistically. By gradually recovering these earlier repressed experiences and understanding them for what they were, the client was able to enlarge his awareness of self and react in a more mature and realistic manner. The interpretations offered by the analyst in relation to the recall of dreams as well as to the associations and behaviors manifested in the therapy sessions, were an important means of helping the patient to obtain insights into his behavior.

The process of the "working through," which took place in the later stages of therapy is somewhat more difficult to describe. Contrary to some views, insights were not obtained in a dramatic "aha" or "Eureka" manner. Rather, it consisted of a more continuous and repetitious process of learning until the patient had fully accepted and integrated the insight or a number of related understandings and insights (Wolberg, 1954). The knowledge gained from therapy had to be worked through and assimilated. Freud particularly stressed this aspect in the process of overcoming the patient's resistance.

> One must allow the patient time to get to know this resistance of which he is ignorant, to "work through" it, to overcome it, by continuing the work according to the analytic rule in defiance of it. Only when it has come to its height can one, with the patient's cooperation, discover the repressed instinctual trends which are feeding the resistance . . . .
> This "working through" of the resistances may in practice amount to an arduous task for the patient and a trial of patience for the analyst. Nevertheless, it is the part of the work that effects the greatest changes in the patient and that distinguished analytic treatment from every kind of suggestive treatment. (Freud, 1914/1950, pp. 375–376)

Psychoanalysis as developed by Freud was the first comprehensive and systematic form of psychotherapy, and although not well received at first by Freud's medical colleagues in Vienna, it soon became the most influential school of psychotherapy. Apart from the fact that Freud attracted many zealous disciples from many parts of the world and that institutes, journals, and organizations were formed to give the movement greater unity and strength, there were no other competing systems of sufficient vitality to rival it. Most of the other emerging orientations tended to be the products of former followers of Freud, but none of the latter appeared to offer as comprehensive a system as Freud did or to be as good an organizer as Freud was. Furthermore, Freud was an astute clinician and observer, as well as a most facile writer, and his system clearly became the dominant one for many years. Although the peak of popularity for psychoanalysis appears to have been reached in the 1960s, much of current psychotherapeutic work reflects the analytic emphasis, and as we will note later, a number of Freud's observations and formulations remain of value in understanding the process of psychotherapy.

OTHER RELATED EMPHASES

A number of the earlier followers of Freud later parted company from the mainstream of psychoanalysis and developed their own approach to psychotherapy. Although Jung and Adler were probably the best known of Freud's earlier disciples who later went their separate paths, neither one exerted the influence on psychotherapy that Freud did.

Somewhat similar comments can be made about figures such as Horney (1939) and Sullivan (1953) in this country. Although Sullivan's influence at first was limited to those who had direct contact with him as a teacher at the Washington School of Psychiatry, his primarily posthumous writings allowed his views to reach a larger audience. Horney was a more popular writer whose books dealt in a more general way with personality and the neuroses, and to a much lesser extent with psychotherapeutic technique. Although the work of these individuals drew some adherents, they did not seriously challenge the influence of psychoanalysis on the field of psychotherapy. A number of practicing psychotherapists may have modified some of their views and procedures as a result of these newer views, particularly in giving greater significance to social factors in disturbed behavior and in emphasizing the relationship between the therapist and client, but basic analytic procedures maintained their popularity. There was no new structure or system that could be viewed as a complete substitute for that of Freud's.

There were some changes influenced by other factors, as well as by these newer views, but these did not necessarily imply significant modification of basic therapeutic concepts. For example, many therapists who were not graduates of official institutes of psychoanalysis did not follow the orthodox procedures of psychoanalysis but utilized psychoanalytic theory. They did not require their patients to recline on a couch or to come for therapy five times per week. Instead, the patient was seated on a chair and appointments made for two or three sessions per week, or even once a week if the therapist had unfilled time and the patient could only afford weekly visits. Sometimes, practical necessities even overrode strongly held theoretical views!

Even though some modifications have occurred over time, many basic postulates of Freud's psychoanalytic views have been followed by psychotherapists designated as psychodynamic. These include the concepts of repressed unconscious conflicts, transference, resistance, and the important role of interpretation and insight in psychotherapy. For example, although Horney took exception to Freud's emphasis on biological factors as opposed to social ones in neurosis, as well as his conceptions of psychosexual development and feminine personality, she accepted the view of unconscious motivation and internalized conflicts as factors in neurotic disorders. Similarly, while Sullivan disagreed with Freud on several issues and developed some of his own concepts and terms, he, too, accepted a basic psychodynamic view of personality disturbance.

To this extent, therefore, there was an important similarity among these views, despite their differences. In most instances, this spoke to an exploratory and uncovering process in therapy along with attempts to provide insight to the client. Although the interpretations among the different groups might differ and the corresponding insights derived by the various groups of clients also might differ, the actual processes or procedures in therapy appeared more similar than otherwise. Thus, although some therapists might label themselves as Freudians, some as Sullivanians or Interpersonal therapists, and some as emphasizing object relations, they might still refer to themselves as analysts or as carrying out psychoanalytically or psychodynamically oriented psychotherapy.

In more recent years, there have also been some other developments within psychoanalysis and psychoanalytic psychotherapy. One of these has been characterized as object relations theory. Instead of Freud's emphasis on repressed conflicts, involving sexual and Oedipal themes, the emphasis in object relations theory is on the importance of interpersonal relations (Blatt & Lerner, 1991; Eagle & Wolitzky, 1992). Although this emphasis is similar to that described for the views of Sullivan, it has developed separately from the work of Klein (1948) and more specifically that of Fairbairn (1952). The term objects, as used here, refers to people, animate objects, rather than material or inanimate objects. "However, a significant part of object relations theory deals with *internalized objects* and *internalized object relations.* In contrast to Freud's psychic world, which is populated by unconscious wishes and defenses against those wishes, Fairbairn's psychic world is populated by internalized objects and internalized object relations" (Eagle & Wolitzky, 1992, p. 127).

Another fairly recent development that appears to have had an impact in this area is the "self psychology" of Kohut (1977). Initially, Kohut viewed self psychology as a development growing out of traditional Freudian theory and as a broadened conception of psychoanalytic theory. Over time, however, Kohut's views increasingly diverged from the traditional psychoanalytic views. "Thus, in all pathology, intrapsychic conflict regarding sexual and aggressive wishes was always secondary to the issue of self-cohesiveness" (Eagle & Wolitzky, 1992, p. 137). Instead of drives and psychosexual stages, the development of the self is the main developmental feature. Thus, there have been several new and somewhat different emphases in more current psychoanalytic views. Of particular importance has been "the increased emphasis on interpersonal relationships and phenomenological experiences as a fundamental data base for the development of a clinical theory of psychoanalysis" (Blatt & Lerner, 1991, p. 164). This has led to a greater interest in the more severe character disorders at the same time that other psychodynamic therapists have developed briefer forms of psychotherapy for less disturbed individuals.

Unquestionably, psychoanalysis and psychodynamic therapies have had a decided influence on the theories and practice of psychotherapy generally. Many of the concepts have been used by therapists who designate themselves as eclectic therapists (Garfield & Kurtz, 1976; Jensen, Bergin, & Greaves, 1990). Furthermore, analytically trained therapists were highly regarded and in the period following the Second World War, representatives of this orientation had positions of leadership in many departments of psychiatry and in clinical psychology programs in this country. However, this has lessened to a discernable degree and other developments, to be mentioned shortly, have had their impact on the field of psychotherapy. Of particular importance, perhaps, has been the relative lack of research on psychoanalysis and traditional forms of psychoanalytic therapy.

CLIENT-CENTERED AND HUMANISTIC EMPHASES

A rather different contribution comes from the work of the late Carl Rogers who was a distinguished clinical psychologist. In the late 1930s, Rogers became dissatisfied with the traditional emphases in psychotherapy and developed his own approach which at first was called "non-directive" counseling and psychotherapy (Rogers, 1942). A later volume was titled "Client-Centered Therapy" and this designation of the therapy has continued (Rogers, 1951).

There are several emphases in this approach that are worthy of note here. Initially, Rogers reacted negatively to the traditional "expert" role of the psychotherapist. Because of the potential similarity to the common roles of the physician and lawyer, the client, consequently, may expect the therapist to do something for him or to tell him what to do. If, in fact, one takes the view that the client himself has the capacity for self-exploration and change, then the traditional helping role is a potential hindrance to the emergence and facilitation of this process. This was one of the reasons that Rogers at first referred to his therapy as non-directive, and in later writings deemphasized the techniques of therapy and stressed instead the personality of the therapist and the client's capacity for change. To a certain extent, also, he tended to place greater emphasis on the feelings of the participants and less on the attainment of insight and cognitions. If the therapist accepts and responds to the feelings of the client, movement toward positive change is likely to result.

Although Rogers continued to emphasize the potential capacity of the individual client to change, he also postulated what he viewed as the necessary therapeutic conditions for positive movement and change in psychotherapy (Rogers, 1957). The latter were essentially desired characteristics of the therapist. Although six such conditions were listed originally by Rogers, the three which have received the most attention and research are: empathy, nonpossessive warmth (originally unconditional positive regard), and genuineness or congruence (Truax & Mitchell, 1971; Zimring, 1991). From the client-centered point of view, these are the sufficient and necessary conditions for change by means of psychotherapy. A therapist who manifests these attributes will facilitate personal growth and positive self-exploration on the part of the client, whereas therapists who are deficient in these qualities may not only impede therapeutic progress, but may actually make the client worse (Rogers, Gendlin, Kiesler, & Truax, 1967).

Although therapists of other persuasions were sometimes critical of Rogers for implying that only his approach centered on the client, it is true that Rogers' emphasis was somewhat different. He did believe in the person's implicit capacity to change and studiously avoided any directive procedures such as expressing disapproval of client behaviors or of giving advice in any form. The therapist's task is to respond accurately, sensitively, and empathically to the communications and underlying feelings of the client. Furthermore, although other therapeutic viewpoints have also mentioned the importance of empathy, warmth, and genuineness on the part of the therapist, none have give them the central importance accorded to them by the client-centered school, nor have they received the intensive study and research which has been characteristic of this orientation. Some of the signal contributions of Rogers and his followers have been the early systematic study of psychotherapy, the introduction of tape-recorded therapy sessions for purposes of research, and the general emphasis on research and its importance for improving the practice of psychotherapy. These individuals in many ways were the significant pioneers in research on psychotherapy, tedious and difficult though the work is. In any event, the importance of the qualities of the therapist in his interactions with the client for the progress of therapy, which has been emphasized by the client-centered school, has general implications for all psychotherapists.

The client-centered approach has also been referred to as one of the humanistic, experiential, or phenomenological approaches to psychotherapy because of its emphasis on the person's perceptions and experiences. Although there are a number of different forms of psychotherapy that are usually included under this general rubric, most differ from client-centered therapy. Most of them also have had relatively little research appraisal although this is beginning to change (Greenberg, Elliott, & Lietaer, 1994).

Although such terms as humanistic, experiential, and existential often lack precise definitions and mean different things to different people, they represent approaches that are more concerned with philosophical views of man and his experience, and less with techniques and empirical findings. Binswanger (1956), Frankl (1965), and May (1958) are representative contributors to this point of view. Although such writers tend to be concerned with the human individual's existence and the experiencing of his present reality as he exists and interacts with his world in the here and now, some, such as Frankl (1965) particularly, have discussed specific techniques of therapy which, though designated differently, closely resemble techniques described by a vastly different approach such as behavioral therapy (Garfield, 1974a).

Although some client-centered therapists have also placed considerable emphasis on the client's current awareness of his experience, or the process of experiencing (Gendlin, 1961), this type of emphasis is not typical of the existentialists. In fact, a study comparing the views of client-centered therapists with those of other orientations indicated that client-centered therapists resembled an eclectic group of therapists more than the humanistic or existential therapists (Garfield & Kurtz, 1975, 1976). However, there is some similarity in the common emphasis on becoming aware of one's own feelings and experiences and being in touch with them. Because of the philosophical orientation of the existentialists and their emphasis on such concepts as "existence" and "being," it would seem that this approach would appeal mainly to clients who themselves are partial to such views, namely, relatively well-educated and culturally sophisticated individuals. This, however, is conjecture in the absence of any studies on this matter.

Another approach that is frequently included in the humanistic-experiential grouping because of its emphasis on the free expression of feelings and the current reality of the here and now is gestalt therapy. Although this approach tended to be viewed as overemphasizing confrontations with the patient, and thus being very different from Rogers' approach, it has undergone significant change in the last 10 to 15 years (Korb, Gorrell, & Van DeRiet, 1989). Some of the emphases of gestalt psychology such as the relation of figure to ground, closure, the formation of gestalts as well as a general holistic emphasis have been stressed more recently. One cannot make valid inferences about a type of therapy from simply having it designated as belonging to some broad grouping such as humanistic or experiential. However, the general emphasis on the feelings and emotional aspects of the patient provided by these forms of psychotherapy is of some potential value.

BEHAVIORAL AND COGNITIVE EMPHASES

Among the relatively more recent contributions to the field of psychotherapy are those that have come from the behavioral and cognitive orientations. Deriving initially from the work of Pavlov on conditioning and then from the later developments in learning theory, the behavioral approach has been one of the most important recent developments in psychotherapy. The behavioral approach has contributed emphases that are quite different from the main features of the more traditional approaches. In contrast to the psychodynamic orientations, the behavioral therapists do not conceptualize or place any emphasis on unconscious motives and conflicts, and generally want nothing to do with such inferred hypothetical constructs. Rather, as their name implies, they prefer to place their emphasis on behavior. The manifestations of the client's difficulties are not to be viewed as symptoms of an underlying conflict, but instead are to be seen for what they are, namely, disturbed or deviant patterns of behavior. Furthermore, the latter are seen as learned behaviors and as the product of faulty learning. The individual has acquired his or her fears, phobias, compulsions, and avoidant behaviors, and what has been acquired by means of learning can be modified by the proper application of the principles of learning. In essence, what has been learned can be unlearned, and there is no reason to postulate unconscious mechanisms and the like when what is involved can be more simply and economically handled by the principles of learning. Thus, behavior therapy appears to be based on postulates and views that are quite the opposite of those advanced by the psychodynamic psychotherapists.

There also appear to be some important differences between the views held by client-centered therapists and those held by the behavior therapists. The role of the therapist is theoretically quite different in these two approaches. The behavior therapist takes on the role of the expert healer. In addition to taking a comprehensive history from the client concerning his current complaints, the initial appearance of the disturbing behavior, the conditions under which the clients' behaviors (symptoms) are more pronounced and the like, the behavior therapist generally tends to direct the therapy. He may give the client instructions in how to relax, assign exercises to practice at home, instruct him in how to visualize particular experiences, and help him to construct a hierarchy of feared situations. In behaving in this fashion, the behavior therapist resembles the physician and other expert healers, and is certainly not behaving in a non-directive role.

The behavior therapists have emphasized a thorough evaluation of the client's problems and then devising a therapeutic or remedial plan which appears appropriate for the specific case. In contrast to the client-centered and psychodynamic schools of psychotherapy, until recently they have paid relatively little formal attention to the personality or personal qualities of the therapist. Such therapist variables as genuineness, empathy, and warmth received little emphasis from behavior therapists, except where positive social reinforcement was deemed necessary, and then it is viewed within a learning theory framework and perceived differently. Nevertheless, although such therapeutic conditions or therapist variables have not been emphasized previously in the behavioral scheme of things, one must not assume that behavior therapists lack such qualities or perform in a cold and mechanistic manner. Most of them do not, and in one study where these therapist conditions were appraised in a group of psychoanalytic therapists and a group of well-known behavior therapists, not only did both groups of therapists manifest relatively high levels of these conditions, but on some variables the behavior therapists actually exceeded their psychoanalytic counterparts (Sloane, Staples, Cristol, Yorkston, & Whipple, 1975). As mentioned earlier, it is more important to examine what therapists actually do, than what they say they do.

In contrast to the earliest behavioral writings, more recent publications have presented a less doctrinaire view. For example, such well-known behavior therapists as Goldfried and Davison (1976), O'Leary and Wilson (1987), and Emmelkamp (1986) have all acknowledged the importance of the therapeutic relationship in psychotherapy. As Emmelkamp stated, "It is becoming increasingly clear that the quality of the therapeutic relationship may be influential in determining success or failure of behavior therapies although well controlled studies are rare" (Emmelkamp, 1986, p. 432).

A significant contribution of the behavioral therapists is their attempt to appraise systematically the client's problem, to formulate the problem in behavioral terms as explicitly as possible, and then to devise a specific therapeutic program for the individual client. Reasonably, one could say that more than in most other forms of psychotherapy, the activities of the therapist are determined by this appraisal of what is required in a given case. Whereas a client-centered therapist would listen to the client and in all instances attempt to express or convey empathy, warmth, and genuineness, the essential therapeutic conditions, the behavior therapist, after appraising the client's problem, would have to decide on what specific procedures should be utilized. While she might use certain preferred procedures such as relaxation and systematic desensitization with a large number of cases, the specific fear hierarchies used would be developed for the particular client. Furthermore, other techniques might be used such as behavioral rehearsal, exposure, assertiveness training, homework assignments, and the like, depending on the problems involved. The tasks in therapy and the appraisal of progress are more clearly defined in behavioral terms and, thus, are more easily understood by the client, as well as being more readily evaluated.

These emphases in behavior therapy, as might be inferred, have not been particularly well received by many therapists of other persuasions, especially the psychodynamic, humanistic, and relationship-oriented therapists, although this has been changing (Arkowitz & Messer, 1984; Birk & Brinkley-Birk, 1974; Feather & Rhoads, 1972; Marmor & Woods, 1980; Wachtel, 1977). The research emphasis of the behaviorists, their publication of positive results, and the relative brevity of the treatment as compared to many other traditional therapies, have all contributed to the impact behavior therapy has had on the current therapeutic scene. Behavioral forms of therapy have been recognized as of particular value in the treatment of problems of anxiety, panic states, and obsessive-compulsive disorders. In addition, behavioral procedures have played a prominent role in the developing field of behavioral medicine and health psychology as well as in attempts to develop psychotherapy integration. More will be said later about this last development.

Although cognitive emphases and approaches to treatment have existed for some time, their relative popularity is fairly recent (Hollon & Beck, 1986, 1994). In fact, the increased interest in such approaches has been quite marked. Not only are there differences within the various cognitive therapies, but there has been a noticeable drawing together of cognitive and behavioral procedures among therapists of both persuasions. As a result, there has also been a greater use of the designation, cognitive-behavioral therapies. In a recent review, Hollon and Beck (1994) describe these developments in the following way:

> The cognitive and cognitive-behavioral interventions differ with respect to their early developmental histories. The cognitive interventions were typically developed by theorists originally trained dynamically and tended to emphasize the role of meaning. In these approaches, it was not so important what a person thinks (or says) as what he or she believes. The cognitive-behavioral interventions, on the other hand, were typically developed by theorists originally trained as behaviorists. In these approaches, thinking tended to be conceptualized in a much more concrete fashion, often being regarded as covert self-statements (private behaviors) that either did or did not occur and that could be influenced by the same laws of conditioning as other overt behaviors. The cognitive approaches tended to take the lead in developing strategies for examining the rationality or validity of existing beliefs, whereas the more behaviorally-oriented cognitive-behavioral approaches tended to focus on the development of strategies for teaching specific cognitive skills.

In fact, both approaches combine cognitive and behavioral elements, albeit in different ways and to different extents, and each can be legitimately considered to belong to the larger family of cognitive-behavioral interventions. Moreover, both approaches have borrowed from the other over the years, blurring the distinctions between them, both conceptually and operationally. (p. 429)

Among the most popular cognitive approaches are the rational-emotive school of psychotherapy developed by Ellis (1962; Bernard & DiGiuseppe, 1989) and the cognitive approach of Beck (1976). In these and related approaches, the cause of disturbed behavior is believed to be faulty thinking or dysfunctional cognitions on the part of the client. The client is unhappy or depressed because she possesses faulty beliefs. These, in turn, lead her to have false expectations about herself and others, and, consequently, she experiences failure and unhappiness. In order for changes to occur, the client's false or distorted beliefs must be given up and more realistic and positive ones acquired. Cognitions, thus, receive relatively more explicit emphasis in these approaches to psychotherapy than they do in most others. The actual role of the therapist and the procedure he follows will also differ from those of other orientations as a consequence. In contrast to the Freudian approach, a rational-emotive therapist will be more active in directly calling the attention of the client to her false beliefs and her need for ridding herself of them. Various other instructions and directions may also be given to the client, including suggestions for actually performing certain activities in the client's life situation outside of the consulting office. The differences between such cognitive therapists and those who adhere to a client-centered point of view should be apparent without further comment.

Although cognitive therapies appear to have been developed independently by therapists who became dissatisfied with the effectiveness of analytically oriented therapy, as noted previously, they have moved more closely in the last few years to some rapprochement and amalgamation with behavioral therapies and procedures. Thus, we have noted increasing discussions of cognitive behavioral therapy (Hollon & Beck, 1986; Kendall, Vitousek, & Kane, 1991; Meichenbaum, 1977). Beck (1976), among others, acknowledges the use and value of behavioral procedures. Several individuals primarily trained as behavior therapists have conducted studies comparing behavioral and cognitive procedures in psychotherapy and have devised new approaches that attempt to incorporate aspects of both behavioral and cognitive therapy (Arnkoff & Glass, 1992; Emmelkamp, 1994; Mahoney & Arnkoff, 1978; Meichenbaum, 1972). Such attempts suggest the possibility that therapists may be able in a somewhat systematic fashion to utilize procedures from more than one school of psychotherapy to improve the effectiveness of psychotherapy.

APPRAISING DIFFERENT ORIENTATIONS
AND EMPHASES

The newcomer to the field of psychotherapy must at times be rather bewildered by the great array of psychotherapies, all claiming to be successful, and all offering apparently different paths to the same goal. In addition to those already mentioned, there are numerous other varieties of psychotherapy which, of necessity, must be omitted here (Binder, Binder, & Rimland, 1976; Corsini & Wedding, 1989; Harper, 1975; Herink, 1980; Morse & Watson, 1977). How does one choose from this vast diversity of offerings? How does one judge which form of psychotherapy is best? If some comprehensive and standardized test were made in which all of the psychotherapies were compared on a common criterion with comparable groups of subjects, one might have at least some possible answers to these questions. However, this has not been done and there does not now exist an agency such as the federal Food and Drug Agency to test the potency and potential harmful effects of the diverse psychotherapies. There is not even a Consumer's Union available in this area although some health maintenance organizations and related groups do attempt to monitor the length and quality of various types of services. The best potential guide is the research literature, but, besides its being widely scattered and limited in many respects, most of the psychotherapies have reported little or no research.

It appears that most psychotherapists follow a particular form of psychotherapy or select their therapeutic procedures on bases other than research evidence. However, no systematic study of this process has ever been made. Consequently, one can only offer some conjectures about what appears to take place, based on personal observation and experience, a few self-reports, and one study of eclectic clinical psychologists (Garfield & Kurtz, 1977).

Some psychotherapists appear to be influenced by the particular approach emphasized during their training, either during their graduate programs or in postgraduate training. Some students may select a particular school or program that is in line with their current preferences. This is probably most likely where a specific institution is known for fostering a particular viewpoint. In such instances, individuals may be attracted to a particular viewpoint for a variety of personal reasons. Either one theoretical viewpoint is intellectually attractive, it appears in accord with one's own personal experience, one has been greatly influenced by an individual of a given persuasion, or the individual's own therapy has made a deep impression on him. After the individual has completed her professional training, she may also modify her views and therapeutic procedures on the basis of her own practice or as a result of attending professional meetings, special institutes, participating in a group, and the like. The individual's personality may also influence how she responds to a particular orientation and how she interprets and adapts it to her own practice. No two therapists of the same school necessarily function in psychotherapy in exactly the same manner (Glover, 1955; Lambert, 1989; Luborsky et al., 1986; Lieberman, Yalom, & Miles, 1973).

In numerous discussions with individuals engaged in psychotherapy, many of them have said that they follow a particular orientation or have evolved procedures for conducting therapy that suits them personally. In most instances, they indicate that they are using procedures they have found to be particularly effective. On the other hand, it appears that at least some therapists are utilizing an approach that they find personally gratifying, and these two aspects are not necessarily identical. For example, some doctoral students have told me that they prefer one type of therapy over another because it is more interesting and exciting than another, or that they deem one specific form of therapy as being rather boring. They do not make any reference to the effectiveness of the respective therapies, but rather to the personal satisfaction secured from using one approach over another—and attempts that are made to have them become more concerned with the former matter are not always successful.

Raymond Corsini in a recent book related how he became a devoted Adlerian (Corsini, 1991). After experiencing therapy with Rogers and working with Moreno in psychodramatic productions, Corsini studied with the well-known Adlerian, Rudolph Dreikurs. One live case presentation by Dreikurs had a tremendous impact on him. "This one incident, together with my personal comfort with Adlerian theory and philosophy, later led me to join Dreikurs' clinic and become an Adlerian" (Corsini, 1991, p. 20). In contrast, the present writer found both positive and not-so-positive features in a number of well-known forms of psychotherapy, and rather early in his career became an eclectic therapist.

Thus, there are many different reasons for individuals choosing certain approaches to psychotherapy, and personal predilections and fortuitous circumstances appear to be as frequent as considerations of proven merit. Although this does appear to be a current reality, there is a need to try to order, appraise, and integrate those procedures that appear to be similar in many of the different approaches or that, on the basis of experience and research, appear to have some therapeutic merit. This is one goal of this book, and the preceding pages have been an attempt to highlight different emphases which have been important in the development of psychotherapy, as well as illustrating some of the wide differences in orientations and procedures.

Taken at face value, the various emphases discussed would appear so different that it would seem extremely difficult, if not impossible, to reconcile them into some ordered fashion. Although this is undoubtedly true to some extent, the task may not be as impossible as it appears. Several attempts at integration have been reported in recent years and there appears to be a greater interest in such attempts currently (Goldfried, 1991; Norcross & Goldfried, 1992). In order to do this, however, it is essential to try to look impartially at a given concept and to examine what it means operationally. One who has been indoctrinated into perceiving a given phenomenon in a specified way may find it difficult to change and perceive matters in a different light. We know from studies of attitude change, as well as from our work in psychotherapy, that it is not an easy matter to change people's views and perceptions, particularly where a person's emotions and personal security are involved. However, change is possible, and it also provides the basis for possible progress. The task appears worthy of the effort, even though the goal may be difficult to attain.

On a very broad level, we have discussed different approaches to psychotherapy that seem to emphasize different aspects of human experience. At least in their written formal presentations, some approaches emphasize behavioral means of effecting change, some stress cognitions as the important avenue to change, while others focus on affective experiences as the crucial variables in psychotherapy. On the surface, these varying approaches appear to be stressing very different pathways to a common goal. However, these different conceptualizations of what occurs may be overly generalized or focused abstractions of what actually takes place. The human being functions as a total organism and it is highly doubtful that one can focus exclusively on cognitions without in some way involving behaviors or affects simultaneously or in some interactive manner. Verbal communications from one individual to another are not simply intellectual messages. They can cause an individual to become angry, frightened, or elated, as well as causing him to strike another person, to run away, or to faint and lose consciousness. The significance of verbal messages are also related to the particular relationships that exist between the individuals involved and to the environmental situations in which these are embedded. Verbal communication, therefore, can be a rather powerful means of inducing changes in people, although there is much that we still need to learn about how to use it for constructive purposes in psychotherapy.

In a similar fashion, although client-centered therapists have emphasized the importance of the therapist's empathy, warmth, and genuineness, and performed most of the research in this area, one cannot state that other therapists do not manifest or incorporate such attributes in their therapeutic work with clients. Although behavior therapists, until recently, seemingly paid scant attention to such therapist attributes in their publications and research, this is no longer the case. Also, as noted earlier, one important study, utilizing scales developed by client-centered therapist-researchers, reported that high levels of such therapeutic variables were manifested by behavioral therapists in their therapy with actual clients (Sloane et al., 1975). In other words, although adherents of a given orientation may make little or no reference to particular variables or procedures in their formal writings, this does not signify that the variables in question are not being utilized. A given theoretical system appears to develop from the particular observations and conceptual formulations of an individual as he tries to organize his particular views of the phenomena in question. He attempts to make them fit together and become a coherent and cohesive system. Once a particular stance or frame of reference is adopted, it will influence the observations and formulations of the individual involved. The individual, of necessity, will have to be selective and concepts which appear to be grossly different or in opposition to the basic concepts held will be slighted or discarded. Consequently, some aspects of psychotherapy will tend to be emphasized by one school and given little or no mention by another.

It is also quite likely that essentially similar phenomena may be described and designated in somewhat different ways by some of the orientations in psychotherapy, as well as receiving different emphases. For example, the particular system of psychotherapy called psychodrama (Moreno, 1946) utilized role playing on the part of the therapist and patient for many years before other therapists made use of this procedure. It appeared later in the writings of behavior therapists under the designation of "behavioral rehearsal." Similarly, one can note the same type of procedure described by an early behaviorist and a more recent existentialist. Dunlap (1932), writing over 60 years ago, described a procedure which he called *negative practice*. This had to do with attempts to correct persistent errors in typing. If an individual frequently typed "teh" instead of "the," instructions to consciously type "teh" appeared to correct the error. In a similar way, Frankl (1965) describes the conscious and deliberate use of a procedure by which a client focuses deliberately on the behavior she wants to avoid, and terms this "paradoxical intention." Other examples of this type could also be secured.

A final point to be considered here is the fact that despite such different formulations and emphases, all of the different varieties of psychotherapy claim to be successful. None claims to be less effective than the others and I have yet to hear a psychotherapist say that his or her own psychotherapy was an inferior form of psychotherapy. This is a phenomenon that has intrigued me for many years and that has influenced my own views of psychotherapy (Garfield, 1957, 1974a, 1974b, 1982, 1987, 1989, 1992).

Although it is conceivable that each of the different varieties of psychotherapy represent a unique and different means of effecting positive change in client behaviors, it appears more likely that the factors or variables emphasized by the different approaches are either similar in how they are received or perceived by the client, or they *are not* the crucial variables responsible for change. In other words, while one school emphasizes insight, another desensitization, and yet another empathy and warmth, it is conceivable that these variables as postulated are not the crucial ones. Rather, there may be other variables or components of these variables that are common to most of the psychotherapies, but which receive little formal attention and emphasis in the different theoretical formulations. One example may suffice for the present, although this topic will receive more attention in a later section of the book.

Let us take the matter of insight. Insight into one's underlying problems is considered important by most psychodynamically oriented therapists. However, what is insight and how is it acquired? An understanding of one's underlying problems is derived by verbal interactions with a therapist and will be influenced by the latter's own theoretical views. Consequently, the insights obtained from a psychoanalyst will be quite different from those obtained by followers of Adler or Horney, or from analysts influenced by more recent developments. In the first instance, it is likely that the individual will gain insight into his sexual or aggressive conflicts deriving from earlier stages of his psychosexual development. Such an insight would very likely not be obtained from an Adlerian therapist. Instead, in such therapy, the client possibly would be given an understanding of the importance of his role in the family, his feelings of inferiority, and his attempts to compensate for these feelings. The followers of Horney, Winnicott, or Kohut (Blatt & Lerner, 1991) provide still other types of insight for their patients—yet, all the patients would supposedly benefit from these very different insights.

It is possible, therefore, that it is not the specific "insights" secured by the patients that are in fact therapeutic, but something else. Furthermore, whatever this something else is, it would appear to be similar among the different approaches mentioned. If we look more closely at this situation, we can at least hypothesize that perhaps one common aspect is that the therapist provides the patient with some explanation for his difficulties. It would appear, hypothetically, that what precisely is told the patient is not of particular import since each of the patients is told something very different. However, the explanation provided and apparently accepted by the client appears to be of some therapeutic value. Apparently then, being given some explanation for one's problems by an interested expert in the role of healer, may be the important common aspect of these divergent therapies (Frank, 1971; Garfield, 1974b, 1991; Torrey, 1972). This is not to say that this is all there is to psychotherapy or that an understanding of one's difficulties is the crucial variable. It is simply an attempt to illustrate how some of the emphasized theoretical postulates of differing schools of psychotherapy may be viewed from a different perspective. It also suggests the possible importance of some potential common aspects of psychotherapy when viewed in this way.

Even the behavior therapists, who say very little about insight in psychotherapy and would feel that it is of little or no consequence in their therapy, can be shown to have something in common with the orientations referred to in our previous illustrations. The behavior therapists who use systematic desensitization generally provide the client with some understanding of the procedures to be used and their rationale. To this extent, therefore, they also provide the client with some insight and understanding of how his problems have developed and how therapy can be expected to modify his current behavior. Although not insight in the traditional psychoanalytic sense, to the extent that such procedures provide the client with an understanding of his difficulties, they may serve a similar function. They both can be viewed also as manifestations of the therapist's knowledge and desire to help the client.

It does not seem wise at this stage in the development of psychotherapy to present only one system of psychotherapeutic procedure, or to cling too tenaciously to any fixed views. At the same time, a simple cataloging of a number of different therapeutic systems, although interesting, does not give any clear or coherent understanding of the psychotherapeutic process. It is the latter that we will strive for in the remainder of the book.

REFERENCES

Arkowitz, H., & Messer, S. B. (1984). *Psychoanalytic therapy and behavior therapy. Is integration possible?* New York: Plenum.

Arnkoff, D. B., & Glass, C. R. (1992). Cognitive therapy and psychotherapy integration. In D. K. Freedheim (Ed.), *History of psychotherapy. A century of change* (pp. 657–694). Washington, DC: American Psychological Association.

Beck, A. T. (1976). *Cognitive therapy and the emotional disorders.* New York: International Universities Press.

Bernard, M. E., & DiGiuseppe, R. (Eds.) (1989). *Inside Rational-Emotive Therapy. A critical appraisal of the theory and therapy of Albert Ellis.* San Diego, CA: Academic Press.

Binder, V., Binder, A., & Rimland, B. (1976). *Modern therapies.* Englewood Cliffs, NJ: Prentice-Hall.

Binswanger, L. (1956). Existential analysis and psychotherapy. In F. Fromm-Reichman & J. L. Moreno (Eds.), *Progress in psychotherapy 1956* (pp. 144–148). New York: Grune and Stratton.

Birk, L., & Brinkley-Birk, A. W. (1974). Psychoanalysis and behavior therapy. *American Journal of Psychiatry, 131,* 499–509.

Blatt, S. J., & Lerner, H. (1991). Psychodynamic perspectives on personality theory. In M. Hersen, A. E. Kazdin, & A. S. Bellack (Eds.), *The clinical psychology handbook* (2nd ed.) (pp. 147–169). New York: Wiley.

Corsini, R. J. (1991). Adlerian Psychotherapy. In R. J. Corsini (Ed.), *Five therapists and one client* (pp. 13–58). Itasca, IL: Peacock.

Corsini, R. J., & Wedding, D. (1989). *Current psychotherapies* (4th ed.). Itasca, IL: Peacock.

Dunlap, K. (1932). *Habits: Their making and unmaking.* New York: Liveright.

Eagle, M. N., & Wolitzky, D. L. (1992). Psychoanalytic theories of psychotherapy. In D. K. Freedheim (Ed.), *History of psychotherapy. A century of change* (pp. 109–158). Washington, DC: American Psychological Association.

Ellis, A. (1962). *Reason and emotion in psychotherapy.* New York: Lyle Stuart.

Emmelkamp, P. M. G. (1986). Behavior therapy with adults. In S. L. Garfield & A. E. Bergin (Eds.), *Handbook of psychotherapy and behavior change* (3rd ed.) (pp. 385–442). New York: Wiley.

Emmelkamp, P. M. G. (1994). Behavior therapy with adults. In A. E. Bergin & S. L. Garfield (Eds.), *Handbook of psychotherapy and behavior change* (4th ed.) (pp. 379–427). New York: Wiley.

Fairbairn, W. R. D. (1952). *Psychoanalytic studies of the personality.* London: Tavistock Routledge & Kegan Paul.

Feather, B. W., & Rhoads, J. M. (1972). Psychodynamic behavior therapy. I. Theory and rationale. *Archives of General Psychiatry, 26,* 496–502.

Frank, J. D. (1971). Therapeutic factors in psychotherapy. *American Journal of Psychotherapy, XXV,* 350–361.

Frankl, V. E. (1965). *The doctor and the soul* (2nd ed.). New York: Knopf.

Freud, S. (1938). The history of the psychoanalytic movement. In *The basic writings of Sigmund Freud.* New York: Modern Library, Random House.

Freud, S. (1950). Further recommendations in the technique of psychoanalysis. Recollection, repetition and working through. In E. Jones (Ed.), *Collected papers* (pp. 366–376). London: The Hogarth Press and the Institute of Psychoanalysis.

Garfield, S. L. (1957). *Introductory clinical psychology.* New York: Macmillan.

Garfield, S. L. (1974a). *Clinical psychology: The study of personality and behavior.* Chicago: Aldine.

Garfield, S. L. (1974b). What are the therapeutic variables in psychotherapy? *Psychotherapy and Psychosomatics, 24,* 372–378.

Garfield, S. L. (1982). Eclecticism and integration in psychotherapy. *Behavior Therapy, 13,* 610–623.

Garfield, S. L. (1987). Towards a scientifically oriented eclecticism. *Scandinavian Journal of Behavior Therapy, 16,* 95–109.

Garfield, S. L. (1989). *The practice of brief psychotherapy.* New York: Pergamon.

Garfield, S. L. (1991). Common and specific factors in psychotherapy. *Journal of Integrative and Eclectic Psychotherapy, 10,* 5–13.

Garfield, S. L. (1992). Eclectic psychotherapy: A common factors approach. In J. Norcross & M. R. Goldfried (Eds.), *Handbook of integrative psychotherapy* (pp. 169–210). New York: Basic Books.

Garfield, S. L., & Kurtz, R. (1975). Clinical psychologists: A survey of selected attitudes and values. *The Clinical Psychologist, 28,* (Spring), 4–7.

Garfield, S. L., & Kurtz, R. (1976). Clinical psychologists in the 1970s. *American Psychologist, 31,* 1–9.

Garfield, S. L., & Kurtz, R. (1977). A study of eclectic views. *Journal of Consulting and Clinical Psychology, 45,* 78–83.

Gendlin, E. T. (1961). Experiencing: A variable in the process of psychotherapeutic change. *American Journal of Psychotherapy, 15,* 233.

Glover, E. (1955). *The techniques of psychoanalysis.* New York: International Universities Press.

Goldfried, M. R. (1991). Research issues in psychotherapy integration. *Journal of Psychotherapy Integration, 1,* 5–25.

Goldfried, M. R., & Davison, G. C. (1976). *Clinical behavior therapy.* New York: Holt, Rinehart and Winston.

Greenberg, L., Elliot, R. K., & Lietaer, G. (1994). Research on humanistic therapies. In A. E. Bergin & S. L. Garfield (Eds.), *Handbook of psychotherapy and behavior change* (4th ed.) (pp. 509–539). New York: Wiley.

Hammer, E. R. (Ed.) (1968). *Use of interpretation in treatment.* New York: Grune and Stratton.

Harper, R. A. (1975). *The new psychotherapies.* Englewood Cliffs, NJ: Prentice-Hall.

Herink, R. (Ed.) (1980). *The psychotherapy handbook: The A to Z guide to more than 250 different therapies in use today.* New York: New American Library.

Hollon, S. D., & Beck, A. T. (1986). Cognitive and cognitive-behavioral therapies. In S. L. Garfield & A. E. Bergin (Eds.), *Handbook of psychotherapy and behavior change* (3rd ed.) (pp. 443–482). New York: Wiley.

Hollon, S. D., & Beck, A. T. (1994). Cognitive and cognitive-behavioral therapies. In A. E. Bergin & S. L. Garfield (Eds.), *Handbook of psychotherapy and behavior change* (4th ed.) (pp. 428–466). New York: Wiley.

Horney, K. (1939). *New ways in psychoanalysis.* New York: Norton.

Jensen, J. P., Bergin, A. E., & Greaves, D. W. (1990). The meaning of eclecticism: New survey and analysis of components. *Professional Psychology: Research and Practice, 21,* 124–130.

Kendall, P. C., Vitousek, K. B., & Kane, M. (1991). Thought and action in psychotherapy: Cognitive-behavioral approaches. In M. Hersen, A. E. Kazdin, & A. S. Bellack (Eds.), *The clinical psychology handbook* (2nd ed.) (pp. 596–626). New York: Pergamon.

Klein, M. (1948). *Contributions to psychoanalysis (1921–1945).* London: Hogarth Press.

Kohut, H. (1977). *The restoration of the self.* New York: International Universities Press.

Korb, M. P., Gorrell, J., & Van DeRiet, V. (1989). *Gestalt therapy. Practice and theory* (2nd ed.). New York: Pergamon.

Lambert, M. J. (1989). The individual therapist's contribution to psychotherapy process and outcome. *Clinical Psychology Review, 9,* 469–485.

Lieberman, M. A., Yalom, I. E., & Miles, M. B. (1973). *Encounter Groups: First facts.* New York: Basic Books.

Luborsky, L., Crits-Cristoph, P., McLellan, A. T., Woody, G., Piper, W., Imber, S., & Lieberman, B. (1986). Do therapists vary much in their success? Findings from four outcome studies. *American Journal of Orthopsychiatry, 56,* 501–512.

Mahoney, M. J., & Arnoff, D. B. (1978). Cognitive and self-control therapies. In S. L. Garfield & A. E. Bergin (Eds.), *Handbook of psychotherapy and behavior change* (2nd ed.). New York: Wiley.

Marmor, J., & Woods, S. M. (1980). *The interface between the psychodynamic and behavioral therapies.* New York: Plenum.

May, R. (1958). Contributions of existential psychotherapy. In R. May, E. Angel, & H. F. Ellenberger (Eds.), *Existence. A new dimension in psychiatry and psychology.* (pp. 37–91). New York: Basic Books.

Meichenbaum, D. (1972). Cognitive modification of test anxious college students. *Journal of Consulting and Clinical Psychology, 39,* 370–380.

Meichenbaum, D. (Ed.) (1977). *Cognitive behavior modification: An integrative approach.* New York: Plenum.

Moreno, J. L. (1946). *Psychodrama Vol. 1* (2nd rev. ed.). New York: Beacon House.

Morse, S. J., & Watson, R. I., Jr. (1977). *Psychotherapies. A comparative casebook.* New York: Holt, Rinehart and Winston.

Norcross, J. C., & Goldfried, M. R. (Eds.) (1992). *Handbook of psychotherapy integration.* New York: Basic Books.

O'Leary, K. D., & Wilson, G. T. (1987). *Behavior therapy. Application and outcome* (2nd ed.). Englewood Cliffs, NJ: Prentice-Hall.

Rogers, C. R. (1942). *Counseling and psychotherapy.* Boston: Houghton Mifflin.

Rogers, C. R. (1951). *Client-centered therapy.* Boston: Houghton Mifflin.

Rogers, C. R. (1957). The necessary and sufficient conditions of therapeutic personality change. *Journal of Consulting Psychology, 21,* 95–103.

Rogers, C. R., Gendlin, E. T., Kiesler, D. J., & Truax, C. B. (1967). *The therapeutic relationship and its impact: A study of psychotherapy with schizophrenics.* Madison: University of Wisconsin Press.

Sloane, R. B., Staples, F. R., Cristol, A. H., Yorkston, N. J., & Whipple, K. (1975). *Psychotherapy versus behavior therapy.* Cambridge: Harvard University Press.

Sullivan, H. S. (1953). *The interpersonal theory of psychiatry.* New York: Norton.

Torrey, E. F. (1972). What western psychotherapists can learn from witchdoctors. *American Journal of Orthopsychiatry, 42,* 69–76.

Truax, C. B., & Mitchell, K. M. (1971). Research on certain therapist interpersonal skills in relation to process and outcome. In A. E. Bergin & S. L. Garfield (Eds.), *Handbook of psychotherapy and behavior change.* New York: Wiley.

Wachtel, P. L. (1977). *Psychoanalysis and behavior therapy.* New York: Basic Books.

Wolberg, L. R. (1954). *The technique of psychotherapy.* New York: Grune and Stratton.

Zimring, F. (1991). Person-centered therapy. In R. J. Corsini (Ed.), *Five therapists and one client* (pp. 59–101). Itasca, IL: Peacock.

CHAPTER 3

The Therapy Client-Patient*

When we consider the variables that can influence the process and outcome of psychotherapy, at least five such variables or factors appear to play potentially important roles. These are the patient or client, the therapist, the particular interaction or relationship that develops in therapy, the type of therapy, and events in the client's life outside of therapy. Without question, client variables play a particularly important part in the therapeutic results secured. Although the contribution of the client to therapeutic outcome is influenced by the type of therapist, the form of therapy, and important events in the client's life, the focus in this chapter will be on the client.

Much has been said and written about the client in psychotherapy and in the past 30 to 40 years a considerable amount of research has been conducted on a variety of client characteristics in relation to both outcome and continuation in psychotherapy (Garfield, 1994). Client variables such as social class, clinical diagnosis, personality, severity and length of disturbance, age, sex, motivation, and expectations for therapy have received some research attention. The increased emphasis on research in psychotherapy is a very positive development for the field. To the extent that findings from research investigations are replicated, we have a reasonably firm base on which to draw conclusions that have implications for practice. In this fashion, as is true in other fields of knowledge, clinical hypotheses and folklore can be supported or found wanting. At the same time, it is important to keep in mind that research on psychotherapy is a complex and difficult process, and that there are problems and limitations in some of the research that has been reported—particularly some of the older studies. We also must keep in mind that although we tend to refer to psychotherapy as if there was just one universal form of psychotherapy, in actuality there are literally hundreds of different forms of psychotherapy. Furthermore, the designations of the therapies (e.g., behavioral, psychodynamic, humanistic) do not necessarily provide us with an adequate picture of the actual therapeutic operations that occur. Also, the therapists used in the various studies have varied in terms

---

*This chapter is based in large part on the author's review of the research literature on client variables in psychotherapy (Garfield, 1994).

of training, experience, and skill. In a similar fashion, a variety of different outcome measures have been used. Thus, our ability to compare studies and to draw reliable or valid conclusions is sometimes limited.

Serious attempts have been made in recent years to improve the quality of psychotherapy research. Since this will be discussed in Chapter 12, only a few comments will be made here. Among the changes made have been the preparation of training manuals for specific forms of psychotherapy. Thus, therapists have been trained to perform the specific forms of therapy being evaluated and their therapy has been monitored to ensure conformity with the manuals. Experienced therapists and carefully diagnosed patients have been used along with a variety of standard evaluation measures. In general, the quality of research has improved and consequently, we shall make reference to research findings where available in our discussion of client, as well as other variables. Where findings are minimal, this will be noted and the author's own views based on his clinical experience will be clearly identified. Now, let us turn our attention to the psychotherapy client.

Clients who seek or are referred for psychotherapeutic help usually are experiencing difficulties or problems in their daily life that appear to be psychological in nature. In some cases, they may even complain of physical or somatic problems for which no physical basis has been found in previous medical examinations. The range of problems brought for psychotherapeutic treatment thus may be quite large and the degree of severity may also vary widely. Although there is no unanimity concerning the type or severity of disorders that can be treated successfully by means of psychotherapy, there appears to be some agreement that problems of anxiety, mild to moderate depression, situational stress, some character or personality difficulties, and the like, generally have positive outcomes. There is much less agreement, as well as less research, concerning the suitability of psychotherapy for psychotic disorders or severe personality disorders, although it may be used along with drugs and medication in the treatment of such disorders as well as in cases of severe depression or anxiety. Thus, to a certain extent, psychotherapy tends to be emphasized as a treatment modality with patients who are not the most seriously disturbed.

Apart from degree of disturbance, clients differ in a number of ways and can be characterized in terms of different characteristics or attributes that presumably may influence therapeutic outcomes. Some of these characteristics, such as sex or gender, are reasonably easy to reliably appraise. Age, for example, can be studied as a continuous quantitative variable. However, when we attempt to appraise inferred client attributes such as motivation for therapy or personality characteristics, the resulting investigation is beset by many difficulties including the reliability and validity of the judgments or appraisals. Even such a widely used clinical designation as schizophrenia suffers from problems of limited reliability (Garfield, 1986, 1993). Consequently, as we review the available data on some of these topics, we may expect to find conflicting results in the various reports in the literature, thus making it difficult to secure reliable and valid generalizations.

Before we examine more specific client characteristics and their relationship to different aspects of psychotherapy, one additional point should be made. In any presentation of a complex phenomenon, it is desirable to discuss the separate component parts. However, it is important to realize that such an analysis cannot fully describe the reality of the total phenomenon or process. In psychotherapy, the client's attributes and behaviors are influenced to an important extent by those of the therapist, and the reverse is also true. However, in analyzing the interaction that takes place, it appears necessary at first to focus on the individual participants and their particular roles and contributions to this interaction. Thus, when we examine client variables in relation to criteria such as outcome or continuation in psychotherapy, we should keep in mind that such findings have been secured from a particular group of clients who received psychotherapy from a given group of therapists. In any given instance, the particular results secured for a client conceivably could have been influenced to some extent by the particular therapist involved. Nevertheless, such findings do provide us with some useful information about what actually occurs in the day-to-day clinical practice of psychotherapy. We shall first review representative findings on client variables in relation to selected aspects of psychotherapy. These data should also help you understand some of the problems and realities of psychotherapy as it currently takes place in the clinical situation. Some of the findings may even be quite surprising—for what occurs in clinical practice may not be quite the same as what is frequently depicted in some of the writings and popular presentations about psychotherapy, or even what a practitioner believes based on her own limited experience.

SELECTION AND ACCEPTANCE OF CLIENTS FOR PSYCHOTHERAPY

Most of the reports on who is selected for psychotherapy tend to come from studies of clinics and from community surveys. There is relatively little systematic information concerning clients treated by private practitioners, although there are a few limited surveys of individuals seen by psychoanalysts. It is very likely that there are important differences in the populations served by the therapists in these different settings. On the basis of some reports, the clientele of the private practitioners of psychoanalysis is made up disproportionately of individuals of the higher socioeconomic and educational levels (Hamberg et al., 1967; Knapp, Levin, McCarter, Wermer, & Zetzel, 1960; Weber, Solomon, & Bachrach, 1985) and one can assume that there is a high degree of selectivity in the patients accepted for such treatment. Community clinics and outpatient departments in hospitals, while having some variation in selection criteria, will generally have a less selected group of patients (Garfield, 1986b; Kadushin, 1969).

Not all individuals who apply for treatment receive psychotherapy. In addition, not all who are actually offered psychotherapy accept it, a finding which many beginning and interested students find hard to understand. In three early studies, approximately one-third or more of the individuals coming to a clinic and judged to be in need of psychotherapy refused treatment after it was offered to them (Garfield & Kurz, 1952; Rosenthal & Frank, 1958; Weiss & Schaie, 1958). Marks (1978) reported that of several hundred patients offered behavioral therapy at the Maudsley Hospital, 23% refused the offered therapy. Comparable results were also obtained by Betz and Shullman (1979) with 24% failing to keep the first appointment. In two studies of outpatients at Boston City Hospital, approximately 40% of the patients failed to show up for their scheduled first appointment (Raynes & Warren, 1971a, 1971b). Almost identical results were reported in a study of a sample of 2,551 cases drawn from 17 community mental health facilities— 40.8% of the cases failed to return after the intake interview (Sue, McKinney, & Allen, 1976). A report of 2,922 students seen at a university counseling center over a period of eight years indicated that almost 49% failed to come to the first therapy session (Phillips & Fagan, 1982). On the basis of such reports, one can anticipate that in most outpatient settings, a relatively large number of patients who have been scheduled for psychotherapy will decline this opportunity by failing to keep their appointments.

Several studies have investigated some of the possible factors related to this nonacceptance of psychotherapy but the results are far from conclusive. A significant relationship between acceptance on the part of the client and client income, and also between acceptance and rated level of client motivation, was secured in an early study by Rosenthal and Frank (1958). A significant correlation also was reported between lower socioeconomic status and the failure of the client to keep his initial appointment by Yamamoto and Goin (1966), but in another study, no significant findings were secured for variables such as sex, education, or age (Noonan, 1973). It was also noted in the latter study that those who failed to keep their first therapy appointment tended to present their problems in a vague and evasive manner as compared with those who kept their appointments.

Two reports based on two different samples of referrals to the Psychiatric Outpatient Department of Boston City Hospital also indicated a large percentage of nonattenders for the initial appointment. In one study of 267 referrals, 42% did not keep their appointment (Raynes & Warren, 1971a). In the first report, it was found that age and race were related to attendance. African Americans and those under 40 were significantly more likely to fail to keep their appointments. No such data were reported in the second study (Raynes & Warren, 1971b), but there appeared to be a relationship between time on the waiting list and nonattendance.

Although some relationship between selected social class variables and rejection of therapy has been secured, there is as yet no completely adequate explanation for this phenomenon. A number of possible hypotheses have been suggested including the following: inadequate motivation to undergo therapy, fear of finding out that one is seriously disturbed, a reluctance to acknowledge that one needs help in resolving personal difficulties, the possible stigma of seeing a mental health professional, and a significant change in one's life situation. The possible causes vary with different individuals. However, research in this area has been limited.

A related aspect pertains to those who appear at clinics but who are not offered psychotherapy. Several studies have reported a positive relationship between social class indices and acceptance for psychotherapy (Brill & Storrow, 1960; Cole, Branch, & Allison, 1962). Somewhat similar findings have been reported for those clients who are referred for psychotherapy as compared with referral for other types of treatment (Lubin, Hornstra, Lewis, & Bechtel, 1973). In the study by Lubin et al., patients with some college education and relatively higher occupational ratings were more frequently assigned to psychotherapy than were individuals with less than 12 years of education and lower rated occupations. In another study of a walk-in clinic, a significant relationship was reported between low socioeconomic status and the frequency of receiving drugs rather than psychotherapy (Shader, 1970).

Several other investigations have also indicated a relationship between social class indices and the type of therapy received. This was clearly shown in the now classic study by Hollingshead and Redlich (1958) of New Haven where long-term psychoanalytic therapy was provided primarily to the middle and upper classes. A survey of mental health activities in Boston also showed that the patients of private psychiatrists are a highly selected group, being predominantly women who have had some college education (Ryan, 1969). Similarly, in New York City, Kadushin (1969) found that social class differentiated the applicants to various clinics and that "the more closely affiliated a clinic is with the orthodox psychoanalytic movement, the higher the social class of its applicants will be" (Kadushin, 1969, p. 51).

A more recent report of 1,582 patients who were accepted and treated at the Columbia University Center for Psychoanalytic Training and Research is generally consistent with the earlier studies (Weber, Solomon, & Bachrach, 1985). "The patients are young, nearly all white, highly educated students, housewives and high vocational achievers." Although two different samples over time were studied and compared, the distribution of patients in terms of income, sex, age, and ethnic background did not change in any significant way. In fact, "The originally high educational level went even higher" (in the second sample) (Weber, Solomon, & Bachrach, 1985, p. 21). Furthermore, patients assigned to psychoanalysis were better educated and tended to be employed in more high status jobs than was the case for patients assigned to psychotherapy. Nearly two-thirds of the patients in the second sample who received psychoanalysis had graduate school experience.

It would appear, therefore, that there is some selectivity in terms of what types of individuals are selected for psychotherapy and that socioeconomic factors play a role in this selection. Furthermore, there also appear to be degrees of selectivity in terms of the nature of the clinic or source of the psychotherapeutic service offered, as well as in the type of treatment offered. Consequently, generalizations about psychotherapy clients in general must be cautious ones in light of variations in selectivity among the different clinical settings. It is possible that with a reduction in governmental funding of clinics and the willingness of third-party payers to provide for treatment, a number of settings and practitioners are less selective than they were in the past. We shall postpone any further consideration of client attributes per se until we have examined some additional aspects of psychotherapy which have relevance for this topic.

THE PROBLEM OF CONTINUATION
IN PSYCHOTHERAPY

One of the intriguing phenomena in psychotherapy, which first attracted my attention over 40 years ago, was that a number of patients, with evident need for psychotherapy, failed to keep their appointments after only a few interviews. They simply dropped out of therapy. While my colleagues at the veteran's clinic in which I was then working did not appear to pay much attention to this phenomenon, I found it both mystifying and perplexing. Such an occurrence was rarely mentioned in the books on psychotherapy. Instead, psychotherapy tended to be described as a rather long process, and despite client resistance and negative transference, there was usually a happy and harmonious ending. This was not my own experience with a moderate number of patients and, as a result, I decided with the aid of a colleague to carry out a study of all of the cases that had been terminated since the inception of the clinic. The results, based on analyzing over 1,000 case files, were quite interesting (Garfield & Kurz, 1952). Although the clinic staff saw themselves as doing psychoanalytically oriented intensive therapy, the median number of interviews of the 560 cases on whom adequate data were available was actually six interviews. In other words, by the sixth interview, half of the patients had terminated their therapy. Furthermore, almost 43% of the patients discontinued before the fifth interview, and only 8.8% remained for 25 or more therapy sessions. This was a startling finding as far as the clinic staff was concerned, although in searching the literature, I did find a few studies published in the preceding four years with comparable results.

There have been a number of additional studies reported since then which have tended to support these findings. I have reviewed this research in previous publications (Garfield, 1986b, 1994). A large number of individuals who begin a course of psychotherapy terminate their therapy after only a few interviews. Furthermore, this pattern of premature termination is found in clinics of the Department of Veterans' Affairs, in psychiatric clinics, in medical schools, in state and community clinics, and in private practice as well, although there have been few reports from the latter source (Koss, 1980; Taube, Burns, & Kessler, 1984).

A previous report by the National Center for Health Statistics (1966) of all those who consulted a psychiatrist during a 12-month period stated that the average number of visits was 4.7. In one study of three urban mental health centers, 37 to 45% of the patients terminated therapy after the first or second interview (Fiester & Rudestam, 1975), a finding also reported by Pekarik (1983). In another study, 43% terminated before the fourth interview (Craig & Huffine, 1976) and in the large scale study by Sue et al. (1976), 23% of the cases dropped out after the first session and 69.6% terminated before the tenth session. Comparable figures were reported in a study of psychiatrists and psychologists in private practice, with 65% and 63% of the patients respectively terminating before the tenth session (Taube, Burns, & Kessler, 1984). More recently, a case review of 138 patients with prepaid mental health insurance and 283 with fee-for-service health insurance at a Health Maintenance Organization (HMO) indicated that 78% completed treatment within 8 sessions (Blackwell, Gutmann, & Gutmann, 1988).

Such findings have been given little attention in most treatises on psychotherapy, yet they are important data. Therapists should have some knowledge of them so that their expectations about the length of psychotherapy are within the bounds of reality. Too frequently, therapists in training have the expectation, derived from diverse sources, that psychotherapy generally is going to be a rather long process and that the client also shares this expectation as well as the student-therapist's enthusiasm for psychotherapy. Thus, when the student in training, in spite of the attempts made to assign "good teaching cases," is faced with the sudden and unexpected departure of his client, he is profoundly concerned. For many years this problem tended to be slighted, but it has received increasing attention in recent years, and as a result, attempts have been made to improve this situation (Garfield, 1978; Heitler, 1976). Reference to this work will be made in a later chapter. Now let us examine some of the research on what types of client variables may be related to early discontinuation. Since the studies in this area have been evaluated in a recent review (Garfield, 1994), no detailed review will be presented here. Rather, we shall review briefly only those findings that appear to be of potentially greatest importance, mention some of the major conclusions, and refer to illustrative studies.

The variables that appear to show the most reliable relationship to continuation in psychotherapy are social class variables, even though the findings are by no means uniform or consistent. A majority of the studies in this area, using such criteria as the Hollingshead Index of Social Class, occupational status or level of education, have found a positive relationship between these indices and continuation in psychotherapy. A greater proportion of those in the lower socioeconomic groups and of lower educational accomplishment drop out of therapy earlier than do their counterparts from higher socioeconomic and educational levels (Garfield, 1994). Individuals with a better education may not only be better informed and more sophisticated about psychotherapy, but to the extent that they are more similar to their therapists in cultural background and verbal communication, an easier and more comfortable relationship between therapist and client may result. As a consequence, upper class clients may appear to their therapist as more suitable and more highly motivated for psychotherapy, as well as the clients' perceiving psychotherapy as a desirable form of therapy.

One additional finding is that lower class patients have missed more scheduled appointments (Weighill, Hodge, & Peck, 1983; Berrigan & Garfield, 1981). In the study by Berrigan and Garfield, missed appointments, as contrasted with cancelled appointments, were related to eventual discontinuation of therapy. This is a finding that psychotherapists should keep in mind. The difference between session cancellations and "no shows" for predicting premature termination from therapy was also emphasized in a study by Tracey (1986).

Although social class variables have shown a relatively consistent relationship to continuation in psychotherapy, a number of other variables that have been studied in this regard have demonstrated little or no such relationship. Sex of client, for example, has been investigated in a number of studies. Although some of the results are mixed, most have revealed no significant differences between males and females in terms of premature termination (Garfield, 1994). Thus, it does not seem that the sex of the client is a significant predictor of continuation in psychotherapy.

Age is another client variable that has received some attention in clinical writings on psychotherapy, although with little reference to continuation. Although some therapists appear to prefer younger patients, the research that has been done does not indicate that age is significantly related to remaining in therapy. In four recent studies, one reported a significant correlation between age and continuation (Greenspan & Kulish, 1985), but the other three found no such correlation (Dubrin & Zastowny, 1988; Gunderson et al., 1989; Sledge, Moras, Hartley, & Levine, 1990).

Another variable that has been investigated is that of psychiatric diagnosis or patient classification. In general, the diagnosis of the patient has not been found to be a significant correlate of premature termination (Garfield, 1994). Thus, neither sex, age, nor psychiatric diagnosis appears to be a significant client variable as far as predicting continuation in psychotherapy is concerned. Race has also been investigated as a possible variable in this connection. However, the problem is a complex one and is often confounded with socioeconomic variables. At present, there do not seem to be sufficient data upon which to base any reliable conclusions (Garfield, 1994; Sattler, 1977). However, two interesting studies can be mentioned here.

In a study by Acosta (1980), 25 Mexican Americans, 25 Black Americans, and 24 Anglo Americans who had previously terminated treatment in a public clinic within 6 sessions were interviewed. Most of them were low-income patients who had received psychodynamic therapy. Seven common reasons for termination were given by all groups and rank ordered in the same way. The four with the greatest frequency were: negative attitudes toward the therapist; therapy of no benefit; environmental constraints; and self-perceived improvement.

In another study of mental health services in Los Angeles County for ethnic minority groups (Sue, Fujino, Hu, Takeuchi, & Zane, 1991), over 13,000 patients were evaluated who represented four ethnic minority groups: Asian Americans, African Americans, Mexican Americans, and Whites. Asian Americans and Mexican Americans were under-represented in the utilization of services whereas African Americans overutilized services and also secured less positive outcomes. Ethnic match of therapist and client was related to length of treatment for all groups and was also related to treatment outcome for Mexican Americans.

Another set of client variables that has received attention pertains to the personality attributes of the client. These have been investigated by a variety of psychological tests and clinical measures. Because of the great variety of techniques used to appraise client personality variables, as well as the numerous methodological problems involved in this research (Garfield, 1994), we will limit our discussion to a few general observations. Before doing so, however, a few comments on research in this and related areas should be presented.

Earlier, the point was made that clinics and practitioners may vary with regard to the selectivity of their patients. As a consequence, samples of patients used for research purposes may not be comparable. Consequently, the consistency of results and the possibility of meaningful generalization from the results obtained are also limited. If the measures used to appraise client characteristics lack reliability or validity, similar problems will be apparent. Furthermore, if premature termination or continuation in psychotherapy is defined differently in various studies, the comparability of results is also hindered. It is possible that the results obtained in any single investigation may be due to chance or to some particular bias or selectivity. In the complicated domain of psychotherapy, any one or all of such possible occurrences may take place and, unfortunately, have taken place. As a result, one tends to find conflicting findings in the literature and failures to replicate earlier findings. As a consequence, although it is important to keep abreast of the research in one's field, it is also important to evaluate the adequacy of this research. One procedure which the author strongly recommends is to treat any single research report as a preliminary report until the findings have been replicated, unless an analysis of the study reveals such significant deficiencies that the results can be safely discarded.

Proceeding with our brief discussion of client personality attributes and continuation in psychotherapy, we can note that the Rorschach Test was used in a number of earlier studies with rather inconclusive results. The same can be said of the MMPI and several other tests. In one evaluation, the authors concluded "that use of the MMPI to make global predictions of persistence in psychotherapy is generally inadvisable" (Walters, Solomon, & Walden, 1982, p. 83).

My own conclusion after reviewing the research on this problem is similar, "In general, the use of psychological tests to predict continuation in psychotherapy has not been very successful" (Garfield, 1994, p. 201). However, one finding reported in three different studies was of some interest. This was that patients who completed test questionnaires prior to therapy were more likely to continue in therapy than were those who failed to complete the tests. It is conceivable that compliance with requests to complete questionnaires may indicate a general pattern of compliance or a greater degree of motivation to cooperate in therapy.

Besides the appraisal of certain personality attributes by tests, a number of other client attributes have been investigated, including suggestibility, anxiety, motivation, expectancies concerning therapy, perseverance, and the like. In many instances, the results of individual studies were never replicated, or were not supported. The clients' motivation for psychotherapy, for example, is one attribute that has been emphasized as an important one in many clinical discussions. However, this view has generally failed to receive much research support. One of the possible explanations is that a psychotherapeutic construct may be used without any precise meaning or definition. Clinicians may refer to a given construct and assume that they all mean the same thing by it, and researchers may use quite different methods of evaluating the supposedly same phenomenon.

The expectations that the client has about psychotherapy may also influence continuation. Although well-educated individuals may be quite knowledgeable about psychotherapy and have realistic expectations about what is to take place, including the respective roles of client and therapist, many other individuals may not. Beginning therapists may overlook or fail to pay adequate attention to this aspect of therapy. Consequently, when seeing a new client during the initial interview, they may not inform the client sufficiently concerning how psychotherapy will take place, how long it may take, or how it may help the client with his current difficulties. They also may not devote adequate time to ascertaining the client's own expectations about therapy or in clarifying them in understandable and unambiguous language. If the client's expectancies are seemingly incongruent with what appears to be occurring in therapy, he or she conceivably could become dissatisfied and withdraw from therapy. If the client expects that the therapist will diagnose his difficulties in short order and then tell him in one or two interviews what needs to be done to rectify his situation, he may be quite dissatisfied to see that the therapist tells him little or nothing and simply wants him to keep talking about himself. A study of patients' expectations about psychotherapy reported some years ago may be of interest here (Garfield & Wolpin, 1963).

In this study, 70 patients, who were referred for outpatient psychiatric treatment and who had no previous treatment of this kind, were asked to complete a detailed questionnaire prior to being assigned for treatment. The median level of education for this group was 12 years. On one item, these patients were asked to select from a number of possible treatments the one that they thought was the preferred treatment for their particular complaint. In contrast to the findings for several earlier studies, 88% of these individuals selected psychotherapy as their treatment of choice, and a majority of them indicated emotional factors as being of some importance in their difficulties. In addition, they indicated that an understanding of one's personal difficulties would be of help with regard to their improvement. Thus, on the basis of their response to these items, these patients appeared to display a positive attitude toward psychotherapy and seemingly had some understanding of it. Nevertheless, on other items their views were quite at variance with those held by most of their therapists. Over one-third of the group thought the therapy sessions would last 30 minutes or less. They apparently had not heard of the "50-minute-hour" and were basing their estimates on the time usually spent with other medical healers. Furthermore, 73% anticipated that they would be showing some improvement by the fifth therapy session, while 70% expected psychotherapy to be completed by ten sessions or less. Although the last prediction, as we have noted earlier, is a fairly accurate one for the majority of patients in psychotherapy, it was not the view held by the professional staff who saw psychotherapy as requiring a larger number of sessions.

A more recent study by Pekarik and Wierzbicki (1986) of the relationship between clients' expected and actual treatment duration secured quite comparable results. The clients both expected and actually attended a small number of sessions. Slightly over 73% of the clients did not remain in therapy beyond the tenth session and about the same number had expected that they would not remain in therapy beyond the tenth session. However, the therapists in this study preferred a longer duration of therapy. In another study of 173 psychotherapists, it was also noted that they overestimated the actual length of treatment and conversely underestimated the actual dropout rates (Pekarik & Finney-Owen, 1987).

Similar findings also have been reported by Kupst and Shulman (1979) who compared professional and lay expectations of psychotherapy. The largest difference was found on the following item: "If I saw a professional helper, I would expect it to take a long time before I solved my problems, maybe years." Whereas only 17% of the lay group agreed with this statement, 96% of the mental health professionals agreed.

Thus, while client expectations may be of some importance with regard to continuation, the reference to the congruence of client and therapist attitudes emphasizes again that psychotherapy involves the interaction of its principal participants. How the therapist views the client in terms of his own expectancies may also affect the process of psychotherapy. If the therapist feels that the client lacks motivation for psychotherapy, is hostile or demanding, and wants the therapist to be the active participant in therapy, conceivably, he may feel that the client is a poor case and indirectly or even directly, influence the client to leave therapy.

In one study, ratings made by therapists after the second session of group therapy indicated that the therapists' estimates of their ability to empathize with a client, their positive feelings toward the client, and their evaluation of the client's ability to form a therapeutic relationship were all related to continuation in psychotherapy (Rosenzweig & Folman, 1974). In another study, the therapists' positive feelings toward clients and their prognoses for treatment were related to continuation, although this was not the case with ratings of psychopathology (Shapiro, 1974). Although these studies are concerned with the perceptions and evaluations of psychotherapists, they do pertain to client attributes as perceived by therapists in the therapy situation. They do not, however, tell us about the relative influence of each of the participants on the specific interaction that occurs or how this process develops. In other words, are the attributes and behaviors of the client the primary factors leading to continuation, or do they act as initial stimuli which cause the therapist to react in certain ways which, in turn, influence the client in how he perceives therapy and subsequently reacts? It seems reasonable to believe that the personal attributes of the client do play a role in continuation, but that the process may be influenced positively or negatively by the personal qualities of the therapist and his manner of responding to the client.

One study of possible interactional correlates of premature termination focused on the relationship of topic determination to premature termination (Tracey, 1986). Topic determination was described as reaching agreement early in therapy regarding the goals and tasks of therapy. A main conclusion reached was: "Whether a dyad continues past the first few sessions is related to how well participants establish mutually agreeable definitions of what each is to do" (p. 787). However, it is also of interest to mention that there were no differences in this regard between continuing dyads that did well in therapy and those that did not.

There are a number of possible reasons that patients may depart early from psychotherapy. Some may actually be helped sufficiently in just a few sessions. Some may be dissatisfied in various ways with the services provided and the clients' perceptions of the therapists' competence and trustworthiness early in therapy also may play a role in continuation (Kokotovic & Tracey, 1987; McNeill, May, & Lee, 1987). The variations in the definitions of premature terminators used in the various studies also limits our ability to draw definitive conclusions. Nevertheless, it does seem reasonably evident that therapists need to be sensitive to the expectations, feelings, and perceptions that the client has about therapy and the therapist and the client should be given a clear explanation of what to expect in therapy. Now let us turn our attention to the important topic of client variables in relation to outcome and improvement in psychotherapy.

CLIENT VARIABLES AND OUTCOME
IN PSYCHOTHERAPY

Although it is important for the client to continue in psychotherapy if the course of treatment is to be completed, the ultimate goal of treatment is the improvement of the client. If the client continues in treatment for a long period of time and shows no change or even gets worse, he or she would indeed have done better to terminate early. However, although positive change and the reduction of discomfort are the common goals of all therapies, none have really claimed to be 100% effective. What most claim is that they help most people or that they are more effective than other types of therapy. Although most people may show positive change, there are those who either show no change, or change for the worse, and we would expect that client differences may play some part in the outcomes secured.

In discussing client variables and outcome, it is important to first emphasize the difficulties inherent in appraising this possible relationship. In addition to the matter of appraising client variables, there is also the difficult problem of evaluating the outcome of psychotherapy. For some therapists, the reduction or disappearance of the client's symptoms or disordered behavior will suffice as the criterion for evaluating outcome. For others, however, the symptoms are merely the surface indications of the more basic underlying problems that need to be remedied. Still others have emphasized the client's self-concept as a basic consideration in evaluating outcome in psychotherapy. It is evident, therefore, that different variants of psychotherapy may appraise different client variables in their appraisal of outcome.

Besides possible differences in criteria of outcome, there is also the matter of how the different outcome criteria are appraised or measured. In actuality, while a variety of outcome measures have been used, many of the same measures have been used by psychotherapists of different theoretical persuasions. Among the most popular have been therapists' judgments or ratings of improvement, client evaluations of treatment, ratings by independent judges, tests, behavioral tasks, and a variety of questionnaires. Because the appraisal of outcome is of such importance, a few of the significant problems in this area will be mentioned. One pertains to the value or validity of the measures used. For example, if a therapist judges a patient to be "very much improved," what changes have actually taken place and how much confidence can be placed in this judgment? Another problem pertains to the agreement or lack of agreement between different judgments or measures of improvement.

What appraisal of outcome does one make if a therapist judges a given client to be improved but the client feels there has been no significant change, a not uncommon finding in psychotherapy research (Garfield, 1994). How does one interpret a positive change on one criterion and no change on another supposedly equally important one? These, it should be noted, are not simply rhetorical questions. Several studies have secured rather low agreement among different criteria used to appraise outcome (Garfield, Prager, & Bergin, 1971; Horenstein, Houston, & Holmes, 1973; Keniston, Boltax, & Almond, 1971; Sloane, Staples, Cristol, Yorkston, & Whipple, 1975). Therapists' judgments of outcome also appear to be more favorable than other criteria, a finding which is not difficult to understand. Finally, apart from the lack of agreement obtained with appraisals of outcome derived from different sources, there is also the related problem of comparing overall judgments of improvement made at the *end* of therapy with scores or ratings based on the *difference* between appraisals made at the beginning and the end of therapy. In the former instance, judges or raters may not recall accurately the initial status of the patient, or may be unduly influenced by the client's overall level of functioning. A client who is only mildly disturbed at the beginning of therapy and changes relatively little may still be judged to be greatly improved at the termination of therapy in comparison with more disturbed clients since the former is functioning at a higher level. Because of such considerations, we can anticipate that deriving reliable generalizations about what kinds of patients respond well to psychotherapy will not be a simple matter.

The first broad group of client variables to be reviewed will consist of social class and demographic variables, and our review will be brief since few studies have been reported. In general, unlike the trend for continuation, there does not appear to be any important relationship between social class and outcome in psychotherapy (Garfield, 1986b; Lorion, 1973; Schmidt & Hancey, 1979). Thus, while the lower class client may be more likely to drop out of therapy, once he or she remains in therapy, the outcome obtained is not noticeably different from that of other groups of clients. Education appears to show a somewhat more positive relationship to outcome, although it is not a consistent finding, and in many of the studies, therapists' ratings have been used as the criterion and sample size has been small (Garfield, 1994).

The results reported on the variables of sex and age also do not show any significant relationship to outcome. Although some psychotherapists, including Freud (1950), have believed that the older patient is less flexible, less educable, and consequently less fit for therapy, there are no reliable data to indicate that the outcomes secured with such individuals are significantly different from those secured with younger individuals (Garfield, 1978, 1994). There also appears to be a more positive view of the elderly at present than previously (Billings & Moos, 1984).

The largest number of studies on client variables in relation to outcome have been concerned with personality variables and, because of their diversity, it is difficult to present a concise summary of the results obtained. Like the studies mentioned in the previous section, many have been based on different psychological tests or batteries of tests with varying groups of clients. As a result, there are a number of conflicting and unreplicated findings which will not be repeated here. A review of such findings is available elsewhere (Garfield, 1994). Instead, some illustrative findings and issues will be presented.

One of the more general findings or conclusions reported in some studies was that those clients who were the least disturbed or had the greatest degree of personality integration or ego strength tended to show the greatest degree of improvement (Luborsky, Chandler, Auerbach, Cohen, & Bachrach, 1971). There were, however, several studies which either failed to obtain such results or which secured the opposite results (Prager & Garfield, 1972; Stone, Frank, Nash, & Imber, 1961; Truax, Tunnell, Fine, & Wargo, 1966). After reviewing some of the studies in this area, Truax and Carkhuff (1967) advanced the hypothesis that patients with the greatest "felt disturbance," evaluated by means of self-report questionnaires, and with the least overt or behavioral disturbance are the individuals who actually improve the most. While this view was congruent with some clinical views, it has not been adequately investigated or confirmed. Before commenting on this further, however, we can examine a few representative recent studies.

In the interesting study by Sloane and coworkers (1975) comparing the effectiveness of behavior therapy and psychoanalytic therapy, some differential results were secured for the two types of therapy. As measured by the

MMPI, the less disturbed patients did better in the psychoanalytically oriented psychotherapy, whereas behavior therapy obtained similar results regardless of the degree of patient disturbance. In this instance, the type of therapy also appeared to be of possible importance with regard to patient degree of disturbance and outcome. Unfortunately, studies of this type have been a rarity.

The long-term project conducted by the Menninger Foundation also reported a positive correlation between ego strength and a global measure of improvement for patients who received psychoanalysis or psychoanalytically oriented long-term therapy (Kernberg et al., 1972). The correlation obtained was not very high ($r = .35$) and the appraisals of ego strength were relative to the population studied. However, if we were to take these results and those of the previous study and generalize, perhaps somewhat dangerously, we might state that ego strength or degree of personality integration may be related to outcome in psychoanalytic therapy, but not necessarily in behavior therapy. Such a conclusion would be of interest if further research would in fact support it.

Without going into great detail, it appears likely that conclusions concerning the relationship of degree of client disturbance or ego strength to outcome is to an important extent influenced by how outcome in psychotherapy is appraised. This point, mentioned earlier, was illustrated clearly in a paper by Mintz (1972), and developed also in a publication by the present writer (Garfield, 1978). In essence, the proposition is that where global judgments of therapy outcome are made by therapists *at the conclusion of therapy,* there exists a high probability of a positive relationship between degree of personality integration or adjustment of the client at the initiation of therapy and outcome. In other words, the less disturbed clients secure the most favorable ratings at the termination of therapy. In contrast, where patient improvement is appraised by the amount of *difference* between test scores or ratings obtained *at the beginning of therapy* and those obtained *at termination,* such a relationship will not obtain, and the results may favor the more disturbed client. The issue is a complex one.

First, let us consider the goal or goals of therapy. Although "cure" is frequently mentioned in medicine, it has appeared less frequently in the area of psychotherapy. Positive change or improvement tend to be the more commonly used terms. However, while practically all of us would agree on client improvement as the goal of therapy, we might differ on how much or what type of change would constitute improvement. Related to this, there has frequently been a stated or implied goal of psychotherapy to the effect that the client's overall personality functioning and adjustment should be enhanced at the completion of therapy. Thus, apart from the patient's specific complaints, there is usually some attention paid to his or her level of functioning. Consequently, when a therapist makes an evaluation of a client's progress at the end of therapy, he is likely to be influenced by the client's overall level of adjustment, as well as by what problems have been helped as result of therapy. A client who enters therapy at a relatively high level of integration and functioning appears more likely to receive a high rating of improvement, whereas an initially much more disturbed client who has shown as much or more improvement but still functions at a lower level than the other client will tend to receive a lower rating. The therapist thus may be influenced more by the client's overall adjustment at the end of therapy than by actual improvement over the course of therapy. As a result, the better adjusted clients would appear to secure the most positive results.

On the other hand, if the *amount* of change resulting from psychotherapy is the actual criterion, and differences between pre- and post-levels of functioning are measured, the results and conclusions may be quite different. Individuals who at the beginning of therapy are relatively little impaired would be near the top of some normative scale of adjustment and would have much less room to move up in this scale than would one who is much further down the scale. To look at it another way, those individuals who are most disturbed deviate the most from the mean level of adjustment manifested by most individuals, or the statistical norm of adjustment. In terms of statistical probability, they have the greatest likelihood on retesting of regressing or moving toward the mean and, thus, of exhibiting greater change than those individuals who are already closer to the mean. As a result, if amount of change is the criterion of outcome, then those who are most disturbed at the outset of therapy are likely to show the largest gains. As already mentioned, all types of results have actually been reported in varying degrees, and the interpretation of these results have also differed.

In recent years, there has been considerable interest in the treatment of depression and several studies have investigated potential prognostic indicators of outcome. In one study, "participants at all levels of depression severity improved markedly, but those who were initially more depressed tended to maintain their relative ranking in posttreatment" (Steinmetz, Lewinsohn, & Antonuccio, 1983, p. 331). A study of interpersonal therapy with depressed patients also found that the best predictor of outcome was the general emotional health of the patient at the beginning of therapy (Rounsaville, Weissman, & Prusoff, 1981). The best predictor of rapid response to treatment also was found to be the level of depression at the beginning of the first treatment session (Beckham, 1989). Burns and Nolen-Hoeksema (1991) also reported that patients who were the most depressed initially also were the most depressed at the end of 12 weeks of cognitive-behavioral therapy.

The research findings on degree of disturbance as a predictor of outcome in therapy thus have been far from conclusive. However, there does seem to be a greater consistency in the more recent findings which indicate that individuals with more serious levels of disturbance have poorer outcomes.

Other personality variables, however, may also be involved. Let us now proceed to a discussion of other client variables in relation to outcome.

Although successful results in psychotherapy have been reported with clients with a wide range of intellectual ability, a number of studies have appeared to indicate a positive relationship between intelligence and outcome. In the review by Luborsky et al. (1971), 10 of 13 studies were listed as showing a positive relationship between intelligence and outcome with correlations ranging from .24 to .46. Meltzoff and Kornreich (1970), however, reviewed 15 studies of which only 7 showed a positive relationship between intelligence and outcome. They also concluded that high intelligence is not a necessary condition for positive outcome in psychotherapy, although it might be of greater importance in some psychotherapies than in others. In psychoanalysis, where candidates apparently may be more rigorously screened, the majority are college graduates or better, and presumably of better than average intelligence (Reder & Tyson, 1980; Weber et al., 1985). On the other hand, behavior therapists do not appear to have been unduly concerned with this issue.

There are a few other points that can be made about this issue. If psychotherapy does involve learning, a view subscribed to not only by the behavior therapists, then it is reasonable to assume that some minimal amount of intelligence is required for successful performance in psychotherapy. However, no precise amount has yet been specified or demonstrated to be the required amount, although it would appear that psychotherapists on the whole prefer clients who possess high intelligence, as well as other desirable qualities (Schofield, 1964). The research data on this matter, however, do not allow one to make any categorical statements. Even if one placed more confidence in the positive results secured and ignored the inconclusive findings, the magnitude of the correlations obtained is rather low. If a correlation of .30 were to be taken as a representative finding, it would still account for less than 10% of the variance. Consequently, a therapist should not place undue emphasis on intellectual ability, although he or she might find it more pleasurable to interact and to discuss psychotherapeutic concepts with highly intelligent individuals.

Another topic of interest that has already been referred to in the section on continuation is that of client expectancies. In the past, this tended to refer to the expectancies the client had about therapy and his expectations of being helped. It was hypothesized that those who had high expectations of being helped might actually do better than those who had negative expectations. Frank and his colleagues were among the earliest to conduct studies of expectations and outcome (Frank, Gliedman, Imber, Stone, & Nash, 1959; Rosenthal & Frank, 1956) and a moderate amount of research has been done since then. The behavior therapists, in particular, conducted studies in which they have tried to manipulate client expectancies experimentally. Several critical reviews of this area have appeared in published form (Lick & Bootzin, 1975; Morgan, 1973; Perotti & Hopewell, 1980; Wilkins, 1971, 1973).

In many studies, expectancies have not been actually measured but inferred, and self-reports have been used to appraise both expectancies and outcome. How expectancies are appraised is of some importance, for in one study significant correlations were secured between high expectancy ratings and self-report measures of outcome, but not between expectancy ratings and a behavioral measure of outcome (Wilson & Thomas, 1973).

Perotti and Hopewell (1980) do not believe that the initial client expectancies for possible improvement, which have been the focus in most studies, have much impact on outcome. However, they do state that the beliefs a client has *during therapy*—that he is improving and is able to handle in better fashion situations which were upsetting previously—are of some importance. In other words, expectancies derived while undergoing therapy are the more significant ones. This appears to be a reasonable hypothesis and at least is congruent with studies that indicate better predictions of outcome after a few early therapy sessions than at pre-treatment assessment (Bandura, Jeffery, & Wright, 1974; Mathews, Johnston, Shaw, & Gelder, 1974).

It has also been suggested that "it may be more correct to assume that client motivation, desire for therapy, and expectations of change may have more to do with prompting the patient to *initially* become involved in therapy than with directly influencing the therapeutic process or its outcome" (Thurer & Hursh, 1981, p. 71). This suggestion appears to be a reasonable one since the pre-therapy expectations of the client will be very much influenced by the client's early experiences in therapy and perceptions of the therapist. Positive expectations can be reinforced or extinguished by the actual experience of therapy and the same would appear likely for negative expectations.

Although the research data and issues on client expectancies may not inspire a strong degree of confidence in the utility of the construct, it does seem as if some of the difficulty is due to the fact that it has been defined in different ways or not defined at all. In some instances, it has been used with reference to the client's beliefs about the success of treatment. In other instances, it has been used to designate the expectations a client has concerning the potential effectiveness of a given therapist. It would appear on the basis of historical accounts of successful quacks in the past, that such expectations may have played a role in their success (Jameson, 1961). Whether we approve of such activities or not, if a variable has some potential influence on outcome, it should be noted. Finally, as mentioned earlier, client expectations have also been mentioned in relation to features of therapy such as the client or therapist role in therapy, the length of therapy, the procedures to be used and the like. If we are going to understand more fully the possible significance of the expectancies of the patient, more attention in research will have to be paid to specifying the type of expectancy under investigation, as well as considering the possible interaction effects of different kinds of expectancies.

A few other topics of possible interest with reference to client variables and outcome can be reviewed briefly before ending this chapter. One concerns the possible importance of the fit between client and type of therapy. In one study, for example, two groups of clients were exposed to two types of therapy (Abramowitz, Abramowitz, Roback, & Jackson, 1974). The clients were classified as "externals" or "internals" in terms of their locus of control as measured by the Rotter I-E Scale. The therapies were designated as "relatively directive" and "relatively non-directive." The findings suggested that externally oriented clients did better with the directive therapy, while the internals performed more successfully in the non-directive therapy. On the other hand, a review of studies that have claimed that internals were more successful in nondirective therapy and externals in directive therapy noted several deficiencies in these studies (Messer & Meinster, 1980).

In another study subjects with a fear of snakes were presented with a videotape of four therapists who illustrated four different types of therapy—systematic desensitization, an encounter therapy, rational-emotive therapy, and a combination of modeling and behavioral rehearsal (Devine & Fernald, 1973). The subjects rated their therapeutic preferences and then were assigned to a preferred, nonpreferred, or randomly selected therapy. Although there was no difference in the overall effectiveness of any of the different forms of therapy, subjects receiving a preferred treatment exhibited significantly less fear than those who received a random or nonpreferred type of therapy.

In a recent study, externalizing depressed patients were found to improve more than nonexternalizing depressed patients in cognitive therapy, whereas the latter group improved most in a form of supportive self-directed therapy (Beutler et al., 1991). Conversely, resistant (defensive) patients improved more in the self-directed therapy, and low resistant patients improved more in the cognitive therapy. Although these results are interesting and suggest the possible importance of interaction effects between type of therapy and client attributes, it is well to remember that therapist variables also play a role in such interactions.

There have also been scattered investigations of client qualities that have been thought to be important in psychotherapy. These have included attributes such as relatability, attractiveness, and likability. However, it would seem that although these terms are used clinically, they need some operational definition before we really know what is meant or can investigate their significance. Nevertheless, they may reflect aspects of psychotherapy that are important. Two early studies found a relationship between therapists' ratings of client likability and their ratings of client prognosis (Ehrlich & Bauer, 1967; Garfield & Affleck, 1961). Furthermore, in the first study, patients who were rated as less likable were three times more likely to be placed on multiple drug regimes than those who received high ratings. In addition, the therapists' ratings of improvement were positively correlated with these ratings. The problem here is determining whether likability influences prognosis or whether patients who are judged to be good candidates for psychotherapy are better liked.

The matter of client-therapist similarity or complementarity has also been discussed in the clinical literature, as well as receiving some research attention. While some psychotherapists may have strong opinions on this matter, the research results are too conflicting and questionable to form any reasonable beliefs on this matter (Berzins, 1977; Garfield, 1978). As Berzins has noted after reviewing this topic in some detail, "there is at present no organized body of knowledge that could serve as an effective guide for implementing matching strategies" (p. 222).

Although it appears obvious that the personal qualities of the patient should be of some significance in psychotherapy and in the type of outcome that is secured, the problem is not as simple as it appears, at least from the standpoint of securing stable results by means of research. The range of client attributes is large, and how they are appraised or evaluated also varies greatly. For such reasons, as well as other methodological ones, replication of findings has not been easy to obtain. It is also difficult to try to order and integrate such a diversity of results. This is particularly true of personality variables. Thus, while we can state with at least some confidence that such variables as social class, age, and sex are of little significance as far as outcome is concerned, conclusions about the importance of the client's degree of disturbance, motivation, likability, and expectations concerning therapy have to be hedged with considerable caution.

On the other hand, as indicated earlier, several studies have indicated that aspects of the client's interactions in the early therapy sessions may have prognostic implications for therapeutic outcome. The therapeutic relationship established early in therapy is obviously of some importance for both continuation and outcome in psychotherapy and involves the therapists as well as the client. However, studies of the therapeutic process have indicated the importance of some client features.

"Patient involvement," representing both positive patient participation in therapy and low manifestations of patient hostility, has been found to correlate positively with outcome in several studies (Gomes-Schwartz, 1978; Kolb, Beutler, Davis, Crago, & Shanfield, 1985; O'Malley, Suh, & Strupp, 1983). In some studies, this positive correlation was noted beginning with the third session. Related to these findings are those summarized by Orlinsky and Howard (1986) indicating that the patient's "openness versus defensiveness" in psychotherapy is related to outcome. The more open patients who become involved in therapy in a collaborative manner appear to be those who secure the best results, but this also takes place in relationship to a specific therapist. A more detailed review of this entire area is available in another publication (Garfield, 1994).

REFERENCES

Abramowitz, C. V., Abramowitz, S. I., Roback, H. B., & Jackson, C. (1974). Differential effectiveness of directive and nondirective group therapies as a function of client internal-external control. *Journal of Consulting and Clinical Psychology, 42,* 849–853.

Acosta, F. X. (1980). Self-described reasons for premature termination of psychotherapy by Mexican-American, Black-American, and Anglo-American patients. *Psychological Reports, 47,* 435–443.

Bandura, A., Jeffery, R. W., & Wright, C. L. (1974). Efficacy of participant modeling as a function of response induction aids. *Journal of Abnormal Psychology, 83,* 56–64.

Beckham, E. E. (1989). Improvement after evaluation in psychotherapy of depression: Evidence of a placebo effect? *Journal of Clinical Psychology, 45,* 945–950.

Berrigan, L. P., & Garfield, S. L. (1981). Relationship of missed psychotherapy appointments to premature termination and social class. *The British Journal of Clinical Psychology, 20,* 239–242.

Berzins, J. I. (1977). Therapist-patient matching. In A. S. Gurman & A. M. Razin (Eds.), *Effective Psychotherapy. A handbook of research* (pp. 222–251). New York: Pergamon.

Betz, N., & Shullman, S. (1979). Factors related to client return following intake. *Journal of Counseling Psychology, 26,* 542–545.

Beutler, L. E., Engle, D., Mohr, D., Doldrup, R. J., Bergan, J., Meredith, K., & Merry, W. (1991). Predictors of differential response to cognitive, experiential, and self-directed psychotherapeutic procedures. *Journal of Consulting and Clinical Psychology, 59,* 333–340.

Billings, A. G., & Moos, R. H. (1984). Treatment experiences of adults with unipolar depression: The influence of patient and life context factors. *Journal of Consulting and Clinical Psychology, 52,* 119–131.

Blackwell, B., Gutmann, M., & Gutmann, L. (1988). Case review and quantity of outpatient care. *American Journal of Psychiatry, 145,* 1103–1106.

Brill, N. Q., & Storrow, H. A. (1960). Social class and psychiatric treatment. *Archives of General Psychiatry, 3,* 340–344.

Burns, D. D., & Nolen-Hoeksema, S. (1991). Coping styles, homework compliance, and the effectiveness of cognitive-behavioral therapy. *Journal of Consulting and Clinical Psychology, 59,* 305–311.

Cole, N. J., Branch, C. H., & Allison, R. B. (1962). Some relationships between social class and the practice of dynamic psychotherapy. *American Journal of Psychiatry, 118,* 1004–1012.

Craig, T., & Huffine, C. (1976). Correlates of patient attendance in an inner-city mental health clinic. *The American Journal of Psychiatry, 133,* 61–64.

Devine, D. A., & Fernald, P. S. (1973). Outcome effects of receiving a preferred, randomly assigned or nonpreferred therapy. *Journal of Consulting and Clinical Psychology, 41,* 104–107.

DuBrin, J. R., & Zastowny, T. R. (1988). Predicting early attrition from psychotherapy: An analysis of a large private practice cohort. *Psychotherapy, 25,* 393–408.

Ehrlich, H. J., & Bauer, M. L. (1967). Therapists' feelings toward patients and patient treatment outcome. *Social Science and Medicine, 1,* 283–292.

Fiester, A. R., & Rudestam, K. E. (1975). A multivariate analysis of the early dropout process. *Journal of Consulting and Clinical Psychology, 43,* 528–535.

Frank, J. D., Gliedman, L. H., Imber, S. D., Stone, A. R., & Nash, E. H. (1959). Patients' expectancies and relearning as factors determining improvement in psychotherapy. *American Journal of Psychiatry, 115,* 961–968.

Freud, S. (1950). On psychotherapy. In *Collected Papers, Vol. 1* (pp. 258–259). London: Hogarth Press and the Institute of Psycho-Analysis.

Garfield, S. L. (1978). Research on client variables in psychotherapy. In S. L. Garfield & A. E. Bergin (Eds.), *Handbook of psychotherapy and behavior change* (2nd ed.). New York: Wiley.

Garfield, S. L. (1986a). Problems in diagnostic classification. In T. Millon & G. L. Klerman (Eds.), *Contemporary directions in psychopathology* (pp. 99–114). New York: Guilford.

Garfield, S. L. (1986b). Research on client variables in psychotherapy. In S. L. Garfield & A. E. Bergin (Eds.), *Handbook of psychotherapy and behavior change* (3rd ed.) (pp. 213–256). New York: Wiley.

Garfield, S. L. (1993). Methodological problems in clinical diagnosis. In P. B. Sutker & H. E. Adams (Eds.), *Comprehensive Handbook of Psychopathology* (2nd ed.) (pp. 27–46). New York: Plenum.

Garfield, S. L. (1994). Research on client variables in psychotherapy. In A. E. Bergin & S. L. Garfield (Eds.), *Handbook of psychotherapy and behavior change* (4th ed.) (pp. 190–228). New York: Wiley.

Garfield, S. L., & Affleck, D. C. (1961). Therapists' judgments concerning patients considered for psychotherapy. *Journal of Consulting Psychology, 25,* 505–509.

Garfield, S. L., & Kurz, M. (1952). Evaluation of treatment and related procedures in 1216 cases referred to a mental hygiene clinic. *Psychiatric Quarterly, 26,* 414–424.

Garfield, S. L., Prager, R. A., & Bergin, A. E. (1971). Evaluating outcome in psychotherapy: A hardy perennial. *Journal of Consulting and Clinical Psychology, 37,* 320–322.

Garfield, S. L., & Wolpin, M. (1963). Expectations regarding psychotherapy. *Journal of Nervous and Mental Disease, 137,* 353–362.

Gomes-Schwartz, B. (1978). Effective ingredients in psychotherapy: Predictions of outcome from process variables. *Journal of Consulting and Clinical Psychology, 46,* 1023–1035.

Greenspan, M., & Kulish, N. M. (1985). Factors in premature termination in long-term psychotherapy. *Psychotherapy, 22,* 75–82.

Gunderson, J. G., Frank, A. F., Ronningstam, E. F., Wachter, S., Lynch, V. J., & Wolf, P. J. (1989). Early discontinuance of borderline patients from psychotherapy. *Journal of Nervous and Mental Disease, 177,* 38–42.

Hamberg, D. A., Bibring, G. L., Fisher, C., Stanton, A. H., Wallerstein, R. S., Weinstock, H. I., & Haggard, E. (1967). Report of ad hoc committee on central fact-gathering data of the American Psychoanalytic Association. *Journal of the American Psychoanalytic Association, 15,* 841–861.

Heitler, J. B. (1976). Preparatory techniques in initiating expressive psychotherapy with lower-class, unsophisticated patients. *Psychological Bulletin, 83,* 339–352.

Hollingshead, A. B., & Redlich, F. C. (1958). *Social class and mental illness: A community study.* New York: Wiley.

Horenstein, D., Houston, B., & Holmes, D. (1973). Clients', Therapists' & Judges' evaluations of psychotherapy. *Journal of Counseling Psychology, 20,* 149–153.

Jameson, E. (1961). *The natural history of quackery.* London: Michael Joseph.

Kadushin, C. (1969). *Why people go to psychiatrists.* New York: Atherton.

Keniston, K., Boltax, S., & Almond, R. (1971). Multiple criteria of treatment outcome. *Journal of Psychiatry, 8,* 107–118.

Kernberg, O. F., Bernstein, C. S., Coyne, R., Appelbaum, D. A., Horwitz, H., & Voth, T. J. (1972). Psychotherapy and psychoanalysis: Final report of the Menninger Foundation's psychotherapy research project. *Bulletin of the Menninger Clinic, 36,* 1–276.

Knapp, P. H., Levin, S., McCarter, R. H., Wermer, H., & Zetzel, E. (1960). Suitability for psychoanalysis: A review of 100 supervised analytic cases. *Psychoanalytic Quarterly, 29,* 459–477.

Kokotovic, A. M., & Tracey, T. J. (1987). Premature termination in a university counseling center. *Journal of Counseling Psychology, 34,* 80–82.

Kolb, D. L., Beutler, L. E., Davis, C. S., Crago, M., & Shanfield, S. B. (1985). Patient and therapy process variables relating to dropout and change in psychotherapy. *Psychotherapy, 22,* 702–710.

Koss, M. P. (1980). Descriptive characteristics and length of psychotherapy of child and adult clients seen in private psychological practice. *Psychotherapy: Theory, Research, & Practice, 17,* 268–271.

Kupst, M. J., & Schulman, J. L. (1979). Comparing professional and lay expectations of psychotherapy. *Psychotherapy: Theory, Research, and Practice, 16,* 237–243.

Lick, J., & Bootzin, R. (1975). Expectancy factors in the treatment of fear: Methodological and theoretical issues *Psychological Bulletin, 82,* 917–931.

Lorion, R. P. (1973). Socio-economic status & traditional treatment approaches reconsidered. *Psychological Bulletin, 79,* 263–270.

Lubin, B., Hornstra, R. K., Lewis, R. V., & Bechtel, B. S. (1973). Correlates of initial treatment assignment in a community mental health center. *Archives of General Psychiatry, 29,* 497–504.

Luborsky, L., Chandler, M., Auerbach, A. H., Cohen, J., & Bachrach, H. M. (1971). Factors influencing the outcome of psychotherapy. *Psychological Bulletin, 75,* 145–185.

Marks, I. (1978). Behavioral psychotherapy of adult neurosis. In S. L. Garfield & A. E. Bergin (Eds.), *Handbook of psychotherapy and behavior change* (2nd ed.). New York: Wiley.

Mathews, A. M., Johnston, D. W., Shaw, P. M., & Gelder, M. G. (1974). Process variables and the prediction of outcome in behavior therapy. *The British Journal of Psychiatry, 125,* 256–264.

McNeill, B. W., May, R. J., & Lee, V. E. (1987). Perceptions of counselor source characteristics by premature and successful terminators. *Journal of Counseling Psychology, 34,* 86–89.

Meltzoff, J., & Kornreich, M. (1970). *Research in psychotherapy.* New York: Atherton Press.

Messer, S. B., & Meinster, M. O. (1980). Interaction effects of internal vs. external locus of control and directive vs. non-directive therapy: Fact or fiction? *Journal of Clinical Psychology, 36,* 283–288.

Mintz, J. (1972). What is "success" in psychotherapy? *Journal of Abnormal Psychology, 80,* 11–19.

Morgan, W. G. (1973). Nonnecessary conditions or useful procedures in desensitization: A reply to Wilkins. *Psychological Bulletin, 79,* 373–375.

National Center for Health Statistics. (1966). *Characteristics of patients of selected types of medical specialists and practitioners: United States July 1963-June 1964.* Washington, DC: Public Health Service Publication No. 1000, Series 10, No. 28.

Noonan, J. R. (1973). A follow-up of pretherapy dropouts. *Journal of Community Psychology, 1,* 43–45.

O'Malley, S. S., Suh, C. S., & Strupp, H. H. (1983). The Vanderbilt Psychotherapy Process Scale: A report on the scale development and a process-outcome study. *Journal of Consulting and Clinical Psychology, 51,* 581–586.

Orlinsky, D. E., & Howard, K. I. (1986). Process and outcome in psychotherapy. In S. L. Garfield & A. E. Bergin (Eds.), *Handbook of psychotherapy and behavior change* (3rd ed.) (pp. 311–384). New York: Wiley.

Pekarik, G. (1983). Follow-up adjustment of outpatient dropouts. *American of Journal Orthopsychiatry, 53,* 501–511.

Pekarik, G., & Finney-Owen, K. (1987). Outpatient clinic therapist attitudes and beliefs relevant to client dropout. *Community Mental Health Journal, 23,* 120–130.

64   The Therapy Client-Patient

Pekarik, G., & Wierzbicki, M. (1986). The relationship between clients' expected and actual treatment duration. *Psychotherapy, 23,* 532–534.

Perotti, L. P., & Hopewell, C. A. (1980). Expectancy effects in psychotherapy and systematic desensitization: A review. JSAS: *Catalog of Selected Documents in Psychology, 10* (Ms. No. 2052).

Phillips, E. L., & Fagan, P. J. (1982). Attrition: Focus on the intake and first therapy interviews. Paper presented at the 90th Annual Convention of the American Psychological Association, Washington, DC, August, 1982.

Prager, R. A., & Garfield, S. L. (1972). Client initial disturbance and outcome in psychotherapy. *Journal of Consulting and Clinical Psychology, 38,* 112–117.

Raynes, A. E., & Warren, G. (1971a). Some distinguishing features of patients failing to attend a psychiatric clinic after referral. *American Journal of Orthopsychiatry, 41,* 581–589.

Raynes, A. E., & Warren, G. (1971b). Some characteristics of "dropouts" at first contact with a psychiatric clinic. *Community Mental Health Journal, 7,* 144–151.

Reder, P., & Tyson, R. L. (1980). Patient dropout from psychotherapy. A review and discussion. *Bulletin of the Menninger Clinic, 44,* 229–251.

Rosenthal, D., & Frank, J. D. (1958). The fate of psychiatric clinic outpatients assigned to psychotherapy. *Journal of Nervous and Mental Disease, 127,* 330–343.

Rosenzweig, S. P., & Folman, R. (1974). Patient and therapist variables affecting premature termination in group psychotherapy. *Psychotherapy: Theory, Research and Practice, 11,* 76–79.

Rounsaville, B. J., Weissman, M. M., & Prusoff, B. A. (1981). Psychotherapy with depressed outpatients. Patient and process variables as predictors of outcome. *British Journal of Psychiatry, 138,* 67–74.

Ryan, W. (Ed.) (1969). *Distress in the City.* Cleveland: The Press of Case Western Reserve University.

Sattler, J. M. (1977). The effects of therapist-client racial similarity. In A. S. Gurman & A. M. Razin (Eds.), *Effective Psychotherapy. A handbook of research.* New York: Pergamon.

Schmidt, J. P., & Hancey, R. (1979). Social class and psychiatric treatment: Application of a decision-making model to use patterns in a cost-free clinic. *Journal of Consulting and Clinical Psychology, 47,* 771–772.

Schofield, W. (1964). *Psychotherapy. The purchase of friendship.* Englewood Cliffs, NJ: Prentice-Hall.

Shader, R. I. (1970). The walk-in service: An experience in community care. In T. Rothman (Ed.), *Changing patterns in psychiatric care.* New York: Crown.

Shapiro, R. J. (1974). Therapists attitudes and premature termination in family and individual therapy. *The Journal of Nervous and Mental Disease, 159,* 101–107.

Sledge, W. H., Moras, K., Hartley, D., & Levine, M. (1990). Effect of time-limited psychotherapy on patient dropout rates. *American Journal of Psychiatry, 147,* 1341–1347.

Sloane, R. B., Staples, F. R., Cristol, A. H., Yorkston, N. J., & Whipple, K. (1975). *Psychotherapy versus behavior therapy.* Cambridge: Harvard University Press.

Steinmetz, J. L., Lewinsohn, P. M., & Antonuccio, D. O. (1983). Prediction of individual outcome in a group intervention for depression. *Journal of Consulting and Clinical Psychology, 51,* 331–337.

Stone, A. R., Frank, J. D., Nash, E. H., & Imber, S. D. (1961). An intensive five-year follow-up study of treated psychiatric outpatients. *Journal of Nervous and Mental Disease, 133,* 410–422.

Sue, S., Fujino, D. C., Hu, L., Takeuchi, D. T., & Zane, N. W. S. (1991). Community mental health services for ethnic minority groups: A test of the cultural responsiveness hypothesis. *Journal of Consulting and Clinical Psychology, 59,* 533–540.

Sue, S., McKinney, H. L., & Allen, D. B. (1976). Predictors of the duration of therapy for clients in the community mental health system. *Community Mental Health Journal, 12,* 365–375.

Taube, C. A., Burns, B. J., & Kessler, L. G. (1984). Patients of psychiatrists and psychologists in office-based practice: 1980. *American Psychologist, 39,* 1435–1447.

Thurer, S., & Hursh, N. (1981). Characteristics of the therapeutic relationship. In C. E. Walker (Ed.), *Clinical practice of psychology* (pp. 62–82). Elmsford, NY: Pergamon.

Tracey, T. J. (1986). Interactional correlates of premature termination. *Journal of Consulting and Clinical Psychology, 54,* 784–788.

Truax, C. B., & Carkuff, R. R. (1967). *Toward effective counseling and psychotherapy.* Chicago: Aldine.

Truax, C. B., Tunnell, B. T., Jr. Fine, H. L., & Wargo, D. G. (1966). The prediction of client outcome during group psychotherapy from measures of initial status. Unpublished manuscript, Arkansas Rehabilitation Research and Training Center, University of Arkansas.

Walters, G. C., Solomon, G. S., & Walden, V. R. (1982). Use of the MMPI in predicting persistence in groups of male and female outpatients. *Journal of Clinical Psychology, 38,* 80–83.

Weber, J. J., Solomon, M., & Bachrach, H. M. (1985). Characteristics of psychoanalytic clinic patients: Report of the Columbia Psychoanalytic Center Research Project (I). *International Revue of Psychoanalysis, 12,* 13–26.

Weiss, J., & Schaie, K. W. (1958). Factors in patient failure to return to clinic. *Diseases of the Nervous System, 19,* 429–430.

Wilkins, W. (1971). Desensitization: Social and cognitive factors underlying the effectiveness of Wolpe's procedure. *Psychological Bulletin, 76,* 311–317.

Wilkins, W. (1973). Expectancy of therapeutic gain: An empirical and conceptual critique. *Journal of Consulting and Clinical Psychology, 40,* 69–77.

Wilson, G. T., & Thomas, M. G. W. (1973). Self versus drug-produced relaxation and the effects of instructional set in standardized systematic desensitization. *Behavior Research & Therapy, 11,* 279–288.

Yamamoto, J., & Goin, M. K. (1966). Social class factors relevant for psychiatric treatment. *Journal of Nervous and Mental Disease, 142,* 332–339.

CHAPTER 4

The Psychotherapist

The psychotherapist is an important variable in psychotherapy, and although the therapist's activities and functions will be a primary focus in much of what follows in later chapters, it is important to offer first some general comments and observations about the therapist's role, training, personal qualities, and impact on the patient.

We can begin by asking: What are the qualities which appear to be necessary in order for an individual to become an effective therapist? It would appear likely that he or she should possess certain personal attributes. We might all agree that a basic attribute would be a deep interest in people combined with a genuine and humane desire to help them with their psychological difficulties. While this would appear to be a basic and desired characteristic, by itself, it would not necessarily be sufficient. Some who seemingly want to help humanity, at the same time, appear to be quite troubled themselves. Other persons with good intentions, by intruding into the affairs of other people, often do more harm than good. We might, therefore, also state that the individual contemplating a career that involves psychotherapy should also possess some reasonable degree of personal adjustment, so that he or she is not overly hampered by personal difficulties which might adversely influence the therapeutic work with disturbed individuals.

Besides these qualities, we would also anticipate that the would-be therapist should be someone who is sensitive to the feelings and communications of the client, displays some warmth and interest in the client and is a good and sympathetic listener—at least up to a point. The therapist also has to explain things to the patient and perhaps provide some direction. Consequently, the therapist should be able to communicate clearly and effectively. If the therapist has to communicate effectively to the client, he or she must not only be a good listener, but must know what to communicate. This, in turn, presupposes some knowledge—in this instance, a knowledge of personality and psychopathology, as well as of psychotherapeutic procedures. If the therapist is to acquire and retain this knowledge, he must also be a good learner and this, in turn, implies that he must be possessed of at least some minimum degree of intellectual ability.

In addition to these personal qualities deemed as desirable for the psychotherapist, a few other qualities also have been considered important. One of these is that the therapist should be a person who commands the trust and respect of the client. If initially the therapist does not inspire the confidence of the client, not only may this affect the expectations which the client has about being helped by the therapist, but he or she may also be more likely to terminate early and/or to seek help elsewhere. The matter of trust also appears to be of particular importance in psychotherapy since the client is expected in most therapies to confide his personal thoughts and feelings to the therapist, no matter how horrible he may believe they are. If a process of openness or self-disclosure is to take place, the therapist needs to be someone in whom the client can have the utmost trust.

Whereas the personal requisites of the psychotherapist mentioned have been cited frequently in many different expositions on psychotherapy, and would appear to reflect some consensus of opinion on this topic, other attributes or specialized knowledge have also been advocated as desirable or essential by particular individuals or groups. There is little to be gained by reviewing these proposals in any detail for they are based on the beliefs of individuals derived from their own particular professional training and experience as influenced by their specific professional affiliation. As mentioned in Chapter 1, most practitioners of psychotherapy are selected and educated initially as members of a given mental health profession. They are trained to be physicians, psychologists, or social workers primarily, and psychotherapy constitutes just one part of their training, although an important one. Their loyalties and their professional identities, as well as their own views, are influenced to varying degrees by their specific professional training. As a result, it is not surprising that individual psychotherapists with different professional training and experience may emphasize certain specific requisites for the psychotherapist, particularly in terms of skills or training, which reflect their own background. In the absence of any empirical test of the actual validity of these postulates, they must be regarded strictly as personal views or hypotheses.

In support of the preceding statement we can refer briefly to the report of an interdisciplinary conference arranged to discuss the ideal training of psychotherapists and the possible recognition of a profession of psychotherapy (Holt, 1971). Although the conference participants were decidedly analytic in their orientation, the professions of psychiatry, clinical psychology, and psychiatric social work were represented. In reading this report, one cannot help but be impressed by the extent to which most of the participants were influenced by their own training and professional affiliation. Thus, apart from some agreement on the desired personal qualities of the therapist already mentioned, psychiatrists believed that some components of medical training including experience in hospital emergency rooms was desirable for all psychotherapists. Some of the psychologists, on the other hand, recommended that all psychotherapists should have training in general psychology and psychological testing. These opinions were largely determined by the professional training and affiliations of the participants and not by any functional analysis of the psychotherapeutic process. Since that time there has been no significant attempt to consider a single profession of psychotherapy.

PERSONAL THERAPY FOR THE PSYCHOTHERAPIST

Another belief that has been strongly held by a number of psychotherapists for many years is that personal therapy is an important requirement for the practice of psychotherapy. Influenced by the views of Freud and the psychoanalysts, many therapists have accepted the rationale advanced for this view that the therapist needs to have an intimate knowledge of himself. He needs to be aware of his own areas of conflict and how he responds to others, so that his own personality and his own problems will not unnecessarily intrude on the psychotherapeutic work with the client. This appears to be a reflection or adaptation of the old adage, "Physician, heal thyself." A related reason for undergoing personal therapy is that by this means the therapist will himself experience the process and be able to empathize better with the client and to understand how the client may experience psychotherapy. To this extent, he or she may be a more sensitive and understanding therapist, as well as a more objective and discerning one.

For such reasons, as well as more personal ones, a large number of therapists have secured personal therapy and have also recommended it as an essential training experience for all future psychotherapists (Greenberg & Staller, 1981). Some believe that it was the single most important part of their training in psychotherapy. It is also a requirement of most psychoanalytic institutes and postgraduate psychotherapy training centers, as well as being recommended in other types of training programs. Nevertheless, opposite views are also held (Holt, 1971). One objection made is that the individual who undergoes personal therapy may be overly influenced by the viewpoints of his own therapist and his own personal experience. Since many of the analytic and postgraduate centers specify that the candidate's therapist must be a member of their institute or approved by them (Rachman & Kauff, 1972), there is a certain amount of indoctrination involved.

Unfortunately, we have little objective evidence on which to base any firm conclusions as to whether or not personal therapy makes a person a better therapist. In the final analysis, one would want to appraise the therapeutic outcomes of therapists who had received personal therapy with a comparable group of therapists who had not.

Although no truly definitive studies on this issue have been reported, a few reports are available. Several surveys of psychotherapists in the United States have shown that a large number of them have undergone some form of personal psychotherapy. In a survey of 855 members of the Division of Clinical Psychology of the American Psychological Association, 63% stated that they had received some personal therapy (Garfield & Kurtz, 1975). Henry, Sims, and Spray (1971) conducted a study of professional psychotherapists and also found that a majority of the therapists had received some form of personal therapy. In their sample, the percentages of therapists who had not undergone personal therapy were as follows: clinical psychologists, 25.2%; psychiatrists, 34.6%; social workers, 35.7%; and psychoanalysts, 2.5%. In this sample of psychotherapists a number of them had had more than one psychotherapy experience. Among the psychologists, 41.2% had had more than one psychotherapy experience, whereas 52.3% of the analysts had had a similar experience. These findings, as well as others (Prochaska & Norcross, 1983), support the belief among many psychotherapists that personal therapy is a desirable (or necessary) experience for psychotherapists.

In the survey by Garfield and Kurtz (1975), the respondents were asked if they would recommend that all clinical psychologists undergo personal psychotherapy. Forty-five percent said "yes," 38% said "no," and approximately 17% were undecided. When those who had had personal therapy were compared with those who had not, the former were significantly more positive concerning the importance of personal therapy. Sixty-five percent of those who had had personal therapy recommended it for all clinical psychologists as contrasted with only 10.5% of those who had not. Generally, those with analytic and Neo-Freudian orientations held the most positive views of personal therapy, whereas the behavioral and learning theory orientations were the least positive. It would appear that one's views concerning the importance of personal therapy as a prerequisite for becoming an effective psychotherapist are very much influenced by one's theoretical views and whether or not the individual himself has undergone personal therapy. However, there are a few empirical studies that can be reviewed briefly.

In the report of a conference on training in psychotherapy, Derner (1960) made reference to some data he had collected on a small number of students in training. He compared the eight students rated by supervisors as being the best therapists over a period of four years with those eight who were ranked as the poorest therapists over this period and was surprised to note that in each group half of the students had had personal therapy and half had not. The ratings of therapeutic competence were thus found to be unrelated to whether or not the therapist had had personal therapy.

In another small study, the hours of personal therapy received by therapists showed an unexpected negative relationship to three criteria of patient change, the Depression, and K scales of the MMPI and changes in the therapists' ratings of client disturbance (Garfield & Bergin, 1971). Although no significant tests were performed because of small sample size, the clients of the therapists who had not had personal therapy showed the largest changes on all of the criterion measures. Furthermore, those therapists who appeared to be better adjusted or less disturbed on certain personality measures also seemed to secure the most change in their clients. Although these findings have to be viewed cautiously since individuals undergoing therapy themselves may be more introspective and self-critical, they suggest the possible importance of the therapist's own level of adjustment in relation to effectiveness in psychotherapy, rather than the significance of personal therapy.

Reference can also be made to two older studies conducted in outpatient clinics of the Department of Veterans Affairs (Katz, Lorr, & Rubinstein, 1958; McNair, Lorr, Young, Roth, & Boyd, 1964). In both instances, there was no significant correlation between the therapists' personal therapy and therapy outcome. This is essentially the conclusion reached in two recent reviews (Beutler, Machado, & Neufeldt, 1994; Clark, 1986).

Before concluding our discussion of personal therapy for the psychotherapist, some additional findings from the study by Henry et al. (1971) are worth mentioning. One concerns the amount of personal therapy received by the therapists in this study. A majority of them received therapy that lasted from four to seven years, ranging from 57% of the psychiatrists to 84% of the psychoanalysts. Personal therapy of this kind is decidedly time-consuming and expensive, and one may ask whether the experience is commensurate with the investment made. Responses to such a question may be made on both personal as well as professional grounds. In the investigation by Henry et al. (1971), the therapists were asked to indicate their satisfaction with their personal therapy on a three-point scale. Thirty-six percent of the psychoanalysts and the psychiatrists, and 46% of the psychologists indicated unqualified satisfaction with their personal therapy; 35% of the psychoanalysts, 18% of the psychiatrists, and 19% of the psychologists indicated qualified satisfaction; and 29% of the psychoanalysts, 46% of the psychiatrists, and 35% of the psychologists indicated that they were not satisfied with their personal therapy. These results speak mainly to personal satisfaction with therapy and not directly to the value of such personal therapy on one's effectiveness as a psychotherapist.

The available data on the relative importance of the therapist's personal therapy as a variable in psychotherapy do not allow one to draw any hard and fast conclusions. However, what data exist do not appear to lend any strong support to the widely held view concerning the importance of personal psychotherapy for effectively conducting psychotherapy. As Clark (1986) has stated, "At present, it has not been empirically demonstrated that personal therapy is beneficial to client outcome" (p. 42). As in other areas of psychotherapy, more systematic and definitive studies are needed.

ADDITIONAL CONSIDERATIONS

We have thus discussed some general qualities which appear to be desirable for the psychotherapist and have also paid some critical attention to the issue of personal therapy as a possible prerequisite for the psychotherapist. As has been emphasized several times already, many of the desirable qualities are based on the beliefs and attempted formulations of a variety of workers in this field. At various times, particularly in terms of conferences or reports devoted to the training of mental health professionals, various lists of the necessary qualifications for entry into the profession have been promulgated (e.g., American Psychological Association, 1947; Holt, 1971; Holt & Luborsky, 1958; Raimy, 1950). Frequently these desired lists of qualifications represent the most highly prized human qualities and virtues. Students who are considering a future career in these professions and who read the recommended personal qualities may not only find themselves rather depressed at their own inability to meet the stated criteria, but they may well wonder if any person is capable of doing so who is merely mortal. An illustration is available from a report of an American Psychological Association Committee on Training in Clinical Psychology (1947). The following were listed as the desirable qualities sought in clinical psychologists:

1. Superior ability;
2. Originality and resourcefulness;
3. Curiosity;
4. Interest in persons as individuals;
5. Insight into one's own personality characteristics;
6. Sensitivity to the complexities of motivation;
7. Tolerance;
8. Ability to establish warm and effective relationships with others;
9. Industry and ability to tolerate pressure;
10. Acceptance of responsibility;
11. Tact;
12. Integrity and self-control;
13. Sense of ethical values;
14. Broad cultural background; and
15. Deep interest in psychology, especially the clinical aspects.

Qualities similar to those just mentioned plus a few additional ones have also been suggested for psychiatrists (Holt & Luborsky, 1958). While no one would decry the attempt to set high standards for any profession, and the work of the psychotherapist would indeed appear to require personal qualities of a high order, it is well to recognize that the attributes listed represent an idealized version of the professional person as well as the aspirations of the profession. It is thus understandable that groups concerned with setting high standards for their professions would strive for standards that reflect the abstracted ideals they associate with their work. Although it is desirable to set lofty goals for oneself and one's profession, it is also important to relate such goals or ideals to some empirically tested standards of performance. Apart from the difficult task of actually attempting to define and appraise the abstract qualities deemed desirable for the profession of psychotherapy, it is also of decided importance to demonstrate that such selected qualities actually are related to the high levels of performance desired. To a large extent, this task has not been adequately fulfilled (Beutler et al., 1994). Let us, therefore, examine some of the work that has been done on the selection of clinical psychologists and psychiatrists for graduate and postgraduate education, as well as more directly related studies of the qualities of psychotherapists in relation to their performance in psychotherapy.

One of the pioneer studies in this area was a large scale investigation sponsored by the Department of Veterans Affairs (VA) shortly after World War II on the selection of individuals for the graduate programs in clinical psychology cooperating with the VA. At this time, there was a critical shortage of trained mental health personnel and the VA was faced with the enormous task of caring for the large number of psychiatric casualties at the conclusion of the war. Among other developments, the VA entered into cooperative arrangements with selected graduate departments of psychology to help select and train individuals to become clinical psychologists, thereby providing a potential pool of psychologists for their own clinics and hospitals. In addition, funds were provided for a research project on the selection of clinical psychologists.

Prospective trainees from many universities came to the University of Michigan where they were intensively studied through tests and interviews (Kelly & Fiske, 1951). All of the popular psychological tests were used, as well as indepth interviews, group exercises, observations, and a final integrative appraisal by experienced clinical psychologists. These selective measures were later correlated with successful completion of the program and ratings of clinical performance during training at VA field stations. On the whole, the results of this large scale enterprise were disappointing. Very few of the predictive measures bore much relationship to the various criteria used and the highest correlations obtained were around .30. While there have been numerous conferences on the training of clinical psychologists since that time, there have been no comparable attempts to appraise and predict successful performance in clinical psychology.

A somewhat similar attempt to study the characteristics of psychiatric residents in training in relation to performance in the clinical situation was carried out at the Menninger Clinic and reported in some detail by Holt and Luborsky (1958). This study was more psychoanalytically and clinically oriented than the one reported by Kelly and Fiske, but in general the results were no more positive. Thus, while leaders in a particular mental health field may demonstrate some agreement in what they believe are the desirable or necessary attributes for the successful performance of their special area of skill, attempts to appraise these attributes and relate them to functional criteria of performance have generally been disappointing.

It is possible to criticize the two studies mentioned previously on certain counts. In the investigation concerning clinical psychologists, the students had been selected for admission to graduate study by different university departments of psychology in terms of their own criteria and selection standards. In most instances, the criteria are deemed to pertain to successful completion of an academic, as well as clinical program, leading to the Ph.D. degree, which is essentially a research degree. That is, the students were not selected solely on the basis of becoming psychotherapists or clinicians. Intellectual and academic criteria were involved to a great extent in their initial selection before they were evaluated at Ann Arbor. The criteria for successful performance at both the university and the clinical training site undoubtedly left much to be desired and varied from setting to setting.

In the study of the psychiatrists in training, other factors also have to be considered. While all of the psychiatric residents received their training and evaluation in one large center with one central administration, the group was already a highly selected one. Initially, they had been admitted to different medical schools on the basis of the latter's academic requirements, and all of the residents had successfully completed their medical school training and then their medical internship. The basic criteria in these instances were not psychiatric or psychotherapeutic ones, but criteria deemed important generally for the practice of medicine. In the second instance, they were selected for admission to the then highly sought after residency program affiliated with the Menninger Clinic where ostensibly psychiatric criteria were used. As in the Michigan project, the results were also influenced by the procedures used for selection and evaluation. The criteria of performance, as in many studies of this type, tended to be the ratings provided by supervisors rather than the actual outcomes secured in psychotherapy. Thus, one could say that both of these important projects were not directly concerned with the selection and performance of psychotherapists per se, although without doubt, the majority of the subjects in these two studies were later involved with psychotherapeutic activities.

More directly related to the matter of therapists' qualities and performance in actual psychotherapy with clients have been the studies carried out by client-centered therapists on the necessary and essential therapeutic conditions for positive outcome in psychotherapy. As mentioned previously, these were termed *Empathy* or *Accurate Empathy, Non-Possessive Warmth,* and *Genuineness* or *Congruence* on the part of the therapist (Truax & Carkhuff, 1967). Empathy referred not only to the ability of the therapist to accurately gauge and understand the feelings that the client was experiencing and trying to express, but also the ability to communicate this understanding to the client. Non-Possessive Warmth, apparently derived in part from Rogers' earlier formulation of Unconditional Positive Regard, pertained to the deep acceptance of the individual as he was. Genuineness referred to the therapist functioning as himself or herself, and without playing any role or attempting to communicate any feelings which he or she was not actually experiencing. The therapist had to be perceived and experienced by the client as a genuine individual and not as a "phony."

These conditions, viewed as the necessary and sufficient conditions for successful psychotherapy, were essentially therapist conditions or qualities of the therapist which were discernable in his or her interactions with the client. Nothing was really said about the importance of the client or patient as a variable in the outcome of psychotherapy. Rather, it was assumed that these therapist conditions were of sufficient power to determine the progress of psychotherapy regardless of the type of client. Perhaps no other formulation of psychotherapy has placed such emphasis on the important role of the psychotherapist. To their credit, however, the client-centered therapists were not content with mere statements or formulations of the desired therapist conditions. They went beyond this point with attempts to define their concepts in operational terms, to create rating scales that could be used to evaluate tape recordings of actual therapy sessions, and to conduct research investigations relating the therapist conditions to various processes and outcome in psychotherapy. This was an important achievement in psychotherapy, for such research is difficult and tedious. It is a way of trying to study therapist qualities as manifested in the actual operations of psychotherapy and relating them to outcome.

Now let us look at some of the results secured by investigations of therapist conditions and outcome in psychotherapy. Truax and Carkhuff (1967) summarized several studies showing the relationship of the rated therapeutic conditions to various measures of outcome. Although most of the findings were quite positive, there were also some findings that were both interesting and perplexing. Whereas all three of the therapeutic conditions were postulated as theoretically necessary for positive outcome, in some of the studies one of the conditions, and not always the same one, was either not correlated with outcome or was negatively correlated with the measures of outcome. This immediately raised the interesting question of how a factor that is supposedly required for positive outcome can in some instances be of no importance or even of negative importance. Another finding of interest was that in some studies two of the therapeutic conditions would show a high inter-correlation but would show either little correlation or a negative correlation with the third therapeutic condition. The high correlation between two of the rated conditions suggests also that they were appraising the same factor rather than different ones.

Truax and Carkhuff (1967) attempted to resolve this unexpected result by taking a somewhat empirical orientation. They suggested that when two of the scales were positively related and the third was not, attention should be given only to the former and the latter be disregarded. In other words, "when one of the three conditions is negatively related to the other two in any given sample of therapists, then patient outcome is best predicted by whichever two conditions are most closely related to each other" (p. 91). Although this procedure conceivably might work for practical or predictive purposes, it makes little theoretical sense, particularly when the two conditions selected would vary from situation to situation and a necessary therapeutic condition correlates negatively with outcome.

Thus, one might well have some reservations about the actual meaning of the three postulated therapeutic conditions and their possible relationship to positive outcome in psychotherapy. Additional research by other investigators has provided additional data that failed to support the claims of the client-centered group. In one study conducted with therapists who were largely eclectic or somewhat analytically oriented, and which used the scales published by Truax and Carkhuff (1967), the results were largely negative (Garfield & Bergin, 1971). While ratings of Empathy and Warmth were positively intercorrelated (.75), both of these scales were negatively correlated with the ratings of Genuineness or Congruence (−.65 and −.66). Here, again, one of the essential conditions was significantly correlated in a negative direction with the other two. Furthermore, when the ratings of the three therapist conditions were correlated with a wide variety of outcome measures, including client, therapist, and supervisor ratings of change, as well as pre-post differences on several scales of the MMPI, not one reached an acceptable level of significance.

The negative results reported above have been followed by other similar results. Mitchell, Bozarth, and Krauft (1977) reviewed this literature and indicated the increase of negative or nonsupporting results. They concluded that it is "increasingly clear that the mass of data neither supports nor rejects the overriding influence of such variables as empathy, warmth, and genuineness in all cases. . . . The recent evidence, although equivocal, does seem to suggest that empathy, warmth and genuineness are related in some way to client change but that their potency and generalizability are not as great as once thought" (p. 483). Parloff, Waskow, and Wolfe (1978) in another review came to the following conclusion:

It must be concluded that the unqualified claim that "high" levels (absolute or relative) of accurate empathy, warmth, and genuineness (independent of the source of rating or the nature of the instrument) represent the "necessary and sufficient" conditions for effective therapy (independent of the outcome measures or criterion) is not supported. (p. 249)

These conclusions, while differing somewhat in their emphases, generally tend to dampen the enthusiasm expressed earlier with regard to Empathy, Warmth, and Genuineness as the essential conditions for facilitating therapeutic change. Although negative findings and the failure to replicate earlier promising results are always disappointing, the failure to substantiate the earlier reports of the client-centered therapists was particularly disappointing for several reasons. One is that the therapist qualities or conditions conceptualized by the client-centered school have been the type of therapist qualities that have also been presumed to be important therapist qualities by therapists of other theoretical persuasions. Although they may at times be stated differently and formulated within somewhat different contexts, attributes such as therapist Empathy, Warmth, and Genuineness would be considered to be desirable and important qualities of all effective therapists. When studies indicate that careful ratings of such qualities do not appear to be significantly related to outcome, feelings of disappointment would be expected. A second reason is that the earlier work in this area appeared to mark a significant step forward in the attempt to make the abstract and often ethereal concepts of psychotherapy operational. The development of rating scales to appraise significant therapist qualities based on actual therapeutic performance and then relating such measures to outcome was of potentially great importance.

Nevertheless, while later research has failed to lend strong support to the very promising findings reported earlier, the general approach of carefully trying to define important therapist characteristics, of developing scales to evaluate these characteristics as they are manifested in the actual interactions with a client in therapy, and then relating the measures of these characteristics to outcome in psychotherapy, is a desirable model to follow. At the same time, it has become increasingly clear that investigators can not focus solely on the therapist. Attention must also be devoted to the patient and the interactions that take place in therapy.

THE THERAPIST AND THE PSYCHOTHERAPEUTIC INTERACTION

We have discussed some of the more general views concerning the qualifications and personal prerequisites of the psychotherapist, as well as reviewing some of the research that has been conducted in this area. As is true in many other areas of psychology and the social sciences generally, there are many orientations and views within the field of psychotherapy, and many of them have never been investigated systematically. When attempts are made to conduct such investigations, more often than not, a number of the prevailing beliefs fail to be substantiated. While this is not the happiest state of affairs, it is not a unique one in terms of historical development and one must see it realistically for what it is—a certain stage in the development of any field. Science advances when old beliefs are gradually replaced by newer beliefs based on more solid supporting evidence. Nevertheless, individuals are more comfortable with authoritative views and certainty. Hope and faith are powerful human forces and they also play a potentially important role in psychotherapy. However, advances in psychotherapy can only take place if we face up to the difficult task of testing our most cherished beliefs.

This important issue has been evident many times in my own career as a clinical psychologist and as a psychotherapist. It has also concerned me in my role as a teacher of psychotherapy. How does one try to convey information and knowledge concerning the procedures and techniques of psychotherapy and at the same time acquaint the student with the state of validated knowledge in our field, the gaps in our knowledge, and the need to take a somewhat critical stance toward views that have failed to be supported or that still lack empirical verification? This is a very difficult task and often is a frustrating one as well. If we present theoretical views or procedures as if they were received from on high or as if they were self-evident truths which do not require any empirical validation, we may inspire a greater sense of well-being and confidence in the student therapist, but is it really desirable in the long run? Do we want to train individuals who believe they have the final word on psychotherapy and are capable of curing all ills? On the other hand, an overly critical emphasis on our lack of knowledge and on the frequent occurrence of negative findings can produce a discouraged or nihilistic attitude which is also undesirable. There is clearly a difficult dilemma presented that is not easy to resolve. It seems best to take an evenhanded but realistic view of our field. We have made noticeable research progress in the past 30 years or so, but there are still gaps in our understanding of the variables that produce positive change. Some of the therapeutic activities that are conducted today may well be ineffective, or even harmful, and there is some evidence in support of this to which we will refer later. At the same time, it is also true that there are many practical situations where action is required and where we must proceed on the basis of whatever knowledge we have, scant though it may be. In some cases, indecision and delay may well be fatal. In some cases, also, the task of carefully collecting and evaluating the data may be a long and difficult one, and practical decisions must be made and action taken before all the findings are in. However, while it may be necessary to act in such instances, it is also important to evaluate our actions and decisions so that in the future we may profit from our past experiences and improve the bases for our future actions.

This issue is an important one for most psychotherapists. The psychotherapist functions as a socially sanctioned healer, and while assuming the role and responsibilities of all healers, he is in some ways unique. There are few professions which make more demands on the personality of the participant than that of psychotherapy and in which the personality characteristics of the individual are considered to be of such prime importance. It is difficult to think of any professional pursuit that requires the kind of intimate and sustained interaction with a client as that of the psychotherapist. Psychotherapists, by the nature of their work, are brought into daily and close contact with all varieties of human suffering. Not only must they have the necessary personal strength to face and cope with such ills, but they must also have some conviction that their efforts are helpful in alleviating the discomforts of the client.

To a certain extent, therefore, the psychotherapist must believe in himself and in his therapeutic procedures. It is very difficult to persist in tasks that you personally believe are of no value. Not only is it important for the therapist to have faith or confidence in himself or his therapy if he is to continue in his life's work, but because of the interactions characteristic of psychotherapy, the beliefs or confidence of the psychotherapist may also have an effect on the patient and his progress in therapy. A therapist who radiates confidence in her ability to help patients may inspire confidence in many of her patients, which in turn may facilitate progress in therapy. If the therapist is overly confident and promises too much, this may backfire and have the opposite result, particularly with some patients. On the other hand, if the therapist is overly pessimistic and indicates little confidence in her procedures, her prophecy may be fulfilled or the client may be done with her quickly. Recall our earlier discussions of client expectations; many of these can be influenced or manipulated by the therapist in therapy to some degree. The therapist is a significant figure to the client and the former's personality, moods, and beliefs, as well as the communications influenced by them can be hypothesized to exert some influence on the client and his progress in therapy.

Consequently, the relationship that develops during psychotherapy is influenced significantly by the personality and skill of the therapist as well as by the problems and perceptions of the patient. Fortunately, increased research attention has been paid in recent years to the importance of this relationship for psychotherapy outcome (Beutler et al., 1994). Sometimes referred to as the *therapeutic alliance* or the helping alliance, the importance of the therapeutic relationship has received increasing recognition from therapists of widely divergent orientations. More will be said about it in the following chapter.

While the psychotherapist needs to be a scientifically responsible and ethical person, she must also be able to inspire a reasonable degree of confidence in the client. She should not make unwarranted statements or promises, but at the other extreme, it would not be helpful to present the client with a summary of the many negative findings culled from the psychotherapeutic literature. Some better solution has to be secured and, in general, each psychotherapist tends to resolve it in his or her own particular way.

My own view on this matter goes something like this. In psychotherapy there are many views, clinical beliefs, and folklore, as well as some reasonably supported facts. When a particular view or procedure has received some empirical or research support, we should note this fact clearly. This type of finding is backed by data and, as a consequence, we can have some confidence in it. The degree of confidence is determined by the kind and amount of research that has been produced in support of a particular method or procedure. For example, we can state with a moderate amount of confidence that outcome in psychotherapy generally is little influenced by the sex or age of the client. We could also state, as another illustration, that recent research findings indicate that a relatively small percentage of clients who undergo psychotherapy appear to become worse than when they started psychotherapy, but that the exact percentage and the precise factors responsible are not yet determined with any conclusiveness (Foa & Emmelkamp, 1983; Lambert & Bergin, 1994; Mays & Franks, 1985; Strupp, Hadley, & Gomes-Schwartz, 1977). On some other items, one can only state that "there appears to be a suggestion that" variable A may influence variable B, but further data are needed. The results of various pretraining programs in psychotherapy, to be discussed later, might be used as an illustration for the preceding sentence since both positive and inconclusive results have been secured.

It can be stated also that in other instances a particular view or procedure has never been investigated and, therefore, must be viewed as an hypothesis or personal belief in need of confirmation. In other instances, the limited and conflicting data available suggest that one must keep an open mind on the problem and hope that further and more definitive data will be forthcoming. The field of psychotherapy is made up of many different kinds of views and findings. With some we may have a fair degree of confidence; with some we may feel the data point us in one direction, but just slightly; and in others we may have to conclude that in the absence of data we are proceeding on what appear to be reasonable or warranted hypotheses or assumptions. Final answers are simply not available, and we must proceed on what appears to be the soundest path possible. In some instances, we can have confidence that our procedures are based on reasonably sound empirical results. In others, we must trust our own judgment and intelligence, recognizing fully what we are doing and the bases for our decisions. Finally, we must be ready to modify our views and even our strongly held beliefs when research data appear to challenge them.

There is also a related issue which has been discussed and debated among psychotherapists of different orientations. This pertains to whether psychotherapy is an "art" or a "science." In one seminar composed of practicum students and their supervisors, one of the student participants made the comment that the discussion revealed our lack of knowledge on this particular issue, and that it highlighted the necessity for research on this problem. Two of the supervising psychotherapists in the group responded in a strong emotional fashion that psychotherapy was an art, would always be an art, and would never become a science. This same view was expressed rather strongly a few years later in a letter published in the *American Psychological Association Monitor:*

> Psychotherapy is NOT a science, it is an art, and is dependent on and expressed through the personality of the psychotherapist. It cannot be objectively measured unless one only views psychotherapy and personality in the mechanical way that is so fashionable among many of our colleagues who are too frightened and too inept to establish an interpersonal relationship of a therapeutic variety with a patient.
>
> Psychotherapy is an art . . . which cannot be quantified. (Lehrer, 1981)

Although it would certainly be very difficult to take the stand that psychotherapy as practiced today is a science, there are many dangers inherent in the view that psychotherapy is fundamentally an art and, therefore, can never be looked at or investigated objectively. To see psychotherapy as solely an artistic enterprise, dependent on the intuitions of the psychotherapist, is to completely remove it from any attempts at objective empirical appraisal or from any means of increasing our understanding of the therapeutic process in order to improve its effectiveness. Rather, we must avail ourselves of all procedures that may offer us a means of increasing the effectiveness of psychotherapy. The scientific model of research has proven its utility in other areas of knowledge and practice, and appears to have definite usefulness in the area of psychotherapy. It has contributed greatly to the advances evident in the field of medicine, and should not be banished because of a biased preconceived view. At the same time, it should be recognized that the more classical models of research must be applied intelligently and modified as necessary if they are to lend themselves to useful application. This is a research issue which we can consider further in Chapter 12. It should be mentioned, however, that in recent years, greater demands for evidence that psychotherapy is effective have been made by governmental and insurance agencies.

ETHICAL AND PROFESSIONAL RESPONSIBILITIES

When the therapist accepts an individual as a client or patient in psychotherapy, he assumes the responsibilities and professional obligations that go with this role. As a member of a recognized profession and as one performing the duties of a sanctioned healer, the psychotherapist is guided by the code of ethics of his or her profession, as well as by society's laws and regulations. Although the various mental health professions may have somewhat different official ethical codes, they are similar in emphasizing the responsibilities that a person has for his or her client. Since these are usually communicated by each of the professions in their training institutions, there is no need to list them here. In general, they tend to emphasize the responsibility of the professional:

- To represent himself and his therapeutic skills honestly,
- To refrain from making false claims or to promise what he cannot deliver,
- To accept only those clients whom he legitimately can expect to help,
- To refer to other qualified persons those cases who fall outside of his field of expertise or who can be handled better elsewhere,
- To charge fees that are within the client's means or are regarded as reasonable,
- To avoid taking advantage of his role in his relationship with the client,
- To respect the confidential nature of the relationship, and
- To regard the client's welfare as a primary concern.

The serious student and practitioner of psychotherapy should be aware of his or her ethical and professional responsibilities, as well as the problems encountered in practice. A nonmedical psychotherapist should be sensitive to problems that might be organic in nature and be ready to make the appropriate referral or seek consultation. This is not as simple a matter as it may seem, for somatic complaints may have other than organic etiology and the proper handling of them may be quite important in the progress of psychotherapy. If a psychotherapist constantly refers his clients, he or she may be indicating a lack of adequacy and self-confidence that could affect the client and the eventual outcome of therapy. On the other hand, if the therapist neglects what may be physical symptoms or interprets them as resistance on the part of the client, he may be failing in his overall responsibility for the welfare of the client. In a similar fashion, a psychiatrist who is organically oriented may rely too heavily on medication, sometimes increasing the dosage instead of fully appraising the psychological nature of the problem and referring the patient for psychotherapy. All practitioners must be well versed in psychopathology and exhibit sound judgment.

There are a few other aspects which appear particularly relevant to psychotherapy, although they are not, perhaps, the exclusive concern of psychotherapists alone. We have already made reference to the higher frequency of close contact between the psychotherapist and his client than is true in most other professional relationships and to the fact that the client usually confides material of a highly personal nature. The client shares very personal matters with the psychotherapist. The therapist may be viewed as a powerful person in whom one places his trust and well-being. As a consequence, the therapist can have significant power or control over such a client. As noted also, the client may develop transference feelings or a strong emotional attachment to the therapist. In such instances, the client may express admiration for the wonderful qualities of the therapist and even bring the therapist gifts. As noted many years ago by Freud, some patients may even express feelings of love for the therapist. This is all very heady stuff, and although psychotherapists may have been instructed to be aware of and to anticipate such behaviors on the part of the client, some may be overly influenced by their own personal needs to pay much attention to these strictures. To be placed in such a role may be too satisfying and pleasurable for some therapists to resist. Furthermore, times have changed greatly since Freud's time and, whereas, as a product of 19th-century Vienna, Freud was horrified to receive confessions of love from some of his female patients, such is not always the case today.

Sexual intimacies and seductions of patients by therapists are clearly unethical behaviors that violate the trust that patients place on the therapist and that can actually produce harmful consequences in patients (Pope, Tabachnick, & Keith-Spiegel, 1987). The current ethical principles and code of conduct published by the American Psychological Association (1992) contain three items in the section on therapy that deal with sexual matters:

4.05 *Sexual intimacies with current patients or clients:* Psychologists do not engage in sexual intimacies with current patients or clients.

4.06 *Therapy with former sexual partners:* Psychologists do not accept as therapy patients or clients persons with whom they have engaged in sexual intimacies.

4.07 *Sexual intimacies with former therapy patients:* (a) Psychologists do not engage in sexual intimacies with a former therapy patient or client for at least two years after cessation or termination of professional services. (b) Because sexual intimacies with a former therapy patient or client are so frequently harmful to the patient or client, and because such intimacies undermine public confidence in the psychology profession and thereby deter the public's use of needed services, psychologists do not engage in sexual intimacies with former therapy patients and clients even after a two-year interval except in the most unusual circumstances. The psychologist who engages in such activity after the two years following cessation or termination of treatment bears the burden of demonstrating that there has been no exploitation, in light of all relevant factors, including (1) the amount of time that has passed since therapy terminated, (2) the nature and duration of the therapy, (3) the circumstances of termination, (4) the patient's or client's personal history, (5) the patient's or client's current mental status, (6) the likelihood of adverse impact on the patient or client and others, and (7) any statements or actions made by the therapist during the course of therapy suggesting or inviting the possibility of a post-termination sexual or romantic relationship with the patient or client. (p. 1605)

Although the ethical principles are clear, there have been several published surveys of violations by therapists, mainly male therapists (Holroyd & Brodsky, 1977; Pope, Keith-Spiegel, & Tobachnick, 1986; Pope, Tobachnick, & Keith-Spiegel, 1987). In these surveys, the percentage of therapists who reported engaging in sexual contact with a client ranged from approximately 2% to 7%. This problem is not limited to psychologists but occurs among psychiatrists and others as well (Gartrell, Herman, Olante, Feldstein, & Localio, 1986). Such instances represent some extreme examples of the intimacy that may develop, particularly in more intensive or long-term psychotherapy, as well as the importance of the therapist's own personal needs as they take precedence over those of the client.

There are also issues of so-called nonerotic physical contact—hugging, kissing, and touching—that also need to be carefully evaluated by therapists (Holub & Lee, 1990). In one study, 30% of humanistic therapists thought that such behaviors might be frequently or always beneficial (Holroyd & Brodsky, 1977). However, the therapist who lets his own needs become predominant over those of the client is behaving in a manner that is both unethical and detrimental to the client's welfare. In our own time where there has been an increased emphasis on openness and strong expressions of affect, as exemplified in the encounter and marathon groups, including nude marathon groups (Mintz, 1971), such incidents may be more likely.

The emphasis among some recent therapeutic orientations on the openness and self-disclosure of the therapist in therapy may also play a role in creating a different type of relationship, one which modifies or diminishes the more traditional professional role of the psychotherapist. Although some such

developments appear to be promulgated by sincere and professionally qualified individuals, they also appear to potentiate the likelihood of undesirable
effects on the part of clients (Hartley, Roback, & Abramowitz, 1976).

Although the previous incidents may be the most dramatic, there are other
instances where the therapist's needs may appear to take priority over those
of the patient's. Because of the nature of the psychotherapeutic enterprise, a
need may be manifested on the part of both patient and therapist to keep the
relationship going regardless of purely therapeutic considerations. Many different reasons may exist for this. Initially, the therapist may want a new client
to continue in therapy because he has many open hours in his schedule and
he would not like to lose this income. The therapist may have the conviction
that additional therapy is desirable for the patient. In a clinic situation, it
may also be a matter of personal pride for the therapist to keep his or her patients coming regularly for therapy instead of having them drop out early.
Student therapists, in the writer's experience, are particularly involved with
their first few clients and will go to great lengths to keep these clients in
therapy whether this is desirable or not. They are willing to see them at any
time of the day or night, and one student was even agreeable to traveling over
an hour to see her client regularly at the client's home when the client showed
no inclination to return for future appointments. Such therapists are understandably crestfallen (and they are not alone!) when a client fails to show up
for a scheduled appointment. They must learn to see that their therapeutic
zeal to help the patient is also a manifestation of their own personal needs,
socially desirable though they may appear to be.

The therapist's needs may also enter in other ways to foster the continuation of the patient in therapy. The therapist may secure personal gratification from having an admiring or grateful patient continue in therapy for a
long period. It is positive reinforcement for the therapist's ego and makes up
for some of the other patients who are less appreciative of the therapist's
services. As a consequence, the therapist may keep some patients in therapy
for a long period on the basis of a mutual reinforcement schedule, but not in
terms of the actual needs of the patient for change. The ostensibly altruis-
tic theme to the effect that the patient "needs me" or needs more therapy
may at times actually reflect some needs of the therapist rather than an objective appraisal of the client's need for continued psychotherapy.

In clinical practice, some therapists appear to keep their patients in therapy for very long periods of time (Stieper & Wiener, 1959). The therapists
in such instances may state that these patients need long-term therapy or
support and that without such therapy many of these patients would have to
be hospitalized. However, in an investigation of this problem in one clinic
where the therapists were told to terminate their cases of many years duration, no unfortunate consequences ensued (Stieper & Wiener, 1959, 1965).
Nevertheless, long-term psychotherapy has been accorded a positive status

in certain circles and it is not uncommon to hear of therapy lasting 10 to 20 years, and referred to with a certain pride by the therapist (Kelman, 1971). The problem is deciding in some relatively objective or reasoned manner whether such long-term therapy is really in the patient's interest or whether it is determined primarily by personal needs of the therapist. At what point should the patient be freed of his or her dependence on the therapist? This remains an issue even though in recent years a number of factors have led to a major reliance on brief forms of psychotherapy.

The major responsibility for seeing that psychotherapy is carried out with the greatest dispatch and in the most efficient manner resides in the therapist. The client, after all, is relatively uninformed and gullible in such matters and can be very much influenced by the therapist. This is particularly true in the case of certain unsophisticated clients who are rather passive and submissive. Therapy may increase the dependency of such clients on the therapist and not only will they be willing to continue therapy for a long period, even at some financial sacrifice, but they may then actually resist terminating therapy. In effect, it has become a way of life for them, and it is difficult for them to give it up. Although the client may very much want to prolong therapy, this does not mean that the therapy has actually accomplished positive gains or has been therapeutic for the client. Instead, it has given him a new crutch and lessened his capacity for independent action. Although it might not be entirely fair to view the therapist's behavior in such instances as unethical, it certainly does not represent competent or acceptable professional performance.

The psychotherapist, therefore, has to be alert to a great many considerations in order to carry out his or her duties in the most responsible and effective manner possible. In addition to displaying a sincere interest in the client and in striving to help him overcome his difficulties, the therapist must also try to be as objective and responsible as possible in appraising the client's problems and in conducting his or her therapeutic work. In an area such as psychotherapy, where despite the appearance of some treatment manuals, there are few explicit and objective guidelines concerning what procedures should be followed in many types of cases and how long treatment should take, the professional and ethical responsibility assumed by the therapist is a heavy one. The particular nature of the psychotherapeutic relationship also would appear to require not only qualities of human sensitivity and empathy, but also those of extreme objectivity in which the client's welfare is the main guide for the therapist's activities. While a knowledge of human personality and behavior, including abnormal behavior, and a knowledge of psychotherapeutic theories and techniques are basic requirements for the effective practice of psychotherapy, by themselves, they are not sufficient. The therapist's personal qualities, including a real and objective concern for the client, an awareness of his own needs and interactions in therapy, a relatively mature personality that does not require undue personal gratification at the client's expense, and a deep awareness of his ethical and professional obligations, are of decided importance. The psychotherapist must also be aware of the lacks in our knowledge of the psychotherapeutic process, be alert to the research in his field, be ready to modify his views when they fail to receive empirical validation and, not least of all, be able to live with uncertainty.

There are a variety of problems that can arise during the process of therapy with difficult and seriously disturbed patients that will test the skill and personal resources of the therapist. Working with individuals who are experiencing personal difficulties and having serious problems of adjustment is a demanding and stressful occupation. Although a majority of clients appear to be helped by psychotherapy, there are those who fail to show improvement and may become a source of concern to the therapist. In one study of the sources of stress for psychotherapists, the two that headed the list were statements made by clients about suicide and the inability of the therapist to help an acutely distressed client to feel better (Deutch, 1984). Concern about a patient's possible suicide was also reported to be the most common fear in a recent survey of 285 therapists (Pope & Tabachnick, 1993) and patient suicide was reported to have a powerful effect on therapists (Chemtob, Bauer, Hamada, Pelowski, & Muraoka, 1989). Many psychotherapists also have concerns about possible hostility and physical attacks by potentially violent patients. Strong emotions and verbal expressions of patients do take their toll on the overall peace and tranquility of therapists (Tryon, 1986) and there has been increasing reference to problems of "burnout" (Farber & Heifetz, 1982).

Another potentially problematic situation that can arise in therapy pertains to serious threats verbalized by clients against other people. In the case of *Tarasoff v. Regents of the University of California,* the Supreme Court of the State of California decided that where a therapist views a patient as a serious threat to others, he or she has a responsibility to protect the potential victim of the danger. In this case, a patient who was receiving therapy at the student mental health clinic several times mentioned the threat of using a gun against a former girlfriend. The therapist did take the threat seriously and informed the campus police. The patient was then taken into custody but released when supervising psychiatrists determined that commitment to an institution was not necessary. However, the patient later killed his former girlfriend.

Pryzwansky and Wendt (1987) have commented on this case as follows:

> While predicting violence is difficult, the court felt that the risk to potential victims outweighs the need of the client. . . . . Practitioners need to be aware that the duty is to "protect" the potential victim, which does not necessarily mean directly warning the person. The protection conceivably

includes other reasonable methods, such as notifying the police, removing instruments/harm, continuous supervision by the family or community, modifying treatment, referral, or even commitment." (p. 96)

Thus, the courts believe that where there is the possibility of serious harm to others being inflicted by a client or patient, the therapist has a responsibility to others that takes precedence over the confidentiality of the therapy situation. This responsibility also needs to be explained to patients. However, despite these potentially negative aspects of the psychotherapeutic role, which occur also in other highly demanding and respected professions, each year many more individuals apply for admission to programs that emphasize psychotherapy than are admitted. On the positive side, helping an individual to surmount problems and to reach a higher level of adjustment provides gratification to the therapist.

REFERENCES

American Psychological Association, Committee on Training in Clinical Psychology. (1947). Recommended graduate training program in clinical psychology. *American Psychologist, 2,* 539–558.

American Psychological Association. (1992). Ethical principles of psychologists and code of conduct. *American Psychologist, 47,* 1597–1611.

Beutler, L. E., Machado, P. P. P., & Neufeldt, S. A. (1994). Therapist variables. In A. E. Bergin & S. L. Garfield (Eds.), *Handbook of psychotherapy and behavior change* (4th ed.) (pp. 229–269). New York: Wiley.

Chemtob, C. M., Bauer, G. B., Hamada, R. S., Pelowski, S. R., & Muraoka, M. Y. (1989). Patient suicide: Occupational hazard for psychologists and psychiatrists. *Professional Psychology: Research, and Practice, 20,* 294–300.

Clark, M. M. (1986). Personal therapy: A review of empirical research. *Professional Psychology: Research and Practice, 17,* 541–543.

Derner, G. F. (1960). An interpersonal approach to training in psychotherapy. In N. P. Dellis & H. K. Stone (Eds.), *The training of psychotherapists.* Baton Rouge, LA: Louisiana State University Press.

Deutch, C. J. (1984). Self-reported sources of stress among psychotherapists. *Professional Psychology: Research and Practice, 15,* 833–845.

Farber, B. A., & Heifetz, L. J. (1982). The process and dimensions of burnout in psychotherapists. *Professional Psychology, 13,* 293–301.

Foa, E. B., & Emmelkamp, P. M. G. (Eds.) (1983). *Failures in behavior therapy.* New York: Wiley.

Garfield, S. L., & Bergin, A. E. (1971). Personal therapy, outcome and some therapist variables. *Psychotherapy: Theory, Research, and Practice, 8,* 251–253.

Garfield, S. L., & Kurtz, R. (1975). Clinical psychologists: A survey of selected attitudes and values. *The Clinical Psychologist, 28,* (Spring), 4–7.

Gartrell, N., Herman, J., Olante, S., Feldstein, M., & Localio, R. (1986). Psychiatrist-patient sexual contact. *American Journal of Psychiatry, 143,* 1126–1131.

Greenberg, R., & Staller, J. (1981). Personal therapy for therapists. *American Journal of Psychiatry, 138,* 1467–1471.

Hartley, D., Roback, H. B., & Abramowitz, S. I. (1976). Deterioration effects in encounter groups. *American Psychologist, 31,* 247–255.

Henry, W. E., Sims, J. H., & Spray, S. L. (1971). *The fifth profession.* San Francisco: Jossey-Bass.

Holroyd, J. C., & Brodsky, A. M. (1977). Psychologists' attitudes and practices regarding erotic and nonerotic physical contact with patients. *American Psychologist, 32,* 843–849.

Holt, R. R. (Ed.) (1971). *New Horizon for psychotherapy.* New York: International Universities Press.

Holt, R. R., & Luborsky, L. (1958). *Personality patterns of psychiatrists: A study in selection techniques* (Vol. 1). New York: Basic Books.

Holub, E. A., & Lee, S. S. (1990). Therapists' use of nonerotic physical contact: Ethical concerns. *Professional Psychology: Research and Practice, 21,* 115–117.

Katz, M. M., Lorr, M., & Rubinstein, E. A. (1958). Remainer patient attributes and their relation to subsequent improvement in psychotherapy. *Journal of Consulting Psychology, 22,* 411–413.

Kelly, E. L., & Fiske, D. W. (1951). *The prediction of performance in clinical psychology.* Ann Arbor: University of Michigan Press.

Kelman, H. (1971). *Helping People. Karen Horney's psychoanalytical approach.* New York: Science House.

Lambert, M., & Bergin, A. E. (1994). The effectiveness of psychotherapy. In A. E. Bergin & S. L. Garfield (Eds.), *Handbook of psychotherapy and behavior change* (4th ed.) (pp. 143–189). New York: Wiley.

Lehrer, A. Letter. *APA Monitor,* 42 (February, 1981).

Mays, D. T., & Franks, C. M. (1985). *Negative outcome in psychotherapy and what to do about it.* New York: Springer.

McNair, D., Lorr, M., Young, H., Roth, I., & Boyd, R. (1964). A three-year follow-up of psychotherapy patients. *Journal of Clinical Psychology, 20,* 258–264.

Mintz, E. E. (1971). *Marathon groups: Reality and symbol.* New York: Appleton-Century-Crofts.

Mitchell, K. M., Bozarth, J. D., & Krauft, C. C. (1977). A reappraisal of the therapeutic effectiveness of accurate empathy, nonpossessive warmth, and genuineness. In A. S. Gurman & A. M. Razin (Eds.), *Effective psychotherapy: A handbook of research* (pp. 482–502). Oxford: Pergamon.

Parloff, M. B., Waskow, I. E., & Wolfe, B. E. (1978). Research on therapist variables in relation to process and outcome. In S. L. Garfield & A. E. Bergin (Eds.), *Handbook of psychotherapy and behavior change* (2nd ed.) (pp. 233–282). New York: Wiley.

Pope, K. S., Keith-Spiegel, P. C., & Tabachnick, B. (1986). Sexual attraction to clients: The human therapist and the (sometimes) inhuman training system. *American Psychologist, 41,* 147–148.

Pope, K. S., Tabachnick, B. G., & Keith-Spiegel, P. C. (1987). Ethics of practice. The beliefs and behaviors of psychologists as therapists. *American Psychologist, 42,* 993–1006.

Pope, K., & Tabachnick, B. (1993). Therapists' anger, hate, fear, and sexual feelings: National survey of therapist responses, client characteristics, critical events, formal complaints, and training. *Professional Psychology: Research and Practice, 24,* 142–152.

Prochaska, J., & Norcross, J. C. (1983). Contemporary psychotherapists: A national survey of characteristics, practices, orientations, and attitudes. *Psychotherapy: Therapy, Research, and Practice, 20,* 161–169.

Pryzwansky, W. B., & Wendt, R. N. (1987). *Psychology as a profession. Foundations of practice.* New York: Pergamon.

Rachman, A. W., & Kauff, P. F. (1972). Directory of postgraduate psychotherapy training facilities. *JSAS Catalog of Selected Documents in Psychology, 2,* 116.

Raimy, V. (Ed.). (1950). *Training in clinical psychology.* Englewood Cliffs, NJ: Prentice-Hall.

Stieper, D. R., & Wiener, D. N. (1959). The problem of interminability in outpatient psychotherapy. *Journal of Consulting Psychology, 23,* 237–242.

Stieper, D. R., & Wiener, D. N. (1965). *Dimensions of psychotherapy: An experimental and clinical approach.* Chicago: Aldine.

Strupp, H. H., Hadley, S. W., Gomes-Schwartz, B. (1977). *Psychotherapy for better or worse: The problem of negative effects.* New York: Jason Aronson.

Truax, C. B., & Carkhuff, R. R. (1967). *Toward effective counseling and psychotherapy.* Chicago: Aldine.

Tryon, G. S. (1986). Abuse of therapists by patients: A national survey. *Professional Psychology: Research and Practice, 17,* 357–363.

CHAPTER 5

Therapeutic Variables in Psychotherapy

It is quite apparent that the different forms of psychotherapy have different theoretical views and emphasize different techniques or procedures that supposedly are derived from the individual theoretical orientations. Their adherents also tend to use different concepts and language to describe what they see as the important variables in therapy that lead to positive outcomes. Any individual who is new to the field cannot help but be somewhat puzzled that forms of psychotherapy that appear to be so different in theory and techniques can all claim to be effective forms of therapy—in fact, actually claim to be the best form of therapy. There are at least two possible explanations. One is that there are many different routes to successful outcome in psychotherapy and that the founders of the different approaches to psychotherapy have each found a unique pathway to the goal. I have sometimes characterized this possibility as "all roads lead to Rome."

A second possibility is that despite different conceptual terminology and procedures, the therapies must have at least some therapeutic variables in common. This would be a partial explanation for the positive claims of the diverse schools of psychotherapy. However, individuals who have become devoted followers of one particular approach have difficulty in accepting this second possibility. Since I am not a follower of any particular school of therapy and believe there is some plausibility to this second hypothesis, I will try in this chapter to describe and discuss those variables that have been emphasized as important in previous works on psychotherapy and to offer an appraisal of their significance. An attempt will be made to emphasize those procedures that appear to be of value to most psychotherapists, regardless of the orientation from which they have been derived. In this chapter, I discuss the selected operational concepts and procedures in a somewhat abstract or conceptual manner, and then show their application where applicable in later chapters on the psychotherapeutic process. The emphasis will be on variables involved in the actual process of psychotherapy.

THE THERAPIST-CLIENT RELATIONSHIP

As already noted, most schools of psychotherapy have tended to place some importance on the relationship that develops in psychotherapy. This is very much influenced by the particular therapist and client who make up the relationship and the interactions that take place. All of the various client and therapist variables discussed in the preceding chapters may be of importance in specific relationships for they are the factors that influence the interactions occurring in psychotherapy.

There are certain factors that appear quite evident. The relationship will develop more positively if both parties regard each other with mutual respect and some positive feelings. If matters are to proceed smoothly at the beginning, the therapist must not deviate too far from the client's expectations about how a therapist conducts his or her business, must manifest a sincere interest in the client, and inspire some degree of confidence and trust in the client. On the other side of the equation, the client should manifest an interest in psychotherapy, a positive regard for the therapist, and a desire to work hard in a collaborative manner with the therapist. Since many clients will not necessarily come to therapy with such attitudes and characteristics, the therapist has a major responsibility to try to structure the situation so that a desirable relationship may take place. She should try to appraise the client as quickly and accurately as possible, and then to respond in an appropriate manner. She should ascertain the client's reasons for seeking therapy and his or her expectations about therapy and being helped. The therapist should also give the client a clear idea of what psychotherapy is and some estimate of how long it will take. She must also be sensitive to any doubts and uncertainties the client may show so that these may be clarified.

The therapist must adapt his or her responses to the particular client. If the client appears to be difficult or unmotivated, or if the therapist responds negatively to the client, the therapist should seriously decide if therapy is desirable and whether or not he or she should accept the client for psychotherapy. This presents a real issue in psychotherapy which will be mentioned only briefly here. On the one hand, if a therapist feels negatively toward a patient or if he sincerely believes that he cannot help a given patient, he may be professionally justified in not accepting the patient for treatment. On the other hand, it is possible that certain types of disturbed individuals who are seen as undesirable cases will not receive treatment, and only the "good" cases will be accepted. This is a difficult matter to resolve since there are reasonable arguments for each side and no easy guidelines to follow.

The initial impressions and interactions of the two participants are, thus, of some importance, for if these are quite negative, the relationship may be terminated before it has any chance to develop. However, if the initial session or sessions proceed without difficulty, there is the likelihood of a deeper relationship taking place in the future. How this relationship is structured and interpreted may vary from one orientation to another, but there are characteristics which would appear to be common to most. Like any other relationship which takes place over a period of time, a common bond develops between the two participants. The scheduled sessions are a regular and important event in the lives of both participants, although they may be especially so regarded by the client.

As therapy proceeds and as the patient comes to trust and value the psychotherapist, the patient begins to reveal and examine himself more openly, to express his true feelings more readily, and to be more responsive to the suggestions, comments, and interpretations of the therapist. The patient, aided by the understanding manner and support of the therapist, is better able to face negative aspects of self and to be motivated to attempt to change older and self-defeating patterns of behavior. Because of this relationship, the therapist is able to exert some influence on the patient, both to have him see behavioral patterns that are maladaptive, and also to try out new patterns that the patient may have been reluctant or afraid to try out previously by himself. To a certain extent, because of the relationship that has developed, the therapist may function as an agent of persuasion or reinforcement for the patient. The patient may be willing to attempt changes because of the support provided by the therapist or in some instances, in order to please the therapist. While the latter instance may not be viewed too positively from some therapeutic orientations, it may be a more adequate occurrence when viewed from a learning theory orientation. For example, if the client is motivated to try out some behavior that he previously avoided and sees that no negative consequences follow this behavior, he is more likely to continue with this positive behavior. To the extent that the disappearance of the negative behavior occurs and is replaced with behavior which facilitates positive adjustment, the goal of therapy is being realized. This is predicated on the behavior being maintained by reinforcement in the client's environment outside of therapy.

While some individuals appear to take an almost mystical view of the psychotherapeutic relationship and would react somewhat negatively to the view of the psychotherapist as a human "persuader" or social reinforcement machine, the social influence role of the therapist has been emphasized by dynamically oriented, as well as behaviorally oriented psychotherapists (Frank, 1973; Krasner, 1962; Strupp, 1973). It would seem reasonable to hypothesize that a person with whom one has formed a rather close relationship and whom one regards with trust and respect can exert considerable influence on the other person. To some extent, therefore, a positive relationship in therapy tends to increase the therapist's influence, for better or for worse, on the client in treatment. The relationship also may be seen as increasing the client's willingness to accept the therapist's explanations for past and current events, as well as to try out new behaviors. The therapist, after all, is an expert in problems of human behavior, is trying to help the client, and the client's hopes for improvement largely depend on the therapist's skills. This, coupled with the therapist's interest and regard for the client, helps to explain in part the potential influence of the therapist in the therapeutic relationship.

The relationship that develops in psychotherapy thus provides a general background or basis for the influence which the therapist brings to bear on the patient. It also helps to motivate the patient to continue in therapy, to attempt to cooperate with the therapist and, eventually, to try out new behaviors. There are other aspects that derive from the relationship and the regular meetings of the two participants. To the extent that the relationship is a positive one, the patient is more inclined to accept the interpretations, explanations, and insights offered or brought out in the therapy sessions. He is also likely to take on some of the values of the therapist and even, perhaps, to model some of his behaviors on those of the therapist. To the extent that the therapist is accurate in his or her perceptions and pronouncements and is a worthy model for the patient, all is well and good. If the opposite is the case, then other less desirable outcomes may be secured.

The psychotherapeutic setting also provides the therapist with an opportunity to observe the actual behaviors of the client. Psychotherapy is not mere talk or intellectual discussion of abstract topics or past events. Although the patient may be on his "good behavior" during the early interviews and be rather cautious in what he discusses, as the relationship develops, he is increasingly able to discuss topics of a more personal nature, and also more readily displays his feelings and characteristic modes of responding. The therapist not only is provided with the opportunity to observe typical behaviors of the client as he interacts with another person, but he can also point out these behaviors to the client and emphasize their probable impact on other interpersonal interactions which the client may have with other people. The fact that the therapist responds to these behaviors in a dispassionate and understanding manner may also increase the possibility of change.

The important role of the therapeutic relationship in psychotherapy has been recognized by adherents of practically all forms of psychotherapy. Even such prominent behavior therapists as Emmelkamp (1986) and O'Leary and Wilson (1987) have emphasized its importance. As stated by Emmelkamp, "It is . . . becoming increasingly clear that the quality of the therapeutic relationship may be influential in determining success or failure of behavioral therapies . . ." (p. 432).

The relationship in therapy also has been called the *therapeutic alliance* or the *helping alliance* by psychodynamic therapists. A number of studies have developed several alliance rating scales for research. Among the best known are the Vanderbilt Therapeutic Alliance Scale (Hartley & Strupp, 1983) and the Penn Helping Alliance Rating Scale (Morgan, Luborsky, Crits-Christoph, Curtis, & Solomon, 1982). There have been various definitions of the therapeutic alliance and Gaston (1990) has made an attempt to reconcile them. According to Gaston, the alliance is composed of four relatively independent dimensions including the patient's capacity to work or engage in therapy, the patient's affective bond to the therapist, the therapist's understanding and involvement with the patient, and the agreement between the two on the goals and tasks of therapy. Gaston has also contributed a review of this research in a multi-authored chapter (Henry, Strupp, Schacht, & Gaston, 1994).

We need not be concerned here with the various issues on the delineation of hypothesized components of the therapeutic alliance. The description of the therapeutic relationship presented previously does include most of the emphasized features of the relationship that occur in psychotherapy. Studies with some of the alliance scales generally have shown a positive correlation with outcome. This generally can be noted by the third or fourth session of therapy and the correlations have tended to fluctuate around .3 and .4. In a meta-analysis of 24 studies, Horvath and Symonds (1991) reported an average effect size of .26 for the working alliance, a reliable but moderate association with therapy outcome. It was also noted that the relation of the working alliance and therapeutic outcome did not appear to be a function either of the type of therapy or of the length of treatment. Thus the therapeutic relationship was positively related to outcome regardless of the type of therapy evaluated. It should be pointed out, however, that if a positive early relationship is accompanied by some indications of progress in therapy, this also may contribute to increased cooperation and a positive attitude toward therapy and the therapist.

The relationship which takes place in therapy, therefore, is a factor of some importance in terms of the potentiality for progress in psychotherapy. If, as already indicated, the relationship is a positive one, the potential for positive outcome would appear to be enhanced. On the contrary, if the relationship is a poor one, then this potentiality would appear to be lessened. The criterion for judging the quality of the relationship is not the comfort, sociability, and enjoyment of the relationship, for such goals can be secured by means of other relationships. Psychotherapy should not be, in Schofield's (1964) terms, "the purchase of friendship." Rather, the criterion has to be positive and adaptive changes in the client. The therapist bears the responsibility to see that the potential influences generated by the therapeutic relationship are used toward this end, and, therefore, he must be constantly aware of what is taking place and how the relationship is being utilized by both the client and himself.

INTERPRETATION, INSIGHT, AND UNDERSTANDING

The concepts of interpretation and insight were mentioned earlier in our discussion of psychodynamic therapies. In this section, an attempt will be made to consider these and related concepts from a more general point of view.

In the psychoanalytic view, interpretations were offered by the analyst as a means of helping the patient to go beyond the surface level of awareness and eventually to come to grips with the unconscious forces motivating his behavior. Whether interpretations dealt with the transference reactions to the therapist, the patient's free associations, his dreams, or his behaviors in or out of therapy, they were essentially explanations offered to the patient. There was, thus, an explicit belief that helping the patient to gain an understanding or insight about his difficulties was an important, if not the most important, means of instituting change in the patient. Although it was recognized that this process was far from a simple one, it was believed that the transference relationship and the understanding provided by the therapist enabled the patient to overcome his natural resistance to such a process, and to gradually accept and act on the basis of his newly acquired insights. Although understanding appears to be primarily a cognitive process, it was recognized that cognitive or intellectual understanding (insight) alone was not very significant, unless in some way, the patient's affects were also involved (Alexander & French, 1946). The assumption made was that insights were essential for progress in psychotherapy and, in fact, such therapies were frequently referred to as insight-oriented or uncovering therapies as contrasted with so-called supportive therapies.

Although Rogers (1942) in his first book on non-directive therapy did emphasize the importance of the client's insights in therapy, in his subsequent writings, this topic received less formal attention. The client-centered school, for the most part, has held the view that important insights follow changes in the self, rather than the other way around (Rogers, 1951). Other orientations, directly or indirectly, also make use of increased client understanding in their therapeutic procedures or theories. In some of the more directive or eclectic orientations, the giving of explanations to the client is one of the techniques utilized (Thorne, 1968). Cognitive therapies also emphasize the distorted perceptions and beliefs of the client as critical factors at the base of the client's difficulties (Beck, 1976; Ellis, 1962). The therapist's task is to get the client to understand his distorted beliefs, and eventually to discard them and to substitute more realistic ones for them. In this process, the therapist essentially points out the client's faulty belief systems and offers him (helps him to obtain) a new and more appropriate set of beliefs and perceptions. In fact, one form of this type of therapy was first named "Rational Therapy" by Ellis (1962).

It thus appears that insights and interpretations, or the offering of some type of understanding to the client by the therapist, are therapeutic variables emphasized by therapists of many different theoretical persuasions. Even the behavior therapists, who pay no formal attention to such dynamically oriented concepts as interpretation and insight, do attempt to provide their patients with some understanding of how their disturbed behavior has occurred and with a rationale for the procedures to be employed in therapy. Furthermore, as mentioned previously, several behaviorally oriented therapists have begun to incorporate cognitive emphases with their behavioral procedures. In all of these instances, some attention is paid to providing the client with some understanding of his difficulties, how they arose, why they persist, and how they can be changed.

Although many of the different approaches to psychotherapy pay some attention to providing the client with an understanding of his or her problems, how they go about this process differs and the insights and understandings provided the client also vary from one orientation to another. At the same time, the different and varied understandings are all presumedly therapeutic in some fashion or other, and this makes for an interesting and also somewhat puzzling situation. How can such different insights or understandings all contribute to positive outcome? In psychoanalysis, the patient tends to be given a Freudian view of his difficulties and past development, and the insights he obtains are based on psychoanalytic concepts. Thus, the patient may gradually accept the explanation from the therapist that his difficulties are based on earlier Oedipal conflicts that have been repressed. Another individual, seeing an Adlerian therapist may gradually come to understand that his problems were influenced by his place in the family, his resulting feelings of inferiority, and his compensatory strivings for power. Still another client seeing a rational-emotive therapist might be told that her difficulties are caused by her irrational beliefs about needing to be perfect and to be loved by everyone. Finally, a behavior therapist would inform her client that his current fears are the result of previous conditioning and that in therapy he will learn responses that are antagonistic to his fears and, as a consequence, these fear responses will gradually be inhibited.

In each of these illustrations, the client is provided with an understanding of his problem from the vantage point of the particular therapist he is seeing. Furthermore, in each instance there is an assumption that the explanation provided is accurate or "true," and that it is helpful to the client. This is an intriguing phenomenon and my thinking about it has been stimulated by the writings of Jerome Frank (1971, 1973). As Frank has formulated it, practically all therapeutic orientations provide their patients with some rationale or belief system to explain their disturbed behavior and there are clear parallels here with more primitive methods of healing. However, the important point is the providing of such a belief system appears to be of therapeutic value to the patient. The fact that the therapist appears to understand the patient's problems and is able to provide this understanding to the patient appears to reduce the latter's anxiety about his problems and to engender hope for alleviating them. When an individual is experiencing discomfort and does not understand what his symptoms signify, what has caused this unhappy state of affairs, or how serious his condition may be, it is reassuring to contact a professional therapist who seems to know what the problem is, what factors are responsible for it, and who also offers a treatment that supposedly can alleviate the patient's situation. Torrey (1972) has stated that the mere "naming" of the patient's disturbance by the therapist is an important therapeutic factor that is common to most therapies.

On the basis of what has just been presented, it seems reasonable to hypothesize that the *precise* nature of the insights and understandings provided by the therapist are of relatively minor importance. What does appear to be of importance is whether or not the client accepts the rationale or explanation offered by the therapist. If the client finds the explanation not quite convincing or incomprehensible, then it is likely that he will not accept it and, consequently, the rationale will have little therapeutic effect. However, if he does accept the explanation of the therapist, it is likely that he will find this reassuring, hopeful, and perhaps helpful. At least doubts, uncertainties, and ambiguity would appear to be partially overcome by such understanding and belief.

It may be that certain clients, for whatever reasons, are more prone to be accepting of some beliefs than of others, and the proper matching of therapy and client might be of some value. It is also possible that the personality characteristics of client and therapist may be important in how readily the therapeutic rationale is accepted in individual situations. Some clients are more readily influenced than others, whereas some therapists are undoubtedly more influential or persuasive than others. In any event, although many variables may be operative in this process, it seems plausible to infer that the providing of an explanation for the client's problems, as well as a rationale for the therapy, may have some therapeutic impact on the client, regardless of the rationale provided.

In discussing this topic with various professional audiences, I have frequently noticed some expressions of discomfort and concern on the faces of some individuals, and have received some critical responses from others. This, perhaps, is understandable. It seems that the implication of what I have presented is not only that some cherished clinical views and theories appear to be without substance, but even more, that the role of the psychotherapist is demeaned. Instead of the therapists' convictions that they are offering explanations to their patients that are theoretically valid, and on which their therapeutic work is apparently based, the therapists are, in effect, told that whatever they tell patients is equally efficacious, as long as the patients believe it. It is the matter of belief and acceptance on the part of the patient that appears to be the important process, and not the actual content of the material provided by the therapist. Viewed this way, the reactions of many therapists to such a presentation is easily understandable. To accept the possibility that it does not matter what you tell the patient as long as you are convincing and the patient accepts what you tell him or her, would appear to smack of potential quackery and salesmanship.

This is not an easy problem to resolve. Certainly a professional person who works with emotionally disturbed people is usually motivated by both humanitarian and scientific ideals and aspirations, and has an understandable expectation that his professional calling is a dignified and honorable one. He or she has a need, also, to have some conviction in one's theoretical beliefs and methods of practice. What has been said about the importance of the patient's acceptance of the rationale provided him for understanding his difficulties would appear to apply also to the psychotherapist. Believing in what he does may be important in how he functions professionally. At the same time, the history of medicine is replete with examples of worthless medicines and practices which, in all good faith and with the best of intentions, were administered to large numbers of people. The interesting thing is that many patients appeared to be helped by pharmacologically ineffective medicines, as accounts and studies of the placebo response inform us (Shapiro & Morris, 1978).

In the light of such issues, I would emphasize that therapists need to keep in mind that our current knowledge of psychotherapy is far from conclusive and that many of our present clinical beliefs and procedures have to be confirmed by empirical research. The very fact that we have so many divergent and conflicting theories and procedures is a reflection of this state of affairs. Consequently, the psychotherapist must strive to keep an open mind concerning developments in psychotherapy. He should be as open with himself about this matter as he would like his clients to be with him in his psychotherapeutic sessions with them and to frankly admit to himself that much of what he does is based on reasonably appearing hypotheses, and not on empirically verified truths. This may be difficult, but it does not necessarily have to create extreme indecision or doubt in the therapist.

At the same time, it appears that at least a significant number of psychotherapists share the view presented by the present writer. For example, in a report of a study of 168 psychotherapists covering a variety of orientations, about half of these therapists believed that the importance of interpretation was greatly overrated (Meehl, 1960). In fact, "Two out of five go as far as to say that 'Under proper conditions, an incorrect interpretation, not even near to the actual facts, can have a real and long-lasting therapeutic effect'" (Meehl, 1960, p. 20). More recently, a certain amount of research has been conducted to evaluate the impact of accuracy of interpretation in psychotherapy. After reviewing some of this research, I came to the following conclusion:

Despite a period of many years and several individualized research attempts, there is no truly strong support for the accuracy of interpretation as a process variable of importance. *The* correct interpretation, after all, is determined by some authority or a group of judges in terms of a specific theoretical orientation . . . In the light of roughly comparable outcomes for different forms of psychotherapy, it is difficult to accept the importance placed on *the* correct interpretation. (Garfield, 1990, p. 276)

A more recent review of the available literature on transference interpretation also reached a quite similar conclusion. "It seems safe to conclude that the available research provides no evidence of any categorically unique benefits of transference interpretations" (Henry et al., 1994, p. 478).

Some related aspects that pertain to the therapist's own feelings about therapy and the interactions in therapy will be discussed more fully later. For now, we can conclude by reiterating the points made earlier: In most therapies, various means are used to provide the patient with some explanation of his difficulties and some rationale for the therapy which is to take place. In some this is done mainly during the early stages of therapy, whereas in others, usually those therapies which take a long period of time, the process occurs over a long period and appears to receive a greater emphasis. Regardless, the patient is given some rationale or belief system, and if reasonably acceptable, it appears to play some role in the progress of psychotherapy. How significant this is and how the process works are as yet not fully understood. Consequently, the importance of insight and understanding in psychotherapy can be viewed as a reasonable hypothesis.

It also appears likely that the potential value in therapy of this variable is interrelated with the client's makeup, his need for an explanation, his view of the therapist, and the type of problem presented. Also of importance in this process is the therapist, his prestige, his own personality, his way of communicating to the client, and his perception of the client. Although this process needs to be more fully investigated, it is important to try to give the client some understanding of his difficulties in a clear and appropriate manner, and to provide him with an understanding of the rationale and procedures of the therapy to be used. It is the impact that this has on the client which has potential significance for psychotherapy, and not necessarily the content of the particular formulation provided.

COGNITIVE MODIFICATIONS

We have commented earlier on the tremendous growth in cognitive emphases and approaches in psychotherapy in recent years and will say a bit more here about the general importance of changing client cognitions in psychotherapy. Although this emphasis overlaps the preceding section on explanations and interpretations in therapy which also involve the goal of changing perceptions and cognitions, it merits some additional discussion.

Although there are many different cognitive approaches with different theories of change and therapeutic strategies, they all "attempt to modify existing or anticipated disorders by virtue of altering cognitions or cognitive processes" (Hollon & Beck, 1986, p. 443). Whether the emphasis be on rational restructuring or changing dysfunctional cognitions, or some other comparable rationale, the critical aspect of therapy involves changing the distorted or irrational cognitions or beliefs of the client. Although many other aspects of the therapeutic interaction are occurring, the role of cognitive change is emphasized by cognitive therapists and perhaps not fully appreciated by noncognitive therapists.

Without question, cognitive change plays a role in the process of therapy and may be more important for some patients than for others. Also, the fact that there is such a diversity of cognitive approaches may indicate that how the therapist goes about the change process is not as important as focusing on the dysfunctional cognitions within a positive therapeutic relationship and using whatever other procedures appear helpful. As we shall note again later, although different emphases, for example, cognitive, affective, or behavioral, conceivably could have different impacts on different individuals, all such aspects of individual functioning are involved in effective change. The human organism is not simply a cognitive, affective, or behaving organism, functioning in some isolated manner, but an organism in which these aspects function in an interrelated fashion. Thus, cognitive aspects are important, but attention also needs to be paid to other equally important aspects of the individual.

CATHARSIS, EMOTIONAL EXPRESSION, AND RELEASE

Early in the history of psychotherapy and at irregular intervals since, some attention has been paid to the role of the release of strong affects or pent-up emotion in psychotherapy. Such patterns had been noted by Breuer and Freud (1950), and at first the "cathartic method" was viewed quite positively. However, Freud came to the conclusion that this procedure did not produce any lasting results, and it was gradually replaced by the particular methods he called psychoanalysis. Although catharsis or abreaction has received less emphasis since that time, it sometimes has a value with selected patients who are acutely anxious or indecisive, or have situationally determined feelings of guilt.

Depending upon the individual case, therefore, catharsis may be of some value in psychotherapy. In a selected number of cases, the client may have engaged in some behavior or gone through some experience which he or she views as very negative or shameful. Because of this, the client is reluctant to share this experience and keeps it to himself. This produces acute and discomforting anxiety or guilt that may finally motivate him to seek professional help. In many instances, the client will not even mention this in the initial interview as a reason for seeking therapy, but will give some other reasons that may be related to the precipitating cause or event. However, as the client learns to trust the therapist, he or she may then recount the disturbing event with considerable affect and, at times, very apparent relief. In some instances, the session in which this occurs may be characterized by very noticeable emotional release and change in the client's outlook of his or her situation and mark a significant point in therapy. It is in many ways similar to a highly emotional confession of guilt which occurs in other situations, as well as in psychotherapy.

When such emotional release occurs in therapy and appears to be instrumental in the patient's improvement, it is capable of making a definite impression on the therapist, even though its occurrence is not frequent. I can recall three such instances. In the most dramatic one, the client was a young man who was highly upset and agitated. He could be heard moving around in the waiting area and pacing restlessly until my office door was opened to admit him. As soon as he was seated, he began an excited and rapid verbal outpouring of his difficulties. Once he started, there was no stopping him. At various points in the session, I attempted to offer some comments of therapeutic wisdom, but to no avail. The client talked without stopping and with agitated expressions of affect for about an hour, releasing very visibly his pent-up feelings. At the end of this, he gave what appeared to be a tremendous sigh of relief, thanked the therapist profusely, and was off—leaving, it should be added, a somewhat frustrated therapist who wanted to provide the client with several choice therapeutic insights, but was unable to do so.

The other cases were less remarkable, but in each instance they involved activities which the individual had not confided to anyone else and which were a source of depressed feelings or guilt to the individual. In each instance, there was noticeable relief on the part of the client in being able to unburden himself of these concerns, sharing them with the therapist, and, as it were, being received in a nonjudgmental, accepting, and understanding manner.

In most cases, catharsis or emotional release alone, was not necessarily the only therapeutic variable in operation. In some instances, it facilitated the client's perceiving his situation in a more realistic manner and helped him to be able to cope more effectively with the situation. In one instance, a certain amount of needed accurate information concerning masturbation was subsequently provided to the client which was both useful and reassuring. However, the emotional release appeared to play a significant part in these clients' subsequent progress in therapy.

Beyond what has already been said, there are no particular cues concerning when catharsis may be a useful component of psychotherapy or how it may best be utilized. I do not believe that the therapist should or can deliberately strive to induce such a response in the client. Rather, the therapist, by his manner and interactions with the client, provides an environment in which clients may feel free to reveal what is disturbing them and express their feelings openly. The therapist, perhaps, can be particularly sensitive to this possibility where the patient appears to indicate acute discomfort of relatively recent origin, but at the same time, does not initially relate these feelings to any particular set of events. Once the beginning of the expression of pent-up feelings is evident, the patient can be encouraged to fully express his feelings and affects. Some other therapists may view catharsis in therapy somewhat differently. Nichols (1974), for example, has described what he termed "brief cathartic therapy" and others have attempted to heighten the emotional level of the therapeutic session as manifested in encounter groups. However, such uses of emotional release or catharsis is not what is being described here.

As already discussed, the therapist in most instances is an important figure to the client who seeks help. To the extent that he or she appears to be an individual who is knowledgeable about psychological problems, has experience in dealing with such problems, and imparts trust and confidence in the patient, the therapist provides a situation where the patient may be freer to disclose the highly personal matters that are disturbing him. As the therapist accepts what the client says without in any way judging him, and as he encourages him to fully express his feelings and to "get things off his chest," the client is more likely to confide in the therapist and to ventilate his pent-up feelings. The client has most likely found his or her concerns acutely discomforting and would like to confide in someone, but has been reluctant to discuss such matters with close friends or relatives. They may be potentially too threatening because of their closeness. The therapist, as a neutral and understanding healer, provides the client with an opportunity for emotional release. Although the amount of release obtained and its significance for the individual client will vary, it is a potential common factor in most forms of psychotherapy.

REINFORCEMENT IN PSYCHOTHERAPY

Although reinforcement as a therapeutic variable has been mainly emphasized by those learning theorists and behavior therapists who stress the importance of operant conditioning, it is also a variable that is utilized in various ways, although less systematically, by other psychotherapists as well. The application of operant techniques and procedures to various settings and populations has increased markedly in recent years (Kazdin, 1978, 1989; O'Leary & Wilson, 1987) but it has received relatively little formal attention from the more traditionally oriented psychotherapists. However, the principles of reinforcement do appear to be applied in the interactions that take place in psychotherapy.

Basically what is implied here is that the therapist tends to positively reinforce those responses of the patient which he views as desirable, and to negatively reinforce or extinguish those responses which he deems to be undesirable in terms of his therapeutic goals. Depending upon the therapist and the situation, the therapist may or may not be aware that he is reinforcing or failing to reinforce a particular client behavior. Those who are stated adherents of operant procedures would fully utilize operant principles and contingencies of reinforcement in a planned and systematic manner. They would also focus more specifically on target behaviors of the patient and attempt to carefully monitor these behaviors in order to observe what changes occur. Many readers probably are familiar with some of the work in this area. The well-known ABA design used in many operant studies will be mentioned briefly for illustrative purposes.

First, a baseline (A) of the behaviors to be modified is obtained by recording the frequency of these behaviors over a given period of time. Then, the operant procedures or programs are introduced and the frequency of the targeted behaviors are once again recorded and any changes noted. If significant changes are noted during the period when the program is in operation (B), the experimental procedures or reinforcements are once again withdrawn for a given period of time (A) similar to the baseline period and the appropriate measures of behavior taken. Generally, the treatment effects diminish and the behaviors revert to their baseline or pretreatment levels. Similar procedures can be used for decreasing undesirable behaviors or increasing specified desired target behaviors. This design allows the therapist to clearly appraise the effects of the particular operant procedures.

There are a number of reasons why many therapists, particularly psychodynamic ones, have shied away from the deliberate use of operant procedures or reinforcement. Target symptoms or behaviors are not the specified focus of therapy for such therapists nor are their therapeutic procedures used to deal directly with them. Related to this are views that this approach is very superficial and that the client is treated as an object or is manipulated by the therapist—views that are repugnant to many therapists. Furthermore, operant procedures would be viewed as limited mainly to changing some behavioral symptoms but as not applicable to more complicated problems that involve the patient's feelings and self views. Implicit also is the view that the therapist should not impose his or her values upon the client or act in a controlling manner. Rather, from this perspective, the client has the responsibility to decide what values he selects and in what directions he shall go.

The therapist, consequently, is an agent who merely facilitates the process of growth and self-discovery. The operant conditioner, on the other hand, is someone who decides what behaviors will be modified, sometimes with and sometimes without the consent of the client, and who then controls the therapeutic situation. As viewed from such a frame of reference, the patient is a passive respondent to the stimuli controlled and manipulated by the therapist.

Finally, operant procedures have been criticized because of behavioral programs in institutional settings where issues of the infringement of the rights of incarcerated individuals undergoing such programs have been raised (Kazdin, 1978).

While many therapists appear to avoid the conscious use of operant procedures, some of their reasons for doing so do not seem to be particularly valid. Like it or not, the therapist is far from being a value-free individual who is completely neutral on all matters discussed by the patient or with reference to the behaviors exhibited in psychotherapy. In fact it seems clear that the majority of therapists do believe that values are embedded in psychotherapy and are reflected in the therapeutic process (Jensen & Bergin, 1988). The therapist, therefore, does have a value system and this does get communicated in some fashion to the client. For example, to the extent that the therapist prefers one therapeutic orientation in preference to others, he has made a value judgment that gets communicated to the client. The client who has undergone psychoanalysis is provided with understandings and a view of human personality which clearly reflect the value system of his analyst. Extreme critics of psychoanalytic training or therapy have even called this process brainwashing. If the analytic candidate does not accept the values of the training institute, he will be found wanting and perhaps dropped from the program (Szasz, 1960). In the case of the patient who resists psychoanalytic interpretations, he will find that his particular form of resistance is hindering treatment and is costing him a fair amount of money. In both instances, submission may be the better part of valour. This may be viewed as a kind of coercion.

Apart from the matter of values, it is also the contention of behavior therapists that many traditional therapists utilize reinforcement and learning principles, but do so in a haphazard, unknowing, and unsystematic fashion. As a consequence, they believe traditional therapists tend to be less efficient and that their therapy requires much longer treatment periods than do behavioral therapies. Therapists may actually reinforce in a positive way the kinds of responses they desire to get from the patient by nodding or verbally signifying acceptance when such responses are forthcoming, and conversely, indicate a negative reaction or disapproval by overt or subtle means when such responses are not made. Thus, although they may not be particularly aware of what they are doing or of their impact on the patient, these therapists are actually "shaping" the responses of their patients. Truax (1966), for example, analyzed the recorded excerpt of one of Carl Rogers' published cases and demonstrated that certain client responses were reinforced by positive reactions from Rogers. These responses could be categorized as responses which were deemed to be desired ones from the client-centered point of view. Furthermore, as the therapist reinforces such client responses by nodding or by saying "hmmm, that's good," or a similar verbal statement, the likelihood of increasing the occurrence of such responses is enhanced. Murray (1956) also provided a similar analysis of one of Rogers' cases and demonstrated that therapist approval and disapproval functions as positive and negative reinforcement.

It is certainly plausible, therefore, that the therapist is capable of influencing the client's behavior. In a general sense, this is an underlying assumption of all psychotherapies, regardless of how they are conceptualized. The important issue is how this process occurs and how it can be used most effectively for the client's welfare.

A related point, made originally by Truax and Carkhuff (1967) is also worth quoting here, "If psychotherapy or counseling is indeed a process of learning and relearning, then the therapeutic process should allow for structuring what is to be learned, rather than depending on what amounts to 'incidental learning,' where the client does not have clearly in mind from the outset what it is he is supposed to learn" (p. 363). The implications of this statement are that, regardless of one's basic conceptualization of the psychotherapeutic process, any changes that take place would involve learning of some kind. If this is so, the therapist should be knowledgeable about this process and utilize it so that learning takes place in the most efficient manner possible.

One obvious implication is that the therapist must be aware of his or her potential influence on the client and in what ways he or she influences the behavior of specific clients. As already indicated, the therapist does influence the client in a number of ways. Besides more directly informing the client concerning what is expected of him and indicating what is in essence desirable client behavior in therapy, the therapist influences the client's behavior during therapy by the way he or she responds to this behavior. Desirable behaviors receive affirmative or rewarding responses from the therapist, whereas responses that are considered to be undesirable are responded to negatively in some fashion or ignored. The therapist may simply indicate approval by gestures such as nodding or smiling, as well as by more overt verbal statements of approval or praise. In a similar manner, responses thought to be retarding of progress in therapy may receive a frown, a show of concern, or an explicit verbal statement of disagreement.

Clearly, the therapist does engage in such behaviors and they do function as reinforcing stimuli for the client. Although different clients will respond differently to the communications of the therapist, most of them will be quite sensitive to them. Not only is the therapist in a position of influence for the reasons already described, but the client's progress is perceived by the client as being largely dependent on the therapist and how he responds to the client. Under such circumstances, it is understandable that the client will be responsive to the differential reinforcements of the therapist.

Consequently, not only should the therapist be aware of his role in influencing the client by means of reinforcement, but it would seem desirable for him to use this knowledge to facilitate the desired changes sought by means of psychotherapy. If this proposition has merit, it does seem surprising that, except for the learning theory oriented therapists, so many therapists are so reluctant to accept it. However, as we noted earlier, there are several reasons why this is so. Perhaps the basic reason is that such a view implies a conscious and deliberate manipulation of the patient which many humanistically oriented therapists perceive as an anathema. Although understandable, this view prevents such therapists from utilizing what appears to be a realistic occurrence in psychotherapy, and one which conceivably explains some of the behavioral processes that take place.

The kind of phenomenon or issue presented here is an important one with implications for other aspects of psychotherapy. However, because many psychotherapists are strongly committed to their therapeutic orientation, it is not an easy task to change their views. Thus, some of the possible implications or applications of the ideas presented here may be rejected, in spite of the fact that they are being implemented with apparent success by some therapists. One such application is using a more direct approach toward attempts to modify the client's behavior in a positive direction by using real life situations in which the behaviors occur, rather than emphasizing in-therapy behaviors per se. Here, also, a very different view is taken from that espoused in most traditional psychotherapies. The more traditional approaches have generally taken what may be termed an indirect approach to modifying the patient's behavior. The belief is that one works with more general organismic variables such as the patient's personality and the underlying causes as the most effective manner of securing behavioral or surface changes. The other view, advanced by the behavioral therapists, is that the most effective way to secure behavioral change is to proceed directly to attempts to change the behavior in question. A view that involves the application of learning principles is much closer to the latter point of view, although it is not necessarily synonymous with it. An illustration of what is implied here may be helpful.

Let us suppose that we have a patient who comes to see us because he is painfully shy in social situations and feels particularly inadequate when around members of the opposite sex. We could postulate that these symptoms are the result of various earlier traumatic experiences and, therefore, therapy will consist of explorations of and associations to earlier repressed events and the gradual attainment of insight, or, from a different orientation, that by the displaying of empathy, genuineness, and nonpossessive warmth on the part of the therapist, the client will gradually enlarge and integrate his views of self and have his experiences become congruent with the new self system. In either instance, the problem behavior and the desired behavior are approached indirectly, and the assumption is made that by means of such a process the desired behavioral change will be obtained. In a more direct approach, however, more attention would be paid to the situations in which the undesired behavior occurs, the kinds of stimuli that produce these reactions, the kinds of cognitions and feelings the patient has, what the patient does in response to these stimuli, and the like. A plan of therapy might then be developed in which the patient would at first play out some of these situations in therapy, but would be encouraged or directed to gradually participate in selected real life situations. He might be encouraged at first to simply engage in conversation or small talk with females for brief periods and in relatively safe situations. Gradually, as he is positively reinforced in these initial attempts and feels generally more secure, he may be instructed to venture into more demanding or initially more threatening social situations. As these behaviors are successful, the patient may eventually be able to ask a woman for a date, to be more at ease, and to interact in a more "normal" and personally satisfying manner. While other interactions with the therapist would also take place, the procedure just described would appear to play a very important part in the therapeutic program and would focus to a great extent on the specific problem and the behavioral change that is sought in therapy. Although it may not always proceed as smoothly and simply as the preceding illustration would suggest, the emphasis on dealing directly with the behaviors to be modified is quite clear. It also calls attention to another point of importance, and that is the emphasis on utilizing the actual life situations of the client as having a more lasting impact or transfer effect than relying exclusively on in-therapy verbal behaviors.

A few other related comments are worth making here before we conclude our discussion of what appears to be an important but still controversial feature of psychotherapy. One aspect concerns what might be termed an organismic-segmental or part-whole emphasis. As pointed out before, the traditional and more indirect approaches appear to believe that the individual as a whole must be worked with or that some dynamic balance of the organism must be changed if any specific parts, subunits, symptoms, or behaviors are to be substantially or "permanently" modified. One proceeds from the whole to the part as it were. The more direct or learning oriented approach deals more specifically with a part or segment, a symptom or behavior of the individual, and attempts to modify it more directly. Although the behavior therapists are mainly concerned with the problem behavior, they frequently also secure appraisals of subjective states or attitudes of their clients. Such data have indicated that when the desired behavioral changes are achieved, other desirable effects may also accompany such changes (Bandura, 1969, 1977). For example, if a person has a fear of leaving his home, his whole style of living is seriously disrupted, as well as his own views of self. If the phobia is overcome, such an individual may also show other changes including increased self-confidence, better relationships with his wife and family, and so on. In this instance, therapy aimed at a specific behavior or aspect of the individual appears to have an irradiating effect that spreads out to influence the total organism.

Only a far wiser man than the writer would venture to state which of these two opposite views encompasses more of the truth. My purpose here is to try to make explicit a very fundamental difference between two important views of psychotherapy. My own evaluation, however, would be influenced greatly by the empirical data provided to support each position as well as the overall economy of the therapy. In this regard, the behavioral view appears to have the edge. However, it is important to emphasize that a sound analysis of the client's difficulties should be made before a plan of treatment is formulated and carried out.

Another aspect that is of some significance pertains to the therapist's view of the psychotherapy he is performing and his satisfaction with it. Besides the fact that many psychotherapists take a negative view of being overly directive in therapy and believe that change comes about solely through the client's initiative, such therapists also view behavioral approaches and procedures as being overly mechanistic. This type of therapy, they believe, can be performed by technicians instead of highly trained psychotherapists. This may be so, but the critical issue really concerns what techniques are most effective in producing the desired changes. If this can be done with properly trained technicians, then this should be considered. However, it does appear that at least some well-known dynamically oriented therapists have begun to make use of behavioral procedures in their therapeutic work as we noted in Chapter 2.

It is evident from what has been presented here that the therapist potentially does have some influence upon the behavior of the client and that how he or she responds and interacts in the therapy session can reinforce certain client behaviors. Since such a process occurs in therapy, it seems desirable for the therapist to utilize this knowledge as explicitly as possible in order to facilitate the goals of therapy.

DESENSITIZATION

Another variable that appears to operate in psychotherapy is *desensitization*. Although this concept has received more systematic attention and formulation in the writing of Joseph Wolpe (1958, 1961), it was also referred to in earlier discussions of psychotherapy (Garfield, 1957; Levine,

1948; Rosenzweig, 1936). Basically, what is referred to here is that as a patient discusses problems that have been troubling him and repeats his concern over time in the accepting climate of the therapeutic session, these problems appear to become less threatening or troublesome. When one broods over matters and does not bring them out in the open for purposes of appraisal or to share with others, these preoccupations become very disturbing and the individual may even appear to magnify their consequences. Unlike the more acute types of discomfort discussed in relation to catharsis, what are referred to here are more like preoccupations, decisions which have to be made, the lack of meeting one's expectations, and the like. Although the specific causal events or patient problems involved cannot be specified very distinctly, the process of desensitization that may occur in psychotherapy seems somewhat clearer.

What appears to occur is that as a patient begins to discuss the events that have been troubling him, they gradually seem to lose their threatening quality. By bringing matters out in the open and looking at them anew, the troublesome events do not appear to be as troublesome as they were previously. Several different hypotheses have been offered to explain this process. One is that by simply sharing such thoughts and preoccupations with the therapist and bringing them out into the open, they become less personalized and hence less threatening. A related view is that by communicating the disturbing items, the client becomes more objective and realistic in appraising his situation. Personalized distortions and magnifications are more readily perceived and thus can be modified with the help of the therapist. Furthermore, the repetition of this material in the therapy situation with no negative reactions, makes the disclosure appear to be less serious than the client perceived it to be earlier. In terms of a learning theory oriented explanation, the client's anxieties about these matters are gradually extinguished as he discusses them in the security of the therapeutic setting and no negative consequences are forthcoming. The fact that the therapist accepts the disclosures of the client without any show of surprise or concern may also contribute to this process of desensitization.

The repeated discussion in therapy of material that the client initially experiences as anxiety-provoking or distressing thus may lessen its anxiety-provoking qualities. Whether the process is one of gradual extinction over time or whether other processes involved is by no means clear. Certainly, during this process the therapist may also offer interpretations and explanations that may help to reduce the client's concerns. However, something akin to desensitization does appear to occur with some patients. As is true with many of the possible variables operating in psychotherapy, desensitization may not always appear to be of major importance in all cases. However, it does appear worthy of note by psychotherapists since the usual verbal interactions occurring within the therapeutic relationship allow the process to take place.

In more recent years, desensitization has received more specific attention as a result of the formulation developed by Wolpe (1958, 1961, 1973) which deals with reciprocal inhibition and systematic desensitization. In terms of Wolpe's view, what has been described already as the process of desensitization would be characterized as unsystematic desensitization. According to Wolpe, if one is to dispel anxiety, some competing process has to be utilized—a process that is antagonistic to it. If an individual is relaxed, by definition he cannot be anxious. This is what is meant by reciprocal inhibition. Wolpe utilized relaxation procedures as part of his therapeutic strategy although other counter conditioners or inhibitors of anxiety have also been used.

In working out his overall approach to therapy, Wolpe developed a procedure that he named "systematic desensitization." The basic objective is to desensitize the patient to the fears or anxieties that have been troubling him. After first giving the patient some training in relaxation procedures in order to develop a response which can "reciprocally inhibit" feelings of anxiety, the therapist and patient jointly prepare a list of the stimuli that arouse anxiety in the patient. The patient is asked to rank these various situations on a theoretical scale of 0 to 100 in terms of their fear arousing values. A hierarchy of such situations is thus arranged from the least disturbing to the most anxiety arousing. When the patient is relaxed, the therapist then asks him to imagine first the situation or scene which is lowest in the hierarchy. If the patient can visualize this scene without any anxiety, the therapist proceeds to the next item in the hierarchy, and so on. If the patient signals that he is anxious when he is visualizing a specific item, he is told to discontinue doing so and to once again relax. The procedure is repeated until the patient can gradually move up the hierarchy of items and visualize what was once a very upsetting scene without any undue anxiety. He has thus become desensitized to the stimuli which earlier provoked severe anxiety.

Although this procedure is different from the more typical psychotherapy sessions referred to in our earlier discussion of desensitization, somewhat similar processes may be involved. Wolpe's approach is obviously a more focused one with a much more explicit emphasis on the process of desensitization. Most other therapists have given relatively little emphasis or attention to it. Although there have been a number of criticisms of Wolpe's theoretical formulations, the empirical results secured by means of systematic desensitization have been relatively good, and perhaps represent the clearest demonstration of the process of desensitization (Davison & Wilson, 1973; O'Leary & Wilson, 1987). Where phobic or anxiety symptoms are the primary complaint, systematic desensitization appears to be a very useful procedure. Where the complaints are less focalized, such a direct procedure may not be necessary and desensitization may take place in interaction with other aspects of therapy.

RELAXATION

Relaxation as a means of alleviating tension and anxiety has been mentioned from time to time in the history of psychological healing. It received attention quite early in relationship to hypnosis and the use of hypnotic procedures in therapy. Over 65 years ago, it received attention in the writings of Jacobson (1929) who developed a program of progressive relaxation. Wolpe (1958) adapted some of Jacobson's procedures in developing his techniques of systematic desensitization and brought relaxation much more into the foreground of psychotherapy. Attempts to utilize relaxation in order to calm people are made in a large number of everyday situations, including psychotherapy.

Although most psychotherapists have tended to view relaxation or attempts to have the client relax as very superficial or temporary palliative measures in therapy, and relaxation procedures constitute just one component in Wolpe's therapy, Goldfried (1971, 1980; Goldfried & Trier, 1974) developed a method of utilizing relaxation as a coping procedure in therapy which can be used along with other procedures.

Goldfried teaches his clients to utilize relaxation as a means of coping with tension and anxiety-provoking situations. Instead of relaxation procedures being learned by the client as a means of being able to progress through a hierarchy of fear-provoking situations in therapy, the client is instructed to use relaxation procedures outside of therapy when faced with threatening real life events. The client is thus provided with a practical means of coping with future situations, and not only with the initial problems presented or worked with in therapy. This is a quite useful procedure for it offers the client a potential method for meeting future problems, and it is not particularly difficult to master. I have used it with some success as an adjunctive procedure in some cases where the individual was shortly to face an anxiety-provoking situation.

To the extent that this procedure also increases the client's self-confidence and allows him to expand the situations he can meet, it would appear to have many self-reinforcing qualities as well. Procedures or experiences in therapy that can be utilized by the client in the real world after therapy is completed and which help him in his subsequent development would appear to be of great potential value (Goldfried & Davison, 1976).

INFORMATION IN PSYCHOTHERAPY

Many patients who seek psychotherapeutic help are, among other things, poorly informed or misinformed on a number of topics which are of some importance in their everyday lives. In a number of instances, providing the correct information in therapy can be of definite therapeutic value. However, for some reason, the imparting of information has not received much attention or been accorded much importance in psychotherapy. Some dynamically oriented psychotherapists, in fact, look with disfavor upon such an activity for it puts the therapist in a non-evocative or directing role which they would try to avoid. The reason in some instances is that activities such as providing information or offering suggestions or even giving a direct answer to a question raised by the patient are perceived by the therapist as constituting supportive psychotherapy. Many of them prefer to engage in an evocative or uncovering type of psychotherapy, which they consider to be a more intensive and desirable type of therapy. In this form of therapy, as we have noted, the emphasis is on the patient's self-explorations and his seeking of solutions, rather than on the therapist's providing him with answers. As a result, therapist behavior that is seen as reinforcing the opposite type of pattern is viewed as undesirable.

It is true that if the therapist helps to structure the situation so that the patient asks questions and the therapist provides answers, the patient will assume that this is the way therapy should be, and other kinds of processes and interactions may in effect be discouraged. Nevertheless, if a reasonable question is asked, or the client appears to suffer badly from misinformation, the therapist can facilitate positive movement by providing the correct information. This is particularly true with regard to matters that cause anxiety or guilt, such as sexual activities and negative feelings toward parents. Where the client has a distinct lack of information on a topic which is relevant to his problems, no amount of uncovering therapy will provide him with the necessary information.

As is true with other aspects of psychotherapy, when and under what circumstances the providing of information may be of therapeutic value depends on the client and the particular problem presented. It should be pertinent to the client's problems and not just a topic of conversation or a response to a request for general information. The therapist must be aware of what the giving of information signifies about his role in therapy and the therapeutic relationship generally. However, he should not overreact or studiously avoid the proffering of information when it may be of value. Some individuals are surprisingly so misinformed about matters such as masturbation, for example, that accurate information offered in a matter-of-fact manner can be extremely guilt-reducing and reassuring. Sometimes, in fact, "knowledge is power."

REASSURANCE AND SUPPORT

Another feature of psychotherapy relates to the reassurance and support which the therapist may provide during psychotherapy. These aspects of psychotherapy, like some of those already discussed, have been viewed and evaluated differently by psychotherapists of different orientations.

Reassurance is a frequently offered human response to individuals who are worried or troubled. As such, it is not something that is unique to psychotherapy, but a form of attempted encouragement offered by friends, parents, and a variety of professional persons. Its place in psychotherapy, however, has been somewhat controversial. Whereas some individuals have accorded it a role in what has been termed "supportive" psychotherapy (Enelow, 1977; Wolberg, 1954), analytically oriented therapists have generally tended to view it as a superficial approach to psychotherapy. To the extent that reassurance is viewed as an activity that fosters an acceptance of a situation and thus avoids further self-exploration, it is seen as countering an uncovering type of psychotherapy, and for this reason is viewed as superficial. Client-centered therapists also have tended to view it negatively since it is usually considered to be a directive form of psychotherapy. Weiner and Bordin (1983) make a distinction between being supportive in psychotherapy and supportive psychotherapy:

> On the other hand, supportive psychotherapy still remains clearly distinct from and should not be confused with the general meaning of being supportive, which may include giving advice, reassurance, and sympathy, or even lending a client money. However supportive or psychotherapeutic such actions may be, they do not constitute psychotherapy, since they involve neither the relationship nor the task elements that define this treatment method. (Weiner & Bordin, 1983, p. 338)

In this latter definition, the word supportive is given a somewhat different definition or emphasis than what is being described here. As already discussed, reassurance when appropriately used within the therapeutic relationship, can have a positive effect, whether it is viewed as an aspect of supportive psychotherapy or not. Reassurance is also acknowledged to be an aspect of therapy present in most forms of therapy (Enelow, 1977; Wolberg, 1954) and it is also viewed in this way by the present writer.

Reassurance can be manifested in the psychotherapeutic situation in different ways. Merely seeing a psychotherapist who accepts the patient's problems as nothing unusual and indicates that they can be treated, can be quite reassuring for many patients. Thus, the manner of the psychotherapist and the way the interview is conducted may convey considerable reassurance and support to some clients. This can be considered a general feature of many psychotherapeutic approaches. That is, without the therapist deliberately attempting to reassure the client, the therapist's manner and communication may be perceived as reassuring. It is important to be aware of this possible influence and not to view reassurance solely as a simple conscious or superficial ploy on the part of the therapist.

The more deliberate use of reassurance on the part of the therapist can be appraised separately. Reassurance would not appear to be a very powerful therapeutic technique, but in certain instances and with certain kinds of clients it may be of some value. Where the client is worried about a current problem due to lack of information or misperception, reassurance, along with the necessary information, may prove helpful. This is particularly so where the client anticipates a negative consequence from some impending action which is clearly overemphasized. The reassurance of the therapist, a clearer understanding of what is actually involved, and the actual occurrence of the event without any dire consequences may suffice to handle the problem situation.

On the other hand, reliance on reassurance when matters are more complex will usually not have positive results. If the individual has a longstanding anxiety or concern about a particular matter and has been offered reassurance by others in the past, it is very likely that reassurance offered by a therapist will be ineffective. This is also one reason why many therapists do not view reassurance as a positive therapeutic technique. Providing reassurance when it is inappropriate will not be a worthwhile procedure and may tend to undermine the client's confidence in the therapist. Like any procedure, reassurance must be used judiciously.

Along with other aspects of psychotherapy, reassurance from the therapist or from the psychotherapeutic situation may provide some feeling of support to the patient who seeks help with his or her personal problems. The fact that one has a potential source of help stimulates feelings of hope and support. The client now has someone to turn to and is not alone in his attempt to cope with his problems. Thus, the client may perceive a source of support in the therapist.

EXPECTANCIES AS A THERAPEUTIC VARIABLE

Since the matter of client expectancies has already been discussed in some detail in the chapter on client variables, only a brief reference will be made to it here as a possible variable in psychotherapy.

The point of reference here is that the client's expectancies, both at the beginning and during the early stages of therapy, may influence the outcome of therapy. Consequently, the therapist must not only be aware of the client's expectations, but he or she should attempt also to foster positive and realistic expectations where possible. Other things being equal, and they probably never are, the patient who has a reasonably positive attitude and expectations about therapy may do better in therapy than one who has an overly and unrealistically positive expectancy or one who has a very negative expectancy for being helped. A positive expectancy would appear to increase the potential reinforcing power of the therapist.

There is also the expectation a client may have for being helped by the therapist. This has been emphasized particularly by Jerome Frank (1973, Frank & Frank, 1991) and appears to play a role in the therapeutic process, regardless of the form of psychotherapy. This may be similar to the positive responses that many individuals make to a placebo or inert form of medication. More will be said about this later in this chapter.

EXPOSURE AND CONFRONTING A PROBLEM

Many individuals develop various types of avoidance behaviors rather quickly and then reinforce these behaviors systematically. If an individual experiences intense fear or anxiety when asked to speak in public, he may, thereafter, studiously avoid all occasions where such an occurrence is potentially possible. Or, if a young and shy individual feels rebuffed and embarrassed in certain kinds of social situations, such situations will be consistently avoided. While the avoidance behavior may be reinforced by protecting the individual from the acute discomfort he may feel in such situations, it also keeps the individual feeling inadequate and upset about his inadequacy. As long as he avoids the situations that are upsetting to him, he will never be able to really overcome his fears and change his behavior. However, if he can be encouraged to enter these situations and to see that the consequences he anticipates are not actually forthcoming, some reduction in fear and an increase in approach behaviors may result.

In writing the first draft of the original edition of this book, I used as the heading for this section, "Facing and Confronting a Problem." The material was based largely on my own clinical experience. However, in preparing the final version for publication, I was aware of the use of "exposure" to the feared stimulus described by behavior therapists and acknowledged this in a footnote with references to some of this work (Gelder et al., 1973; Marks, 1978). Since that time, guided exposure has become a recognized therapeutic procedure for such anxiety disorders, particularly agoraphobia (O'Leary & Wilson, 1987). Thus, if the individual can be brought to face the fearful stimuli without any negative consequences occurring, the fear will rapidly diminish and approach behaviors will be strongly reinforced.

Something like this also may explain the positive results secured in such other therapeutic procedures as systematic desensitization, implosive therapy, and modeling, as well as in some others. For example, in a number of studies where systematic desensitization has been compared with implosion, similar results have been secured with the two procedures even though they differ greatly in their theoretical assumptions (Gelder et al., 1973). Somewhat comparable findings have been reported in studies comparing modeling and systematic desensitization (Bandura, Blanchard, & Ritter, 1969; Erdwins, 1975). It is hypothesized here that what is common in all of these approaches, and what may be the variable of importance, is the fact that in all of them the client is in some way confronted with the disturbing situation and finds that no catastrophic consequences result. O'Leary and Wilson (1987) similarly conclude, "The critical component of techniques such as systematic desensitization, flooding, and modeling is systematic exposure to the anxiety-eliciting material" (p. 176).

Where it is possible to help the individual to face disturbing situations with a high probability of no negative consequences, a potentially very therapeutic experience in therapy may ensue. The procedures for accomplishing this can vary, depending upon the case and the circumstances. There is still some debate about whether this should be done gradually or whether there should be a frontal attack on the problem with the patient actually confronting the feared situation with relatively little delay. Although the evidence is far from clear, the writer prefers the former approach since if the more direct confrontation fails, it may actually increase the patient's fearful behavior and present additional problems in therapy (Wolpe, 1973). However, if the client sees that it is possible for him to face a troublesome situation, each time that he is able to do so lessens its threatening qualities, increases his self-confidence in meeting the situation, and very likely contributes to a general increase in his self-esteem. Also, "According to self-efficacy theory, treatment methods, whatever their nature, are effective because they increase expectations that the client can cope with threatening situations" (O'Leary & Wilson, 1987). Visible evidence of improvement facilitates an increased expectancy of positive outcome in psychotherapy on the part of the client, which is also of some benefit.

TIME AS A THERAPEUTIC VARIABLE

Another potential variable in psychotherapy that does not receive sufficient attention is that of time. It is quite difficult to estimate its role in psychotherapy because it generally is not an isolated or controlled variable. Instead, in the therapeutic situation, it interacts with all other possible variables.

In general, when time is alluded to in discussions of psychotherapy, it is in reference to the fact that a certain amount of time is required for the process of psychotherapy to take place and that it cannot be unduly hurried. From the psychoanalytic viewpoint, time is required for the development of the transference relationship, to overcome resistances, and to work through and to integrate the various insights secured in psychotherapy. Time is referred to in this sense also when mention is made of long-term or intensive psychotherapy. Time is viewed then as a necessary medium through which other variables are allowed to operate, although not necessarily as a directly influencing variable.

There are, however, some other aspects to consider. One can conjecture that in some cases an individual who is upset or disturbed may simply get over this discomfort on his own without any therapeutic help whatsoever. He may, for example, by some means of self-appraisal, self-talk or self-analysis, find his situation less upsetting or his perception of it changed. What seemed very depressing yesterday may seem less so today. Besides the sheer passage of time, if there is such a thing, external events may also intervene to modify the situation. Dim prospects for acceptance into graduate school or the attainment of suitable employment may be radically changed by the receipt of positive news and one's whole outlook correspondingly changes.

Whatever may actually occur or be instrumental in this type of change in the person, it does appear that such occurrences do take place without any formal psychotherapeutic intervention. Such a phenomenon has been recognized and given some attention with regard to two particular matters in the area of psychotherapy. One observation made in the past concerning the matter of improvement in psychotherapy with children is that children, as developing organisms, can be expected to show certain changes as a result of the process of maturation. Thus, if a child has certain fears or wets his bed, there is a high likelihood that these symptoms will disappear as he grows older. The passage of time allows certain maturational changes to take place in the normal process of growth and development. Consequently, if a child with such problems and at a certain stage of development received psychotherapy, the resulting improvement could be the natural result of maturational processes rather than of psychotherapy.

A similar point has been made with regard to the evaluation of outcome in psychotherapy generally. This view, frequently referred to as spontaneous recovery or remission, and borrowed from medicine, has been particularly espoused by the British psychologist, Eysenck (1952, 1966), and just as strongly criticized by a number of others (Lambert, 1976; Subotnik, 1972). This view is that certain disturbances may have a time-limited quality and that after a certain period of time, the individual shows a spontaneous recovery or improvement. It is known that many physical illnesses run a particular course and, except in the more serious ones, the individual in most cases will recover without specific treatment. It is postulated that psychological disorders, such as neurotic disturbances, may exhibit similar characteristics. Consequently, some critics of psychotherapy have stated that much of the improvement judged to be due to psychotherapeutic intervention, is really due to the self-limiting nature of the disorder and the remission which occurs over time.

My point in raising this matter here is not to debate the issue of the effectiveness of psychotherapy, which will be discussed in a later chapter, but to note the possible significance of time as a potential variable in psychotherapy. On the one hand, the passage of time may allow certain self-regulating or recuperative processes within the individual to take place and, thus, lead to improved adjustment, aided or unaided by psychotherapy. Here the important variables would be organismic ones residing mainly within the person. On the other hand, in some instances, the variables of importance would be real life events or environmental stimuli outside of the organism, but ones that exert a positive influence on the individual. These would thus be situational variables, and could include a variety of events that are capable of influencing the individual in a significant manner. These latter ones could include interactions with other people who may actually function as quasi-therapeutic figures for the person involved, such as, for example, a friend, minister, or supervisor. In these instances, the situation becomes more complicated, for we may have therapeutic variables involved even though the therapeutic agents are not formally identified as such.

There are a couple of points which are worth emphasizing here. One is that events which go on outside of the therapeutic hour may be of considerable importance as far as changes in the client are concerned. Most therapists see their clients only one or two hours during the week. At the same time, however, therapists are inclined to attach very great importance to the influence of these hours. Although this may be a valid inference in some cases, it is also important to recognize that the patient is interacting with a number of people in many different situations during the great majority of his waking hours, and some of these may be of great importance for him. Changes ascribed to psychotherapy may actually be the result of factors occurring outside of the therapy sessions. A reconciliation with a former girl friend or a promotion at work can have a significant positive effect on a person. The therapist should attempt to appraise such matters as accurately as possible and to strive to be objective in evaluating what changes occur. However, it is something which usually does not receive adequate attention, even in psychotherapy research. A related point, therefore, is that some of the changes thought to be derived from psychotherapy may actually be brought about by factors outside of psychotherapy, and clearly this is a matter of some significance if we are to appraise adequately the results of psychotherapy. It is for such reasons, among others, that one cannot accept therapists' judgments of outcome as valid measures.

It is also possible, as noted previously, that the client is helped by the essentially psychotherapeutic activities of someone who is not the formally designated therapist. In such instances, as Bergin and Lambert (1978) have pointed out, the improvement is due to the psychotherapeutic influence of others, and is not the result of spontaneous remission. However, in such instances, the formal psychotherapy should not be considered as responsible for the changes or outcome secured.

Finally, in terms of the present discussion, proper attention should be paid to the type of client and the problem presented. It seems reasonable to hypothesize that problems which are of recent origin and in which situational factors appear to play an important role, may be more responsive to time and changing situations than other types of problems. If, for example, an individual is having marital difficulties which are very upsetting to him and which appear to be the primary reason for his seeking therapy, the problem might be resolved by factors occurring outside of therapy. Two cases supervised by the writer may illustrate this. In one, a middle-aged woman sought psychotherapeutic help because she had become acutely upset and depressed by her husband's decision to divorce her. She felt very much rejected and abandoned. She dominated the therapy sessions with her verbal outpourings, gave the therapist little opportunity to offer any comments, and generally was not considered to be a very good psychotherapy candidate. However, after a few weeks, her husband changed his mind and a reconciliation followed. Although she verbally expressed her thanks for the therapist's help and probably did secure some gratification and release from the cathartic outpourings in therapy, the critical factor did seem to be the events which occurred outside of therapy.

In another case, a young man was being divorced by his wife to whom he had been married for ten years. In this instance, the divorce took place while he was in therapy and the early stages of therapy were concerned with his acceptance of this reality. Although this case was very different from the preceding one and went on for a longer period of time, outside events again played a very important part in the client's overall state of adjustment. In this case, the passage of time and the opportunity for the client to discuss his situation in therapy appeared to be of some importance in his overcoming his feelings of personal loss. However, securing a new female friend after the divorce appeared to be a most significant factor in raising his mood, even if this was not always sustained. Thus, time may be a factor that allows the hypothesized variables in psychotherapy to exert their influence on the client, but, it may also allow other extraneous variables to exert their influence as well. A recognition and understanding of such occurrences, however, should not lead one to devalue the general usefulness of the therapist's interactions with his clients. Rather, it should foster an awareness of viewing the client's total situation in relation to the therapy.

THE PLACEBO RESPONSE

The final variable to be discussed in this chapter is the enigmatic placebo response, one of the most interesting and perplexing phenomena in the history of the healing arts. To a large extent the placebo response has been used to designate unexpected or unexplained therapeutic results. Its most formal definition and use has occurred in the field of pharmacology and in the testing of the effects of various drugs. Traditionally, the placebo has been an inert pharmacological substance which is made to look like the active drug. In double-blind research, one group of patients is given the drug and another comparable group is given the placebo. Neither the therapists nor the patients know which pills contain the active medication and which are the placebos. If the rate of improvement is significantly greater with the drug, then the drug is considered to have a definite therapeutic effect. However, if both groups of patients show similar amounts of improvement, then the positive response is considered to be a placebo effect, and the drug is judged to be lacking in effectiveness. All responses which cannot be explained on the basis of actual drug effects are thus considered to be placebo responses, that is, due to some unknown and nonpharmacological causes. Such unknown causes have generally been thought to be psychological in nature, and while unknown or unanticipated psychological causes of patient change may be disappointing to the pharmacologist, they are of decided interest to the psychologist.

In a general way, the placebo response has been considered to be a nonspecific response in psychotherapy, that is, one which comes about without direct reference to the planned interventions of the therapist. In the case of a patient who is given a placebo pill and shows a decrease in his symptoms, it has been believed that the mere taking of a pill may have some suggestive therapeutic effects on the patient. The mere appearance of receiving medication from the physician may be sufficient to indicate to the patient that he is receiving treatment and that he should be better as a consequence. It may also convey the idea that his illness is understood and that there is a treatment for it. Consequently, undue concern may be brushed away and hope for recovery generated. The therapist's manner and the patient's personality may also contribute to the placebo effect, although the research data are rather conflicting (Shapiro & Morris, 1978). If the therapist is a recognized authority or has an imposing manner, or if he confidently tells the patient that the medication is very effective and will soon rid him of his discomfort, placebo effects may be heightened. In a related fashion, if the patient has a great deal of confidence in the doctor or is very much impressed by him, or is in other ways rather suggestive or impressionable, more pronounced placebo effects may be secured. It should be mentioned also, that although positive placebo effects have tended to receive the greatest amount of attention, negative placebo effects have also been obtained.

The placebo response, ubiquitous and enigmatic, has received a fair amount of study and discussion from both pharmacologically and psychologically oriented investigators. Its precise nature is still not fully understood, although it has appeared to play an important role in the history of medical and related therapeutics. An interesting and comprehensive review has been provided by Shapiro and Morris (1978), which most readers should find both informative and provocative. Consequently, no attempt will be made here to even review some of the literature on this topic. We will simply call attention to its implications for psychotherapy.

It can be noted that a number of psychotherapists react quite negatively to the entire concept of the placebo response. With some justification, they point out that the concept is vague and appears to include a variety of causes and effects. Also, whereas many hypotheses have been advanced to explain the presumed placebo effect, systematic studies have not always lent support to these hypotheses. Although all of this is certainly true, the reaction is sometimes overly strong. To the extent that a number of studies of the effects of both drugs and psychotherapy have indicated positive changes for groups provided with some form of placebo control, it does appear that some kind of influence process is activated by placebos of various kinds. Even in studies where the drug or the type of psychotherapy evaluated secures significantly better results than the placebo control condition, some positive results tend also to be secured with the latter. The fact that the more sophisticated research projects in psychotherapy have utilized a placebo control also attests to its potential importance in psychotherapy. Many psychotherapists, however, seemingly tend to feel that acknowledging that there is such a phenomenon as the placebo response is somehow a criticism of their work and of psychotherapy in general. My own speculation is that it tends somehow to disconfirm the therapist's own firmly held beliefs about what produces change in psychotherapy. If a certain amount of the change can be attributed to the placebo response, then the therapist conceivably may have to acknowledge that many of his efforts and procedures perhaps were actually unessential, and this is a difficult thing to accept.

At the same time, critics of psychotherapy have emphasized the positive responses to placebos as evidence that psychotherapy is not much more effective than a placebo (Prioleau, Murdock, & Brody, 1983). Although this is an important issue for research evaluating the effectiveness of psychotherapy which we will review in a later chapter, a few comments on this matter deserve mention here.

Relatively similar findings have been reported in a major meta-analysis of 475 studies (Smith, Glass, & Miller, 1980) and in the large scale NIMH Collaborative Study of the Treatment of Depression (Elkin et al., 1989). In these instances, the effects of a placebo response were positive but were approximately about half of the size of the effects of the psychotherapies evaluated. Although frequently the therapies studied did not obtain statically significant superior results as compared to the placebo, the relative size of the effects secured have been relatively consistent and have favored psychotherapy. I have commented on this pattern in a previously published article as follows:

My point is that whatever general features placebo conditions may have, they tend to produce positive results, even though it is less than that produced by a regular form of psychotherapy. Therefore, part of the positive effect secured by psychotherapy may be due to such hypothesized variables as seeing a therapist, the creation of hope, and the passage of time. These could be viewed as potential process variables, and perhaps they represent, or are related to, the therapeutic relationship in general.

The remaining portion of the effect size claimed for the psychotherapies would be attributed to the specific therapeutic variables that are part of the particular form of psychotherapy (e.g., interpretation, reflection, empathy). (Garfield, 1990, p. 278)

In other words, although some have interpreted selected findings on this issue as indicating that psychotherapy is no more effective than a placebo, I have interpreted the overall differences in the findings as indicating a positive general effect for the placebo and a greater effect for psychotherapy that may also incorporate the general effects of a placebo. These hypotheses appear plausible and will be discussed again later.

We can conclude this chapter by emphasizing that if positive changes occur in psychotherapy which do not appear to be the result of our planned procedure, it would seem worthwhile for us to investigate the possible causative factors involved. If the therapist's confidence in his procedures can be shown to have a positive effect on outcome, the therapist should act accordingly. We should want to do anything that maximizes positive outcome and increases the effectiveness of therapy, even if it is not in line with our preconceived views. We can also be aware that many individuals who seek our help in psychotherapy suffer from demoralization and being accepted for therapy by a sensitive and competent therapist increases hope and helps to restore morale (Frank, 1973). Many potential therapeutic variables can come into play during the process of psychotherapy with some playing a more important role depending on the particular client and therapist. Those described in this chapter appear to be of some importance in most forms of psychotherapy.

REFERENCES

Alexander, F., & French, T. M. (1946). *Psychoanalytic therapy.* New York: Ronald.

Bandura, A. (1969). *Principles of behavior modification.* New York: Holt, Rinehart and Winston.

Bandura, A. (1971). Psychotherapy based upon modeling principles. In A. E. Bergin & S. L. Garfield (Eds.), *Handbook of psychotherapy and behavior change.* New York: Wiley.

Bandura, A. (1977). Social learning theory. Englewood Cliffs, NJ: Prentice-Hall.

Bandura, A., Blanchard, E. B., & Ritter, B. (1969). The relative efficacy of desensitization and modeling approaches for inducing behavioral, affective, and attitudinal changes. *Journal of Personality and Social Psychology, 13,* 173–199.

Beck, A. T. (1976). *Cognitive therapy and emotional disorders.* New York: International Universities Press.

Bergin, A. E., & Lambert, M. J. (1978). The evaluation of therapeutic outcomes. In S. L. Garfield & A. E. Bergin (Eds.), *Handbook of psychotherapy and behavior change* (2nd ed.). New York: Wiley.

Davison, G. C., & Wilson, G. T. (1973). Processes of fear reduction in systematic desensitization: Cognitive and social reinforcement factors in humans. *Behavior Therapy, 4,* 1–21.

Elkin, I., Shea, T., Watkins, J. T., Imber, S. D., Sotsky, S. M., Collins, J. F., Glass, D. R., Pilkonis, P. A., Leber, W. R., Docherty, J. P., Fiester, S. J., & Parloff, M. B. (1989). National Institute of Mental Health Treatment of Depression Collaborative Research Program. General effectiveness of treatment. *Archives of General Psychiatry, 46,* 971–982.

Ellis, D. (1962). *Reason and emotion in psychotherapy.* New York: Stuart.

Emmelkamp, P. M. G. (1986). Behavior therapy with adults. In S. L. Garfield & A. E. Bergin (Eds.) *Handbook of psychotherapy and behavior change* (3rd ed.) (pp. 385–442). New York: Wiley.

Enelow, A. J. (1977). *Elements of psychotherapy.* New York: Oxford University Press.

Erdwins, C. F. (1975). *A comparison of three behavior modification procedures including systematic desensitization and vicarious modeling.* Unpublished Doctoral Dissertation, Washington University, St. Louis, MO.

Eysenck, H. J. (1952). The effects of psychotherapy: An evaluation. *Journal of Consulting Psychology, 16,* 319–324.

Eysenck, H. J. (1966). *The effects of psychotherapy.* New York: International Science Press.

Frank, J. D. (1971). Therapeutic factors in psychotherapy. *American Journal of Psychotherapy, XXV,* 350–361.

Frank, J. D. (1973). *Persuasion and healing* (2nd ed.). Baltimore, MD: Johns Hopkins University Press.

Frank, J. D., & Frank, J. B. (1991). *Persuasion and healing: A comparative study of psychotherapy* (3rd ed.). Baltimore, MD: Johns Hopkins University Press.

Freud, S. (1950). On the history of the psychoanalytic movement. In *Collected Papers, Vol. 1.* London: The Hogarth Press and the Institute of Psychoanalysis.

Garfield, S. L. (1957). *Introductory clinical psychology.* New York: Macmillan.

Garfield, S. L. (1990). Issues and methods in psychotherapy process research. *Journal of Consulting and Clinical Psychology, 58,* 273–280.

Gaston, L. (1990). The concept of the alliance and its role in psychotherapy: Theoretical and empirical considerations. *Psychotherapy, 27,* 143–153.

Gelder, M. G., Bancroft, J. H. J., Gath, D. H., Johnston, D. W., Mathews, A. M., & Shaw, P. M. (1973). Specific and non-specific factors in behavior therapy. *The British Journal of Psychiatry, 123,* 445–462.

Goldfried, M. R. (1971). Systematic desensitization as training in self-control. *Journal of Consulting and Clinical Psychology, 37,* 228–234.

Goldfried, M. R. (1980). Psychotherapy as coping skills training. In M. J. Mahoney (Ed.), *Psychotherapy process. Current issues and future directions* (pp. 89–119). New York: Plenum.

Goldfried, M. R., & Davison, G. C. (1976). *Clinical behavior therapy.* New York: Holt, Rinehart and Winston.

Goldfried, M. R., & Trier, C. S. (1974). Effectiveness of relaxation as an active coping skill. *Journal of Abnormal Psychology, 83,* 348–355.

Hartley, D., & Strupp, H. (1983). The therapeutic alliance: Its relationship to outcome in brief psychotherapy. In J. Masling (Ed.), *Empirical studies of psychoanalytic theories* (Vol. 1, pp. 1–27). Hillsdale, NJ: Erlbaum.

Henry, W. P., Strupp, H. H., Schacht, T. E., & Gaston, L. (1994). Psychodynamic approaches. In A. E. Bergin & S. L. Garfield (Eds.) *Handbook of psychotherapy and behavior change* (4th ed.) (pp. 467–508). New York: Wiley.

Hollon, S. D., & Beck, A. T. (1986). Cognitive and cognitive-behavioral therapies. In S. L. Garfield & A. E. Bergin (Eds.), *Handbook of psychotherapy and behavior change* (3rd ed.) (pp. 443–482). New York: Wiley.

Horvath, A. O., & Symonds, B. D. (1991). Relationship between working alliance and outcome in psychotherapy: A Meta-analysis. *Journal of Counseling Psychology, 38,* 139–149.

Jacobson, E. (1929). *Progressive relaxation.* Chicago: University of Chicago Press.

Jensen, J. P., & Bergin, A. E. (1988). Mental health values of professional therapists: A national interdisciplinary survey. *Professional Psychology: Research and Practice, 19,* 290–297.

Kazdin, A. E. (1978). The application of operant techniques in treatment, rehabilitation, and education. In S. L. Garfield & A. E. Bergin (Eds.), *Handbook of psychotherapy and behavior change* (2nd ed.). New York: Wiley.

Kazdin, A. E. (1989). *Behavior modification in applied settings* (4th ed.). Pacific Grove, CA: Brooks/Cole.

Krasner, L. (1962). The therapist as a social reinforcement machine. In H. H. Strupp & L. Luborsky (Eds.), *Research in psychotherapy* (Vol. 2). (pp. 61–94). Washington, DC: American Psychological Association.

Krasner, L. (1963). Reinforcement, verbal behavior and psychotherapy. *American Journal of Orthopsychiatry, 33,* 601–613.

Krasner, L. (1971). The operant approach in behavior therapy. In A. E. Bergin & S. L. Garfield (Eds.), *Handbook of psychotherapy and behavior change.* New York: Wiley.

Lambert, M. J. (1976). Spontaneous remission in adult neurotic disorders: A revision and summary. *Psychological Bulletin, 83,* 107–119.

Levine, M. (1948). *Psychotherapy in medical practice.* New York: Macmillan.

Marks, I. (1978). Behavioral psychotherapy of adult neurosis. In S. L. Garfield & A. E. Bergin (Eds.), *Handbook of psychotherapy and behavior change* (2nd ed.). New York: Wiley.

Meehl, P. E. (1960). The cognitive activity of the clinician. *American Psychologist, 15,* 19–27.

Morgan, R., Luborsky, L., Crits-Christoph, P., Curtis, H., & Solomon, J. (1982). Predicting the outcome of psychotherapy by the Penn Helping Alliance Rating method. *Archives of General Psychiatry, 39,* 397–402.

Murray, E. J. (1956). A content-analysis method for studying psychotherapy. *Psychological Monographs, 70,* (13, Whole No. 420).

Nichols, M. P. (1974). Outcome of brief cathartic psychotherapy. *Journal of Consulting Psychology, 42,* 403–410.

O'Leary, K. D., & Wilson, G. T. (1987). *Behavior therapy. Application and outcome* (2nd ed.). Englewood Cliffs, NJ: Prentice-Hall.

Prioleau, L., Murdock, M., & Brody, N. (with commentary) (1983). An analysis of psychotherapy versus placebo studies. *The Behavioral and Brain Sciences, 6,* 275–310.

Rogers, C. R. (1942). *Counseling and psychotherapy.* Boston: Houghton Mifflin.

Rogers, C. R. (1951). *Client-centered therapy.* Boston: Houghton Mifflin.

Rosenzweig, S. (1936). Some implicit common factors in diverse methods of psychotherapy. *American Journal of Orthopsychiatry, 6,* 412–415.

Schofield, W. (1964). *Psychotherapy, the purchase of friendship.* Englewood Cliffs, NJ: Prentice-Hall.

Shapiro, A. K., & Morris, L. A. (1978). The placebo effect in medical and psychological therapies. In S. L. Garfield & A. E. Bergin (Eds.), *Handbook of psychotherapy and behavior change* (2nd ed.). New York: Wiley.

Smith, M. L., Glass, G. V., & Miller, T. I. (1980). *The benefits of psychotherapy.* Baltimore, MD: Johns Hopkins University Press.

Strupp, H. H. (1973). On the basic ingredients of psychotherapy. *Journal of Consulting and Clinical Psychology, 41,* 1–8.

Subotnik, L. (1972). Spontaneous remission: Fact or artifact? *Psychological Bulletin, 77,* 32–48.

Szasz, T. S. (1960). Three problems in contemporary psychoanalytic training. *Archives of General Psychiatry, 3,* 82–94.

Thorne, F. C. (1968). *Psychological case handling* (Vols. One and Two). Brandon, VT: Clinical Psychology Publishing Company.

Torrey, E. F. (1972). What Western psychotherapists can learn from witchdoctors. *American Journal of Orthopsychiatry, 42,* 69–76.

Truax, C. B. (1966). Reinforcement and nonreinforcement in Rogerian psychotherapy. *Journal of Abnormal Psychology, 71,* 1–9.

Truax, C. B., & Carkhuff, R. R. (1967). *Toward effective counseling and psychotherapy.* Chicago: Aldine.

Weiner, I. B., & Bordin, E. S. (1983). Individual psychotherapy. In I. B. Weiner (Ed.), *Clinical methods in psychology* (2nd ed.) (pp. 333–388). New York: Wiley.

Wolberg, L. R. (1954). *The technique of psychotherapy.* New York: Grune & Stratton.

Wolpe, J. (1958). *Psychotherapy by reciprocal inhibition.* Stanford: Stanford University Press.

Wolpe, J. (1961). The systematic desensitization treatment of neuroses. *Journal of Nervous and Mental Disease, 132,* 181–203.

Wolpe, J. (1973). *The practice of behavior therapy* (2nd ed.). New York: Pergamon Press.

CHAPTER 6

Common and Specific
Factors in Psychotherapy

The problem of what procedures, interactions, or variables produce or facilitate positive change in psychotherapy is of critical importance for understanding and improving the therapeutic process. It is a matter that has interested me for many years and Chapter 5 presented my views of what appear to be some of the basic variables that are operative in psychotherapy. Although the emphasis in psychotherapy has appeared to be on the presentation of different theoretical and procedural systems of psychotherapy (Corsini & Wedding, 1989), I was impressed with the potentially common threads that seemed to run through these diverse systems and by the fact that therapists in practice behaved in ways that were not specified by their theoretical orientations.

Earlier publications which influenced my thinking were those by Rosenzweig (1936), Levine (1948), Heine (1953), and Rosenthal and Frank (1956). All of these suggested the possibility of at least some common elements occurring in diverse forms of psychotherapy, and I subsequently made reference to several common factors in psychotherapy in an earlier textbook on clinical psychology (Garfield, 1957). Jerome Frank and his colleagues also referred to such phenomena as "non-specific" factors in psychotherapy (Frank, 1973; Stone, Imber, & Frank, 1966), since they were not specific to any particular form of therapy. This term has been used to refer to therapeutic effects not directly due to the specified treatment procedures. Frank (1971) also discussed common and specific factors in psychotherapy, which reinforced my own views. Because I regard this issue as being extremely important, the present chapter is devoted to a fuller discussion of it. It also serves as an elaboration of the preceding chapter.

A basic hypothesis advanced in this chapter is that despite many apparent differences in theoretical orientations and procedures, many of the divergent schools of psychotherapy rely on essentially common factors for securing some of the changes believed to occur in their respective psychotherapeutic endeavors. Although each of the schools may emphasize specific factors or processes which are considered to be unique to their particular form of psychotherapy, an examination of what actually may be occurring allows for an alternative interpretation. This was exemplified in our previous discussion of the role of insight and understanding in psychotherapy. Although the different orientations in psychotherapy may provide different types of understanding, it is not these specific insights that appear to be of some potential value in psychotherapy, but rather, the provision of a rationale for explaining the patient's problem which may be the important variable. Thus, it is not necessarily the precise explanation offered by a particular school that is potentially therapeutic, but the more general process of giving the client some kind of understanding of what is troubling him and his acceptance of this explanation.

To the extent that all approaches claim to be successful in alleviating the problems of those seeking their help, it seems plausible to assume that there may be variables or processes common to most approaches which are the operative ones instead of the different specific ones advanced by the separate approaches. Although this view is offered as a hypothetical one, it is one that appears to have some plausibility, is congruent with research findings on outcome in psychotherapy (Gelder et al., 1973; Lambert & Bergin, 1994; Luborsky, Singer, & Luborsky, 1975; Sloane, Staples, Cristol, Yorkston, & Whipple, 1975) and is one which is worth considering in more detail.

A somewhat similar view of the psychotherapeutic process was also presented by Lennard and Bernstein (1960) in their analysis of psychotherapy as a social system. One of the conclusions drawn from their study was the following:

> First we saw that despite major differences in the outlook and the behavior of each therapist and each patient, there are major similarities among therapist-patient pairs in terms of the way the interaction unfolds longitudinally. This finding raises many questions for those who tend to stress differences between therapists in their theoretical orientation and who overemphasize the importance of the "school" to which a therapist belongs as the determinant for what transpires during therapy. It could be claimed that specific acts (techniques) occurring in one kind of therapy and not in another are the significant factors in the "cure" of the patient. From this point of view, it is the "differences" in therapy which count. However, we are inclined to disagree that this is wholly true. If emotional illness is the result of long and continued faulty interaction from childhood on between the patient and a wide variety of his role partners, then it is hard to see how one or another circumscribed aspect of therapist behavior could provide the necessary restorative experience. We believe that the most important contribution of therapy lies in the experience, in the total and recurrent pattern of patient and therapist interaction, extending over an enduring period. The enormous amount of similarity in the therapeutic systems suggests to us that what is shared by different therapist-patient pairs may be at least as therapeutic as that which is unique. (pp. 193–194)

I agree with the view expressed by Lennard and Bernstein (1960) "that the most important contribution of therapy lies . . . in the total and recurrent pattern of patient and therapist interaction." However, this is a global type of statement advanced to explain the evident similarity among the different therapeutic approaches. In order to understand this similarity, we must look for the therapeutic variables that account for change and that presumably are common among the differing forms of psychotherapy. Despite the growth and proliferation of the psychotherapies, there has been a slow but steady recognition of the potential importance of common factors in psychotherapy (Frank, 1971, 1973; Garfield, 1973, 1980, 1982, 1991, 1992; Staples, Sloane, Whipple, Cristol, & Yorkston, 1975; Torrey, 1972). Even such well-known psychodynamic researchers as Strupp (1977) and Luborsky (Luborsky, Crits-Christoph, Mintz, & Auerbach, 1988) have acknowledged the likelihood of common factors in psychotherapy. In a somewhat comparable development, behavior therapists have shown more interest in the influence of expectancy and placebo effects on outcome in systematic desensitization (Brown, 1973; Kazdin & Wilcoxon, 1976; McReynolds, Barnes, Brooks, & Rehagen, 1973) and others have suggested that common variables may be operative in hypnosis and behavior therapy (Spanos, Moor, & Barber, 1973). The importance of managing interpersonal issues in systematic desensitization also was emphasized by Braff, Raskin, and Gersinger (1976). "Systematic desensitization takes place within the larger framework of a therapeutic alliance in which careful attention to interpersonal factors is crucial" (p. 794).

Barrett, Hampe, and Miller (1978) also offered an interesting observation based on their own research:

It would seem redundant to state that reciprocal inhibition therapy and play therapy are two different techniques. To a large extent, though, the activities conducted under these two names are quite similar, so much so that in our own research we found it possible and profitable to describe a generic set of procedures that we found ourselves using no matter which kind of treatment we were using. Moreover, these common procedures probably accounted for the fact that we obtained no differential treatment effect. One treatment *was* the other. Therefore, it appears to us that the first step is that of discovering and describing those procedures that are common to nearly all child treatments and assessing their impact. Once the impact of these procedures is known, we can determine whether those maneuvers that are exclusive to one type of therapy add anything beyond the "G" variable. (p. 431)

Rosenthal and Bandura (1978) also comment about common features in discussing various symbolic procedures in behavioral therapies:

Similar information and meaningful inferences can be drawn from many permutations of input. Hence, it is not surprising if symbolic modeling produces much the same results as related guidance techniques bearing other labels like systematic desensitization, role-playing, and flooding. Nominal format differences may prompt contrasting brand-names that emphasize superficial distinctions but obscure basic commonalities. Ordinarily, all such methods share a number of important treatment features which overlap substantially in form, organization, substance, and functional consequences.

The author's own eclectic approach, as exemplified in the first edition of this book has been characterized as a "common factors" approach. It was of particular interest to me that two recent volumes to which I was invited to contribute had sections on eclectic and integrative approaches to psychotherapy with subheadings entitled "Common Factors" (Norcross & Goldfried, 1992; Zeig & Munion, 1990). Over time, some changes do take place.

Thus, gradually there has been a greater recognition and acknowledgment of possible common factors operating within the various forms of psychotherapy, although proponents of the different approaches to psychotherapy continue to emphasize the unique values of their own approach.

It is also worth emphasizing that the view of common factors advanced here and illustrated in the previous chapter is by no means considered to account for all of the possible variables operating in psychotherapy. There are also more specific variables that may be particularly effective in working with certain types of problems. We will discuss such possible variables later. However, let us now proceed to consider more fully the existence of common factors in psychotherapy.

COMMON FACTORS IN PSYCHOTHERAPY

Having advanced the proposition that there may be common factors operating among the various psychotherapies, let us begin by looking at the most likely or obvious similarities among them. All psychotherapy begins when an individual experiences a degree of discomfort or difficulty that finally motivates him or her to consult a therapist. Thus, all of the psychotherapies have in common a disturbed individual who seeks help. They also utilize a therapist who is perceived generally as a socially sanctioned healer. The act of seeking help and receiving the therapist's reassurance that the therapist will undertake to help him is also of some potential therapeutic significance. As we noted earlier, such action may generate considerable hope in the patient that his situation may change for the better. This process is also one that appears to occur in most of the psychotherapies.

Most psychotherapies also utilize verbal means of communication and interaction between the therapist and client, but since it is what is communicated and how the communications are made which appear to be important, nothing more need be said here about the means of communication per se. However, in all therapies, the client is afforded an opportunity to tell the therapist about his problems, to confide personal matters, and generally to unburden himself of those matters which have been troubling and perplexing him. The therapist, in most instances, will manifest an attentive interest in what the client has to tell him and may also ask questions or seek elaborations of material being discussed. The therapist may also indicate his interest and professional concern by nodding his head, by reflecting on some of the client's statements and feelings, and by noting down some of the client's statements. Such responses of the therapist conceivably may indicate to the client that the therapist understands his problems, that he has encountered such problems before, and that there is indeed some hope or possibility of positive change. Such common features of psychotherapy may indeed have some therapeutic effect on the client. Besides generating a more optimistic outlook on the part of the client, they may also signify an important turning point in the patient's current life situation. He is not facing, alone, some unknown difficulty about which he knows little and may be apprehensive. Instead, he now has the understanding support of someone who has agreed to help him in overcoming his difficulties. To the extent, also, that most of the psychotherapies provide the client with regularly scheduled appointments, the client has the assurance of knowing that he will see his therapist at a fixed time and can look forward to such meetings. There is, thus, a promise of continued support and help.

Some of the other common variables which may be operating in psychotherapy have already been discussed in the previous chapter and can be merely mentioned in brief form here. In most of the psychotherapies, the client develops a relationship with the therapist. Although the importance of the relationship may be stressed in some forms of psychotherapy and receive less formal emphasis in others, the fact that a relationship does form and take place in therapy seems quite evident and is generally acknowledged today. It is true that the type of relationship which occurs may be influenced by the particular type of therapy, but, again, there appear to be features which are common to most. In any good relationship, there will be mutual respect and regard for the other person, and this appears to hold also for the relationship that occurs in psychotherapy, regardless of the type of therapy offered. The "good" therapist in any variety of psychotherapy would also be expected to show those qualities which have been considered as desirable and as facilitating the therapeutic process, whether the therapist be a client-centered, cognitive, behaviorally oriented, or dynamically oriented therapist. Since, perhaps, this may not appear readily apparent to some readers, it may be worthwhile to elaborate a bit on it here.

There have been a few studies of the therapy behavior of some well-known psychotherapists in which the differing styles of these therapies were clearly apparent and were in conformity with the tenets of the different schools they represented. In one interesting experiment, the same client was interviewed by Carl Rogers, Fritz Perls, and Albert Ellis, representing the client-centered, gestalt therapy, and rational-emotive approaches, respectively (Zimmer & Cowles, 1972). The therapy behaviors of each of these well-known therapeutic leaders was what one would have anticipated from knowing their work. They operated on the basis of different premises, their personality styles were distinctively different, they appeared to influence the client in different ways, and they actually functioned in a different manner. For example, an analysis of the transcribed interviews showed very marked differences in therapist verbal behavior, particularly between Ellis and Rogers. In the case of Rogers, he was less directive and authoritative, more reflective, and the majority of the verbal utterances made during the session were made by the client. In contrast, Ellis performed in a much more directive and authoritative manner, and dominated the session in terms of verbal output. Other differences could also be noted, but these will suffice.

One might, on the basis of what has just been presented, question the previous assertion about common factors in the therapeutic relationship and ask what these therapists had in common. First of all, in spite of their differences, each of the therapist was an acknowledged authority and leader of a particular school of psychotherapy. To this extent, they all had some potential influence on the expectancies of the client. Second, each of them had strong convictions about the utility and validity of their own form of therapy, an attribute that may have been communicated to the client and have had some effect on her. Finally, while the client did perceive each of the therapists differently, and had different reactions to them, she did mention both positive and negative features of her interactions with all three of them. Unfortunately, since this was a filmed demonstration, and not a study of regular therapy, no conclusions can be offered concerning the relative effectiveness of the three therapists with their different approaches, or concerning what components of the different therapies were most important in their effect on the client. However, to the extent that the client did respond positively to certain attributes of the three therapist-therapy combinations, there was, again, a common feature in all three. The client saw all three as helpful, even though they were different and functioned in different ways. One could argue that each of the different therapists was utilizing a different but equally effective therapeutic procedure, or one could state that in spite of the apparent differences, the client responded to whatever procedures the therapists offered as long as she viewed them as being a means of helping her. Neither view can be supported or rejected on the basis of this particular example.

Another source of support for the view concerning common factors comes from the interesting study reported by Sloane and his collaborators (Sloane et al., 1975). Three well-known and experienced behavior therapists were compared with a comparable group of psychoanalytically oriented therapists. Each therapist saw 10 patients over a four-month period of therapy and 30 patients were used as a wait-list control group. Although the control group also showed some significant gains on selected measures of outcome, on the whole, both therapy groups showed significantly greater change on ratings of primary symptoms. However, the two therapy groups did not differ significantly from each other. Although the two groups of therapists followed the characteristic procedures of their respective orientations and were clearly differentiated in this regard, as appraised by sample recordings of actual therapy sessions, they secured essentially similar overall outcomes in their psychotherapeutic work. While this, in itself, is a most interesting finding, there were some others that were even more interesting or surprising.

A tape recording of the fifth interview for all the therapists was analyzed in terms of several of the therapeutic conditions specified by the client-centered therapists. In this analysis, five therapist-offered conditions were rated. The behavior therapists showed significantly *higher* levels of depth of interpersonal contact, accurate empathy, and therapist self-congruence (genuineness), but there were no differences between the two groups of therapists on unconditional positive regard and depth of interpersonal exploration. The authors of this report found these findings to be quite surprising:

in view of the fact that behavior therapy has been at times characterized as a rather impersonal process with little regard for the patient as a human being in contrast to the close empathic relationship of psychotherapy. However, both groups of therapists showed high levels of these variables. (Sloane et al., 1975, pp. 148–149)

These results are of particular interest for our present discussion. Not only did the two very different forms of therapy secure quite comparable results in terms of outcome, but the behavior therapists also exhibited high levels of positive therapist qualities in their therapy—even though such matters receive practically no formal emphasis in presentations of their approach to therapy. In other words, although behavior therapists had tended to place little formal emphasis on the therapeutic relationship as a significant variable in psychotherapy, in their actual work with clients they appear to develop as good relationships as are secured by therapists of other orientations in which considerable emphasis is placed on the therapeutic relationship.

There were also some other findings of interest in the study by Sloane et al. (1975) that are worth quoting here:

> The successful patients in both therapies placed primary importance on more or less the same items. The following items were each termed "extremely important" or "very important" by at least 70 percent of successful patients in both groups:
>
> 1. The personality of your doctor.
> 2. His helping you to understand your problem.
> 3. Encouraging you gradually to practice facing the things that bother you.
> 4. Being able to talk to an understanding person.
> 5. Helping you to understand yourself.

In addition, at least 70 percent of the successful psychotherapy patients rated as extremely or very important:

> 1. Encouraging you to shoulder your own responsibilities by restoring confidence in yourself.
> 2. The skill of your therapist.
> 3. His confidence that you would improve. (pp. 206–207)

These views of the patients are particularly intriguing in light of the postulated theoretical premises of the therapies studied. As Sloane and his collaborators pointed out,

> Nearly all these items can be classified as "encouragement, advice, or reassurance," factors common to both behavior therapy and psychotherapy. None of the items regarded as very important by the majority of either group of patients describes techniques specific to one therapy. . . . Most noticeable is the great overlap between the two groups, suggesting that, at least from the patient's point of view, the effectiveness of treatment was due to factors common to both therapies rather than to any particular theoretical orientation or techniques. (p. 207)

All in all, as these investigators themselves pointed out, the findings of this study do appear to support the view that there are common factors operating in both behavioral therapy and psychoanalytically oriented therapy which are of potential significance as far as outcome is concerned. In a study of cognitive-behavioral therapy, patients were requested to list the positive factors they believed were important in their therapy (Murphy, Cramer, & Lillie, 1984). The most frequently listed factors were: advice (79 percent); talking to someone interested in my problems (75 percent); and encouragement and reassurance (67 percent)—some of the common factors mentioned previously. Although such factors have been viewed as superficial by some therapists, who perhaps work with a select group of patients, they were considered important by the predominantly lower socioeconomic class of patients in this study.

Somewhat comparable results were reported in an earlier study by Ryan and Gizynski (1971). They interviewed fourteen patients who had received behavioral therapy, most of whom had shown definite improvement in therapy. "The patients felt, and the authors would agree, that the most universally helpful elements of their experience were the therapists' calm, sympathetic listening, support and approval, advice and 'faith'" (p. 8). Feifel and Eells (1963) reported that the patients they studied stressed the personal qualities of the therapist and the opportunity to discuss their problems as variables of importance, whereas the therapists emphasized their therapeutic techniques in this regard.

Thus, it appears reasonable to believe that many different psychotherapies use a number of similar procedures or interactions that have an impact on the client, although they are not particularly emphasized in the formal description of the therapy. Furthermore, these conceptually neglected variable may actually be of some importance in whatever outcomes are secured. What is really needed is research which goes beyond any particular orientation and which examines other possible variable (common ones) that may be therapeutic. Many therapists appear to be locked in by their particular orientation, although the situation does appear to be changing. It is extremely important to go beyond the postulated variables being studied and to study the behavior of the therapist and her interactions with the client or patient. As Davidson and Seidman (1974) noted in a previous review,

> important variables have been selected a priori and any others systematically left out of investigative efforts. There is no real sense of an effort toward discovery, rather only the application of a conceptually closed paradigm to a new content area. (p. 1008)

We can be even briefer in discussing the next few variables which may be common to most of the psychotherapies since they have been discussed in more detail previously. The matter of insight and understanding has been alluded to several times already and should by now be a familiar topic. The only point to be made now is that the variety of rationales and explanations offered to the client by the different schools of therapy is a fascinating area for study in its own right. The significant aspect which is common to all of the orientations is the importance of the client's acceptance of the rationale provided him. Although one may question philosophically the value of adhering to a false set of beliefs, there is little question that having some belief system allows the individual to order and explain his experiences, thus providing him with some semblance of security. Where the individual has hitherto been unable to understand certain aspects of himself, with resulting anxiety, the explanations provided by the therapist are not only reassuring but may also help him to interpret and explain future events. Thus, the understandings provided in psychotherapy may also function as a coping mechanism for the individual. As long as it seems meaningful to the individual, it has some potential utility.

Catharsis and release also appear to occur in most of the verbal psychotherapies, and to the extent that such a process is not deliberately sought or induced by the therapist, it may even occur as an unexpected or distracting event in therapy. In one description of a case receiving behavior therapy, the client insisted on talking about a particular event to the therapist and not following the particular instructions for that session. The therapist, to his credit, however, allowed the client to express himself, and there was considerable emotional release followed by significant positive movement in the therapy. Desensitization, similarly, would appear to occur in many different kinds of therapy where the client is given the opportunity to examine certain problems repeatedly. As already mentioned, even if desensitization is not formally recognized as a process or specific attention paid to it, some desensitization may take place.

Another aspect of psychotherapy that appears to be common to most approaches, but which has not been stressed particularly, is that the therapist has the opportunity to observe and react to the characteristic behaviors of the client. Whereas some therapists may become overly involved with the verbal content of the client or his expression of feeling, many do pay attention to the behavior the client exhibits in the therapy session. To the extent that this is done, there is some communality among the different approaches on what may be dealt with, even if different interpretations of the behavior are offered. If the client is habitually late to therapy, is always sarcastic in his comments to the therapist, continually asks the therapist what he should do, or, worst of all, is behind in paying his fees, to the extent that these behaviors are commented on and discussed by the therapist, a common procedure is being used. Furthermore, dealing with the actual current behaviors of the client may be more effective than mere verbal discussions of a more abstract nature.

The client may also receive reassurance and support from the therapist, directly or indirectly, which encourages him to try out new behaviors. To the extent that some of his attempts along these lines are successful, the client is reinforced in his efforts to change. Whether this reassurance and encouragement is provided by the empathic communications of the therapist, by the insights secured in therapy, by the direct encouragement of the therapist, or by specific instructions or exercises provided by the therapist, the common feature in all is that the client is motivated to attempt new behaviors which he or she previously avoided.

A related feature of most therapies is that they all in various ways attempt to modify the patient's perception of himself and his world. In most successful psychotherapy, a key feature is the patient's change or reorganization of his perceptual reality. Although this may actually be more a result of successful therapy than a therapeutic variable per se, it is still worth noting here. It would seem that the recent emphasis on cognitive approaches in therapy are very much linked to attempts to modify the perceptions of the client (Hollon & Beck, 1986; Rosenthal & Bandura, 1978). In spite of different stated emphases, many of the different forms of psychotherapy actually do try to change the perceptions as well as beliefs of the client.

It does seem, therefore, that in spite of apparent differences in the theories and methods of the various approaches to psychotherapy, there may be a number of common factors that are operative in most of them. Furthermore, it appears also that these factors may in fact play an important role in producing some of the positive changes which are presumed to take place in psychotherapy. If this actually is so, it may be worthwhile to pay more attention to these common therapeutic factors than to rely exclusively on one of the theoretical formulations provided by the current schools of psychotherapy. Although the latter provide a rationale for carrying out psychotherapy, they carry a certain amount of unnecessary excess baggage. As in the first edition, I will again compare the present situation to the one described by Charles Lamb in his classic essay, "A Dissertation on Roast Pig." In this amusing essay, Lamb describes how an accidental fire burned down the cottage of the swine-herd, Ho-ti, in ancient China and everything was burned, including the pigs. Until now, people had eaten raw pork, but Ho-ti and his son accidentally tasted the roasted pig and discovered that it was vastly more delicious than raw pig. After this, Ho-ti built and subsequently burned down other cottages so that he could continue to enjoy roast pig. This practice was observed by others and, consequently, Ho-ti and his son were brought to trial and the obnoxious roast pig presented as evidence in court. The members of the jury touched the burnt meat and brought their burnt fingers automatically to their lips, thus tasting the delicious roast pig. To the surprise of all, the verdict of "Not Guilty" followed.

Lamb continues his delightful description of this historic event as follows:

The judge, who was a shrewd fellow, winked at the manifest iniquity of the decision: and when the court was dismissed, went privily and bought up all the pigs that could be had for love or money. In a few days his lordship's townhouse was observed to be on fire. The thing took wing, and now there was nothing to be seen but fire in every direction. Fuel and pigs grew enormously dear all over the district. The insurance-offices one and all shut up shop. People built slighter and slighter every day, until it was feared that the very science of architecture would in no long time be lost to the world. Thus this custom of firing houses continued, till in process of time, says my manuscript, a sage arose, like our Locke, who made a discovery that the flesh of swine, or indeed of any other animal, might be cooked (burnt, as they called it) without the necessity of consuming a whole house to dress it. Then first began the rude form of a gridiron. Roasting by the string or spit came in a century or two later, I forget in whose dynasty. By such slow degrees, concludes the manuscript, do the most useful, and seemingly the most obvious, arts make their way among mankind. (Lamb, 1935, p. 110)

Although roast pig is much tastier than raw pig, it is very inefficient to roast a pig by burning your house down. If we can produce some better conceptualizations of the variables that appear to be important in successful psychotherapy, then it is also likely that our procedures could become more effective and efficient. It is also likely that the great proliferation of therapeutic approaches would gradually diminish.

SPECIFIC FACTORS IN PSYCHOTHERAPY

Just as there may be common factors in psychotherapy which operate in most of the psychotherapies, so may there be specific factors or procedures that are of particular value in treating specific kinds of clinical problems. Consequently, an effective therapeutic approach would utilize the basic common factors already discussed in a more deliberate manner than they are now employed, plus some specific procedures selected for the particular case at hand. Thus, instead of utilizing one general approach for all patients regardless of the type of problem they present, greater attention would be paid to the use of selected procedures for the individual patient. This would appear to call for some significant changes in the way psychotherapists are trained and in the way they carry on their psychotherapeutic work. It would signify a more systematic and eclectic approach to psychotherapy in general, something which may not be easily forthcoming. Although it does appear if a majority of psychotherapists actually function as eclectics (Garfield & Kurtz, 1977; Jensen, Bergin, & Greaves, 1990), their eclecticism would not necessarily follow the formulation presented here.

Although many of the therapeutic approaches may secure positive outcomes largely because of common psychotherapeutic factors, some of the approaches appear to have particular value for certain kinds of problems. This seems to be the case particularly with regard to certain types of behavioral and cognitive-behavioral approaches. A considerable amount of the research reported by behavior therapists has been concerned with a variety of anxiety and phobic disorders. Such behavioral procedures as systematic desensitization, implosion, and modeling have to a significant extent been developed or utilized for overcoming phobic behaviors. Consequently, if a given client consults a psychotherapist because of phobic symptoms, it would be wise to utilize a behavioral approach. Speaking in a very general way, procedures taken from systematic desensitization, modeling, and exposure therapy would appear to be effective ones to use. They could also be combined or integrated for certain cases, particularly where in vivo procedures could be used. More detailed descriptions of these and other behavioral procedures are available elsewhere (Emmelkamp, 1986; O'Leary & Wilson, 1987; Wolpe, 1973); no attempt to present such procedures will be made here. It appears that some specific procedures may prove to be more effective with certain kinds of phobias than others. Considerable progress has been made in recent years in the treatment of anxiety disorders by cognitive-behavioral therapists (Barlow, 1988; Hollon & Beck, 1994). Of particular interest has been the work with patients suffering from panic disorders (Barlow & Cerny, 1988). Although these different behavioral approaches themselves utilize some of the common therapeutic factors mentioned previously, they do appear to have some specific values as well. More than other approaches, they deal directly with the client's problem and quickly help him or her to engage in behaviors that confront the disturbing stimuli. Because of this, as well as the relative speed with which they produce change, they would appear to be the treatment of choice for such problems.

Before proceeding, it would be well to elaborate on what has just been said and to offer some comments which apply to psychotherapy generally. In some instances, the client does in fact appear to have a focal or specific problem such as a specific phobia, and in these cases a straight behavioral approach may be effective and sufficient. However, in other cases, the problems may be more complex, and some other therapeutic plan may be more effective. Here, the important consideration is the proper appraisal of the client and his problem, so that the most appropriate therapeutic plan can be devised. While the proper diagnosis and evaluation of the client has been emphasized by many psychotherapists of different orientations, it has not really led to uniquely different procedures being applied to the different cases. Actually, the matter of adequate assessment of the client's problem is of the utmost importance, since it should determine the kinds of procedures selected for use with the individual case. Also, because the eclectic therapist is willing to use a larger array of procedures than is typically the case of a psychotherapist who follows only one particular approach, he must have some basis for deciding what procedures will be used in each case. Furthermore, the evaluation of the client's problem is not limited to the initial interview with the client at the start of therapy, but is a continuous process throughout therapy. Not only may the client present new problems later in therapy which she was reluctant to discuss at the beginning, but the extent of the problem may not be as clear initially and the therapist may be in a better position to evaluate it once the process is underway. This may necessitate some change in the procedures being used. The following example may illustrate what is involved here.

A young man consulted the writer about sexual difficulties, particularly, premature ejaculation. In the next session or so, he discussed this particular problem in some detail and it appeared that a straight-forward behavioral approach similar to one described by Wolpe (1973) might suffice for this client. However, as the sessions continued, it became clear that what the client was describing was something that had occurred many years in the past and which he brooded over and presented as something recent. What subsequently became clearer was a general inadequacy in approaching women and in establishing relations with them. This seemed more fundamental than the past occurrence of premature ejaculation, and consequently, this became a focus of therapy. His current activities were discussed and he was encouraged to make appropriate approach behaviors to the women with whom he had contact. As these proved to be successful, his interactions became more realistic and satisfying. He also brought up some difficulties he had in dealing with his father. In addition to allowing him to ventilate some of his negative feelings toward his father, and to change some of his perceptions concerning this relationship, we discussed some possible explanations of why these distorted perceptions had occurred and continued. The client also participated in some role-playing sessions prior to going out of town to visit his parents. A successful visit on this occasion was also of therapeutic value in reinforcing changes secured earlier, confirming perceptual and verbal changes with changed behavior. Shortly thereafter, therapy was terminated with the feeling on the part of both participants that positive change had occurred. What appeared to be of primary importance in this therapeutic intervention was an increase in the client's self-efficacy (Bandura, 1977).

One of the important contributions from the behavioral camp has been to clarify problems which appear to result from deficits within the individual, as contrasted with other types of disorders where the individual has the necessary skills or behaviors in his repertoire but is prevented from utilizing them because of fears and avoidance behaviors. In the latter case, deconditioning the client or substituting approach behaviors for avoident ones may be sufficient to allow the individual to function effectively. However, where the individual is deficient in certain skills or behaviors, merely getting him to overcome his fears or engage in approach behaviors may not be sufficient. The individual may have to be taught new social skills in order to improve his level of adjustment. A simple example comes to mind.

A young man complains that he is depressed at his lack of social success with women. "When they see me coming, they turn away." Some of this is easily comprehensible. The individual is extremely unattractive, untidy, in fact, dirty, and a very marked body odor is evident when he gets close to you. One could treat all these as surface symptoms and of little real importance, but the fact remains that the individual's lack of personal hygiene would be offensive to most people. He also seems quite unaware of why people avoid him. The most direct approach, and one which seems quite sensible, is to work with the client on understanding his obvious deficiencies and how to improve his appearance. He could be told to bathe more frequently, to wear clean clothes, and so on. This may not require a very sophisticated knowledge of psychotherapy or personality dynamics, but it might lead to some positive changes. The individual might also be helped in attaining social skills that may help him in meeting others and in his social interactions generally. Similar examples are available elsewhere (Goldfried & Davison, 1976; Leitenberg, 1976).

A somewhat related area is that of assertiveness training. These rather forthright procedures have been used by behavior therapists where the client has significant problems in being able to express or to assert himself in certain situations. The procedures used have included relaxation, systematic desensitization, behavioral rehearsal, modeling, and practical exercises in real life (Wolpe & Lazarus, 1966). Assertiveness training is included here as another example of a specific factor or treatment package in psychotherapy because it has been developed for a particular problem, that is, lack of assertiveness.

There are a number of other clinical problems that have been dealt with rather successfully and efficiently by use of behavioral techniques, including fear of public speaking, enuresis, school phobias, and other specific behavioral disturbances. Thus, where a specific behavioral problem is at issue, it would appear desirable for the therapist to consider devising a therapeutic program which would utilize appropriate behavioral techniques for handling the problem (Goldfried & Davison, 1976; O'Leary & Wilson, 1987). In the case of children with behavioral disturbance where the role of the parent appears to be of decided importance, work with the parents along behavioral lines would also appear to be of value. Since children are very much under the influence of the parents, and the latter tend to be significant reinforcing agents for their children, an approach of this type should be more effective than the traditional one to one therapy frequently offered in the past. The family interactions should be observed and the parents dealt with directly. They can also be used as therapeutic agents in the overall therapeutic program (Ollendick, 1986; Patterson, 1971; Patterson & Gullion, 1976).

Another possible example of a specific type of therapeutic approach or factor is what has been referred to as crisis intervention or crisis psychotherapy (Ewing, 1978; Garfield, 1989; Koss & Butcher, 1986). Such therapies have developed out of attempts to apply theories of crisis to individuals undergoing specific current crisis situations. Thus, they are aimed at specific types of problems and tend to be more structured brief forms of psychotherapeutic intervention.

While these crisis oriented forms of therapy may vary in some respects, they share a common emphasis on the current crisis as a focus of therapy, on the coping mechanisms of the individual, and on attempts to restore the individual to his or her previous level of adjustment as quickly as possible. The therapy tends to be more structured, to have a specific focus, to be brief, and to require a more active stance on the part of the therapist. Another emphasis is that the client should be seen as soon as possible after a crisis is experienced in order to prevent the individual's symptoms of difficulty from becoming more fixed.

A brief form of crisis or emergency therapy would appear to be of specific value in obvious crisis situations where the person is acutely upset, experiencing discomfort, or where there is some threat to the person's life or to others.

Thus, as described in the preceding pages, there are certain features of psychotherapy as currently practiced which appear to be common to most of the different forms of psychotherapy and which appear to be responsible for some of the changes which are reported to take place in psychotherapy. Although these common factors have received relatively little attention in the past they have been increasingly recognized as important in recent years (Glass & Arnkoff, 1988; Lambert, Shapiro, & Bergin, 1986). At the same time but generally less well-developed and delineated outside of the behavioral and cognitive-behavioral therapies, there are also some therapeutic approaches and procedures which appear to be particularly well suited for treating certain specific types of problems. For this reason, some of them have been identified as specific factors in psychotherapy. For most psychotherapeutic endeavors, many of the common factors described would be utilized as basic variables in the psychotherapeutic process. In many instances, also, some selected specific factors would be utilized as well. However, in some cases, although common factors would play a part in the psychotherapy, particular attention would be focused on the specific techniques or factors which appear to be particularly suitable for the individual problems presented.

As some readers may have already recognized, the approach being advanced here has many similarities to the scheme produced by the British psychologist, Charles Spearman, for viewing intelligence. In this writer's opinion, it has been a fruitful conception for the understanding and appraisal of intellectual functioning, and it appears to also hold some potential utility for a better understanding of the psychotherapeutic process (Garfield, 1991). As presented here, it is admittedly crude and unsystematic, but, at the same time, it appears worthy of consideration. The future goal of helping to make psychotherapy a more efficient and effective process would appear to lie in a clearer recognition that different procedures are required for different kinds of problems and that one approach cannot be all things to all men and women. While there are common features among individuals who seek help, and there are also common factors which appear to be of value in psychotherapy generally, there are also specific factors which need to be understood and applied in different kinds of cases. A better knowledge of the common and specific factors in psychotherapy should be of value in securing more effective outcomes in our therapeutic endeavors.

Finally, it is well to remember that positive outcome requires a therapist who is capable of selecting and effectively using the various common and specific therapeutic variables. Although not as much research has been conducted on therapist skill and effectiveness as on the types and techniques of therapy, it seems quite apparent that not all psychotherapists are equally skillful. In fact, Lambert (1989) has hypothesized that the lack of differences revealed in the research on outcome comparing different types of psychotherapy, suggests both common factors and the range of therapist skill in all therapeutic approaches.

REFERENCES

Bandura, A. (1977). Self-efficacy: Towards a unifying theory of behavioral change. *Psychological Review, 84,* 191–215.

Barlow, D. H. (1988). *Anxiety and its disorders: The nature and treatment of anxiety and panic.* New York: Guilford Press.

Barlow, D. H., & Cerny, J. A. (1988). *Psychological treatment of panic.* New York: Guilford Press.

Barrett, C. L., Hampe, I. E., & Miller, L. (1978). Research on psychotherapy with children. In S. L. Garfield & A. E. Bergin (Eds.), *Handbook of psychotherapy and behavior change* (2nd ed.) (pp. 411–435). New York: Wiley.

Braff, D. L., Raskin, M., & Geisinger, D. (1976). Management of interpersonal issues in systematic desensitization. *American Journal of Psychiatry, 133,* 791–794.

Brown, H. A. (1973). Role of expectancy manipulation in systematic desensitization. *Journal of Consulting and Clinical Psychology, 41,* 405–411.

Corsini, R. J., & Wedding, D. (1989). *Current psychotherapies* (4th ed.). Itasca, IL: Peacock.

Davidson, W. S., & Seidman, E. (1974). Studies of behavior modification and juvenile delinquency: A review, methodological critique, and social perspective. *Psychological Bulletin, 81,* 998–1011.

Emmelkamp, P. M. G. (1986). Behavior therapy with adults. In S. L. Garfield & A. E. Bergin (Eds.), *Handbook of psychotherapy and behavior change* (3rd ed.) (pp. 385–442). New York: Wiley.

Ewing, C. P. (1978). *Crisis intervention as psychotherapy.* New York: Oxford University Press.

Feifel, H., & Eells, J. (1963). Patients and therapists assess the same psychotherapy. *Journal of Consulting Psychology, 27,* 310–318.

Frank, J. D. (1971). Therapeutic factors in psychotherapy. *American Journal of Psychotherapy, 25,* 350–361.

Frank, J. D. (1973). *Persuasion and healing* (2nd ed.). Baltimore: The Johns Hopkins Press.

Garfield, S. L. (1957). *Introductory clinical psychology.* New York: MacMillan.

Garfield, S. L. (1973). Basic ingredients or common factors in psychotherapy? *Journal of Consulting and Clinical Psychology, 41,* 9–12.

Garfield, S. L. (1980). *Psychotherapy. An eclectic approach.* New York: Wiley.

Garfield, S. L. (1982). Eclecticism and integration in psychotherapy. *Behavior Therapy, 13,* 610–623.

Garfield, S. L. (1989). *The practice of brief psychotherapy.* New York: Pergamon.

Garfield, S. L. (1991). Common and specific factors in psychotherapy. *Journal of Integrative and Eclectic Psychotherapy, 10,* 5–13.

Garfield, S. L. (1992). Eclectic psychotherapy: A common factors approach. In J. Norcross & M. R. Goldfried (Eds.), *Handbook of integrative psychotherapy* (pp. 169–201). New York: Basic Books.

Garfield, S. L., & Kurtz, R. (1977). A study of eclectic views. *Journal of Consulting and Clinical Psychology, 45,* 78–83.

Gelder, M. G., Bancroft, J. H. J., Gath, D. H., Johnston, D. W., Mathews, A. M., & Shaw, P. M. (1973). Specific and non-specific factors in behavior therapy. *The British Journal of Psychiatry, 123,* 445–462.

Glass, C. R., & Arnkoff, D. B. (1988). Common and specific factors in client descriptions of and explanations for change. *Journal of Integrative and Eclectic Psychotherapy, 7,* 427–440.

Goldfried, M. R., & Davison, G. C. (1976). *Clinical behavior therapy.* New York: Holt, Rinehart & Winston.

Heine, R. W. (1953). A comparison of patients' reports on psychotherapeutic experience with psychoanalytic, nondirective and Adlerian therapists. *American Journal of Psychotherapy, 7,* 16–23.

Hollon, S. D., & Beck, A. T. (1986). Cognitive and cognitive-behavioral therapies. In S. L. Garfield & A. E. Bergin (Eds.), *Handbook of psychotherapy and behavior change* (3rd ed.) (pp. 443–482). New York: Wiley.

Hollon, S. D., & Beck, A. T. (1994). Cognitive and cognitive-behavioral therapies. In A. E. Bergin & S. L. Garfield (Eds.), *Handbook of psychotherapy and behavior change* (4th ed.) (pp. 428–466). New York: Wiley.

Jensen, J. P., Bergin, A. E., & Greaves, D. W. (1990). The meaning of eclecticism: New survey and analysis of components. *Professional psychology: Research and practice, 21,* 124–130.

Kazdin, A. E., & Wilcoxon, L. A. (1976). Systematic desensitization and nonspecific treatment effects: A methodological evaluation. *Psychological Bulletin, 83,* 729–758.

Koss, M. P., & Butcher, J. N. (1986). Research on brief psychotherapy. In S. L. Garfield & A. E. Bergin (Eds.), *Handbook of psychotherapy and behavior change* (3rd ed.) (pp. 627–670). New York: Wiley.

Lamb, C. (1935). *The complete works and letters of Charles Lamb.* New York: Modern Library.

Lambert, M. J. (1989). The individual therapist's contribution to psychotherapy process and outcome. *Clinical Psychology Review, 9,* 469–485.

Lambert, M., & Bergin, A. E. (1994). The effectiveness of psychotherapy. In A. E. Bergin & S. L. Garfield (Eds.), *Handbook of psychotherapy and behavior change* (4th ed.) (pp. 143–189). New York: Wiley.

Lambert, M. J., Shapiro, D. A., & Bergin, A. E. (1986). The effectiveness of psychotherapy. In S. L. Garfield & A. E. Bergin (Eds.), *Handbook of psychotherapy and behavior change* (3rd ed.) (pp. 157–211). New York: Wiley.

Leitenberg, H. (Ed.). (1976). *Handbook of behavior modification and behavior therapy.* Englewood Cliffs, NJ: Prentice-Hall.

Lennard, H. L., & Bernstein, A. (1960). *The anatomy of psychotherapy: Systems of communication and expectation.* New York: Columbia University Press.

Levine, M. (1948). *Psychotherapy in medical practice.* New York: Macmillan.

Luborsky, L., Crits-Christoph, P., Mintz, J., & Auerbach, A. (1988). *Who will benefit from psychotherapy?* New York: Basic Books.

Luborsky, L., Singer, B., & Luborsky, L. (1975). Comparative studies of psychotherapies. *Archives of General Psychiatry, 32,* 995–1008.

McReynolds, W. T., Barnes, A. R., Brooks, S., & Rehagen, N. J. (1973). The role of attention-placebo influences in the efficacy of systematic desensitization. *Journal of Consulting and Clinical Psychology, 41,* 86–92.

Murphy, P. M., Cramer, D., & Lillie, F. J. (1984). The relationship between curative factors perceived by patients in their psychotherapy and treatment outcome: An exploratory study. *British Journal of Medical Psychology, 57,* 187–192.

Norcross, J. C., & Goldfried, M. R. (Eds.). (1992). *Handbook of integrative psychotherapy.* New York: Basic Books.

O'Leary, K. D., & Wilson, G. T. (1987). *Behavior therapy. Application and outcome* (2nd ed.). Englewood Cliffs, NJ: Prentice-Hall.

Ollendick, T. H. (1986). *Child and adolescent behavior therapy.* In S. L. Garfield & A. E. Bergin (Eds.), *Handbook of psychotherapy and behavior change* (3rd ed.) (pp. 525–564). New York: Wiley.

Patterson, G. R. (1971). Behavioral intervention procedures in the classroom and in the home. In A. E. Bergin & S. L. Garfield (Eds.), *Handbook of psychotherapy and behavior change* (pp. 751–775). New York: Wiley.

Patterson, G. R., & Gullion, M. E. (1976). *Living with children: New methods for parents and teachers* (Rev. ed.). Champaign, IL: Research Press.

Rosenthal, D., & Frank, J. D. (1956). Psychotherapy and the placebo effect. *Psychological Bulletin, 53,* 294–302.

Rosenthal, T., & Bandura, A. (1978). Psychological modeling. In S. L. Garfield & A. E. Bergin (Eds.), *Handbook of psychotherapy and behavior change* (2nd ed.) (pp. 621–658). New York: Wiley.

Rosenzweig, S. (1936). Some implicit common factors in diverse methods of psychotherapy. *American Journal of Orthopsychiatry, 6,* 412–415.

Ryan, V., & Gizynski, M. (1971). Behavior therapy in retrospect: Patients' feelings about their behavior therapists. *Journal of Consulting and Clinical Psychology, 37,* 1–9.

Sloane, R. B., Staples, F. R., Cristol, A. H., Yorkston, N. J., & Whipple, K. (1975). *Psychotherapy versus behavior therapy.* Cambridge: Harvard University Press.

Spanos, N. P., Moor, W., & Barber, T. S. (1973). Hypnosis and behavior therapy: Common denominators. *American Journal of Clinical Hypnosis, 16,* 45–64.

Staples, F. R., Sloane, R. B., Whipple, K., Cristol, A. H., & Yorkston, N. J. (1975). Difference between behavior therapists and psychotherapists. *Archives of General Psychiatry, 32,* 1517–1522.

Stone, A. R., Imber, S. D., & Frank, J. D. (1966). The role of non-specific factors in short-term psychotherapy. *Australian Journal of Psychology, 18,* 210–217.

Strupp, H. H. (1977). A reformulation of the dynamics of the therapist's contribution. In A. S. Gurman & A. M. Razin (Eds.), *Effective psychotherapy. A handbook of research* (pp. 3–22). New York: Pergamon Press.

Torrey, E. F. (1972). What western psychotherapists can learn from witchdoctors. *American Journal of Orthopsychiatry, 42,* 69–76.

Wolpe, J. (1973). *The practice of behavior therapy* (2nd ed.). New York: Pergamon Press.

Wolpe, J., & Lazarus, A. A. (1966). *Behavior therapy techniques.* Oxford: Pergamon Press.

Zeig, J. K., & Munion, W. M. (Eds.) (1990). *What is psychotherapy? Contemporary perspectives.* San Francisco: Jossey-Bass.

Zimmer, J. M., & Cowles, K. (1972). Content analysis using fortran: Applied to interviews conducted by C. Rogers, F. Perls, and A. Ellis. *Counseling Psychology, 19,* 161–166.

CHAPTER 7

The Beginning Phase of Psychotherapy

In the preceding pages we have discussed some of the basic features and components of psychotherapy. Hopefully, the presentation has provided a basis and structure for understanding the actual interactions that occur or that are planned in order to achieve positive outcomes in psychotherapy. In the next three chapters our focus will be on the psychotherapeutic process as it develops from the beginning stages to its termination.

Although the therapeutic process may be viewed and conceptualized in different ways, six basic aspects have been described as common to all forms of therapy (Orlinsky, Grawe, & Parks, 1994). These, briefly, are as follows:

1. The formal aspect: Therapeutic contract agreements on arrangements, roles, and goals of therapy.
2. The technical aspect: Therapeutic operations.
3. The interpersonal aspect: Therapeutic bond.
4. The intrapersonal aspect: Self-relatedness. The responsive self-experience of the individuals participating in therapy.
5. The clinical aspects: In-session impacts. The effects within therapy sessions of the therapeutic interactions.
6. The temporal aspect: Sequential processes. Essentially, the course of therapy.

We have already discussed most of these aspects of therapy process in our discussion of client, therapist, and therapeutic variables in psychotherapy. However, we shall now focus more specifically on the therapeutic process from its initial stages until termination. Therefore, let us begin with the initial interview.

THE INITIAL INTERVIEW

As already noted, most psychotherapy takes place because an individual, after experiencing some discomfort or dissatisfaction, decides that his discomfort will not disappear by itself and seeks some type of help for it.

Depending upon his situation, he may discuss the matter with his wife or with a friend who has previously received psychotherapy, or he may consult his family physician. Eventually, he may be directed to a particular clinic or to a specific therapist. In such instances, the potential client appears to take the initiative, himself, for seeking therapeutic help. In other instances, the individual may come to the clinic or the psychotherapist only after some urging or pressure from other individuals or agencies. Parents frequently are urged to seek treatment for their children by school officials when their children are viewed as problems in the schools. In some instances, one marital partner may threaten divorce if the spouse does not seek professional help; in other cases, a judge may require psychotherapy or counseling as a condition of probation; and in some instances, a family on welfare will decide finally to accede to the request of their social worker that they seek help at a nearby clinic.

Although all of these cases may appear to be in need of some kind of treatment and may make an appearance at the therapist's office, their reasons for seeking treatment differ. It is important to be aware of such differences and to try to ascertain the patient's reasons for seeking help, as well as why he or she seeks such help at this particular time. The therapist needs to understand the conditions that have led the patient to take this action. There is little sense in making serious preparations for therapy if it seems clear that the patient is really not interested in seeking help or in being helped, but is merely acceding to outside pressures. It is best to get this clarified in the opening session and face whatever the reality of the situation is.

Another important matter to clarify in the initial session is what the client views as his problem or disturbance. A serious attempt should be made to clarify just what the client would like to see changed in order that both participants agree on the explicit goals of therapy. If the client's complaints are vague or unclear, the therapist should strive to clarify them so that he or she has a clear understanding of what the client seeks in therapy. Not infrequently, the client may present a variety of complaints that in some ways may resemble a long shopping list. To give an implicit acceptance of all of these as matters that will be resolved in therapy is not a good procedure. Instead, the therapist should ask the client which of the problems he considers to be the most important or troublesome so that they can focus on them. Even though the nature of the client's main problems may change later in therapy, it is desirable that the issues or problems be stated as clearly as possible and that they be understood by both parties to the undertaking. Although some therapists appear to favor an approach that allows the client to verbalize freely with little intrusion from the therapist, this approach is limited if the therapist does not fully understand what the client is saying. I have found that beginning therapists in particular are sometimes hesitant to stop the client at a certain point and frankly admit that they do not understand what the client is trying to communicate. Particularly in the initial interview, the therapist needs to be aware of what the client is saying about his problems and what he conceives the goals for therapy are. If the therapist does not have an accurate idea of what it is that requires modification or change, it is not likely that he will be able to devise the most effective therapeutic approach. Also, if the client is asked to indicate the relative importance of the problems he presents, the therapist has a better understanding of what is most disturbing to the client and how the priorities of treatment can be arranged.

The therapist usually will also want to secure other related information. She will want to know when the client's difficulties started or began to be viewed as a problem by him. It may be worthwhile also to find out if the client's difficulties are related to particular situations or people. If the client's current living or family situation appears to play a role in his current problems, it would be prudent to explore this in more detail as well.

The setting in which the psychotherapist works will also influence to some degree how he interacts with the client and what information or clarification is sought. If it is a clinical setting in which the patient is first seen by an intake worker, then a certain amount of background information concerning the patient and his problems will be secured. It is unnecessary to essentially repeat this information gathering process. Rather, the therapist can simply ask the patient to tell him, in the patient's own words, what he sees as the main problems. Unless there are ambiguities in the report of the intake worker or there are certain areas that the therapist would like to have elaborated, the therapist can focus more directly on matters pertaining to therapy. If the therapist is conducting the initial interview, more attention would be devoted to the areas mentioned previously. However, I, personally, do not believe it is essential to get a traditional type of social case history for every client, unless there are particular problems presented. If the patient's complaints appear bizarre or there is a possible question of serious pathology, then the necessary inquiries and appraisals should be made. Otherwise, I would secure only the information that seems necessary for evaluating the client's problems and planning a possible approach to therapy. In other words, the focus is on psychotherapy.

The initial session, therefore, provides the client with the opportunity to present and discuss his problems with the therapist, as well as allowing the therapist to clarify these matters and to make some appraisal of the client. It is well for the therapist also at this time to ascertain the client's expectations about psychotherapy, both about matters pertaining to outcome and also about how therapy takes place. Just as there should be clarification and agreement about what problems will be tackled in therapy, there should also be clarification and agreement about what will occur in the sessions ahead. As was emphasized in a previous chapter, the client and the therapist may have quite divergent expectations about psychotherapy and it is important that these be clarified and discussed at the initial session. It is particularly important to find out what the client's expectations are so that the therapist can respond in an appropriate way. As a general rule, it is wise not to take anything for granted, but to be as explicit as possible. In this way, few false assumptions will be made. It is quite easy to assume with certain clients that they are knowledgeable about certain matters, only to discover that one's assumptions were incorrect. The writer, for example, recalls seeing an intelligent and well-educated woman for the initial interview and on the basis of some of her remarks assumed that she anticipated therapy would continue for a long time. Because my own appraisal of her problems indicated that matters could be handled in about 10 to 12 interviews, the client was informed that although she might have other expectations, the therapist believed that therapy would require only 10 to 12 sessions. The woman was, in fact, quite startled by this statement of the therapist and responded that she had only counted on about 5 sessions! The moral of this incident is that it is always wise to test assumptions wherever possible.

In the initial interview, therefore, the therapist should ascertain the patient's expectations about psychotherapy and attempt to orient the patient to what will take place in the light of the information he has secured. He must be careful to appraise the patient's reactions to what he has told him so as to bring out any feelings of disappointment or apprehension. An attempt should be made to clarify and work through these feelings in order to see if there is a viable basis for therapy. It is the author's personal conviction that therapy should proceed from a basis of clear understanding and agreement between the two participants. If the patient has reservations about what the therapist has told him about therapy, it is best to try to bring these feelings out in the open in the hope of resolving them. On the other hand, if the patient had expectations concerning a particular kind of therapy which the therapist does not provide, it is best to acknowledge this at the start, and perhaps, have the patient seek help elsewhere. Even this, however, should be done in a sympathetic and understanding manner, so that the individual does not feel "put down."

After the patient's problems and expectations have been clarified, the therapist should provide him with some brief understanding of how therapy will proceed, how long it may be expected to take, what will be expected of the patient, and similar matters. Thus, the patient will be informed as to what awaits him in the future and points of difference can be resolved. If the therapist is undecided about the future course of therapy or if there is some discrepancy between his and the patient's estimate of how many sessions are required, it may be desirable to compromise by agreeing on a trial period over a specified number of sessions. Increasingly, I have found this type of approach to be a useful one, providing one does this in a decidedly honest manner, and that it is not actually a means of seducing one into long-term psychotherapy. In essence, one can state that while 15 to 20 sessions may be required, the therapist is not completely sure about this, but a more precise appraisal will be possible after 4 or 5 sessions, at which time both parties can reappraise the situation and come to some new agreement. Freud, himself, encountered situations where he deemed it wise to undertake what he termed a trial analysis, and this seems to be an appropriate procedure in a certain number of cases.

In addition to the above matters, other matters of a more practical nature also have to be settled at the time of the initial interview. These include such things as the fee for the sessions, how they will be paid, the time for scheduling regular interviews in the future, the importance of being on time for appointments, and the like. The patient should also be given an opportunity toward the end of the session for asking questions about any of the matters which had been discussed previously and, perhaps, what his reaction has been to these matters. The therapist should also be observing the patient throughout the interview to note characteristic mannerisms and patterns of behavior and how he or she responds to the particular topics discussed. Sometimes the patient may verbally assent to something but his facial features and bodily gestures may indicate a more negative response. Depending on the situation and what is discussed, the therapist may simply note this and file it away mentally, or may indicate to the patient that while he said "yes," he didn't seem really confident about his assurance. In this way, the issue can be explored further. The therapist's observations of the patient along with the verbal material communicated allow him to reach some judgment about the patient, to formulate some predictions about the course of therapy, and to reach a decision concerning the acceptance of the patient for therapy. If the therapist has serious reservations about being able to help the patient or if for whatever reason he does not want to work with him, he should face this straightforwardly and inform the patient in an appropriate manner. If at all possible, he should suggest several other alternative sources of help which the patient might be able to contact.

The client also attempts to size up the therapist during the initial interview. Whatever fantasies the client may have had about what kind of person the therapist might be are now confronted with reality. If the discrepancies are too great, the patient conceivably may be disappointed and drop out of therapy. However, this does not appear to be a very significant problem in terms of the general appearance of the therapist per se. Of more importance is the impression created by the therapist in terms of what he tells the client about therapy, how he attends to the client's account of his problem, and how he generally responds to the client's concerns. If he communicates sincerity, interest, and competence, the client in most instances will respond favorably, will adjust his expectations accordingly, will generate a more hopeful attitude toward the future, and will look forward to cooperating with the therapist in their mutual therapeutic endeavor.

Thus, the initial interview and the initial phase of therapy are of definite importance for setting the proper stage for what is to take place subsequently. If this is carried out well, the process of psychotherapy should develop without unusual difficulties. However, if this is not done, and if ambiguities and misunderstandings are not resolved early in therapy, then there is a greater likelihood of premature termination and perhaps a slower rate or lack of progress altogether. The initial interview, or interviews if this seems necessary, should clarify the client's questions and expectations concerning therapy, and should result in some sort of mutual agreement between therapist and client at the end of the session or sessions. In fact, at the very end of the session, it is worthwhile for the therapist to summarize this mutual agreement and understanding.

Before proceeding to the next aspect of the psychotherapeutic process, it may be well to emphasize one point which the writer believes is of some importance for all psychotherapists and would-be psychotherapists. This is to never make the mistake of accepting what the patient tells you as the actual truth of what has occurred. This statement has frequently been received quite negatively by my students, so I had better hasten to explain what I mean by this statement. Essentially, what the patient tells the therapist about his experiences are his *perceptions* of events and his *perceptions* of others. While it is very important for the therapist to understand how the patient views the world about him, it also is essential that he remember that these are perceptions and not necessarily the true reality of the situation. It is essential that the therapist keep this in mind, for the two are not necessarily the same; and, if the therapist does not differentiate them, he could conceivably reinforce patient attributes which are not desirable. In more extreme cases, such as severe paranoid disorders and the like, this distinction is more readily apparent and there is no problem in distinguishing between the patient's perceptions that are clearly distorted and the actual stimuli and environmental events to which he reacts. However, in the large majority of cases seen in outpatient psychotherapy, the matter is much less apparent. When the patient describes his employer, or his wife, or any particular event, the therapist has only the patient's description for what has occurred. In essence, the patient presents his side of the story and usually we have no other account of the events depicted. It should be kept in mind, therefore, that we are getting just the patient's view of whatever he is recounting to us, and that while this is the base from which we work, we must not assume that what the patient tells us always has some external validity. These accounts or reports of the patient represent his perceptions, influenced also by what he is willing to recount to us at a particular time. If, as sometimes happens, the therapist does have occasion to talk to the patient's spouse, he may be quite surprised at receiving a very different account of the events previously described by the patient. In fact, the therapist may have difficulty in recognizing the spouse that he sees from the description previously provided by the patient. In some instances, these discrepancies are quite dramatic indeed.

Since the preceding account may appear to be quite obvious to some readers and, therefore, unnecessary, or, on the other hand, to imply that the writer believes all patients are liars, it seems worthwhile to elaborate and illustrate what has been said. If we saw a patient who told us that he was being followed by strange creatures from Mars who were spying on him, we most likely would not accept this account as an accurate one. In trying to understand the patient, however, we would want him to tell us all that he could about these strange experiences, and we would attend to his verbalizations with interest and no apparent disbelief. However, if we saw a man or a woman as a patient who described his or her respective spouse as cold, unaffectionate, and lacking in understanding, we are less inclined to remind ourselves that we are dealing with the perceptual report of the patient and not with the "true facts" of the case. The important thing is that the therapist should strive to be an objective observer and participant in the process of psychotherapy. Although he should try to understand why the patient sees things as he does, and should also be able to empathize with him, he does not have to give up his objective view of the situation. The therapist must not get caught up in the patient's perception of his situation and lose the objectivity required for helping the patient reorganize his own perceptions in order to function more adaptively.

The therapist's personal response to the patient is also a factor of some importance in this regard. If he responds in a very positive manner to the patient and identifies with him, he is more inclined to accept the patient's view as correct views, and to be very sympathetic and empathic, but also, perhaps, to lose objectivity. Surprisingly, if the therapist responds negatively to the patient, he or she is more likely not to accept the report of the patient as being accurate. In this instance, the patient by his own behavior indicates to the therapist how he may influence others to react negatively to him. However, the therapist has to be aware of his or her feelings in such cases and not to let such feelings interfere with the handling of the case. Besides the loss of objectivity, the communication of negative feelings, as distinguished from pointing out the consequences of the patient's behavior, may have a detrimental effect on the therapeutic relationship and subsequent progress.

A few actual clinical examples may illustrate what has been described above. One client with whom the writer worked for several years described his wife early in therapy as slovenly, unattractive, stupid, culturally illiterate, and lacking in understanding, to state matters briefly. Toward the end of therapy, the wife had somehow become attractive, intelligent, and considerate. Since the therapist never had the opportunity of meeting the client's wife, he could form no accurate picture of her or decide which, if any, of the client's descriptions were accurate. He could only conclude that in both instances he was dealing with the client's perceptions of his wife, and that it was these perceptions with which realistically he had to respond.

The writer also recalls many clinical staff conferences in which professional colleagues gave reports to the effect that a patient had a domineering mother, rejecting father, or a shrewish wife. When he inquired if the clinical worker had seen the mother, father, or wife, the invariable answer was, "No, this is how the patient described them." The description of a person by another may differ quite significantly from how that particular person is actually perceived by others, but somehow this difference is frequently overlooked. Thinking back, the writer can recall an experience early in his career which made him sensitive to the issue being discussed here. One psychiatric colleague in an outpatient clinic for veterans would frequently expound on his cases in the intervals between appointments. This colleague, who gave the impression of being quite involved with his cases, appeared to make a recurrent comment about many of them. This was something like, "Oh, this patient really has a bitch of a wife." After a number of such instances, I asked him one day if he had in fact seen the wife in question. His response was that he had not, but the type of wife the patient had was clear from what the patient had told him. I was intrigued by this since most of my patients did not seem to be married to "bitches." Being also very much influenced by psychodynamic views at that time, I made inquiries concerning my colleague's wife since I thought this might be influencing his own perception of his patients' accounts, but from all I could gather, he was happily married and had a good relationship with his wife. So much for theoretical insights.

The final illustration that seems worth mentioning here occurred in an outpatient staff meeting and was a rather unusual one. A husband and wife had come to the psychiatric clinic because they were having serious difficulties. Each was seen separately for an intake interview by two different psychiatric residents, and the staff meeting was held to consider the two applications for treatment. As it happened, the resident who had seen the husband presented his case first. In brief, his account was that the husband was trying valiantly to support and keep his family going. However, this was a difficult task for in spite of his working at two jobs, his wife was so completely inadequate. Although he brought in enough income, she was a poor manager of the household and could not run it efficiently. Besides squandering money, she did not take proper care of either the house or their two young children. When the husband came home, the house was a disorganized mess, there was no supper ready for him and the children were usually dirty and hungry. This will serve as a brief synopsis of the resident's report of the husband's interview.

The response by the clinic staff was one of great sympathy and desire to help this poor unfortunate and mistreated person. Consequently, there was a unanimous decision that he be accepted for psychotherapy, the greatest positive recognition that the staff could accord him. It was now the turn of the second resident to give his report on the wife, and it seemed as if both the facts of the case and the outcome were easily predictable. However, we were in for a surprise. The resident seemed somewhat perplexed and at first wanted to check to be sure that the right cases were being discussed. When this was confirmed, he began his presentation. According to his account, based on the interview with the wife, the wife was having a most difficult time trying to take care of her children properly and to maintain some semblance of adjustment. Her husband was frequently out of work, did not give her sufficient money with which to clothe and feed the children, would frequently go on alcoholic binges when he had money, and was physically abusive to both her and the children. If her mother had not given her money from time to time, she and the children would actually have had to go hungry on many occasions. When the presentation was finished, there was somewhat of a hush and then some rather angry reactions toward the husband. The sympathies of the staff had swung entirely away from the husband toward the wife, and now there was a strongly negative view expressed with regard to the husband. As a result, it was decided to offer the wife psychotherapy, and to change the previous unanimous decision to accept the husband for psychotherapy. He was now considered unsuitable for psychotherapy! It was as if the husband had deceived the staff and, consequently, was being punished. Although there were many interesting aspects of this staff conference, the point of interest for the present discussion is that the entire staff was very much swayed by and based their professional decisions on reports of the perceptions of the parties involved, and were not at all aware of or concerned about matters of fact or truth. In essence, they accepted the wife's version as the true one, without in any way seeing that both reports were similar in being unsubstantiated. No further comments need be offered.

THE DEVELOPING RELATIONSHIP AND EARLY PROBLEMS IN PSYCHOTHERAPY

As therapy proceeds, there is initially a continuing process of appraisal on the part of both participants as they begin to form some sort of relationship. If the initial interviews have clarified the nature of the problems to be dealt with, the client's expectations about psychotherapy, and the procedures to be followed, there should be a reasonably sound basis for the development of a mutual working relationship in therapy. In the subsequent early interviews, each participant has a chance to test out his earlier impressions of the other and to see if matters are proceeding as each might have anticipated. If these sessions are not perceived by the client as meeting his expectations or needs, he may express his dissatisfaction or he may show his displeasure in other ways. He may cancel appointments, he may ask about the use of medication, he may inquire if there are any quicker ways to be helped, or he may fail to keep appointments and drop out of therapy. If the therapist notes any cues which suggest dissatisfaction with therapy, it would be well to try to bring the topic up for discussion and clarification.

The therapist needs to be an astute observer of the client's behavior in the therapy situation and to be sensitive to any communications from the client that appear to pertain to the therapy process or interactions. Even though the therapist initially has tried his best to ascertain the client's expectations about therapy, and has appeared to reach a mutual understanding with the client of what is to follow, some clients may still entertain somewhat distorted and wishful hopes for therapy which are not being fulfilled. Consequently, the therapist always has to be alert to the explicit and implicit communications from the client, and particularly when these pertain to the process of psychotherapy, itself, the therapist should attempt to bring out and clarify the client's possible dissatisfactions. If a client should make some passing reference to an aspect of the current therapy and then go on to discuss some other topic, it would be well for the therapist to go back to this reference and try to ascertain what the client really meant by that particular statement. Sometimes, comments with a negative implication for therapy are rather disturbing to the therapist, and if the client goes ahead to discuss other matters, the therapist may remain silent. However, this does not appear to be a wise procedure, particularly at the early stages of therapy. Beginning therapists, particularly, appear to find this aspect difficult to handle and defend themselves against any queries from their supervisors by stating that they did not want to interrupt the client's flow of communication. Nevertheless, in such instances, the client's possible dissatisfaction or doubts about therapy are not explored, and a matter of importance for the relationship is left unresolved.

The early periods of therapy following the initial interviews are also those in which the roles of the participants become clarified. After the initial interview in which the therapist plays a prominent role in structuring what takes place, the therapist in most therapies, with the possible exception of behavior therapy, will allow the patient to determine the content of what is to be discussed. At this stage of therapy, the patient should be encouraged to talk freely and to ventilate whatever feelings he or she may need to express. This seems desirable for several reasons. As indicated earlier, there may be matters which the patient did not feel free to discuss with the therapist initially. However, as the patient begins to feel more secure and to place his trust in the therapist, he may begin to divulge more intimate and troublesome matters. Providing an atmosphere in which the patient feels free to share his concerns with the therapist also may facilitate some emotional release or catharsis, as well as contributing to a process of desensitization. The opportunity to bring up new concerns may also change the focus or goals of therapy in a more realistic manner as far as the patient's real problems are concerned. Finally, such structuring of the roles in therapy helps to signify the important role of the patient in determining what is to be discussed, as well as reinforcing the fact that no matter how troublesome the topic, the therapist is sympathetic, willing to listen, but does not function as a moralistic judge of the patient's behavior. It also indicates the role of the therapist as listener and reflector of feelings, which is important at this stage of therapy, and de-emphasizes the role of the therapist as someone who will necessarily provide direct answers and instructions. The role of the therapist may change as the need for such change occurs, depending upon the requirements of the individual's case. However, during the early stages of therapy, the opportunity for client expression appears worth fostering and reinforcing.

At this stage of therapy where the relationship is being formed, it is important that the therapist be perceived in a positive way by the client. If the therapist is perceived in this fashion, his or her potential impact on the client is more likely to be of some consequence. The various processes already referred to in terms of hope, optimism, and motivation to change are more likely to become operative. Consequently, it is important for the therapist to convey interest, respect, warmth, competence and genuineness in his interactions with the client. This should not be a staged performance, for most clients are able to detect insincerity on the part of the therapist and, on the whole, such behavior tends to have a negative rather than a positive effect. If for any reason the therapist believes she cannot work effectively with a particular client, she should try to analyze the possible reasons for this, and if necessary, refer the client elsewhere.

As therapy proceeds at this stage, each of the participants is able to form a clearer picture of the other and to anticipate certain expected behaviors on the part of the other. The client, for example, may get a better idea of what is expected of him and the kind of person that the therapist is. He will also observe what kind of material the therapist seems interested in and what kinds seem not to be received so well. Depending upon the type of personality he has, he may try to respond in ways he believes will please the therapist, or he may become antagonized by the way the therapist is conducting the therapy and is responding to him. Thus, some clients may tend to agree with everything the therapist says, while others will take the opposite stance. Interpretations of any kind, no matter how bizarre, will be accepted by some clients, while others will tend to reject even rather mild statements of inferred criticism. The range of client reactions to the behavior and pronouncements of the therapist may be expected to vary widely and they will influence not only what type of relationship develops, but the progress of therapy as well. The therapist, as a consequence, must be an astute observer of the client's behavior and constantly be alert as to how the client is responding in the session. Just as the client begins to form some picture of the therapist, a similar process takes place with regard to the therapist. With each additional session, he has another opportunity to see how the client responds to his various interactions and to perceive some of the client's characteristic patterns of behavior. As these become clearer in therapy, he is in a better position to evaluate the impact of his behaviors on the client and also to anticipate how the client will respond to various verbal interventions.

As the therapist secures a better understanding of the kind of person the patient is, he can adapt his particular approach or pattern of interaction accordingly. The therapist generally has several sources of information that allow him to form some hypotheses about the patient. The patient has certain kinds of complaints and he also gives the therapist some account of how these problems developed. In recounting this, the patient generally provides some information about his current life situation, and how he sees the world around him. In addition, how the patient tells his story and how he presents it to the therapist is also quite informative. Does he merely give a sketchy outline of past events, does he leave out references to important people in his life situation, does he have to be prompted to recall or include certain information, does he imply that his current difficulties are primarily the fault of others, or does he believe that there must be some organic or physical cause for his difficulties?

The style of the patient's communication, therefore, may tell us as much or more than the content per se. Most important, however, is the opportunity the therapist has to observe the behavior of the patient as he participates in the therapy situation. To paraphrase an old Chinese proverb, "One behavior is worth a thousand words," and although outwardly psychotherapy consists largely of verbal behavior, there are other kinds of behaviors and behavioral cues manifested in the psychotherapeutic situation. Actually, the patient will display in the therapy situation many of his characteristic patterns of behavior and it is exceedingly important that the therapist understand this and respond appropriately to such cues. The patient may be extremely deferential and obsequious, he may be overly demanding and critical, he may bestow lavish praise on the therapist, he may be anxious and tense throughout the interview, or he may have difficulties talking about a particular topic. The patient may also ask very personal questions of the therapist, may attempt to treat him as a personal friend or professional colleague, or constantly ask when is he going to get better. In other instances, the patient may give somewhat more indirect personal cues, but ones which, nevertheless, the therapist should note and respond to as he believes necessary. For example, if after a few sessions, the patient asks the therapist how long he has been practicing or how many patients actually have been helped by his procedures, the query should not be regarded as polite conversation or as a simple request for information. Such a communication would appear to express doubts about the effectiveness of the therapist's approach and the likelihood of the patient's being helped. Since this has very important implications for the patient's attitudes and expectations about therapy and for the developing relationship, it would be important for the therapist to bring out the patient's implied concerns and to attempt to clarify them if at all possible.

The behaviors and related cues which the patient exhibits in therapy are thus very important communications and sources of data for the therapist. The therapist has to be attentive to them and to respond to them in some appropriate manner if therapy is to progress satisfactorily. If, for example, the patient's praise of the therapist is really too lavish and out of proportion to what has been accomplished, it would appear desirable for the therapist to point this out to the patient, painful though this may be for many therapists. If the therapist is going to try to change the distorted perceptions and maladaptive behaviors of the patient, then it is best to deal with them as they actually occur in the therapeutic situation. Here is an opportunity to deal with actual behaviors as they occur in a real life situation. To the present writer, this provides a much better chance to try to modify patient perceptions, cognitions, and behaviors than merely talking about past events that the patient recounts, but to which the therapist has not been a participant-observer.

The behaviors that occur in therapy are actual behaviors which take place in the "here and now" between the two participants, and thus they should not be easily discounted or dismissed. Assuming that the therapist is an objective observer, the behaviors that occur in therapy and which are discussed constitute a part of the reality of the patient and the therapist. They are not fantasies or constructions of the therapist, but can be pointed out and, as it were, documented by the therapist. One does not have to present any theoretical interpretations which may be misunderstood or rejected by the patient. The latter may be reluctant to face up to the implications of his behavior. However, if the behavior displayed by the patient is quite clear, it is very difficult for him to deny or disavow it. For example, the writer recalls an initial interview with a young man. After describing some specific problems of concern, the patient mentioned an additional problem with which he would like to be helped—namely, to become more assertive in his interactions with others. This took the writer completely by surprise, since in terms of the patient's overt behavior in this interview, assertiveness would have been the last thing he would have considered to be a problem for this young man. My response was, "*You* want to be *more* assertive?" After the writer expressed this questioning view of assertiveness as a problem for therapy, there was very little discussion. The patient smiled, said he understood what the therapist was referring to, and that he agreed with him.

Although some therapists may believe that the writer's behavior in this instance was too confrontative in nature at this beginning phase of therapy, it was (and is) the writer's view that the patient's behavior was very clear, that it was important at the outset to try to clarify the goals of therapy, and that by this straightforward approach the therapist was indicating clearly that therapy was to be concerned with problems that needed help and not anything that the patient merely might mention. Since the patient was actually quite assertive in this interview, it seemed important and potentially therapeutic to point out the realities that were taking place right at the outset and not to accommodate any distortion or attempted controls on the part of the patient. Although the writer is both a biased observer and reporter of this incident, his behavior did appear to have a positive influence on the therapy which followed.

There are a few additional points that the writer would like to make in this regard. Although my psychoanalytically oriented colleagues will take exception, I do not believe that it is necessary or desirable to bring in the concept of transference in dealing with the manifested behaviors of the client. Whether the client developed such behavioral patterns when he was a child in response to his parents is beside the point, and although explaining it to him in this way may be satisfying to the therapist as a means of demonstrating his knowledge of personality theory, it will not necessarily change the client's behavior. In fact, in some instances where such an etiology is inferred by the therapist, it may be denied by the patient and followed by considerable debate until the patient overcomes his "resistance" and accepts the interpretation. Telling the patient that he is responding to the therapist as he has previously responded to his father is not of any critical importance at this point in therapy. The important fact is that the patient is responding in a particular fashion to the therapist right now and, to the extent that this type of behavior is both characteristic of the patient and has negative consequences, it is important that the patient be aware of his behavior and try to modify it. The negative consequences of the current behavior and the need for change are the essence of the matter.

Another aspect which should be kept in mind is that the therapist should avoid having a preconceived and fixed view of both the client's problems and of his handling of the case. Although, as indicated earlier, it is desirable to have as clear goals for therapy as possible and to formulate some plan for therapy, the therapist should be ready to modify his or her own perceptions and formulations as required by the continued contacts with the clients. What seemed very clear initially may seem less clear as therapy progresses, and other problems may also come to the fore. Certain behavioral patterns that were not very evident at the beginning of therapy may become visible as the patient becomes more involved in therapy or as he feels more secure in his relationship with the therapist. The writer also feels strongly that preconceived notions of the "dynamics" of a case based on the initial complaints of the client should not be held too rigidly and/or forced down the client's throat. Rather, they should be seen as possible hypotheses which may be confirmed or rejected by subsequent events in therapy. In fact, the model of the scientific approach of having hypotheses that are viewed as working hypotheses only, and which require subsequent confirmation if they are to be retained, is a good one for all psychotherapists to follow.

The early stages of psychotherapy are thus important for a number of reasons. They allow the therapist additional opportunities to appraise the patient and to observe characteristic patterns of behavior. As the therapist gets to know the patient better, she is better able to plan and adjust her therapeutic procedures accordingly, and, eventually, to take a more directive role in therapy if this seems indicated. During this period, furthermore, the therapist has to be particularly alert to any possible communications from the patient concerning therapy or the therapist, so that any misperceptions or negative reactions can be clarified. It is in the very early stages of therapy that such a problem as continuation in therapy is most critical, and the therapist has to alert to any cues from the patient that may indicate dissatisfaction or disappointment. Such feelings and attitudes on the part of the patient also impede the development of a positive relationship with the therapist which is of basic importance both for continuation, and for subsequent progress in therapy. The therapist, however, should not attempt to keep the patient in therapy by making unrealistic promises or by catering to any demands of the patient, regardless of their therapeutic implications. Although such behaviors on the part of the therapist conceivably may keep the patient in therapy for awhile, in the long run they are self-defeating and not in the best interests of the patient.

The therapist also has to be attentive to such possible problems as the client's being late for appointments, the cancellation of appointments, and of even greater significance, the failure to show up for a scheduled appointment. The therapist should not ignore such behaviors but should comment on them, and if the client does not volunteer an answer, a further query should be made. Reasonable explanations for being late or for cancellations should be accepted without any further comment from the therapist. The fact that the therapist notices and comments on such behavior is sufficient to indicate that it is of some importance in therapy. However, if such behavior occurs again, then it may have to be discussed in greater detail and its negative implications for therapy pointed out to the client. Failure to keep an appointment without notifying the therapist appears to be a more serious matter and would appear so even to the client. It is also predictive of premature termination from therapy (Berrigan & Garfield, 1981). Consequently, this is something which has to be discussed with the client and an attempt made to ascertain the reasons for such behavior. It is quite important that the therapist in such instances clearly differentiates his role from that of a parent or authority figure who has caught someone in a misdeed and is considering possible punishment. The therapist's concern has to be in terms of the implication of the client's behavior for psychotherapy. He is not questioning the client because he has misbehaved or is being impolite and inconsiderate. Whereas the latter implications are certainly there, the focus should be in terms of what this signifies for psychotherapy and what reasons there may be for possibly avoiding the therapeutic session. The therapist must not act in a punitive fashion and must clearly communicate that the concern is a therapeutic one. It is understandable that the therapist may be upset at such behavior for in a real sense it is a negation of his therapeutic efforts, but again, he has to strive for objectivity and reflect this in his concern for the therapeutic relationship. The usual matters of politeness and social etiquette do not apply in this situation.

Missing appointments appears to reflect a lack of desire to continue in therapy or dissatisfaction with the way therapy is going. It is likely that the client may have already communicated such feelings in subtle ways which may have been overlooked by the therapist. When such a pattern occurs, therefore, it may be useful for the therapist to review his therapy notes and recollections of previous sessions in order to discover any possible indications or causes for this behavior which may have been overlooked previously, and to formulate some possible hypotheses for the client's behavior. In discussing the matter with the client, the therapist should be alert for any possible indication of dissatisfaction which the client may not want to verbalize openly. The therapist then should try to construct some formulation of the problem and attempt to resolve it as constructively as possible. If, in fact, the therapist feels there are valid external reasons for the cancellation or missing of appointments, the relationship can proceed on a more clearly understood basis in which both parties have discussed a mutual problem and secured some resolution of it. However, if the discussion of the problem shows that the client has considerable misgivings about therapy or is continuing on an erratic basis because of pressure from others, a serious discussion about whether it is feasible to continue should be undertaken. This should be conducted in a manner that allows the client to make a decision to withdraw from therapy, if he is so inclined, without any feelings of guilt or of letting the therapist down. If necessary, the therapist, himself, should make the suggestion for terminating therapy at this point and also inform the client that if he should later feel otherwise and want to resume therapy, the therapist would be happy to see him. Although this may not be easy for some therapists to do, it appears better to terminate a problematic therapy in this joint fashion than to have therapy terminated by the client's failure to appear for repeated appointments. Although there is little research on this matter, self-terminated cases may be less likely to return for help in the future.

Finally, if a client misses two successive appointments without notifying the therapist, it is probably best to acknowledge this obvious lack of interest in continuing psychotherapy. A letter can be sent to the client stating that in view of his missing the last two scheduled appointments, the therapist assumes he is not interested in continuing therapy at this time. Consequently, the case is officially being closed. However, the letter can also state that the client may contact the therapist in the future if he so desires.

The preceding pages, hopefully, provide you with some understanding of what is involved in the relatively early stages of psychotherapy and of the therapist's role and responsibilities in this undertaking. It is also a worthwhile procedure for the therapist early in therapy to clearly state the client's problems as the client sees them, the therapist's own formulations on this matter, and his goals and plans for therapy. By writing these down in his notes, the therapist not only clarifies these matters for himself by having to formulate them as clearly as possible, but he also has a record of them to which he can readily refer. At a later stage, he may have reason to add, subtract, or in other ways to change his original plans. However, the original complaints which have brought the client into therapy should be a main focus both in guiding therapy, and in evaluating the subsequent outcome. If a client seeks out therapy because he is afraid to leave his house and at the end of therapy it is noted that the client now gets along better with his wife at home, but is still afraid to leave his house, one cannot view the therapy as really being successful. Noting down clearly at the outset what changes are sought is thus a guide to therapy and a basis for evaluating the effectiveness of one's therapy.

It is also desirable for the psychotherapist to record his predictions about the future course of psychotherapy with each client and then put them away until the case is terminated. In this way, the therapist can check the accuracy of his formulations and predictions, and perhaps, as a result, modify and improve some of his views of the psychotherapeutic process. This can be quite a sobering experience for the therapist. For example, I once noted down my prediction that a given patient was too somatically preoccupied to be a motivated and involved patient in psychotherapy, and would drop out of therapy before the eighth interview. As it turned out, he stayed in therapy with me for almost four years and never missed an interview! I also learned a fair amount from this case. I also have learned that many of my predictions were not supported by the subsequent events in psychotherapy, and this has led me to modify some of my views over the years. The more specific and concrete the prediction one makes, the easier it is to support or reject it, and conversely, certain predictions about the dynamics of the case cannot be verified or rejected unless the predictions are translated into some kind of behavioral or operational terms. There is one possible danger, perhaps, in making such predictions, in that a therapist might try to make his predictions come true, a self-fulfilling prophecy as it were. However, this does not appear too likely, and a therapist who would deceive himself in this fashion would probably deceive himself in others as well.

Before concluding this chapter, it may be well to add a few additional comments about some other problems which the therapist should be alerted to during the first few interviews. As a general rule, the therapist should take the responsibility for the direction in which therapy should move. Consequently, he should be sensitive to patient behaviors in therapy which somehow seem to be opposite to the agreed upon goals of therapy, or which appear to be headed in directions which he believes are undesirable. Since the behaviors and interactions which occur in the early interviews may well set a pattern for later ones, it is important that the therapist intervene constructively in order to try to set therapy on an appropriate course. If, for example, the patient avoids talking about the problems for which he or she seeks therapy, it is appropriate for the therapist to point this out and to explore with the patient the possible reasons for this. Similarly, if a patient has been asked to engage in some behaviors outside of therapy, to practice relaxation at home, or to role play a particular situation, and obviously fails to do so, this has to be faced openly and its implications discussed. This, of course, has to be done in a manner which is not overly critical of the patient and which makes him defensive. However, it should be done, and it can be presented as something directly related to the mutually agreed upon goals of therapy.

What has just been presented is not meant to imply that if no progress occurs it is the patient's fault. Although this may sometimes be the case, it is also too frequently used as a rationalization by the therapist. What is being stressed here is that the therapist has the responsibility for trying to keep therapy on a goal-directed course. If the patient is beginning to show behaviors or patterns which appear to block proper progress, then the therapist has to take the initiative in correcting the situation. In some instances, if the therapist's attempts appear to be unsuccessful, then a more direct confrontation as to the patient's real desire to change and the desirability of continuing therapy should be faced. It seems better to face this situation early in therapy than to allow the therapy to drift aimlessly and eventually to be terminated on an unhappy note. The writer very vividly recalls one patient who talked incessantly about all kinds of topics but avoided those of more direct concern. I made several unsuccessful attempts to intervene, but then allowed the patient to continue in this matter, hoping that the situation would change. No real progress was made, however, and therapy was finally discontinued with dissatisfaction on the part of both participants. In this instance, the therapist was not forceful enough in trying to restructure what was occurring in therapy, and he allowed the early pattern to persist. It is possible that I may not have been successful even if I had confronted the patient more forcefully, but at least, I would have forced the issue more clearly into the open. In any event, the therapist should try to gauge the way therapy is proceeding in the early stages and modify his or her approach accordingly.

The early stages of psychotherapy, therefore, are of vital importance in the therapeutic process and early indications of progress frequently are prognostic indicators of ultimate outcome (Luborsky, Crits-Christoph, Alexander, Margolis, & Cohen, 1983; Marks, Gelder, & Bancroft, 1970; Mathews, Johnston, Shaw, & Gelder, 1974).

REFERENCES

Berrigan, L. P., & Garfield, S. L. (1981). Relationship of missed psychotherapy appointments to premature termination and social class. *The British Journal of Clinical Psychology, 20,* 239–242.

Luborsky, L., Crits-Christoph, P., Alexander, L., Margolis, M., & Cohen, M. (1983). Two helping alliance methods of predicting outcomes in psychotherapy. *Journal of Nervous and Mental Disease, 171,* 480–491.

Marks, I. M., Gelder, M. G., & Bancroft, J. H. H. (1970). Sexual deviants two years after aversion. *British Journal of Psychiatry, 117,* 173–185.

Mathews, A. M., Johnston, D. W., Shaw, P. M., & Gelder, M. G. (1974). Process variables and the prediction of outcome in behavior therapy. *British Journal of Psychiatry, 125,* 256–264.

Orlinsky, D. E., Grawe, K., & Parks, B. K. (1994). Process and outcome in psychotherapy—Noch einmal. In A. E. Bergin & S. L. Garfield (Eds.), *Handbook of psychotherapy and behavior change* (4th ed.) (pp. 270–376). New York: Wiley.

CHAPTER 8

The Middle and Later
Phases of Psychotherapy

As therapy progresses beyond the beginning stages the role and activity level of the therapist may change as he tries to deal with the client's difficulties. As described earlier, during the early interviews the therapist may be quite reflective of the client's feelings, as well as encouraging the client to express himself as fully as possible. However, depending upon the client and the nature of the problem presented, the therapist may become more active in certain ways. It may be at least partially correct to say that whereas common therapeutic factors dominate the early interviews, as therapy proceeds more specific factors are called into play. The relative emphasis of these two groups of factors, as well as when specific factors may be emphasized particularly, will vary with the individual client. In some instances, more specific procedures may be employed quite early, say the third interview or so, whereas in others, they may not come to be employed for several more interviews. It should also be remembered that what may be regarded as specific factors or approaches may also have a more general effect. If the therapist, for example, initiates the procedure of systematic desensitization, he is not only using a specific procedure for a specific type of problem, but by the very fact of directly doing something in a concrete manner for the client, he may also be generating hope and fostering confidence in the therapist.

In contrast to some traditional approaches to psychotherapy where there is a greater emphasis on a central dynamic conflict whose solution is expected to have a generalized effect and thus to influence a variety of more specific behaviors, the eclectic approach described here calls for a more diversified use of procedures, depending upon the types of problems presented. As a corollary of this, the role of the therapist is also different and, again, depends on the requirements of the case. To the extent that the therapist may want to employ several rather specific procedures as therapy progresses, his role will change into a more directive one. Any procedure that is deemed potentially useful may be used, and if a particular approach does not appear to be effective, a different one can be tried. This differs from such approaches as client-centered therapy or psychoanalysis. In psychoanalysis, for example, a major emphasis would be on free association and interpretation as the procedures for all cases, and while the analyst might be more verbally active as therapy progresses, the same procedures would be followed throughout. In client-centered therapy, the emphasis is placed on the necessary and sufficient conditions of therapist empathy, warmth, and genuineness, and the therapist's role theoretically would be consistent throughout therapy. In the eclectic approach described here, however, the therapist plays a more active role as the therapeutic relationship is developing and as therapy proceeds.

The therapist in this approach has to have a clear conception of what the goals of therapy are in each case so that appropriate procedures and techniques can be devised and applied. To this extent, the eclectic therapist has much in common with behavior therapists who also use a similar approach in appraising their clients and devising a therapeutic program which seems suitable for them. However, as already stated, an eclectic therapist does not limit himself to just behavioral approaches. There is much more emphasis on the therapeutic relationship and on the common factors in psychotherapy. However, in any given case, if the problem appeared to be quite specific and readily treated by means of a behavioral procedure primarily, then such a procedure would be used.

THE CONTINUING PSYCHOTHERAPY PROCESS

Let us now, however, discuss a bit more specifically what may occur as psychotherapy continues beyond the beginning stages. The client has had an opportunity to disclose the matters which are disturbing him and the changes he would like to see take place, he has had some opportunity for the expression and release of feelings, and he has had an opportunity to appraise the therapist and form some sort of relationship or "therapeutic alliance." The therapist, on his part, has been able to form a clearer picture of the client as an individual, to note some characteristic patterns of behavior, has become alert to possible difficulties in therapy, and has begun to plan his procedures for the therapy which is to follow. He has a potentially wide array of techniques and procedures that he can use. The only strictures are that the therapist select procedures that are applicable to the case in hand, and that he be reasonably informed and proficient in their use.

Among the procedures that the therapist can use are those described previously that have been developed by cognitive behavioral therapists. For example, training in relaxation procedures has been used successfully to help clients with symptoms of anxiety, tension and even hypertension. Furthermore, such learning and practice can occur outside of the therapy hour in the actual real life environment in which the client lives. Also, as mentioned earlier, if relaxation is taught as a coping procedure which the client can use in meeting future problematic life situations, successful performance can be quite therapeutic.

An example will help illustrate what has been described thus far. Let us take the case of a young man who calls in for an appointment because he would like some help with his personal problems. During the interview, he appears despondent and unhappy about his current situation. He is in his mid-20s, is working, and living at home with his parents. Besides his parents, there are no others living with him at home. He has recently broken off with the "only girl friend" he has ever had. At first he mainly verbalizes his feelings of being unhappy and discouraged. While he feels that life should treat him better than it has, the discontent seems to be of rather recent origin. As the initial session proceeds and he is given an opportunity to present his problems, a few things appear to be reasonably clear. He expresses some dissatisfaction about still living at home with his parents and being treated at times as if he were still a young boy. Nevertheless, although he has thought of moving out on his own, he has never put his thoughts into action. He gives the impression of being a somewhat shy person who is not very assertive. The main reason, however, for his current despondency appears to be the break-up of the relationship with his girl friend, which was of some significance to him. He feels strongly rejected and this event seems to have had a pervasive influence on how he views both himself and his current situation.

Although this individual is somewhat deferential and submissive in relating to the therapist, he also gives the impression of being interested in therapy and in trying to do something about improving his state of affairs. He has had no difficulties on his job and is willing to pay a moderate fee in line with his income. It was the therapist's impression that this young man was a reasonable candidate for psychotherapy and that arrangements could be made for future interviews. The individual did not appear to be seriously depressed; rather, his despondency seemed to be situational and very much related to his rupture with his girl friend which stirred up feelings of personal inadequacy as well as depression. Consequently, the therapist attempted to present some summary and formulation of what had been presented as a tentative basis of agreement with the suggestion that these might become more specific during the next interview. It was stated that the patient was currently despondent with his present life but that the loss of the girl friend appeared to be the event that largely accounted for his feelings. Therefore, this relationship would have to be explored in more detail. It also seemed that he was quite ambivalent about his home situation and this would also have to be evaluated. Finally, it appeared also that he lacked confidence more generally in his interpersonal relations, and felt he wasn't able to assert himself in some situations where such behaviors would have been beneficial. These were then set up as three problem areas that the patient felt were important and that we would attempt to work with in therapy. In answer to the patient's question about how long therapy would take, the therapist informed him that while one could not always give a precise answer, it did seem that approximately 10 to 15 sessions might be sufficient. The patient was also informed that we would be better able to judge this matter after 4 or 5 sessions. Since the patient had no particular expectations about what would take place in therapy, but was willing to do "whatever was requested," little time was spent on this matter.

Because the initial interview is of particular importance, it has been presented in greater detail than the remainder of the therapy in this brief illustrative case. In the second interview, the patient was encouraged to go into more detail about the problem areas designated previously and to express his feelings as fully as possible. This he did reasonably well, devoting most of the time to describing his relationship with his former girl friend. During this session, the patient was the active participant and did most of the talking. The therapist primarily responded by reflecting the patient's feelings, emphasizing an occasional point made by the patient, and occasionally asking a question for purposes of clarification. From the therapist's standpoint, at least, the session went well and the patient was involved with his retelling of his experiences. At the third interview, the patient appeared to be noticeably less despondent and during the interview appeared to be organizing his own perceptions and understanding of what had taken place. This was noted and verbally reinforced by the therapist. Some of the patient's difficulties in his relationship with his former girl friend also became clearer during this interview and attention was drawn to them by the therapist in a noncritical but questioning manner—"Do you think that perhaps some of the difficulties you are describing were due to the fact that you always asked your girl friend to make the decisions, and that she felt you should make them?" Thus, in this interview, the therapist became more active in suggesting possible characteristic behaviors of the patient which might account for some of his difficulties. At the same time, he demonstrated close interest in the patient and what he was saying, as well as reinforcing the patient's attempts to examine his patterns of behavior in the past and to see how his behaviors contributed to the problems encountered. Some attention to increased awareness and understanding were thus important components of this session.

In the next few interviews, the patient's lack of assertiveness became highlighted even more as he began to discuss his problems at home. Attention was paid to his desire to be independent, but also that at the same time he enjoyed having his mother take care of certain of his needs. Certain references also were made to his somewhat similar behavior in therapy. Although the patient was cooperating very well in therapy and was motivated to try and change his behavior, he not only tended to be very respectful of the therapist, but also very careful not to disagree with him, even when he might not fully agree with him. Thus, apart from discussing characteristic behaviors of the patient, an attempt was made to illustrate what was being discussed with reference to the behaviors manifested in the therapy sessions. This seemed to make an impression on the patient and he verbalized the need for becoming more assertive. As a result, two specific procedures were used. He was encouraged to be aware of his lack of assertiveness in his interactions with others, and to clearly label the situations where more assertive behaviors would have been more beneficial. Along with this, he was encouraged to try to assert himself in these situations. In addition, some role playing or behavioral rehearsals were attempted in the therapy situation. Desirable behaviors were verbally reinforced by the therapist. Gradually, the patient became more assertive in the therapy situation and apparently, from his verbal reports, more assertive outside the therapy situation.

The above excerpt should provide at least some brief illustration of how the therapist may proceed in working with a client and how different emphases and procedures may be employed at different stages as psychotherapy progresses. Different cases would require somewhat different emphases although the general overall pattern might be quite similar. In some cases, I have suggested or instructed clients to carry out a specific task as a means of overcoming certain avoidance behaviors. For example, I had one male client who was particularly shy in relating to women. I instructed him to seat himself at a table in the college dining room that was occupied mainly by women students. I also told him to engage in conversation with his fellow students and to repeat the procedure on successive days. Since he attended a small college emphasizing the arts, following my suggestion was not unduly difficult. On the whole this procedure proved to be beneficial and the client became more self-assured in relating to women.

As already mentioned, there are numerous procedures that can be used constructively in working with diverse cases in psychotherapy. There are instances in which asking patients to keep a diary or a record of certain incidents or activities can be helpful. Individuals with weight problems can keep a diary of the foods eaten, the time the eating has occurred and the circumstances. Marital couples can record events or situations that seem to lead to serious arguments or to periods of positive feelings and relationships. It is important, however, for the therapist to discuss such homework assignments or tasks with clients and to secure their cooperation. It is certainly unwise to force an activity on a client who responds negatively to it. In the latter case, however, the negative response may be indicative of problems in therapy or the relationship in therapy and would merit further appraisal.

The important features in this process are that the therapist provide a climate which is potentially therapeutic in terms of the hypothesized common factors in psychotherapy and which facilitates the patient's own motivation for change, and then selects specific procedures in terms of the patient's particular problems. If the hope for improvement generated in the beginning stages of therapy is accompanied by some tangible signs of progress, then the patient is thereby reinforced in his efforts for change and progress is enhanced (Garfield, 1986).

EVALUATING PSYCHOTHERAPEUTIC INTERACTIONS AND PROGRESS IN THERAPY

Although the focus at the beginning of therapy is on gaining a clearer picture of the client and his problems, on allowing the client an opportunity to express himself as fully as possible, to develop a tentative plan for the therapy, and to gradually select more specific procedures in terms of the problems presented, as therapy continues, the therapist has to consider additional aspects. As a continuing process, he should be appraising how therapy is proceeding and what progress is being made. Are matters going along in line with the expectations the therapist has or do there appear to be some unexplained problems or lack of progress? Without being overly compulsive about the situation, the therapist should keep an eye on the overall pattern and progress of therapy. If all has gone quite well in the beginning stages of therapy, unusual problems may not be forthcoming, but it is best for the therapist not to become complacent. Sometimes, a marked improvement in the client early in therapy may be the result of some situational factors which may be of a temporary nature. When the external situation changes, the client's progress may also be interrupted and in fact show a downward dip. As in all problems encountered in psychotherapy, the therapist has to appraise the situation as adequately as possible, and to utilize this appraisal to modify his/her approach in therapy if this seems desirable. If new problems should crop up as therapy proceeds, then again, the therapist has to evaluate what is taking place and react accordingly.

It is not possible to describe all of the various interactions that may occur as therapy continues, nor can one provide concise guides for appraising progress during the ensuing stages of psychotherapy. If the published results of outcome in psychotherapy are taken at face value, the best prediction seems to be that about two-thirds of those who continue in psychotherapy will show some improvement, or state that they are somewhat better than they were at the beginning of therapy (Lambert, Shapiro, & Bergin, 1986). While there are a number of issues and problems connected with the very difficult task of evaluating outcome in psychotherapy, we can postpone any discussion of these matters until a later time. For the present, let us accept the proposition that not all clients will improve as a result of psychotherapy and that perhaps a third or so may fall into this category. This at least gives the therapist some sort of reference point for having his own expectations about therapy be somewhat realistic, although it seems quite reasonable to assume that some therapists may be more successful than others (Crits-Christoph et al., 1991)—an assumption which most psychotherapists appear to hold in the belief that they are part of the former group. One can at least keep this average figure in mind as a matter of reasonable expectancy.

In addition to the possible *rate* of anticipated improvement, one should also consider the *amount* of improvement that might be expected. Obviously, this matter would be expected to be influenced by a number of factors pertaining to the individual case. More severe types of psychopathology would be considered more difficult to treat and probably to have a poorer prognosis for therapeutic gain. Other factors which have been mentioned also are the chronicity of the disorder, the duration of the problem, the situational elements involved, the client's personality resources, and his/her motivation for treatment. Thus, to be realistic, any prognosis would have to be based on some kind of adequate appraisal of the client. However, granting this, one can again have recourse to research findings as one means of securing some general level of reasonable expectation about degree of improvement. This also is a complicated matter which we will gloss over for the present and simply look at the results reported in typical investigations. To go into such problems here would divert us from the focus of our present discussion. What results have been reported suggest that maximum improvement or total "recovery" is secured in a small percentage of cases, noticeable improvement is secured in a large percentage of cases, smaller amounts of improvement in perhaps a smaller percentage of cases, and in a relatively small percentage of cases, the client becomes worse (Avnet, 1965; Lambert, Shapiro, & Bergin, 1986; Mays & Franks, 1985; Meltzoff & Kornreich, 1970; Strupp, Hadley, & Gomes-Schwartz, 1977). Without debating these data further, and accepting them as tentative facts, the therapist has to realize that in most instances the client may still have some complaints or difficulties that have not been fully resolved at the time therapy is terminated. At a recent symposium, for example, such experienced and well-known therapists as Hans Strupp and Arnold Lazarus emphasized that expectations about improvement had to be realistic and moderate (Norcross, 1993).

Although the preceding view and the reasons for it may not be very happily received by therapists and would-be therapists, it is the writer's view, as already emphasized throughout this volume, that the therapist has to be, or should strive to be, an objective observer, and should be informed about the research in his or her field. In research studies which use such descriptive terms as "Recovered" to indicate restoration to maximum level of functioning or the complete disappearance of all symptoms, the percentage of patients who rate themselves in this way rarely exceeds 10 percent (Avnet, 1965). In a related fashion, where numerical ratings of outcome are used, the percentage of patients who receive the top rating is also around 10 percent or so, and the mean rating of all patients is clearly below this figure (Sloane, Staples, Cristol, Yorkston, & Whipple, 1975). In some reports, also, which report statistically significant gains as a result of therapy, the measures used to appraise outcome still indicate significant pathology or below normal functioning (Kazdin, Bass, Siegel, & Thomas, 1989; Kendall & Norton-Ford, 1982; Levis & Carrera, 1967). Such findings have to be considered by the therapist as a background for his own expectations and appraisal of the therapy he is conducting.

As indicated earlier, however, the therapist should attempt to evaluate the progress of therapy with each individual case as therapy proceeds and not just at the end of therapy. If therapy does not appear to be progressing satisfactorily, the therapist should try to discover what is causing the impasse and what can be done to modify the situation so that a more fruitful course is followed. In exploring the situation, the therapist may consider possible events in the client's current life situation, certain features of the client which may not have been correctly evaluated previously, possible deficiencies in the techniques or procedures employed, or possible factors in the relationship influenced by how the therapist is being perceived by the client. Unfortunately, there are no simple instructions that a therapist can follow in such instances, and in some cases, he may not be able to fully ascertain what is blocking the progress in therapy or be able to rectify the situation. Sometimes the cues that are provided may not be overly clear, or the therapist may be unwilling to recognize them. For example, in one case that the writer was supervising, the client asked a question about therapy at the end of the session and was told to bring it up at the next session because her time was up. The question was how therapy was going to bring about constructive change. Although the therapist was instructed to be alerted to this type of query, he made no reference to it in the next session when the client failed to bring it up. In the following interview, the client again made a similar reference toward the end of the session and the matter was again postponed by the therapist. In this case, therapy was not progressing very well, and one of the possible reasons was that the client had some resentment toward the therapist for not answering her requests about the ongoing therapy. The therapist obviously was not very eager to face her implied criticisms and, consequently, let several opportunities for clarifying matters go by the board. When he finally brought up the matter at the subsequent interview, the client was able to express her feelings as well as her expectations about the therapist. The therapist then acknowledged his failure to respond adequately to her queries, and a clearer focus of what was to follow was derived. This did seem to improve the relationship and facilitate progress.

Sometimes, a given patient may indicate several problems which are of concern to him. Depending on the situation, some may be handled concurrently, or the therapist may decide to concentrate first on the one problem which appears most important or which appears most remediable. As therapy continues, it may be important to re-evaluate the original plan and, in some cases, to re-order the priorities originally established. For example, in one case, the client had mentioned being overweight as a very disturbing problem and as being related to her feeling depressed and sleeping a great deal. Since the therapist inferred that her low self-esteem was probably related to her overweight condition and that attention to this problem might help the former condition, as well as providing a specific program that the client could follow early in therapy, he suggested that the client get a notebook and record all that she ate and the times for doing so. The client agreed to this, but subsequent events lessened the importance of following this procedure. A more important problem was disclosed in the subsequent interview, and although the client did keep an account of her eating habits, she obviously was more concerned with other matters and her eating problem was relegated to a minor role. The therapist decided not to make an issue of this matter, and instead, the major emphasis was placed on the more significant problem. As this began to show decided improvement, the client, herself, announced that she had decided to follow a diet and stated with some satisfaction that she had already lost seven pounds. In this instance, the therapist thought it beneficial to modify his plans as new material was presented by the client and to allow the client to deviate from a previously agreed upon plan. If the situation had been one in which more significance were attached to the program of weight loss, the therapist's behavior might have been different. However, in general, when a client does not appear to be following through on something that has been mutually agreed upon, it is wise not to force the issue immediately, but to wait and see if some possible reasons for this may be ascertained. At a later point, one may have a better understanding of the client's behavior and thus be better able to deal with it. Although it is desirable for the therapist to have some plan and hypotheses to guide his or her therapeutic approach, the therapist also has to be flexible and be able to modify the therapeutic plan if circumstances indicate that this is necessary. Throughout therapy, therefore, the therapist constantly has to monitor and evaluate how therapy is going and to see if there appear to be any difficulties which require attention or a modification of approach.

THERAPISTS' PERCEPTIONS OF THE THERAPEUTIC PROCESS

Another point worth mentioning here pertains to the therapists' perceptions and feelings as he works with a given patient in psychotherapy. Although psychotherapy may appear to be a glamorous occupation to many people in which the therapist seemingly penetrates the deepest layers of the human psyche and does marvelous wonders for suffering humanity, in real life it does not appear to be quite so glamorous. Psychotherapy, like many other professional occupations, can be very demanding and sometimes a very tedious, frustrating, and even disheartening undertaking (Deutsch, 1985; Hellman, Morrison, & Abramowitz, 1986). What is sometimes depicted in popular accounts of psychotherapy does not necessarily correspond to the actual interactions which occur in therapy sessions. Miraculous cures are hard to come by and anyone who has listened to countless tapes of therapy sessions for either teaching or research purposes can tell you that not many of them are particularly exciting. This may be somewhat different for the therapist who is personally involved with the case at hand than for the observer, but even so, various factors will influence the therapist's perceptions of the case and his responses to it.

By the very nature of things, the therapist will perceive different patients in different ways and the demands of each of them will also vary. The therapist, as a person, will also respond differently to different patients, regardless of the professional aspects of the case. Some patients convey respect and admiration for the therapist, some are very likable and attractive individuals in their own right, and some seem to take to therapy very well, responding with definite and discernible progress. In such cases, therapy is likely to be a pleasurable undertaking for both parties, and the therapist may secure understandable gratification from his work. These kinds of patients make therapy seem worthwhile and provide the intermittent reinforcement necessary for keeping the whole enterprise going, even if other factors might also play a role in the patient's improvement. Anyone who has worked as a psychotherapist and has observed positive changes take place and received the grateful thanks of patients or their relatives, knows how gratifying and reinforcing such experiences are. However, such experiences, unfortunately, may not necessarily constitute a majority of the experiences which most therapists have, and to fail to acknowledge this is to place one's head in the sand. Except in the case of very prestigious clinics or therapists, who can afford to be very selective in the patients they accept for treatment, most therapists will tend over time to see a variety of patients who vary widely on almost any aspect of personality and psychopathology. A number of these will be considered as difficult or trying cases by most criteria, or as unmotivated or poor candidates for psychotherapy; yet, they also need help and need to be seen by some helping individual.

If a psychotherapist had complete freedom in selecting the cases with which he would like to work, it is conceivable that for purely selfish reasons he would select only those cases that he likes, finds personally gratifying, or with whom he feels there is a high probability of success. Things being what they are, this is not possible in most situations. Therapists need a reasonably full case load to earn the kind of income they feel entitled to, and clinic case loads also have to be maintained. Besides these matters, there are many people with serious psychological problems who are in need of help, and mental health workers have been trained and designed to provide this service for society. If the situation should change drastically and the demand for services diminish, there would be other types of problems which these professions would have to face. Be that as it may, most therapists probably have a heterogeneous group of patients, although there are differences, as noted earlier, in the clientele of different clinics and therapists. As a consequence, most therapists can be expected to have some patients who present particular problems for them (Deutsch, 1984). Generally, the difficulties will become more apparent as therapy progresses and as certain of them are brought into sharper focus. Before discussing this problem further, let us make a few additional observations about the perceptions and feelings of the therapist as he interacts with his patients in the therapeutic situation.

As indicated in the preceding paragraph, psychotherapy is a serious and demanding undertaking. This holds for the client as well as for the therapist, but it is the therapist who has the ultimate responsibility for seeing that therapy moves along and that some progress is made. The therapist, by the very nature of his role, takes on a significant responsibility when he accepts someone as a psychotherapy client. He also has to give a lot of himself in this undertaking since psychotherapy involves a constant interaction with another person. The interaction is also a somewhat unique one in that the focus is on the other individual's personal difficulties and problems. The psychotherapist is thus privy to human suffering and to private confidential matters of some importance to the client. Furthermore, he must be very attentive during the therapy session, not only to the content of the material the client relates to him, but to the behaviors of the client as well, and be ready to offer appropriate responses when indicated. Thus, the therapist must be in an alert state during the session. If the therapist has a reasonable number of patients, it should be apparent that his work demands considerable attention and effort on his part. It is conceivable, too, that the therapist may be affected by how the therapy with a particular client is going, by his remaining store of energy during the latter part of his day, by pressures from his own personal and professional life, and by specific kinds of problems which may take place from time to time.

In terms of what has just been described, it is important that the therapist not only be able to understand the communications and behaviors of the client, but that he also be aware of his own perceptions and reactions to the client and the possible factors influencing them. Certain kinds of clients may influence the therapist in certain ways, even though the therapist seemingly strives for objectivity in his dealings with the patient. The therapist, for example, may respond in a somewhat deferential manner to a very "important client" and be more reluctant to confront this client than he would another client, even when this would appear to be required. He may also be too hesitant in dealing with a client who holds the threat of a suicidal attempt over him, or conversely, he may try to demonstrate his therapeutic competence by being too confrontative with a very disturbed individual who is unable to cope with such confrontations. He may see some clients as overly demanding and thus not respond to some demands which are essentially reasonable. The therapist also may not always be aware that he looks forward to certain appointments with clients and with some apprehension to others. This is to say that the therapist, in spite of his erudition and skill, is still human and he, too, must be aware that his judgments and evaluations of clients are based on his perceptions, which at times may be somewhat biased by factors occurring in therapy or outside of therapy.

Once therapy is underway, the kinds of problems mentioned previously, as well as others, may make their appearance, depending upon the particular case and the type of relationship established. Consequently, when the therapist is aware of a problem in therapy he must not only evaluate possible client factors but also, his own possible contribution to what is taking place. Far too frequently in psychotherapy, the blame for the impasse or the failure in psychotherapy tends to be placed on the client. The client was overly defensive, was resistive to psychotherapy, or was poorly motivated—these are the kinds of comments one hears not infrequently at case conferences or discussions of psychotherapy. One gets the impression that it is the client's fault when things do not go well in therapy. While this may certainly be the case in some instances, it is not always so. It does, however, appear to make the therapist and his or her colleagues feel better about the poor outcome secured. In one case conference that the writer attended, a report of a therapy interview was presented concerning a case in which no real progress had been obtained after some 30 interviews. The therapist in his presentation was highly critical of his client and very frustrated with regard to his interactions with his client. This client was not accepting any of the therapist's psychodynamic interpretations and was seemingly blocking all of the therapist's attempts to help him. To the writer, it seemed as if a real impasse had been reached much earlier in therapy, that the client was obviously dissatisfied with the lack of any progress, and that the frustrated therapist was openly hostile to the client for his lack of progress. The participating staff members, however, tended to place most of the responsibility for lack of progress upon the client, and the clinic director even apologized to the therapist for assigning him such a poor case. In this particular case, some of the difficulties were apparent much earlier and should have been responded to at that time. The therapist should also have been more aware of his own perceptions and feeling about the client, and have tried to modify his approach to the client instead of persisting in what appeared to be a fruitless procedure.

When a patient demonstrates or persists in certain behaviors which the therapist believes are undesirable and as interfering with the therapeutic process, the therapist would be wise to try to ascertain the possible reasons for such behaviors. Is this behavior characteristic of the patient usually, or is the patient responding in part to events occurring in therapy? That is to say, if a patient begins to be overly critical of the therapist because he does not understand what is going on in therapy or because he does not see any visible progress, is this behavior simply a manifestation of the patient's essential negativism and criticality, or is there some justification for the client's criticism? If the therapist is able to appraise both how he has been perceiving the client in his interactions with him as well as how the client may perceive what is occurring in therapy, he may be better able to understand why the client is reacting in this negative and critical manner. He is then in a much better position to evaluate the current problem, to clarify it with the patient, and, hopefully, to do something to rectify it.

There are no specific rules that can be laid down for the intermediate or later stages of psychotherapy beyond the more general ones already discussed. Sensitivity, objectivity, and constant scrutiny and appraisal of what is occurring in therapy would appear to be required of the psychotherapist. He has to be aware of his own role and influence as they may affect the patient, and he must avoid placing undue blame on the patient when therapy is not progressing as he would like it to progress. He must also be very much aware of any feelings he has toward specific clients, particularly as these may affect his professional objectivity and handling of the case. For example, does the therapist reach a decision to increase the frequency of interviews for one patient and decrease the frequency for another patient for "valid" therapeutic reasons, or for some other reasons. Similarly, does he go out of his way to change the appointment schedule for one patient but steadfastly refuse to do so for another patient. Constant vigilance would appear to be required for good therapeutic management as well as for liberty.

CONSISTENCY AND FLEXIBILITY IN THERAPY

Above all, it would seem that the therapist has to be reasonably flexible as therapy proceeds. This should not be interpreted to mean that the therapist simply flies by the seat of his free associations or intuitions. The therapist should have some hypotheses to guide him and some tentative plan for therapy. However, as already emphasized, he has to be ready to test his hypotheses as time goes on and be willing to modify them in the light of new observations and information. Particularly when things are not going well or when problems arise, it would be desirable to evaluate the situation in therapy, to seek the reasons for this, and to modify one's plans accordingly. Furthermore, even if one is convinced that his interpretation of events is absolutely correct, it does not seem wise to persist in the face of consistent difficulties and lack of progress. A search for other explanations may be worthwhile. Again, it should be stressed that what is being referred to here does not signify a shifting from pillar to post on the part of the therapist, or a lack of some unified approach to the patient. Rather, the therapist should not adhere to a rigid formulation, derived either from theory or from his inferences about the patient, and persist in trying to ram this down the patient's throat. A too rigid adherence to some theoretical view about the patient's dynamics or focal problem can lead to frustration on the part of both therapist and client, and produce no meaningful change in the patient. The patient, if she is docile enough, may eventually agree with the therapist's formulations, but no particular positive change in the patient necessarily will be forthcoming. In other instances, the patient may well decide that he is wasting his time and money and leave therapy.

One other point should be mentioned here and this pertains to the consistency of the therapist's role in psychotherapy. Since the writer has stated that the therapist's role at various stages of therapy should vary in terms of activity and related matters, this may be seen as contradicting some views of therapy where consistency in the therapist's role is advocated. Client-centered therapy, for example, delineates a consistent role for the therapist in terms of providing maximum amounts of empathy, warmth and genuineness, and in avoiding making suggestions or being in any way directive in therapy. Other viewpoints in therapy also believe that inconsistency in the therapist's role leads to confusion or even an impairment of the therapeutic endeavor. This is particularly true in those therapies which emphasize the importance of the patient's role as an active one in psychotherapy and believe that it is not desirable for the therapist to behave in a way which will interfere with the patient's responsibility for securing change. Related to this is the feeling that sudden changes in the therapist's activity or role in therapy may be confusing to the patient since he has adapted to a certain style of the therapist and if the latter suddenly behaves in a very different manner, the patient may be uncertain as to what has produced this change and as to what is now going to take place in therapy.

While the above points are not without some merit, the writer has come to take a somewhat different view. It is true that in any relationship the individuals involved gradually form some consistent picture of each other and build up certain expectations concerning the behavior of the other person. When there is an occasion where the anticipated behaviors are not forthcoming or where very different behaviors are manifested, the individuals involved may be rather surprised. However, such unanticipated change or surprise is not always a negative matter, for on some occasions the surprise may be a very positive one, indeed. Although consistency is an important characteristic in many interactions, its value has to be appraised in the light of the specific situation. Too much consistency can be viewed as rigidity and, of course, too little consistency may lead to chaos. There are certain matters in which the therapist has to be reasonably consistent and others in which overtly his role may be superficially inconsistent or changeable. In such matters as expressing interest in trying to help the client overcome his difficulties and in being a person the client can trust, it seems important for the therapist to behave consistently. To do otherwise, would appear to seriously and negatively influence the client's hopes for improvement and the collaborative relationship deemed desirable for progress in therapy. Even in this matter, however, the therapist should be honest in how he views the situation for if the client detects a lack of sincerity, his trust in the therapist will suffer and influence his attitudes toward the therapist and therapy as well. However, in other aspects, a change in the therapist's role to becoming more active and instituting certain procedures which appear to be desirable, are inconsistent only in a strict behavioral sense. Such changes are not capricious ones, but ones which are taken in terms of a certain plan of therapy, and a suitable explanation can and should be provided to the client. From this point of view, what takes place is not a drastic change in the therapist's role, but instead represents a planned stage in therapy. It can be noted, too, that Alexander and French (1946) also advocated changing roles for the therapist depending on the client's problem, but their emphasis differed from that which is presented here.

How changes in therapeutic procedures are instituted in psychotherapy has to be considered and planned in terms of the individual patient, his particular problems, and the personality of the patient. In some instances, therapy can proceed in a very quick and efficient manner. Usually, the patient in such cases is well integrated, the presenting problems are reasonably clear and specific, and the indicated procedures can be followed with good effect. In other cases, however, the situation may be very different. There may be a multiplicity of complaints, some of them may be rather vague or diffuse, and the individual appears to be quite inadequate in many respects. In such cases, considerably more time may have to be spent in initial explorations, in trying to delineate the problems more specifically, and in a more general evaluation of the patient. If there appear to be features of the patient's personality and behavior that are central to his difficulties or which may constitute problems in therapy, then these may require special attention early in therapy or throughout therapy. If a patient, for example, is overly critical of everyone he discusses in the initial interviews, the therapist would do well to keep this in mind. If this is indeed a general characteristic of the patient, the therapist should at least entertain the hypothesis that the patient will at some point become overly critical of him, and he should be prepared to deal with it as the occasion requires. Depending upon the particular case and the stated goals of therapy, this behavior may be handled lightly, or it may become an important focus of therapy even though it was not mentioned as a problem initially by the patient. In a somewhat similar fashion, a patient who appears overly servile and dependent has to be responded to in a manner appropriate to his personality, as well as to his stated problems. In such cases, the therapist has to be alert to the problem of not fostering or reinforcing the patient's dependent behavior. If he decides to institute certain procedures, he should attempt to involve the patient in discussing what procedures seem desirable and discuss also possible procedures for helping the patient become more independent and assertive.

From what has been described, it should be evident that the therapist has to be a very alert and active participant in the therapeutic process. He has to appraise his clients as accurately as possible, devise some initial plans for therapy, be able to modify his plans when this seems indicated, and to monitor the process of therapy as it takes place. To be maximally effective, the therapist has to be flexible and to utilize whatever procedures seem potentially useful for the given case. He should not sit back and place all the responsibility on the client, nor should he follow the same approach with every client.

THE LATER STAGES OF PSYCHOTHERAPY

At some point, therapy begins to enter its later stages or final period and considerations about possible termination may begin to emerge. How this is handled will be determined in large part by how therapy was structured at the beginning and whether any specific time limits were set initially. In the latter case, there is usually a more specific termination point which acts as a very concrete guide for both participants, and may have a significant influence on how psychotherapy progresses. Although it appears that time-limited therapy is not utilized by the majority of therapists and is viewed rather negatively by a number of them, it has some special features which are worth mentioning. To begin with, time-limited therapy provides the client with a clear idea of how long therapy will take. The particular time limits are decided by the therapist or are a matter of clinic policy, and may vary from setting to setting. Some clinics have offered a brief type of time-limited therapy which takes from 6 to 10 interviews (Harris, Kalis, & Freeman, 1964). This may constitute a general procedure for most patients, or it may be utilized only for selected cases, for example, those who are facing a particular crisis situation or those who are felt to be unsuitable for longer term therapy (Butcher & Koss, 1978). In one clinic, for example, all patients were seen initially for therapy which lasts seven sessions and the intake process has been streamlined so that the patient is able to begin therapy without some of the usual delays which occur in many clinical settings (Levanthal & Weinberger, 1975). Those patients who are judged to have made sufficient progress are terminated at the end of the seventh session. Those who are considered to require further treatment may then be continued in therapy or referred elsewhere. This actually seems like a very sensible procedure since approximately two-thirds of the cases appear to be sufficiently improved to be discharged after the seventh interview.

The setting of a time limit for psychotherapy not only removes some of the ambiguity surrounding the length of treatment, but it also appears to set a goal for the client. Several pioneers of time-limited therapy have stressed this aspect (Rank, 1936; Schlien, 1957; Taft, 1933). The patient and therapist are provided with a finite period in which to secure whatever progress they hope to secure. It may thus act as a motivating variable in therapy, and to the extent that a specific amount of time is indicated, it may also generate a positive and hopeful attitude on the part of the patient. Several studies have indicated that time-limited therapy is actually as effective or more effective than unlimited psychotherapy (Gurman & Kniskern, 1978; Luborsky, Singer, & Luborsky, 1975; Muench, 1965; Schlien, Mosak, & Dreikurs, 1962). A more recent review of research on brief psychotherapy has also concluded: "Comparative studies of brief and unlimited therapies show essentially no differences in results" (Koss & Butcher, 1986, p. 662). Even if comparable results are secured for the two types of therapy, the fact that time-limited therapy is seemingly more efficient in terms of the time required would appear to make it a desirable type of therapy.

There are two additional comments on time-limited psychotherapy that can be mentioned here. Some therapists, like the writer, respond positively to brief psychotherapy in general but do not favor setting the same time limits for all patients. The latter are by no means identical. Some learn faster than others, some are more highly motivated, and some have fewer external stresses and stronger support systems. On the other hand, with the increase in managed health care and health maintenance organizations, there is a greater probability of time limits being placed upon therapists.

Where no clear time limit has been set in psychotherapy, it is likely that the client will raise some question about possible termination if the therapist does not do so himself. If the question is raised, the therapist should respond to this query, and if he has not anticipated the matter of termination, or if it comes along before any previously stated termination date, it should be explored with the client. As stated earlier, any question or comment which pertains directly to therapy should be responded to immediately, but a question about possible termination is particularly important. The client's reasons for bringing this matter up, even in a passing fashion, should be ascertained by the therapist and the matter fully discussed. Whereas such a communication from the client indicates that he has been thinking about termination, the therapist needs to find out why this is so.

In a number of instances, the client's comment or query about the possible cessation of therapy may signify that he feels he is getting along quite well and that he, himself, has been thinking that therapy should be approaching its end. If the therapist has also been in the process of reaching a similar conclusion, then the matter of termination should be discussed and a mutual agreement on it can be secured. In such an instance, the client, as it were, has anticipated the thinking of the therapist, and the matter can be resolved with little difficulty. We shall discuss such problems and related ones pertaining to termination of therapy in more detail in the next chapter. However, if the matter of termination seems to be premature or to possibly indicate something else, then the therapist has a very different issue to confront and he needs to discover what is motivating this particular response on the part of the client.

There conceivably may be a number of different reasons why the patient may at a certain point in therapy ask the therapist about how much longer therapy will last. If the patient has never been given any clear idea about this, it seems to be a reasonable question. Most individuals like to have some idea of how long a particular activity will take and most organized activities have a clearly stated or generally recognized time limit. University programs are considered to be four-year programs, mortgages are given for a specified period of time, football games have one hour of playing time, and so on. Furthermore, most people do not tolerate ambiguity very well. Thus, if the patient has not really been given an adequate indication of when therapy might be completed, this matter can be discussed and some suitable answer provided. If a patient's query about any matter seems reasonable, it is the writer's view that it should be judged and responded to in this fashion, and that it need not necessarily be viewed as dynamically motivated resistance to therapy. On the other hand, if this is not the case, then the matter must be handled differently.

In some instances, the patient may indeed raise some question about the termination of therapy before any such consideration would be presumed to be appropriate. If, in fact, this occurs relatively early in therapy, and there has been very little movement or change thus far, it would appear to be a rather unusual and unexpected query, and thus in need of an explanation. The therapist in such a situation should be quite forthright in stating that he is rather puzzled or surprised by this question and wonders why the patient has raised it. If this move on the part of the patient masks a more direct concern about lack of progress or any other concerns about therapy, it is desirable to bring the matter out in the open and try to clarify it. Sometimes the patient may have misunderstood or misinterpreted an earlier statement of the therapist and the issue can be clarified without much difficulty. In some instances, the patient may have had certain expectancies about therapy which were never clearly verbalized, and, therefore, an opportunity now can be provided for clarifying these views of the patient's. There may be many different reasons why the patient makes such a comment, and these can only be ascertained by suitable inquiry on the part of the therapist. If the patient's query does imply an impatience with lack of progress, then it is an issue of some importance. Does the therapist perceive the situation in the same way as the patient does? If not, why not? If the therapist believes that therapy is progressing satisfactorily and the patient has the opposite perception, then it would appear that the therapist has not been very effective in understanding the patient's perceptions and communications with regard to therapy. In such an instance, it is imperative that the therapist try to ascertain the reasons for this unhappy state of affairs and why he has been insensitive to the real feelings of the patient. If this can be cleared up, then therapy may be able to continue on a better understood and sounder basis. If not, it will remain as a problem, but at least if it is discussed, the therapist may be more aware of it and the patient may have a more specific idea of how long therapy may be expected to take and what kinds of progress may be anticipated.

If the patient is very dissatisfied, he may be inclined to terminate therapy, either by informing the therapist of his decision, or by simply failing to return for subsequent appointments. In these instances, the therapist has to accept the decision of the patient, but perhaps he/she may learn something from the experience and be in a better position to handle such problems in the future.

It sometimes happens in psychotherapy that the patient actually progresses much more rapidly than was originally anticipated. The patient's problems diminish noticeably, his/her situation looks brighter, and in general, life seems worth living again. Sometimes the unexpected improvements can be explained by the therapist. For example, the problems of the patient may have been influenced primarily by a specific crisis in the patient's life which has been largely overcome, or there has been a significant change in the patient's life situation which has, along with therapy, contributed to a real change in the patient's functioning.

In other instances, the possible reasons for the patient's rapid and unexpected improvement are not at all clear, and this may mystify the therapist. It is interesting that such unanticipated progress has been viewed by some dynamically oriented therapists as a rather negative development in psychotherapy instead of as an unanticipated happy occurrence. Such therapists have labeled this type of phenomenon as an escape or "flight into health," and have tended to view it as a serious form of resistance (Menninger, 1958). The reasoning here is that if the patient claims he is well, there would then appear to be no further reason for continuing in therapy; thus, the patient is able to remove himself from the self-analysis and confrontation which further therapy implies. Consequently, such therapists are not very pleased when a patient of theirs states that he is over his difficulties, is getting along very well, and sees no need for any further therapy. Although this would appear to be a perfectly rational view for most people, it is not so regarded by such analytically oriented therapists. They would make some attempts to interpret the patient's behavior as an attempt to flee from therapy, point out that many of the real sources of his difficulties have not been uncovered, that he is foregoing an opportunity to really come to grips with his problems, and that while his current symptoms may have appeared to clear up, this is expected to be a temporary phenomenon. Furthermore, even if the patient's symptoms do not return, he can anticipate the appearance of other symptoms, since the causes of the symptoms have not been brought to light.

Although the matter of flight into health has received attention in the publications of analytically oriented clinicians, the writer is unaware of any attempt to study this problem in any systematic manner. Admittedly, the incidence of this phenomenon is unknown and probably quite infrequent. Consequently, it would be a somewhat difficult problem to investigate. Nevertheless, in the absence of any real empirical studies, we have to be aware of the fact that we are dealing with theoretical inferences and hypothetical constructs. The writer's views are no better in this regard and the reader is hereby alerted to this fact. However, it does appear that more than one view can be taken to interpret or explain a given phenomenon and, that in the absence of any compelling evidence in support of one particular point of view, one should have an open mind and entertain more than one hypothesis.

It is possible that there may be some instances of patient behaviors which could reasonably be interpreted as flights into health. This, however, should not be taken to mean that all rapid or unanticipated improvements in patients undergoing psychotherapy are, therefore, to be considered cases which fall into this category. This would appear to be utterly unfounded and a clear instance of how a particular theoretical view may be blindly adhered to by a therapist with the resulting attempt made to push this interpretation and have it accepted by the patient. Too much of this kind of therapy appears to occur, unfortunately. Once the therapist has made an interpretation derived from his theoretical position, this interpretation is regarded as "the truth" by the therapist, as well as by some of his likeminded colleagues, and the attempt is made to force this view or "insight" on to the patient. Any nonacceptance on the part of the patient is then viewed as resistance. What is exemplified here is a rigid adherence to one hypothesis and a failure to entertain other hypotheses. However, having made this criticism, let me continue with the present topic.

It would appear possible to examine each case in which there is an unexpected report of improvement by the patient and to evaluate it in the light of whatever facts are available and whatever inferences are reasonable. If it actually does appear to the therapist that there is really no noticeable improvement in the patient, but the latter claims that there is and believes there is no further need for therapy, then the therapist should respond in some appropriate manner. In this instance, the patient may indeed be communicating a desire to leave therapy, and it would be worthwhile for the therapist to try to discover the reasons for this behavior on the part of the patient. Does the latter find therapy threatening, is he disappointed in the therapist, has he been encouraged by someone else to seek another kind of therapy or a different therapist, or exactly what accounts for his apparent reason for stating he is well and wants to end his therapy? Although the therapist should try to ascertain the possible motives for the patient's decision, and then to try to deal with these in a constructive manner, it does not appear wise for him to argue with the patient or try to convince him that he is making a bad mistake in running away from therapy. This only may make it more difficult for the patient to be honest in his dealings with the therapist in the future if there were a need to do so. If no resolution is possible, it seems best to accept the inevitable, to wish the patient well, and to offer him the opportunity to contact you in the future if he should ever feel the need to do so.

However, if after considering the patient's reasons for bringing therapy to an end, the therapist feels that the patient's case has merit, he should then acknowledge this and go ahead to discuss an early termination. If this is brought up early in the interview, it may be that this can be the last interview if this seems warranted. Otherwise, a mutually agreed upon date in the future can be set for the terminal meeting. I see nothing wrong in such a procedure if the patient does appear to be functioning better and if he clearly indicates that he is satisfied with the way things are going. The therapist, if he believes it is feasible, can go over the list of the patient's initial presenting complaints and ask the patient how these affect him currently. However, if the patient indicates that they are under control and do not constitute real problems for him presently, it seems best to accept the possibility that the patient may actually be better and that further therapy is not required.

Psychotherapy at present is far from being completely understood, and as a consequence, in the same way that we may encounter problems which were not anticipated earlier in therapy, it is conceivable that occasionally we will encounter some positive developments which are quite unexpected. This has occasionally been the writer's experience and it would seem likely that other therapists may have had similar experiences. The fact that we may be unable to predict such occurrences or to fully account for them, is an indication that our knowledge of the psychotherapeutic process is far from complete.

Consequently, when a client shows some improvement and asks questions about when therapy is going to terminate, it seems worthwhile to discuss this matter fully, and if termination seems reasonable, to consider an early end to therapy. If the therapist does not respond favorably to such a comment, he should evaluate very thoroughly why he responds as he does. There are undoubtedly reasons why he is reluctant to have the client terminate, and these may be quite varied. Among them are that the therapist, himself, has become overly involved with the client, that he resents the client's reaching such a decision before he has, that he has set goals which the client has not reached, or even that cases are scarce and he would like to keep his clients for longer periods of time. As a general policy, it seems wise to be attentive to the statements and communications of the patient, and to accord greater weight to them than to one's own theoretical views, heretical though this may sound. If, during what the therapist may regard as the early or middle stage of therapy, a patient indicates that he is sufficiently improved to want to terminate therapy, the therapist should modify his views and accept the possibility that termination is a reasonable decision. Nothing is really lost and much may be gained by such a decision. If the patient is able to function adequately, it is better for him to leave therapy and function independently. If the decision is premature, the patient can always return for additional sessions. On the other hand, to indicate to the patient that you do not agree with his own self-appraisal is to diminish his self-esteem, possibly increase his own concerns about himself, and even to affect the relationship in therapy. Now, however, let us turn to the next chapter and consider the matter of termination or rather, the termination phase of psychotherapy.

REFERENCES

Alexander, R., & French, T. M. (1946). *Psychoanalytic therapy.* New York: Ronald.

Avnet, H. H. (1965). How effective is short-term therapy? In L. R. Wolberg (Ed.), *Short-term psychotherapy.* New York: Grune & Stratton.

Butcher, J. N., & Koss, M. P. (1978). Research on brief and crisis-oriented therapies. In S. L. Garfield & A. E. Bergin (Eds.), *Handbook of psychotherapy and behavior change* (2nd ed.) (pp. 725–767). New York: Wiley.

Crits-Christoph, P., Baronackie, K., Kurcias, J. S., Beck, A. T., Carroll, K., Perry, K., Luborsky, L., McLellan, A. T., Woody, G. E., Thompson, L., Gallagher, D., & Zitrin, C. (1991). Meta-analysis of therapist effects in psychotherapy outcome studies. *Psychotherapy Research, 1,* 81–91.

Deutsch, C. J. (1984). Self-reported sources of stress among psychotherapists. *Professional psychology: Research and practice, 15,* 833–845.

Deutsch, C. J. (1985). A survey of therapists' personal problems and treatment. *Professional psychology: Research and practice, 16,* 305–315.

Garfield, S. L. (1986). Research on client variables in psychotherapy. In S. L. Garfield & A. E. Bergin (Eds.), *Handbook of psychotherapy and behavior change* (3rd ed.) (pp. 213–256). New York: Wiley.

Gurman, A. S., & Kniskern, D. P. (1978). Research on marital and family therapy. In S. L. Garfield & A. E. Bergin (Eds.), *Handbook of psychotherapy and behavior change* (2nd ed.) (pp. 817–901). New York: Wiley.

Harris, M. R., Kalis, B. L., & Freeman, E. H. (1964). An approach to short-term psychotherapy. *Mind, 2,* 198–206.

Hellman, I. D., Morrison, T. L., & Abramowitz, S. I. (1986). The stresses of psychotherapeutic work: A replication and extension. *Journal of Clinical Psychology, 42,* 197–205.

Kazdin, A. E., Bass, D., Siegel, T., & Thomas, C. (1989). Cognitive behavioral therapy and relationship therapy in the treatment of children referred for antisocial behavior. *Journal of Consulting and Clinical Psychology, 57,* 522–535.

Kendall, P. C., & Norton-Ford, J. D. (1982). Therapy outcome research methods. In P. C. Kendall & J. N. Butcher (Eds.), *Handbook of research methods in clinical psychology* (pp. 429–460). New York: Wiley.

Koss, M. P., & Butcher, J. N. (1986). Research on brief psychotherapy. In S. L. Garfield & A. E. Bergin (Eds.), *Handbook of psychotherapy and behavior change* (3rd ed.) (pp. 627–670). New York: Wiley.

Lambert, M. J., Shapiro, D. A., & Bergin, A. E. (1986). The effectiveness of psychotherapy. In S. L. Garfield & A. E. Bergin (Eds.), *Handbook of psychotherapy and behavior change* (3rd ed.) (pp. 157–211). New York: Wiley.

Levanthal, T., & Weinberger, G. (1975). Evaluation of a large-scale brief therapy for children. *American Journal of Orthopsychiatry, 45,* 119–133.

Levis, D. J., & Carrera, R. N. (1967). Effects of ten hours of implosive therapy in the treatment of outpatients: A preliminary report. *Journal of Abnormal Psychology, 72,* 504–508.

Luborsky, L., Singer, B., & Luborsky, L. (1975). Comparative studies of psychotherapies. *Archives of General Psychiatry, 32,* 995–1008.

Mays, D. T., & Franks, C. M. (1985). *Negative outcome in psychotherapy and what to do about it.* New York: Springer.

Meltzoff, J., & Kornreich, M. (1970). *Research in psychotherapy.* New York: Atherton Press.

Menninger, K. (1958). *Theory of psychoanalytic technique.* New York: Basic Books.

Muench, G. A. (1965). An investigation of the efficacy of time-limited psychotherapy. *Journal of Counseling Psychology, 12,* 294–299.

Norcross, J. C. (Chair) (1993, August). *Lasting lessons from psychotherapy practice: Six psychologists reflect.* Symposium conducted at the meeting of the American Psychological Association, Toronto.

Rank, O. (1936). *Will therapy.* New York: Knopf.

Schlien, J. M. (1957). Time-limited psychotherapy: An experimental investigation of practical values and theoretical implications. *Journal of Counseling Psychology, 4,* 318–323.

Schlien, J. M., Mosak, H. H., & Dreikurs, R. (1962). Effect of time limits: A comparison of two psychotherapies. *Journal of Counseling Psychology, 9,* 31–34.

Sloane, R. B., Staples, F. R., Cristol, A. H., Yorkston, N. J., & Whipple, K. (1975). *Psychotherapy versus behavior therapy.* Cambridge: Harvard University Press.

Strupp, H. H., Hadley, S. W., & Gomes-Schwartz, B. (1977). *Psychotherapy for better or worse: An analysis of the problem of negative affects.* New York: Jason Aronson.

Taft, J. (1933). *Dynamics of therapy in a controlled relationship.* New York: Macmillan.

CHAPTER 9

Terminating Psychotherapy

We have already anticipated the matter of termination by discussing the matter of unanticipated improvement and earlier than expected termination. However, in the majority of cases, this will not occur. Consequently, it becomes important during the final stages of therapy for the therapist to gauge the client's progress, to anticipate a possible time for termination, and to discuss this with the client in terms of reaching some mutual agreement on the matter.

The particular problems of termination will vary with the type of client, the length of therapy, the type of therapy, and the kind of relationship that has developed in therapy.

A very dependent client, as might be anticipated, has more difficulty in separating from therapy and in severing his relationship with the therapist than do less dependent clients. For a number of reasons, the therapist should avoid behaviors that tend to foster the client's dependency on him. Where the client appears to be a highly dependent individual, a discussion as to a time for future termination should be initiated as soon as possible. This allows the client to prepare for it as best he can, and his possible concerns about leaving therapy and being on his own can be dealt with during the later stages of therapy. Time-limited therapy has the advantage of fixing a definite time for termination at the beginning of therapy, but this is not a procedure that many therapists follow and it is not always possible. Consequently, the therapist has to be alert to signs of improvement and indications that a possible terminal date for therapy needs to be discussed.

One's goals for therapy will also influence one's estimate of the time required for therapy and its eventual termination. As psychotherapy is currently practiced, there is a wide range in the time therapy is expected to last. Analysts and analytically oriented psychotherapists at one end of the scale tend to think in terms of years as their units of time, whereas most behavior therapists and those who practice time-limited or brief therapy, at the other end of the scale, think in terms of weeks. A period of therapy lasting a year is regarded by some as a moderately long period of therapy, but is regarded by others as brief psychotherapy (Sifneos, 1965). Generally, long-term therapy which lasts several years is reputed to have a goal of personality reconstruction, whereas the briefer therapies aim at treating the patient's presenting complaints or resolving current conflicts. We will discuss some of the different emphases and issues pertaining to brief and long-term psychotherapies in Chapter 11. Therefore, we will omit further discussion of therapeutic goals except to point out that they both theoretically and practically can influence the length of therapy, thereby presenting somewhat different problems with regard to termination.

In more traditional, dynamically oriented therapy, considerable emphasis is placed on evaluating and satisfactorily resolving the transference relationship. Weiner and Bordin have described this issue very succinctly:

> Once a client has made substantial progress toward the goals of the treatment and reached a point of diminishing returns, two other considerations help determine when psychotherapy should be terminated. First, any lingering transference elements in the treatment relationship must be resolved, so that client and therapist can complete their work together primarily on the level of the real relationship. Clients who leave psychotherapy harboring unexpressed feelings toward their therapists may continue to be troubled by them, just as they were troubled by other unfinished psychological business when they entered the treatment. To avoid merely exchanging one set of problems for another, the therapist should work through all aspects of the transference relationship before the treatment is stopped.
>
> Second, clients should appear capable of continuing on their own to engage in the kinds of self-observation that they have profited from in the treatment. . . . Hence when improved clients whose transference reactions have been worked through begin to use their sessions less for discussing unsolved problems than for recounting problem situations that they have already brought to a satisfactory resolution by themselves, the time has come to consider terminating the treatment contract. (Weiner & Bordin, 1983, p. 372)

Where therapy takes a long time, it would appear that, regardless of theoretical assumptions, the patient becomes more dependent and attached to the therapist and the therapy. As a result, termination becomes more of a problem and more time is spent on discussing it in therapy. In brief therapy, where more specific goals are attained in a relatively short period of time, the possible problems of termination are generally quite less and little time need be spent on them. The patient's personality also interacts with the length and type of therapy so that in some instances a more intensive relationship is developed in long-term therapy, and it cannot easily be dissolved or terminated.

For the reasons just mentioned, the matter of termination has received more theoretical and clinical discussion in the dynamically oriented and long-term psychotherapies than it has in most of the other forms of psychotherapy (Freud, 1950; Glenn, 1971; Weiner, 1975; Wolberg, 1954). In fact, termination is not viewed as a particular problem or topic of importance in the briefer therapies, and it appears plausible, therefore, that the length of therapy is a critical variable in creating the problem. Theoretical notions of separation also play a role in the matter of termination in the psychodynamic therapies (Glenn, 1971).

Putting aside differences among the different therapeutic approaches for the moment, let us look more generally at the possible clues the therapist may receive that suggest that termination should be considered. The most obvious one is that the patient's complaints have disappeared. If the patient recounts evidence of continuous progress and satisfaction with therapy, then the therapist clearly should consider termination in the near future and bring the matter up for discussion. If the patient agrees readily to an early end to therapy or even mentions that he had been wondering about this, too, a definite date can be agreed upon and therapy terminated forthwith, as already mentioned in the preceding chapter. In the present instance, however, the improvement is more in line with the therapist's expectations and termination is the final step in what has been occurring in therapy. Unless the therapist believes in interminable psychotherapy, all psychotherapy, good or bad, has to have an ending.

In some cases, the client, while showing some improvement, does not communicate it as clearly as in the previous case. However, the client seems to have relatively little of importance to talk about and seems preoccupied in a positive way with his current life activities. When the therapist pursues this further, it does appear that while all of the client's problems have not been fully resolved, he is functioning quite well and feels optimistic about his future situation. In other words, the client does not feel he has any significant problems and believes he can handle those he has. When the matter of possible termination is mentioned, such a client may make the comment that he has also thought about this and that essentially therapy has served its purpose.

The groups of cases mentioned above present no problems with reference to termination. There are other cases, however, which do. Some of these are the dependent type of person referred to earlier, while with others therapy has not always progressed in a uniform or clear manner. With very dependent individuals, even in cases of noticeable improvement, it is important that therapy not be prolonged unnecessarily and that the patient be alerted and reminded of termination as early as possible. Although such patients may at times be overtly laudatory of the therapist, he should, as much as possible, avoid behaviors that reinforce the dependency patterns of the patient. Clues about such matters will be apparent early in therapy so that the therapist should be able to anticipate probable problems and plan some strategy for dealing with them. If possible, and frequently it is, some time indication should be given at the beginning of therapy. The frequency of interviews also should be set with such possible problems in mind. If reasonable progress appears to be in the making, the therapist should mention some probable date for termination to the patient so that this reality can begin to be faced as soon as possible. Also, if after the mention of termination, the patient seems to be very fearful or apprehensive about termination, it is sometimes a good procedure to gradually reduce the frequency of visits so that the patient's attachment to therapy is diminished and he is able to see that he can function adequately without the support of the therapeutic relationship.

Some case illustrations may be useful here. Many years back, when the writer was more involved with long-term therapy than he is at present, he worked with a very dependent individual who had a variety of somatic and interpersonal complaints. The patient was seen on a weekly basis and after several months he asked if he could be seen more than once a week. When asked why he thought this was necessary, he said that he thought it might facilitate therapy and increase the rate of improvement. While the therapist attempted to reflect the patient's concerns about therapy and the desire for more rapid improvement, he stated that he did not believe it was wise or necessary to increase the frequency of the interviews. It might make the patient too dependent on the therapist and time was an important factor in therapy anyway. The patient reluctantly had to accept this, although he mentioned the same issue once again a short time later. Over a period of two and a half years, during which time his dependency problem, as well as other important aspects, were given considerable attention, the patient eventually showed definite improvement. Despite the improvement, when the topic of termination was brought up, the patient expressed clear concern and wanted termination delayed. After some discussion, the therapist offered a plan of decreasing visits to facilitate the termination process. The next appointment would be in two weeks, the following one in three weeks, the one after that in one month, the next in two months, and the final session three months later. The patient agreed to give this plan a try and it worked out very successfully. In this case, it was believed worthwhile to stagger the visits with increasing time intervals so the patient could adapt more readily to leaving therapy. The patient's personality, plus the length of therapy, were both factors in making termination a problem in this instance.

In another case, a young intelligent woman with some difficulties in her interpersonal relationships was seen by me for fifteen sessions and made considerable progress. After discussing her progress in the thirteenth session, she agreed with my suggestion to terminate after two more sessions, with the last session scheduled two weeks after the next to last session. When seen at the fifteenth session, she stated that things were progressing well but she would feel more secure if we set up one future appointment. Since the idea of termination seemed still to be of some concern to her, I agreed with her request and set an appointment for one month later. About two weeks before our scheduled appointment, she called to tell me that her life was going along quite well, and she now felt that she did not need the additional appointment. I agreed, wished her well, and also told her she should feel free to call me in the future if she had any problem. Therapy thus was terminated in an amicable manner in which the therapist responded to the initial concerns of the client about leaving therapy and to her later expression of confidence to continue on her own.

In general, it seems like a good procedure to make some reference to a possible or indicated termination date some time before the time occurs. In some instances, this will merely be a reference to the tentative date mentioned as a possibility in the beginning interviews. As such, it is a reminder to the patient that therapy is not an endless process and that a finite number of sessions remain. It conceivably may also act as a possible motivation for the patient to apply himself conscientiously to making the most of his remaining sessions. If no particular time indication has been given at the beginning of therapy, it may be worthwhile at a certain stage later to discuss with the patient how he is progressing. This will allow for some exchange as to how therapy is moving, and in the light of this, some possible statement of what remains to be done and the necessary time for this. In this way, the matter of termination is approached in a reasonable manner and the idea of a natural termination point for therapy is communicated. Such a discussion also allows the patient to clarify his or her remaining goals for therapy and perhaps to indicate a shorter remaining period than that mentioned by the therapist. If this is agreed upon, both the remaining goals and the termination point become more specific and therapy can proceed to its end with a clearer understanding by both participants.

If, on the other hand, the patient feels that either little progress has been secured or that he or she would like to spend more time on a particular problem, these matters can also be discussed and their validity or utility evaluated. The instance of lack of progress is a more complicated one generally and needs to be appraised very carefully. If the patient's complaints appear justified, and the therapist has no ready solutions at hand, this should be discussed quite openly and frankly. The alternatives available should be indicated and the patient allowed to make a decision, including termination, if this is one of the alternatives. In the case of a request for additional sessions, the therapist should also evaluate this request. If it seems reasonable and specific problems are mentioned which are within the scope of therapy, a new tentative termination date can then be set. If, however, the request appears to reflect concerns about leaving therapy, these concerns should be brought to the fore and perhaps a staggered plan of appointments or similar plan should be proposed.

On the other hand, if the patient should bring forth a completely unexpected problem as a basis for continuing psychotherapy, such a statement needs careful appraisal on the part of the therapist. I have had some patients who verbalized what was their real reason for seeking therapy after their first two or three sessions, and I have viewed this as the patients using the first few sessions as the basis for deciding whether to trust the therapist with their real problem. However, if a patient brings up a new problem after what the therapist has considered to be a reasonable period of therapy, this is a rather unexpected and surprising turn of events. Has the therapist misjudged the case? Is the new problem a real problem or is it an attempt to prolong therapy? Clearly, in such an instance, a serious reappraisal of the case is called for.

Whereas some proponents of long-term psychotherapy believe that termination is a potential traumatic event for a large number of patients because of separation anxiety, this does not appear to be a particular problem for most patients. Since most of the psychotherapy is in fact brief therapy, as we noted in an earlier chapter, termination is not a particular problem and the therapist does not have to spend any significant period of time on it. However, as mentioned before, it is worthwhile to make a clear reference to termination several weeks before the anticipated time. In most instances, the client will acknowledge this and that is all that is required. If, however, there is some other reaction to this information, the therapist can proceed to clarify it with the client. It also seems worthwhile to refer to the terminal interview once again in the interview which precedes it.

Termination can be a problem, however, when the therapist without any warning whatsoever tells the client that the current interview will be the last one. Even where therapy has been taking place for only a brief period of time, such an announcement can have a very negative effect on the client. He is just beginning to know the therapist and to place some trust in him, when suddenly the rug is yanked out from under him. In the case of patients who have been in therapy with the therapist for some time, the sudden announcement that therapy is to be terminated today or that the therapist is leaving and the patient is being transferred to another therapist can be quite devastating. It is for such reasons that it is always best to anticipate possible termination and to share this with the patient. The sudden and unexpected departure of the therapist is a negative experience for the patient and should be avoided as distinctly irresponsible and unprofessional behavior, yet the writer can recall a few actual instances of such behavior. In one case, the patient had been seeing his therapist for about a year and a half when the therapist announced that this was his last session with the patient since he was leaving the clinic and going into private practice. Clearly, this kind of case management or unplanned shock treatment could have been avoided, and it would have been distinctly better for all parties concerned. This case was transferred to the writer and it required a fair amount of time for the patient to fully release the hostility he had for his previous treatment and to learn to trust his new therapist. It should be remembered that most individuals who seek out some form of psychotherapeutic help usually have feelings of low self-esteem and of not being highly regarded by others. A sudden notice of the therapist's termination without just cause or of the patient's transfer to a different therapist is not only very poor professional practice, but it can be viewed as another rejection by the patient with accompanying negative effects.

There is one other topic which also needs to be discussed before we conclude our discussion of termination from psychotherapy. This has to do with decisions about possible termination when inadequate progress has resulted. Although termination would appear to be a natural consideration where progress has been obtained, decisions as to termination when little or no progress has been obtained is a more problematic and difficult issue to resolve. Nevertheless, it is one that has to be faced in a certain number of cases.

In spite of the best of intentions on the part of the therapist, there are instances where the client and his problems appear resistant to change. The reasons may be diverse and frequently may not be fully understood. In some cases, the fault may appear to lie with the client. He may give the impression of lacking suitable motivation for change or his particular patterns of behavior may seem to be so deeply ingrained that there is little positive response to the various procedures attempted by the therapist. In other instances, the home and family situation of the client may be so utterly poor and overwhelming that whatever therapy is attempted seems woefully weak by comparison. Thus, in a certain number of cases, client or related situational variables may seemingly be the possible reason for lack of progress. As already mentioned, it is not infrequent that the blame for lack of therapeutic progress is placed on the client, and in some instances, this may be justified. Some presentations of psychotherapy have in fact emphasized the suitability of the client as a necessary condition for progress in therapy (Strupp, 1973).

In a certain percentage of psychotherapy failures, it is also true that the cause would appear to be the lack of skill on the part of the therapist or the use of inappropriate or ineffective procedures and techniques. The therapist may be lacking in the necessary requisites or skills and consequently handle the case in a poor and inappropriate fashion. There are numerous examples that could be given here and some have already been presented in previous sections. The therapist may have misjudged the personal strengths of the patient, he may have been too passive in his approach, he may have been too critical of the patient, and he may have failed to use more appropriate techniques. Whatever the reason, there are many instances where the main cause of lack of progress appears to be deficiencies in the therapist, and while many therapists may be unable to see the errors or limitations in their own work, they are able quite readily to see the inadequacies in the work of other therapists.

It is also likely that in some cases the lack of progress is caused mainly by a poor fit between therapist and patient, or what we can refer to as interaction variables. The styles and expectancies of the two participants may be too discrepant or the particular approach used by a therapist may be poorly suited to a given patient. This type of problem has been increasingly recognized in recent years although we have not advanced very far in our practical procedures for coping with it (Kiesler, 1971; Strupp, 1980). Ideally, the type of therapist and the type of treatment would be selected in terms of the specific client and his or her problems. This appears to be a desirable goal, but in practice, the patient usually is referred to a therapist by someone he knows, or in a clinic setting, is assigned to the therapist who has an opening in his or her schedule. The kind of treatment approach selected will depend on the theoretical preference of the available therapist. As a consequence of this situation, the therapeutic relationship that develops between a particular therapist and patient pair may not be that which is most desirable, and progress consequently may be less than satisfactory.

For the reasons just mentioned, it is conceivable that therapy may not proceed in a positive manner and after a certain period of time the lack of progress becomes quite apparent. This is clearly a problem situation which the therapist must evaluate carefully in order to ascertain what factors may be responsible. It is not good practice to allow therapy to drift aimlessly and the therapist has the responsibility for trying to rectify the situation. If he does perceive some possible reasons for the lack of progress, he can then react accordingly and attempt to improve the situation. In some instances, he may have been incorrect in his appraisal of the patient or misjudged the severity of his problems. The procedures the therapist is using may be inappropriate or inadequate, and will need to be replaced by others. If the therapist feels that he does not fully understand the lack of progress secured, it may be worthwhile to discuss this openly with the patient and to find out his views. If there do not appear to be any answers or solutions to the problem at hand, it seems desirable to discuss the matter of possible termination with the patient. In essence, the therapist's communication would go something like this. In spite of the best intentions of both parties, the patient has shown little improvement over a reasonable period of time. The therapist has examined the situation and tried to discover the possible reasons for this, but without success. He has tried a different procedure and discussed the matter with the patient in the hope of being more successful. However, little progress has been secured and this should be faced openly and realistically, even though it is disappointing to both therapist and patient. Consequently, the therapist believes he should discuss with the patient the feasibility of continuing therapy. If the patient agrees that termination seems to be reasonable, this should then be agreed upon. It can also be stated that the patient can see how he gets along without therapy, that he might continue on his own with some procedures which appear to be worth continuing, and that he could arrange for an occasional visit in the future if he believes this would be helpful.

If the patient should ask about other sources of possible therapeutic help, the therapist should accommodate him by providing several names of clinics or therapists. On the other hand, if the patient should indicate that in spite of the lack of any real progress, he would like to continue with the therapist in psychotherapy, the therapist should explore the patient's feelings about this and then, perhaps, agree to continue seeing the patient for a fixed number of interviews in order to see if any change will occur. The number of additional interviews should be relatively brief, and the ultimate decision about termination should be made when these interviews have been completed.

The above statements have been rather categorical in nature for the purpose of illustrating what might actually occur in a hypothetical case. What is actually done will have to be determined by the therapist in terms of his best judgment and appraisal of the particular case. What is being stressed here is that the therapist should constantly be evaluating the progress of his psychotherapy and modifying his approach as the situation appears to demand. Furthermore, if after a reasonable period of time, therapy shows little sign of progress and the therapist is unable to rectify the situation or to institute a new approach with some probability of success, then the therapist has the responsibility to consider terminating the patient's therapy. Some therapists may take exception to this view and believe that it is the mark of a frustrated therapist who, in essence, is rejecting his patient and turning him out into the cold. This may be the case in some instances, but it should not becloud the point being made here, nor should it be a rationalization for keeping a patient in therapy for unnecessarily long periods of time when there is no visible sign of progress.

Although there has been very little research on this problem, it does appear that some therapists are very reluctant to let their patients terminate therapy regardless of progress or lack of progress, and one hears of people being in therapy for 20 years or more. This seems, to the writer, to be a rather deplorable type of situation in which the dependency of the patient upon the therapist has been reinforced to an astonishing degree. One must really feel important if another human being cannot exist without him. In a study of one clinic, for example, it was discovered that some patients had been in psychotherapy for a very long period of time (Stieper & Wiener, 1959). When the matter was investigated further, it was found that a small number of therapists accounted for most of these patients. Furthermore:

When four judges roughly predicted who the 'long-term' therapists in the study would be, their pooled rankings correlated .79 with the criterion, suggesting a predictable dimension in the area of 'dependency nurturing.' The judges characterized the long-term therapists in these ways: therapist primarily desires to 'help,' and this feeling can be sustained indefinitely; tends to personalize relationship; tends to aim for marked changes in very sick patients; desires to succeed with intensive therapy; and needs to feel appreciated and effective (as a person and as a therapist). None of the comments made by the judges suggested that the therapists were dealing with chronic patients who required interminable support. (Stieper & Wiener, 1965, p. 66)

When the clinic administrators decided that it was desirable to close the cases, the therapists in question stated that these patients had been kept out of the hospital for many years and that to terminate their psychotherapy would lead to their hospitalization. However, the patients were discharged and a follow-up study made of them (Stieper & Wiener, 1959, 1965). Their rate of hospitalization and relapse was no different from that of any comparable group of patients and most of them continued to function without their therapy and without requiring hospitalization.

Rosenbaum (1964) in a thoughtful article has also discussed that problem. Among other things, he emphasized the importance of the therapist's attitudes towards therapy and how they may influence decisions concerning early termination from therapy.

> If the therapist believes that hours spent in therapy and weeks spent in personal growth change are necessarily proportional, he may encourage the patient to remain in treatment after the patient is capable of consolidating his gains on his own. These considerations include, for young therapists in private practice, the simple need to make a living. (p. 507)

Therapists in training are particularly likely to become involved with their cases and to resist possible termination, even when the case is a difficult one with many problems. In one instance, for example, where a number of difficulties had been encountered in therapy, and progress was somewhat limited, the client inquired about when the therapist thought they would be ending therapy. This was done somewhat indirectly and as the client, after a pause, made an additional comment, the therapist did not respond to the previous query. Instructed to do so in the next session and to explore what the client's feelings were on this matter, the therapist did refer back to the client's previous query concerning when therapy might end. In response, the client stated that she had been able to handle the problems for which she sought therapy and thought this might be a reasonable time to think about termination. The therapist, however, did not respond favorably or really directly to this view, but indicated that there should be further discussion. In effect, the therapist was reluctant to let go of his client, even though it seemed feasible to discuss termination at this point. Although there was room for further improvement, the fact that the client felt well enough to broach the topic of ending therapy, and that, on the basis of what had already taken place, the therapist was in no position to promise further change, a decision to terminate therapy was eminently reasonable. After this interview, the client missed a number of appointments, the interviews that followed were rather unproductive, and therapy was eventually terminated. It might have been better to have listened to the client and to have agreed on a mutual decision to terminate therapy. As Rosenbaum (1964) remarked, "the therapist should let the patient define mental health, improvement, or relief in his own terms" (p. 507).

No one likes to acknowledge failure in any undertaking of importance. However, unless one is successful 100 percent of the time, and the probabilities of this are very slight, one has to acknowledge some failures in his activities from time to time. The athlete is not always successful, the surgeon is not always successful, and neither is the psychotherapist always successful. Consequently, it is best to face reality directly and not to take refuge in various belief systems or rationalizations. When a patient does not show satisfactory progress, one can do what he can to rectify the situation, but if this is not successful, the facts must be faced and the idea of termination entertained. It is the writer's contention that in the long run this is the fairest and most justified way to treat one's patient. Hopefully, such instances will include only a small portion of those patients with whom the therapist attempts to work with in psychotherapy. In the majority of instances, the matter of termination will be a natural culmination of the therapeutic process in which the patient has secured some positive gains.

The discussion of the process of the termination of psychotherapy and its potential problems presented in this chapter has had as its central focus the welfare of the individual patient. In the field of psychotherapy, as in other professional or clinical areas, all workers may not agree on what is the best plan or procedure for a given case. This is particularly true where the research findings are rather limited. In the present instance, the material presented is based largely on the author's own clinical and supervisory experience, and only secondarily to the small amount of existing research. The issue of termination, however, appears likely to be settled increasingly by neither therapists nor researchers but by insurance companies and governmental agencies—at least in the United States. In such instances, arbitrary time limits may be set for terminating therapy. Although a case for time-limited therapy can be made, and has been made for certain types of problems (Garfield, 1989), one can question the value of setting such limits for all individuals.

In concluding this chapter, the following statements on termination can be offered as a concise summary of the points emphasized:

1. The therapist should make some reference to termination well before the last therapy session and be sure that the client is fully aware of what is to occur.
2. The therapist needs to consider the particular client, the length of therapy, and the type of relationship developed.
3. The therapist must be cognizant of his or her role in the relationship and handle matters accordingly. The welfare of the client always must be given the main priority.
4. In considering termination, the therapist should evaluate whatever decisions and referrals seem most appropriate.

5. In most cases, termination can be handled smoothly and without any particular stresses or strains. It should be looked forward to as a natural and desirable goal (Garfield, 1989, p. 129).

REFERENCES

Freud, S. (1950). Analysis terminable and interminable. In *Collected papers, Vol. V.* (pp. 316–357). London: Hogarth Press and the Institute of Psycho-Analysis.

Garfield, S. L. (1989). *The practice of brief psychotherapy.* Elmsford, NY: Pergamon.

Glenn, M. L. (1971). Separation anxiety: When the therapist leaves the patient. *American Journal of Psychotherapy, 25,* 437–446.

Kiesler, D. J. (1971). Experimental design in psychotherapy research. In A. E. Bergin & S. L. Garfield (Eds.), *Handbook of psychotherapy and behavior change* (pp. 36–74). New York: Wiley.

Rosenbaum, C. P. (1964). Events of early therapy and brief therapy. *Archives of General Psychiatry, 10,* 506–512.

Sifneos, P. E. (1965). Seven-years experience with short-term dynamic psychotherapy. *Proceedings of the 6th International Congress of Psychotherapy,* Selected Lectures, (pp. 127–135). London 1964, Basel/New York: S. Karger.

Stieper, D. R., & Wiener, D. N. (1959). The problem of interminability in outpatient psychotherapy. *Journal of Consulting Psychology, 23,* 237–242.

Stieper, D. R., & Wiener, D. N. (1965). *Dimensions of psychotherapy: An experimental and clinical approach.* Chicago: Aldine.

Strupp, H. H. (1973). On the basic ingredients of psychotherapy. *Journal of Consulting and Clinical Psychology, 41,* 1–8.

Strupp, H. H. (1980). Success and failure in time-limited psychotherapy. Further evidence (Comparison 4). *Archives of General Psychiatry, 37,* 947–954.

Weiner, I. B. (1975). *Principles of psychotherapy.* New York: Wiley.

Weiner, I. B., & Bordin, E. S. (1983). *Individual psychotherapy.* In I. B. Weiner (Ed.), *Clinical methods in psychology* (2nd ed.) (pp. 333–338). New York: Wiley.

Wolberg, L. R. (1954). *The technique of psychotherapy.* New York: Grune & Stratton.

CHAPTER 10

Theoretical Emphases and Issues

Now that we have surveyed the general features of the psychotherapeutic process, it is worthwhile to relate this description to some of the more general points made earlier. We shall consider again the matter of common and specific therapeutic variables, the emphasis by different schools of psychotherapy on cognitive, affective, and behavioral features, and some of the more recent developments concerning specific forms of therapy for specific disorders. Some of the possible implications of recent developments in health care in the United States will also be noted.

COGNITIONS, AFFECTS, AND BEHAVIORS

When individuals describe the nature of psychotherapy they generally make reference to verbal communications and interactions between therapist and client. To a large extent, psychotherapy has been a verbal therapy and has been referred to as "the talking therapy." However, since many of the problems dealt with are not purely verbal or cognitive problems, some individuals may wonder how verbal means of therapy can be used to overcome problems of an emotional or behavioral nature. This is particularly true in those cases in which there are also somatic complaints that have been diagnosed as "psychosomatic" in origin. Many therapists in training have a rather difficult time in providing a suitable answer to their client's query as to how psychotherapy is going to bring about a change in their condition. This is particularly true if the clients are relatively uneducated and not psychologically sophisticated. Beginning therapists tend to respond in an overly general and vague manner, couching their responses in abstract or technical terms. A typical response by psychotherapy trainees is that the client will have an opportunity to understand his problems, to talk about them, and to express his feelings, a response that may mystify the client and even lead him to conclude that such therapy is not for him.

An incident that occurred early in the writer's own experience may illustrate this issue. Working in a veteran's outpatient psychiatric unit, I was impressed with the large number of patients who dropped out of therapy very early. After a discussion of this problem, the clinic director agreed to let me see every patient who was recommended for psychotherapy after the intake interview. My objective was to orient the patient to his future psychotherapeutic treatment. I recall explaining to such a patient that we wanted to acquaint him with psychotherapy, the new treatment which he would be receiving the following week. In the midst of my very informative explanation, the patient got up from his chair, said he wanted "treatment, not talk," and departed. Needless to say, my good intentions were not positively reinforced. Nevertheless, the issue of how primarily verbal or cognitive therapies can lead to significant changes in human behavior and adjustment is an important one and worth discussing in terms of the major emphases in contemporary approaches to psychotherapy.

COGNITIVE EMPHASES IN PSYCHOTHERAPY

Early in the development of psychotherapy an important emphasis was placed on cognitive aspects. Although emotional reactions to therapy and to the analyst were considered to be important, their resolution was primarily by verbal and cognitive means. The verbal associations of the patient and the essentially cognitive interpretations offered by the therapist were considered the main techniques of therapy and were the means by which such emotional or affective phenomena as resistance and transference were overcome or resolved. Freud, himself, stated that while the voice of the intellect was gentle or soft, it was persistent and ultimately reached the patient. Nevertheless, the question of how cognitions or cognitive procedures actually produced changes in the patient's behavior and affects was never very clearly explained.

Some analysts also were aware of the possible limitations of such cognitive aspects. In several sources, one finds references to the effect that intellectual insight alone was not adequate for securing significant improvement in therapy (Alexander, 1963; Alexander & French, 1946). For example, a patient might secure what appeared to be profound insights into his problems and their causes, and could also verbalize them adequately, but still manifest his original symptoms even after years of therapy. The phenomenon must have occurred with sufficient frequency to have received the attention and discussion it did. Clearly, and correctly, it was viewed as a serious problem in analytical therapy. Some more recent appraisals of the role of interpretation and insight in analytically oriented therapy also have questioned their importance. Recent research on transference interpretation appears to challenge many long-held assumptions (Henry, Strupp, Schacht, & Gaston, 1994).

Although some people may appear to profit from the verbal-cognitive interactions which occur in psychotherapy, some apparently do not. Furthermore, we do not really understand either why some respond favorably to such interventions and some do not, or what is actually involved in this process. Are there some cognitive procedures that are applied effectively in the favorable cases of outcome and poorly or ineffectively applied in the cases of poor outcome, or is the type of problem or type of client the variable of importance here? No precise answer can be given here although it would appear that both of the possible answers suggested are at least partially correct or tenable. However, it is also tenable to consider that other factors may have played a role in therapy which did not receive as much explicit recognition or emphasis as the cognitive variables emphasized in the particular theoretical view of therapy utilized. As already discussed in the chapter on common factors in psychotherapy, influences may occur in therapy which are not officially recognized or emphasized by a particular school of psychotherapy.

Although insight-oriented therapy has appeared to rely on a cognitive approach in seeking to effect change in psychotherapy, such therapy was a long-term procedure in which insights were to be secured gradually as the relationship in therapy developed, and as repressed material slowly reached the patient's awareness. In more recent years, newer cognitive therapies have appeared that deal more directly with cognitions, are relatively brief, and which are based on different theoretical views of personality disturbance. One of these is Rational-Emotive Therapy or R.E.T., developed by Albert Ellis (1962; Ellis & Dryden, 1987). Ellis, after becoming dissatisfied with psychoanalysis, gradually worked out his approach which stressed that the client's maladjustments were largely due to distorted or unrealistic perceptions and cognitions. Since these cognitions of the client appeared to be causing the client's difficulties, Ellis believed that it was best to work with them directly and to help the client replace them with more realistic beliefs and expectations. Because of this emphasis, his therapy was first called Rational Therapy. Later, he pointed out that cognitions were intimately related to emotions and that emotional disorders could be caused by unrealistic or distorted cognitions. As a result, he renamed his therapy R.E.T.

Ellis also came to the view that many unhappy and disturbed individuals had common distorted views and beliefs which were at the basis of their discontents. These included the beliefs that they should be universally loved, that they had to be admired by everyone, that they had to be successful in every activity, and the like. As a result, many such unrealistic expectations could be anticipated and the therapist could deal with them directly and expediently. No time had to be wasted in trying to explore hypothetical unconscious conflicts or dealing with transference reactions. The therapist's role was an active and confrontative one in which the false beliefs of the client were exposed and constantly pointed out and demonstrated. In this approach to therapy, therefore, cognitions were explicitly recognized as factors of central importance in affecting therapeutic change. The distorted beliefs were identified, the patient was directly confronted with them as the causes of his difficulties, and he was persuaded to give them up and to replace them with more realistic views. Cognitions were also recognized as influencing emotions. Although patients were also directed to engage in certain behaviors and activities outside of therapy, this feature did not receive as much theoretical emphasis as the more purely cognitive aspects. However, in a recent brochure, Ellis has included an emphasis on behavior.

Since the appearance of R.E.T. on the therapeutic scene, there have been other forms of therapy appearing with a strong emphasis on cognitive factors as variables for affecting change. One prominent example is the cognitive therapy developed by Aaron T. Beck (1976). Originally an outgrowth of his work with depressed patients, Beck has extended his views to include therapeutic work with other types of disorders including anxiety and personality disorders (Beck & Emery, 1985; Beck et al., 1990). Although Beck's approach has a number of similarities with that of R.E.T., it also has some unique features which need not be spelled out here. Beck also places more explicit emphasis on combining behavioral techniques with his cognitive approach.

Another related development which was alluded to briefly in an earlier chapter is what is now referred to as cognitive behavior therapy. This movement was facilitated by the work of Bandura (1969) whose influential book stressed the importance of symbolic mediating processes in behavior modification. As the name implies, this development has been one in which attempts have been made to combine some cognitive features of therapy with either standard or modified behavior therapy procedures. Some of the individuals prominent in this development have been Goldfried (1971; Goldfried, Decenteceo, & Weinberg, 1974); Mahoney, (1974; Mahoney & Arnkoff, 1978); and Meichenbaum (1977). Meichenbaum, for example, conducted some research studies in which a combination of R.E.T. and systematic desensitization was purportedly more effective than systematic desensitization alone in treating such conditions as fear of public speaking and examination anxiety (Meichenbaum, 1972; Meichenbaum, Gilmore, & Fedoravicius, 1971). More recently, he has developed a cognitive-behavioral approach for coping with stress called Stress Inoculation Training (Meichenbaum, 1985). Thus, several behaviorally oriented therapists have come to recognize cognitive variables as being of some importance in their therapeutic work and have made attempts to include such variables along with their behavioral procedures. This compliments the use of behavioral procedures by the more cognitively oriented therapists. Such developments appear to offer some convergence of theories and techniques, and, hopefully also, to offer some promise for the development of more effective therapeutic procedures.

The Behavioral Emphasis in Psychotherapy

As already noted, the development of behavior therapy has been a decidedly vigorous and important development in psychotherapy. Arising from a more rigorous tradition and background in psychology and being quite critical of earlier approaches, particularly the psychodynamic ones, which emphasized unconscious motivation and inferred hypothetical personality constructs, the behavior therapists have placed their emphasis on observable behavior. From this point of view, it is the individual's maladaptive behavior which is causing the individual to experience difficulties and which has to be modified if he/she is to function more adequately. Consequently, it is behavioral change which is sought and this can be handled directly without having to go back into the client's early childhood or to deal with inferred conflicts and related matters. Furthermore, the process is more efficient since one deals directly with the problem at hand, and changes in the client's behavior can be appraised objectively. There is also a strong emphasis on the importance of objective empirical evaluation of the therapy that is carried out.

The behavior therapy movement, at first rather slow in getting started, has progressed vigorously in the last 30 years or so, and in many ways has been somewhat of a revolution within psychotherapy. Some psychotherapists, in fact, have viewed behavior therapy as distinct and outside of the field of psychotherapy, but there are few who take this view today.

Apart from the research emphasis and the accompanying stress on the objective assessment of outcome in therapy, an emphasis of some importance in this field, the behavior therapists have accorded behavior the significant place in psychotherapy which it merits. Even if one does not wholly agree with a behavioristic point of view, one cannot argue convincingly against the important goal of behavioral change as a desirable outcome in psychotherapy. Furthermore, if behavioral change is a desired goal in many cases, it is also perfectly reasonable to consider procedures which deal directly with the behaviors in question.

Although the doctrine of ascertaining the cause of a person's disturbance in order to fully treat the disturbance effectively has a definite appeal and also some merit, it is important to consider whether this is universally necessary. Although it is true that similar appearing symptoms may have different causes and, consequently, might require different kinds of treatment, one may not always be able to discover the actual cause, nor is it necessary to go over all of the possible past events in a person's life which theoretically might pertain to the development of the symptom in order to treat it. Diagnostic evaluation is important in deciding what the problems are and in formulating a treatment program. However, once this is done, then the most direct and efficient form of treatment should be used.

In any event, there is no good reason to fail to consider a therapeutic approach or procedure that deals directly with the behavior one wants to change and which appears to offer promising results. Furthermore, concerns about the emergence of substitute symptoms when the original symptom has been rather successfully dealt with do not appear to be justified (Baker, 1969; Nolan, Mattis, & Holliday, 1970; Paul, 1967; Ullman & Krasner, 1965). This concern, therefore, does not appear to be a valid one.

The emphasis on behavior is a salutary one which in many ways had been neglected in psychotherapy previously. Where behavior disorders specifically are a major referral problem, behavioral procedures and clear attention to behavioral considerations would appear called for in most instances. In those cases in which new skills or patterns are required for more effective functioning, it is not sufficient merely to discover why the individual has failed to acquire normal social skills, or to help him to express his feelings about his lack of such skills. He must be helped to learn the necessary behavior patterns and to be able to apply them to the socially relevant situations. Such a procedure clearly involves principles of learning and behavior, even though personal attitudes, beliefs and feelings may also be related to the behaviors in question.

To the extent, therefore, that previous psychotherapies had tended to emphasize feelings and cognitions, the emphasis on behavior provided by the behavior therapists can be seen as a much needed corrective emphasis. Even though behavior therapy may not be the cure all and end all for psychotherapy that some of its staunch advocates proclaim it to be, it will have made a significant contribution to the field if the behavior of the individual is accorded its proper importance. At the same time, it can be stated again that, except perhaps in certain cases, to focus exclusively on only one aspect of human functioning is to neglect other aspects which are also of critical importance. Some awareness of this, as we have noted, has already been evident in the development of so-called cognitive behavior therapy. While this appears to be a potentially worthwhile development, it also may be somewhat incomplete or limited in not giving attention also to other aspects of the individual's adjustment, particularly, affective aspects.

Affective Emphases in Psychotherapy

Although most traditional psychotherapies recognized the importance of emotional or affective factors in the genesis of personality disturbance, as well as in therapy, affective aspects have not received as much explicit attention in terms of therapeutic techniques. Many therapists have been aware of the importance of emotional expression and release in therapy and have been aware that something is amiss when the therapy sessions have been devoid of emotional expression on the part of the client. However, such matters did not receive the explicit emphasis given to cognitive variables in the dynamic or the cognitive therapies, or to the emphasis on behavioral variables provided by the behavior therapists. At times, confrontations have been instituted with clients in order to arouse emotional reactions, and a number of therapists have been aware of the potential values of emotional release and catharsis, but, again, these aspects of therapy have generally been accorded less importance in most therapeutic approaches. Some analysts have also referred to emotional re-education as a feature of their therapy, but descriptions of how this process is presumed to operate are far from clear (Alexander & French, 1946; Wolberg, 1954).

Thus, while there has been some recognition of the importance of emotions and of affective change in psychotherapy, the procedures for inducing such change have not been very clear and the main emphasis appears to have been placed on other types of variables. Yet, disturbed emotional states, including the rather painful experiences of anxiety, apprehension, and depression, have been the most distinguishing and identifiable features of the so-called neurotic disorders which have been the focus of most forms of psychotherapy in the past. Perhaps, because of this lack, the encounter and marathon groups attained a certain degree of popularity in the recent past. These approaches placed great emphasis on the free and full expression of feelings and emotions. Openness and frankness in all interactions were stressed, and except for physical violence, no holds were barred in the scheduled sessions. One aim of the encounter movement appeared to be to remove most of the individual's acquired inhibitions. Various games and techniques were used in order to foster strong emotional expression including that of having the participants shed all of their clothing and participate in so-called "nude marathons" (Mintz, 1971). If many of the other therapeutic approaches seem to neglect the expression of emotions and the release of affect, some of the encounter and marathon groups appeared to emphasize them with a vengeance! Group pressure was used to force emotional expression and disclosure from members of the group, and in some of the encounter groups the leader quite overtly challenged members thought to be not sufficiently involved or self-revealing (Lieberman, Yalom, & Miles, 1973).

Although these types of encounter groups and related developments may be seen as attempts to emphasize an important aspect of the human condition which had not received sufficient emphasis in traditional forms of psychotherapy, their approach did appear too one-sided. Although emotional factors play an important role in the individual's overall adjustment to his life situation, they do not constitute the essence or totality of human existence. To emphasize openness and free expression of emotions and feelings at the expense of intellectual, behavioral and other aspects of the individual's functioning is to single out and stress one component at the expense of the others. Furthermore, in a comprehensive study of encounter groups, those groups which did not provide adequate cognitive explanations or rationales to their participants were judged as less satisfactory than those which did (Lieberman et al., 1973).

Not only are such approaches potentially one-sided in their emphasis, but some may produce potentially serious negative consequences. In the well-conducted, large scale study of a variety of encounter groups by Lieberman et al. (1973), in which rather stringent criteria were set up for judging casualties resulting from the encounter experience, nine percent of the participants were considered to fall into this category. Because the encounter group leaders knew they were being observed and because 25 of the 104 casualty suspects could not be reached by phone, Lieberman and his coworkers (1973) believe that the incidence of casualties secured is a conservative estimate. The types of psychological casualties included psychotic decompensation, depression, and anxiety symptoms. Although other reports of encounter groups have not been as negative, the studies reported have generally contained a number of methodological weaknesses (Hartley, Roback, & Abramowitz, 1976). The intensity of the experience sought in the encounter or marathon group may be simply too much for some of the participants to handle adequately. In effect, some group members are forced to participate and disclose at a rate which is actually beyond their capacity or tolerance level and may thus suffer negative consequences. Although the type of emotional expression and release may appear similar to that described earlier for catharsis, the setting is very different, and because of the external pressures brought upon the individual for open emotional display, the two processes are not identical.

While there appear to be limitations in the emphasis on emotional expression and openness in past encounter groups, nevertheless, emotional variables are of potential importance for the psychotherapeutic process. To the extent that the encounter movement has focused attention on these aspects of therapy, albeit to an exaggerated degree, they may have had a partially positive impact on correcting some neglected features of psychotherapy. Since the person is a cognitive, feeling, as well as behaving organism, theoretical as well as practical considerations would indicate that the person should be viewed in terms of all his or her attributes, and not just one. In the section which follows, some preliminary attempt will be made to sketch out some possible implications of this view.

THE PLACE OF COGNITIONS, AFFECTS, AND BEHAVIORS IN PSYCHOTHERAPY

As we have seen, the various approaches to psychotherapy and behavior change appear to have emphasized a particular channel of change or aspect of human experience in their overall psychotherapeutic approach. Some seem to place great emphasis on cognitive means of promoting change, some on the release of feelings and openness, while others focus primarily on a behavioral approach. Although the various groups of therapeutic approaches differ in these ways in terms of their theoretical orientations and therapeutic procedures, they, nevertheless, all claim to be successful forms of psychotherapy, and have their own body of staunch followers. At the same time, as the preceding discussion has indicated, each of these emphases would appear to neglect or underplay significant aspects of human functioning. Clearly, this is a matter which requires further consideration.

If one reasonably can hypothesize that all aspects of human personality and behavior are of potential importance in most attempts to secure positive change by means of psychotherapy, then several subsidiary hypotheses also appear tenable. One hypothesis, presented previously, is that the stated theoretical views of the different schools of psychotherapy are really not the "true" explanations of the changes reportedly secured in psychotherapy. Rather, the results may be due to common factors in all or most of the psychotherapies which are not explicitly recognized in the theoretical views presented. This hypothesis would also allow us to consider two related corollaries. One is that in varying degrees the different types of psychotherapy may actually utilize psychotherapeutic variables which do not receive much formal emphasis in their presentations of therapy. For example, behavior therapists may establish close emotional relationships with their patients, as suggested by the research of Sloane, Staples, Cristol, Yorkston, and Whipple (1975), and they may also provide opportunity for emotional release. In addition, they utilize cognitions in giving the patient a rationale for therapy, as well as for understanding how his/her symptoms may have developed. Thus, although the formal emphasis is on behavior, these other aspects may also play a role in the therapy and in the type of outcome secured. As already noted in Chapter 5, behavior therapists have in recent years acknowledged the importance of the therapeutic relationship in securing positive outcome. Similar examples could be provided for the other approaches, but are not necessary here.

Another corollary of our hypothesis is that certain individuals whose problems are mainly of a behavioral, cognitive, or affective type, or who respond best to an approach featuring one of these emphases, may secure better results with one approach than another. To the extent, however, that each approach receives a somewhat random group of patients, the overall results become somewhat similar for most of the different psychotherapeutic approaches. These, it should be made clear, are simply hypotheses, but are interesting nevertheless, and are not in conflict with existing research findings.

A final hypothesis to be entertained here is that to the extent that most of the psychotherapies tend to stress their particular emphasis and related procedures, their therapeutic effectiveness is less than the maximum effectiveness possible. By failing to utilize all the significant channels of human interaction and influence, each of the psychotherapies is less powerful than it might be and has variable degrees of effectiveness depending upon the type of case being seen. To become more effective, a psychotherapeutic approach would have to pay more systematic attention to all important aspects of human functioning: cognitive, affective, and behavioral. In a related fashion, more specific approaches could be developed for particular kinds of problems in which the major emphasis was placed on those aspects which seemed most important. For example, in overcoming specific fears or in attempting to develop necessary social skills, a major emphasis would be placed on behavioral procedures. However, cognitive and emotional aspects would not be neglected. In other instances, affective aspects or cognitive ones might be emphasized to a greater extent. The approach used would be tailored to the individual case so far as possible, drawing upon all relevant procedures, and being cognizant of human personality and behavior.

It is the writer's belief, that in practically all the therapies that are relatively successful, what actually occurs is not necessarily what is described by the formal theories and procedures of a particular school. Many other processes may be involved but these go on incidentally and without any clear or acknowledged recognition of what may actually have occurred. Although the formal description of a particular therapeutic approach may in essence focus on one part of the elephant, and serve to identify that approach, operationally what actually takes place may include other parts of the elephant as well. This, however, may be done erratically and without any clear recognition of the totality of the processes involved. Consequently, our therapeutic procedures may be less efficient and less successful than they might be if we were to enlarge our understanding of the variables that are important in the therapeutic process and develop our procedures accordingly. In order to accomplish this goal, we shall have to give up our segmental and partisan approaches to psychotherapy and to recognize clearly that progress can only be made if we give proper attention to the totality of human functioning. Man and woman are organisms in which cognitions, emotions, and behaviors are interrelated and integrated aspects of their being and, while particular aspects may be pronounced in certain types of psychopathology, an effective approach to psychotherapy has to be aware of this interrelationship and to utilize this awareness constructively. It appears likely that many of the psychotherapies have developed in an attempt to compensate for apparent lacks in existing approaches. However, in this process, they have tended to stress in their own approach the lacks or deficiencies perceived in others, and in so doing, have neglected some of the potential positive features of the approaches they have attempted to rectify. Nevertheless, in the final analysis, psychotherapy is best viewed as a complex cognitive, affective and behavioral learning process.

SPECIFIC THERAPEUTIC EMPHASES FOR PARTICULAR PROBLEMS

Thus far in this chapter we have noted the particular emphases of some important approaches to psychotherapy and have commented on their relative disregard of other potential therapeutic variables. The point was made that the human organism does not function in an isolated manner as an emotional, cognitive, or behaving organism, but as a total human being, and that actually most therapies do include other emphases of aspects of human functioning even though they may be given little formal attention. It was the author's view that this point was important to make along with the recognition of possible common factors among the psychotherapies.

At the same time, as mentioned previously, it is also important to recognize that the different forms of psychotherapy may be particularly helpful for certain patients with certain problems. Thus, although the common therapeutic factors play an important role for all forms of therapy, the specific emphases or factors of some approaches may be indicated for particular cases. This view has received increased acceptance in recent years. In essence, what kind of therapy is best suited for what kinds of clinical problems?

Of all the different psychotherapeutic approaches currently plying their wares in the therapeutic market place, the behavior therapists and the cognitive-behavioral therapists appear to have made the most progress in attempting to devise procedures to fit the problems of the individual client. Behavior therapists, for example, have distinguished between behavioral deficits and behavioral excesses as one broad type of differentiation and have developed different procedures for handling these two categories of problems. Behavior therapists first try to specify the behaviors that either are to be diminished as problem or undesirable behaviors, or which are to be shaped or increased as the desired behaviors. The particular program of reinforcement or punishment will be developed for the individual case. Attention is paid to the reinforcement history of the individual so that potentially effective reinforcements can be selected for use in the behavior change program. Furthermore, the program can be monitored to check on its effectiveness and appropriate changes made if this seems necessary. Attempts are also made to analyze complex behaviors, to separate them where necessary into their most important component parts, and to devise separate procedures for these specific components of the problem behaviors.

While the specific procedures which make up systematic desensitization have by now become somewhat routinized, nevertheless, in most instances the particular fear hierarchy is developed in terms of the individual client. The attention to specific problems has also led a number of behavior therapists to attempt to deal with a great variety of clinical problems and to develop programs and techniques for dealing with them. Although these individuals have had a certain theoretical framework, they have not limited themselves to a particular group of techniques. They have analyzed a problem situation and then selected or devised techniques which appeared potentially useful for dealing with the problem at hand. In the past relatively few years, they have attempted to devise procedures for improving the ward behavior or specific behaviors of chronic psychotic patients, autistic children, delinquents, criminals, school phobics, persons with learning disabilities, and a variety of others (Barlow, 1988; Emmelkemp, 1994; Kazdin, 1989; O'Leary & Wilson, 1987; Ollendick, 1986). What is being emphasized as desirable here is the close attention and analysis paid to the problem and to the particular procedures devised or used. These are specific programs for specific problems. Furthermore, the behavior therapist will usually not limit himself or herself to just one type of behavioral technique, but will use as many as are deemed useful for securing the desired changes.

Perhaps at this point it may be well to present a summary of one case treated by behavior therapists that is a dramatic and pointed illustration of how specific procedures were devised to save a child's life. In this instance, a young infant of about nine months of age was hospitalized because of severe and continuous vomiting resulting in a serious loss in weight which threatened the infant's life (Lang & Melamed, 1969). The infant had been hospitalized on three previous occasions because of this condition. A variety of diagnostic tests had been done and a number of treatments tried, but with no apparent success. As a result, the physicians involved in the case consulted the psychology department.

Although the infant had attained a weight of 17 pounds at the age of six months, at the time Lang and Melamed were consulted, he weighed only 12 pounds, he was in a critical condition, and was being fed through a nasogastric pump.

The infant was first observed by the psychologists for two days during and after normal feeding periods. Most of the food was regurgitated within ten minutes of each feeding. In order to obtain a clearer picture of the patterning of the infant's response, electromyograph (EMG) activity was monitored at three sites—on the underside of the chin, the upper chest at the base of the throat, and straddling the esophagus. In this way a precise picture of the patterning of the infant's muscular responses associated with vomiting could be ascertained, and the schedule for aversive conditioning worked out accordingly. "The authors were concerned with eliminating the inappropriate vomiting, without causing any fundamental disturbance in the feeding behavior of the child" (Lang & Melamed, 1969, p. 4). It was fortunate that the child did not vomit during feeding, and that sucking behavior, which usually preceded the vomiting, could be distinguished on the EMG.

After this two-day observation and monitoring period, aversive conditioning procedures were instituted. As soon as vomiting occurred, a brief but repeated shock was administered and was continued until the vomiting response was terminated. Based on the observation of a nurse and the confirmation by the EMG, shock was administered "at the first sign of reverse peristalsis," and a tone was presented coincident with each shock presentation. After only two sessions, shock was rarely required. By the sixth session, the infant did not exhibit any vomiting during the testing procedures. He was discharged from the hospital six days after the final conditioning trial. At this time, the infant's level of activity had increased, there was evident a steady gain in weight, and the infant showed more interest and response to his environment. One month after being discharged from the hospital, he was eating well, he looked healthy, and his weight was up to 21 pounds. One year after treatment, the child continued to be healthy and alert.

As is apparent, this was a very serious intervention on the part of these behaviorally oriented psychologists. The child's physical state was precarious, all previous attempts at trying to alleviate the child's vomiting and to help him retain his nourishment had failed, and the psychologists were brought into the case at what appeared to be the last possible moment. Because the situation was a critical one, whatever was to be done had to be done very quickly. The therapeutic procedures devised by Lang and Melamed under these very unusual and trying conditions turned out to be highly effective and the child's life was saved. Furthermore, as indicated, follow-up investigations after the treatment was concluded indicated that the child's health and development subsequently were quite normal. This case is a very clear demonstration of a specific treatment plan developed by very creative therapists to deal with a specific and serious clinical problem. These therapists did not rely on a traditional procedure which they were in the habit of using with all of their cases, but used their wisdom and ingenuity to devise procedures appropriate for the problem which was presented to them. Furthermore, it also illustrates how one case can very convincingly provide evidence of the effectiveness of the therapeutic procedures used without even having recourse to a control group!

Besides the very dramatic illustration of the specificity of effective therapeutic intervention provided by Lang and Melamed (1969), there are many other illustrations in the behavior therapy literature that could also be offered. Many of these are much less striking in terms of the kind of problem dealt with, but they also illustrate the attempts of therapists to devise and utilize specific therapeutic procedures to best meet the needs or requirements of the individual case.

As a further illustration of such work, we can mention briefly some of the differing kinds of therapy procedures that have been developed for some specific kinds of commonly occurring problems.

Behavioral approaches were first developed with reference to a variety of phobic behaviors. Reciprocal inhibition, or systematic desensitization, based on a counter-conditioning theory, was one of the first groups of techniques to receive clinical recognition. With the passage of time, other procedures such as flooding, modeling, and guided participation were also developed. All of these procedures had in common the arrangement of specific therapeutic steps for overcoming specific fears of particular individuals, and they generally involved exposure to the fear provoking stimulus.

With the relative success of such behavioral approaches, a variety of other procedures have been developed in recent years for overcoming a number of different problems. For example, response prevention and bringing patients into contact with the stimuli that triggered compulsive rituals has been relatively effective in reducing ritualistic behaviors (Marks, 1978). The treatment of sexual disorders, influenced by the work of Masters and Johnson (1970), has involved procedures for reducing anxiety, the training of sexual skills, the modification of attitudes towards sexual activity and the like. Specific procedures are used also for such different problems as premature ejaculation, erectile failures, ejaculatory failures and anorgasmia (LoPiccolo, 1975). Operant procedures also have been developed and applied to a variety of problematic behaviors ranging from delusional speech and social withdrawal to such behaviors as hyperactivity, academic performance, and anti-social activities (Kazdin, 1989). Practically all of these programs emphasize a careful study of the behaviors to be modified, the conditions that appear to be sustaining these behaviors, the institution of procedures for changing the behaviors, and methods for carefully monitoring the effects of the therapeutic procedures. Thus, the focus tends to be on the analysis of the individual case and the adapting of procedures to meet the requirements for the case at hand. In the case of unassertive behavior, for example, the procedures found helpful include the changing of beliefs about oneself and the expectations concerning others, role-playing, modeling, and practice in real life situations. In cases of obesity, a treatment package may include adhering to a prescribed caloric intake, eating at only certain times and at certain places, recording all food eaten and the time this was done, regular recording of one's weight, positive reinforcement for weight loss, and the like. Thus, procedures and treatment packages have been developed for specific problems, and although these have not always been successful, they augur well for future therapeutic developments.

AN ECLECTIC APPROACH TO SPECIFICITY IN PSYCHOTHERAPY

Although the preceding sections may appear to reflect a particular bias on the part of the writer in favor of behavior therapy, this is not really the case, nor is an advocacy of behavior therapy a goal of this chapter. Rather, it is the author's conviction that one has to have an open mind on all matters and to evaluate a particular view in terms of its apparent adequacy and on the basis of the evidence presented in support of that view. In terms of the behavior therapists, one has to admit quite frankly that they have been a very enterprising and inventive group of therapists who have tackled a variety of difficult problems with enthusiasm and resourcefulness. In fact, they have devoted attention to very difficult clinical problems which most of us in the field of psychotherapy have preferred to ignore or avoid because they seemed hopeless (e.g., chronic schizophrenia, childhood autism). One can't help but admire this kind of professional activity. Also, as has already been stressed, the attempt to devise specific treatments for specific problems appears to be a most desirable attribute. Besides these features, the behavior therapists deserve recognition for their attempts to evaluate their results in a systematic fashion and to report their findings in the published literature. These all deserve positive recognition and acknowledgment. However, while an open-minded and conscientious psychotherapist would want to be acquainted with the developments occurring in behavior therapy and to utilize some of its techniques and procedures, he need not limit himself solely to behavioral techniques. Instead, he may pay more attention than the behaviorists to the possible common factors in psychotherapy and to other aspects as well.

An eclectic approach to the use of specific procedures in psychotherapy has already been discussed in the chapter on common and specific aspects of psychotherapy. However, we can add some further comments. A basic consideration is that the therapist evaluate the client and his problems as adequately as possible and then to have very clear and explicit goals for therapy. The more concretely and specifically the goals can be stated, the more readily can a program of therapy be devised for the particular client. The therapist may also have to consider the priority of goals and what procedures should be used in the early stages of therapy. The particular constellation of factors in any given case will tend to determine what or how many procedures should be instituted initially. In some cases, the therapist may want to delay instituting certain therapeutic procedures because, in spite of the client's statements, the problems mentioned do not appear to be of prime importance. In other cases, the therapist may decide that it is best to start a program of relaxation or systematic desensitization immediately. It may be in the latter case that a particular fear is judged to be a very critical problem, or that while the problem is not of the highest importance, it is worth doing something concrete that may have relatively quick results in order to increase the client's overall feeling of adequacy and hopefulness of change.

In any event, clarifying and specifying the goals of therapy, and then deciding on what particular approach and procedures might be feasible, would constitute the initial phase of therapy. The eclectic therapist would be differentiated from most therapists who adhere to one approach only by the attempt at greater specification of goals and procedures, and by his willingness to use specific procedures from any orientation, including behavioral ones, if they seem appropriate to the case at hand. He would be differentiated from the behavior therapist by his greater attention to common, cognitive, and affective variables in therapy and by his willingness to use other techniques besides strictly behavioral ones.

Although the eclectic therapist would appear to have the advantage of having a broader orientation to psychotherapy and potential access to a wider variety of therapeutic techniques and procedures than his school-oriented colleagues, it must also be acknowledged that his path is less clearly illuminated. There is some personal comfort for the therapist in believing in and adhering to a given theoretical system. He can follow certain stated procedures and explain certain phenomena in terms of his theoretical system. This is of no little importance, for over and over again the writer has been impressed with the fervor which some adherents of particular viewpoints cling to or espouse their specific orientation. Not infrequently, such individuals are unable to shift their views and to accept the emphases of other viewpoints, even in the face of supporting evidence. Just as patients appear to get some therapeutic benefit from the naming or explaining of their problem by the therapist, so do many therapists get some personal benefit from the specific structure and explanations provided by their theoretical system. A unified theoretical view does have this benefit for the psychotherapist. The eclectic therapist, however, has much less of this kind of support, and this is something of a disadvantage. However, he or she can make use of any technique which appears to be therapeutically worthwhile and, potentially, can provide the most flexible approach to psychotherapy. For the time being, the eclectic therapist will have to place a considerable amount of his or her confidence on empirical results and tenable hypotheses instead of a unified and developed theory of psychotherapy. However, this appears to be a defensible and justifiable stance in the light of our present knowledge and theoretical development in the field of psychotherapy.

Although the absence of a unifying and guiding theory has its drawbacks, an awareness of one's limitations and of the gaps in our current knowledge is, in the long run, a positive thing—even though it may make for uncertainties. It is better to see the situation for what it really is than to have what may be an incorrect or biased orientation.

An eclectic approach to psychotherapy also allows the therapist to pay appropriate attention to the individual requirements of the client for therapy and to select those specific, as well as general, procedures which the specific case requires. In fact, such an approach necessitates specificity, not only in terms of the individuality of the client, but in the understanding that any single approach to therapy is not the best approach for all clients.

The therapist has to be selective in his choice of procedures and to devise a plan of therapy which utilizes whatever specific procedures seem warranted. There are a few other aspects that can also be mentioned before we leave the present topic. One is that it appears important for the therapist to keep a proper perspective on whole-part relationships when working with any client. By this we mean that the significance of any particular problem of the client has to be viewed and understood in terms of its particular importance for the individual as a whole. The same holds for the use of any specific treatment procedure. A corollary of this is that the therapist has to be alert to the impact any particular feature of therapy has on the client, to evaluate the situation accurately, and to be able to modify his approach accordingly. Perhaps some examples will be useful.

Although one has to begin with the patient's complaints at the initial starting point for psychotherapy, two patients who appear to give comparable reasons for seeking therapy may not be precisely the same. Let us take two individuals who verbalize a fear of flying or that they are socially inadequate, or have some other complaint. In one case, the fear of flying, for example, may be the main or sole complaint, whereas in the second case, it may be just one of many. Even if the therapist should decide on the use of a procedure such as systematic desensitization (SD), he might handle the two cases quite differently. In the one instance, SD may suffice as the main therapeutic approach and therapy could last for only a short time. There would appear to be little need for any other interventions. However, in the hypothetical second case, progress might be slow, and there would appear to be a need for other interventions as well. More opportunity might be allowed for the patient to discuss feelings of inadequacy, some need for assertive training might be indicated, and perhaps even the need to involve the spouse in the therapy. Thus, the two therapeutic programs would gradually evolve quite differently. In some instances, a specific type of therapy for a particular problem, if successful, can have a more generalized and important effect upon the patient. A patient who has overcome his fear of flying, for example, may also show an increase in overall self-esteem and confidence. In another case, this may not occur, the results may be more focalized and limited, and other attempts will have to be made to secure these additional outcomes. Conversely, in some cases, more general improvement in such aspects as self-confidence and positive self-image may allow the patient to progress more rapidly on specific problems.

The therapist has to be sensitive to whatever clues are manifested by the patient so that emphases and procedures can be flexibly modified. The writer recalls one case he supervised where initially there appeared to be one central complaint, fear of driving in traffic. The case appeared to be ideally suited for SD and the therapist attempted to follow this procedure.

This patient, however, appeared very anxious and fearful when in the clinic, and this should have provided some awareness to the therapist that what might be involved here was not a simple case of a specific phobia. The patient, furthermore, was very fearful of closing her eyes as part of the training in relaxation. The therapist, while partially aware and concerned about this, did not adequately evaluate the situation and only slight gains were achieved by means of SD. In this case, no adequate assessment was made of other aspects of the case, and consequently, the attempt to push through with one approach was relatively unsuccessful.

In summary then, an eclectic approach places responsibility on the therapist to make an adequate appraisal of the client and his problems and to work out some plan for therapy which seems initially appropriate for the particular client. The therapist selects those procedures which on the basis of empirical evidence seem to be most effective for the specific problems presented by the client. In the absence of research data, the therapist has to rely on his own clinical experience and evaluations, or on his best clinical judgment, realizing that he should evaluate his work as therapy proceeds. Once therapy is underway, the therapist should monitor the client's progress and make whatever modifications seem to be necessary in order to facilitate positive movement in therapy.

REFERENCES

Alexander, F. (1963). The dynamics of psychotherapy in the light of learning theory. *American Journal of Psychiatry, 120,* 441–449.

Alexander, F., & French, T. M. (1946). *Psychoanalytic therapy.* New York: Ronald.

Baker, B. L. (1969). Symptom treatment and symptom substitution in enuresis. *Journal of Abnormal Psychology, 74,* 42–49.

Bandura, A. (1969). *Principles of behavior modification.* New York: Holt, Rinehart and Winston.

Barlow, D. (1988). *Anxiety and its disorders: The nature and treatment of anxiety and panic.* New York: Guilford.

Beck, A. T. (1976). *Cognitive therapy and the emotional disorders.* New York: International Universities Press.

Beck, A. T., & Emery, G. (1985). *Anxiety disorders and phobias: A cognitive perspective.* New York: Basic Books.

Beck, A. T., Freeman, A., Pretzer, J., Davis, D. D., Fleming, B., Ottaviani, R., Beck, J., Simon, K. M., Padesky, C., Meyer, J., & Trexler, L. (1990). *Cognitive therapy of personality disorders.* New York: Guilford.

Ellis, D. (1962). *Reason and emotion in psychotherapy.* New York: Lyle Stuart.

Ellis, A., & Dryden, W. (1987). *The practice of rational-emotive therapy.* New York: Springer.

Emmelkamp, P. M. G. (1994). Behavior therapy with adults. In A. E. Bergin & S. L. Garfield (Eds.), *Handbook of psychotherapy and behavior change* (4th ed.) (pp. 379–427). New York: Wiley.

Goldfried, M. R. (1971). Systematic desensitization as training in self-control. *Journal of Consulting and Clinical Psychology, 37*, 228–234.

Goldfried, M. R., Decenteceo, E. T., & Weinberg, L. (1974). Systematic rational restructuring as a self-control technique. *Behavior Therapy, 5*, 247–254.

Hartley, D., Roback, H. B., & Abramowitz, S. I. (1976). Deterioration effects in encounter groups. *American Psychologist, 31*, 247–255.

Henry, W. P., Strupp, H. H., Schacht, T. E., & Gaston, L. (1994). Psychodynamic approaches. In A. E. Bergin & S. L. Garfield (Eds.), *Handbook of psychotherapy and behavior change* (4th ed.) (pp. 467–508). New York: Wiley.

Kazdin, A. E. (1989). *Behavior modification in applied settings* (4th ed.). Pacific Grove, CA: Brooks/Cole.

Lang, P. J., & Melamed, B. G. (1969). Case report: Avoidance conditioning therapy of an infant with chronic ruminative vomiting. *Journal of Abnormal Psychology, 74*, 1–8.

Lieberman, M. A., Yalom, I. D., & Miles, M. B. (1973). *Encounter groups: First facts.* New York: Basic Books.

LoPiccolo, J. (1975). Direct treatment of sexual dysfunction. In J. Money & H. Musaph (Eds.), *Handbook of sexology.* Amsterdam: ASP Biological and Medical Press.

Mahoney, M. J. (1974). *Cognition and behavior modification.* Cambridge, MA: Ballinger.

Mahoney, M. J., & Arnkoff, D. B. (1978). Cognitive and self-control therapies. In S. L. Garfield & A. E. Bergin (Eds.), *Handbook of psychotherapy and behavior change* (2nd ed.). New York: Wiley.

Marks, I. (1978). Behavioral psychotherapy of adult neurosis. In S. L. Garfield & A. E. Bergin (Eds.), *Handbook of psychotherapy and behavior change* (2nd ed.). New York: Wiley.

Masters, W. H., & Johnson, V. (1970). *Human sexual inadequacy.* Boston: Little, Brown & Company.

Meichenbaum, D. (1972). Cognitive modification of test anxious college students. *Journal of Consulting and Clinical Psychology, 39*, 370–380.

Meichenbaum, D. (Ed.) (1977). *Cognitive behavior modification: An integrative approach.* New York: Plenum.

Meichenbaum, D. (1985). *Stress inoculation training.* Elmsford, NY: Pergamon Press.

Meichenbaum, D. J., Gilmore, J. B., & Fedoravicius, A. (1971). Group insight versus group desensitization in treating speech anxiety. *Journal of Consulting and Clinical Psychology, 36*, 410–421.

Mintz, E. E. (1971). *Marathon groups: Reality and symbol.* New York: Appleton-Century-Crofts.

Nolan, J. D., Mattis, P. R., & Holliday, W. C. (1970). Long-term effects of behavior therapy: A 12-month follow-up. *Journal of Abnormal Psychology, 76*, 88–92.

O'Leary, K. D., & Wilson, G. T. (1987). *Behavior therapy. Application and outcome* (2nd ed.). Englewood Cliffs, NJ: Prentice-Hall.

Ollendick, T. H. (1986). Behavior therapy with children and adolescents. In S. L. Garfield & A. E. Bergin (Eds.), *Handbook of psychotherapy and behavior change* (3rd ed.) (pp. 525–564). New York: Wiley.

Paul, G. L. (1967). Insight versus desensitization in psychotherapy two years after termination. *Journal of Consulting Psychology, 31,* 333–348.

Sloane, R. B., Staples, F. R., Cristol, A. H., Yorkston, N. J., & Whipple, K. (1975). *Psychotherapy versus behavior therapy.* Cambridge: Harvard University Press.

Ullman, L. P., & Krasner, L. (1965). *Case studies in behavior modification.* New York: Holt, Rinehart and Winston.

Wolberg, L. R. (1954). *The technique of psychotherapy.* New York: Grune & Stratton.

CHAPTER 11

Brief and Long-Term Psychotherapy

As is frequently true with many aspects of psychotherapy, there is no unanimity of opinion concerning the optimum length of psychotherapy. Although Freud expressed concern about the length of psychoanalysis in his article, "Analysis terminable and interminable," he was not very positive about attempts to shorten it (Freud, 1950, Vol. 5). Because of the theoretical views of psychoanalysis, it was not a procedure that could be significantly shortened. In fact, as Schmideberg (1958) remarked some years ago, "Psychoanalysis has been practiced on an increasingly large scale for the last 50 years; the length of individual treatment has become longer and longer, amounting sometimes to 5, 10, and 15 years" (p. 236). In the Menninger study of psychoanalysis and psychoanalytically oriented psychotherapy, for example, the mean number of sessions was 835 for psychoanalysis and 289 for psychoanalytically oriented therapy (Bergin & Lambert, 1978).

Such therapies are long-term therapies and are not for everyone. In fact, they are mainly for those well-educated individuals who are interested in rather intensive self-appraisals and have the time and money to engage in such therapy. Most individuals, however, appear to want their treatment to be brief and, as was pointed out in Chapter 3, expect that in actuality their therapy will not require more than a few weeks or months. Thus, there is a wide range in the length of current psychotherapeutic treatments, in the expectations of the clients served, and in the goals of treatment. Until fairly recently, one could assert that most psychodynamically oriented psychotherapy tended to be long-term psychotherapy (concerned with producing insights into repressed conflicts) and that only behavior therapy (concerned with changing problem behaviors) or crisis-oriented therapies were essentially brief therapies. The situation today is quite different. Whereas previously the emphasis appeared to be on rather long-term therapy, the emphasis today, despite the unhappiness of a number of therapists is clearly on brief therapies, generally therapy that lasts for approximately 20 to 30 sessions. Let us review briefly some of these developments.

DEVELOPMENTS IN BRIEF PSYCHOTHERAPY

Among the earliest workers who seriously attempted to shorten the length of psychotherapy were two well known psychoanalysts, Ferenczi and Rank (1925). These early followers of Freud favored a more active role on the part of the therapist and going beyond just providing interpretations. They also advocated a focus on current life problems and even setting time limits in therapy. Freud reacted negatively to these views and further progress in brief therapy was quite limited.

In the 1940s, Franz Alexander and Thomas French, the director and associate director, respectively, of the Chicago Institute of Psychoanalysis, also tried to promote a greater interest in brief psychotherapy. In 1944, Alexander organized and led a meeting at his institute on brief psychotherapy. In a published report of that meeting, Alexander was quite outspoken in his views:

> Recently many psychoanalysts, puzzled by the great discrepancy between the length of treatment, frequency of interviews and therapeutic results, have felt the need for a thorough, critical examination of the therapeutic factors . . .
> Occasionally, one or two psychotherapeutic interviews, rich in emotional experience and insight, may have a more revelatory effect upon certain patients than months of analysis have on others. (Alexander, 1944, p. 3)

Two years later, Alexander, French, and colleagues at the Chicago Institute of Psychoanalysis published their *Psychoanalytic Therapy. Principles and Application* (Alexander & French, 1946). The book was a serious attempt to develop principles and procedures for making psychotherapy more efficient. Although it did not appear to be very warmly received by many traditional psychoanalysts, it did have an important impact on the field of psychotherapy. Some other works on brief psychotherapy were also published in the 1940s, but seemed to have relatively little impact. These included Frohman's *Brief Psychotherapy* in 1948 and Herzberg's *Active Psychotherapy* in 1946. I made some reference to these two volumes in my textbook on clinical psychology (Garfield, 1957), but cannot recall seeing many references to them in other publications. In general, these new ideas suggesting modifications of traditional approaches to psychotherapy had relatively little acceptance. One interesting study conducted by Avnet and appearing in a book on brief therapy edited by Wolberg in 1965 is worth mentioning here. In this study, 2,100 New York City area psychiatrists were invited to participate in time-limited psychotherapy of 15 sessions as part of a group health insurance project. Nine hundred of these psychiatrists refused to participate despite having favorable attitudes towards such insurance. Most of them said that they did not engage in short-term therapy or that they could not help people in such a brief period of time. Furthermore, of those psychiatrists who participated in the study, in 94 percent of their cases further therapy was recommended when the 15-session limit was reached—a recommendation, incidentally, which was not followed by most of the patients to whom it was offered.

Ratings of outcome were also secured from the psychiatrists and from 740 patients about 2.5 years after completion of treatment. Although such ratings are subjective, they have been used frequently in the past. In this instance, 81 percent of the patients saw some improvement, with 17 percent indicating that they had recovered. The ratings of the psychiatrists were almost as good, with 76 percent of the patients rated as improved and 10.5 percent as recovered. Thus, although most of these psychiatrists favored psychotherapy of longer duration, their own ratings of outcome of the brief therapy conducted was quite favorable. It is also interesting to point out that about 30 percent of the psychiatrists did attempt some modification of their procedures in order to secure results in less time. They modified their objectives, became more active and directive, and even considered this a learning experience. As I have commented elsewhere, "It would seem, therefore, that with the right set of motivating circumstances, some therapists can become more flexible and innovative" (Garfield, 1989, p. 8).

There were some other developments pertaining to brief psychotherapy in the 1960s that can also be noted briefly. In the aftermath of World War II with the large number of psychiatrically disturbed veterans in the United States, there was an increased awareness of the lack of trained personnel and facilities to care for individuals with psychiatric problems. In addition to programs for training additional mental health personnel and the availability of federal and state funds for the establishment of community mental health centers, a number of innovative programs for crisis intervention and emergency care were developed. The latter programs were developed so that individuals in crisis situations could obtain immediate treatment, thus preventing the possibility of the problem becoming chronic. Among these pioneering programs were the brief therapy approach (one to six sessions) of Bellak and Small (1965) that provided around the clock emergency service and the program developed at the Langley Porter Neuropsychiatric Institute in San Francisco (Harris, Kalis, & Freeman, 1963, 1964; Kalis, Freeman, & Harris, 1964). In the latter program, consisting of up to seven sessions, the therapists believed that the therapy was sufficient for about two thirds of the patients seen. The remaining cases were deemed to require additional therapy.

There were also a number of other reports published in the decade of the 1960s which do not need to be mentioned here but are available elsewhere (Garfield, 1989). Like those already mentioned, the emphasis in these programs tended to be on a current crisis or problem as the focus of therapy.

Several of these reports also mentioned the use of a specific time-limit in therapy that was explained to the patient at the start of therapy.

The interest in brief therapy has continued to grow along with the growth and increased acceptance of psychotherapy generally. Furthermore, as the dominance of psychoanalysis has diminished and the rise in popularity of behavioral, cognitive, and eclectic approaches has occurred, the emphasis on long-term psychotherapy has been replaced to a significant degree by the increase in briefer forms of therapy. This has also led to a large variety of approaches to brief psychotherapy.

THEORETICAL DIVERSITY IN BRIEF PSYCHOTHERAPY

Although a primary emphasis in many of the forms of brief therapy in the 1960s was on crisis intervention and brief therapy that did not exceed 10 sessions, some forms of brief therapy were appearing that were both longer and not focused solely on crisis situations. Interestingly, several were psychodynamic in orientation. One of the early psychodynamic approaches to brief therapy was developed at the Tavistock Clinic in London by Ballint (Ballint, Ornstein, & Ballint, 1973) and Malan (1963, 1976). The emphasis was placed on one focal conflict with particular attention to the interpretation of transference reactions, especially parent-transference links. Another well-known approach is that of Sifneos (1965, 1981) who named his approach "Anxiety Provoking Brief Therapy." Sifneos has emphasized unresolved Oedipal conflicts, separation problems, and grief reactions as the psychodynamic foci of therapy. His therapy can last from 2 to 12 months and he has very specific selection criteria, including a circumscribed chief complaint, above average intelligence and psychological sophistication, and motivation to change.

Another prominent psychodynamic brief therapy is that of Mann (1973). He adheres to a time limit of 12 sessions and emphasizes conflicts of separation and individuation. Still another relatively well known psychodynamic form of brief psychotherapy is that of Davanloo (1978). He maintains a specific focus in therapy and emphasizes rapid, systematic challenges to resistance in order to facilitate high levels of affective and cognitive functioning throughout therapy. In general, he appears to function in a quite confrontative manner and to use a trial period of therapy. Another somewhat different dynamic approach is that of Strupp and Binder (1984). They emphasize an interpersonal focus organized around the narrations in therapy and the interpretations of the relationship in therapy. Also emphasizing the therapeutic alliance is Luborsky (1984). His approach, however, focuses on the interpretation of what he has called the "Core Conflictual Relationship Theme." Accuracy of interpretation is reported as positively correlated with outcome.

As is evident from even this very brief listing of psychodynamic variations on a theme of brief psychotherapy, the designation of psychodynamic therapy is a rather broad one and there are what appear to be important differences among the forms of brief therapy described. Another well-known form of brief therapy that emphasizes interpersonal relations but is usually not included as a form of "psychodynamic" therapy is the approach referred to as "Interpersonal Psychotherapy" (Klerman, Weissman, Rounsaville, & Chevron, 1984). This approach is more eclectic, recognizes common elements in psychotherapy, emphasizes the current life situation of the patient, and attempts to restore a sense of group belongingness.

Besides the brief therapies mentioned, there are behavioral and cognitive approaches that explicitly or otherwise are brief psychotherapies. One of the advantages mentioned for behavior therapy early in its development was that it was a briefer and, therefore, more efficient form of psychotherapy than the more traditional forms of dynamic therapy. Cognitive and cognitive-behavioral forms of psychotherapy also have been brief and time-limited approaches to therapy, and like the brief dynamic therapies, there have been several different varieties (Hollon & Beck, 1994); Lewinsohn & Hoberman, 1982). Also, when some comparative studies of the different varieties have been made, the differences in outcome have been very slight, a general finding that reflects some of the emphases in the present book. The latter trend is also reflected in some eclectic approaches to brief psychotherapy, one of which has been published by the present author (Garfield, 1989).

Thus, there has been a noticeable increase in the number of different theories and orientations in brief psychotherapy in the past 25 years. What is also worth noting is that for several of these approaches specific training manuals have been developed and some have been developed for the treatment of specific disorders. For example, in the large-scale study of depression coordinated by our National Institute of Mental Health (Elkin, Parloff, Hadley, & Autry, 1985), manuals were developed and used for the two brief psychotherapies evaluated: Cognitive Psychotherapy (Beck, Rush, Shaw, & Emery, 1979) and Interpersonal Psychotherapy (Klerman et al., 1984). We shall say more about the role of such manuals in the research and training of therapists in Chapter 12.

BASIC FEATURES OF BRIEF PSYCHOTHERAPY

There are a number of features that characterize effective brief psychotherapy. Some are general therapeutic variables that have been described earlier as being important in all successful therapy and need not be repeated here (e.g., a good therapeutic relationship, a skilled therapist, the use of appropriate procedures, and the like). However, there are some features that are unique or of major importance in the practice of brief psychotherapy.

A very basic and obvious one is that the therapy can't go on forever—by definition, the therapy has to be brief. Whether the therapy is time-limited, with a specific time limit announced in advance in terms of weeks or months or in terms of number of sessions, or whether some range of sessions, not exceeding 20 to 25, is indicated, the therapy will be considered brief psychotherapy. Although there is no unanimity on the number of sessions that define therapy as brief therapy, a commonly accepted limit is 25 sessions (Koss & Butcher, 1986). Brief therapy is usually conducted for weeks instead of years. Consequently, the therapist in brief psychotherapy has to take a very active role in therapy. He or she cannot sit back and rely mainly on the client's free associations to move therapy along or to wait for developments to occur spontaneously. The therapist has to direct the therapy if the desired objectives are to be secured within the expected time. To client-centered and psychoanalytically oriented therapists, directive forms of psychotherapy may not be very well regarded. However, it is perfectly realistic and essential for conducting brief therapy. It is important to emphasize that directive or directed therapy need not in any fashion imply a lack of sensitivity, empathy, or caring for the welfare of the patient. In actuality the therapist has to be particularly sensitive and tuned into the patient's problems in order to facilitate the progress of therapy as quickly and efficiently as possible.

As previously noted, most forms of brief psychotherapy tend to have some particular type of focus. In my own view of psychotherapy, the goals focused on should be the clients', and not the therapist's. Generally, also, the focus is on the here and now. If therapy is to be brief, not much time can be spent on detailed retrospective accounts of the individual's past history. In most cases, the problem or problems which have motivated the client to seek psychotherapeutic help can be a focus for initiating therapy. Also, as indicated in the earlier chapter on the initial phase of psychotherapy, if the problem presented initially by the client is not actually the main reason for seeking therapy, the latter will be brought forth in early sessions if a positive therapeutic relationship has been established. In such a case, a change in the focus of therapy is clearly warranted.

The therapist constantly has to evaluate the process of therapy and the interactions that take place during the therapy session. Although this should occur in all types of therapy, it is particularly important in brief therapy if unusual impediments to progress in therapy are to be overcome. By sensitive and perceptive attention to what takes place in therapy, the therapist can make whatever modifications appear feasible and desirable in order to facilitate therapeutic progress. It is important, also, for the therapist to attempt to engage the patient as an active collaborator in the therapeutic work.

Providing homework assignments and guidance are also common features of many forms of brief psychotherapy since they tend to facilitate and speed up potential progress.

Although certain features of therapy are emphasized in conducting brief psychotherapy, the general basic principles of psychotherapy emphasized throughout this book apply as well. As in most forms of psychotherapy, the therapist has to convey genuine interest in the patient and a feeling of competence if progress is to be secured. Brief psychotherapists, as well as all psychotherapists, should try to help patients develop coping skills or problem solving procedures that can be used to handle difficulties that may arise in the future. After all, therapy does not solve all problems once and forever, but, hopefully, can help the individual to understand and be able to cope better with future problems.

In essence, therefore, brief therapy contains the essentials of any effective form of psychotherapy, but is focused on conducting therapy quickly and efficiently. Furthermore, in terms of the eclectic approach described here, it means being flexible and using whatever procedures seem appropriate and potentially useful for the particular case. Brief psychotherapy is also in line with the current economic realities of third-party payments and related developments as well as the surveys of the actual length of most of the psychotherapy conducted in this country. Consequently, for a variety of reasons, brief forms of psychotherapy have become the modus vivendi of most therapists and therapeutic settings.

Although there are still a number of psychotherapists who prefer to engage in long-term psychotherapy, who view brief forms of psychotherapy as rather superficial "covering up" types of therapy, and are very critical of the current emphases and pressures to conduct brief therapy, there is little question that brief therapy will continue to be the modal type of psychotherapy.

SOME ISSUES CONCERNING BRIEF PSYCHOTHERAPY

As noted, there are differing views concerning the suitability and merits of brief psychotherapy for most patients. Some therapists believe that brief therapies are mainly useful for mild or situational problems that tend to have good prognoses and are not appropriate for seriously disturbed individuals. Although adequate research on this issue is lacking, it does appear that brief psychotherapy is not the treatment of choice for psychotic individuals and those with severe personality disorders. At the same time, one may question whether long-term psychotherapy is a truly effective treatment for such disorders. It is important to remember also that in discussing psychotic, borderline, and severe personality disorders, we are talking about very broad and gross categories that cover a wide range of human personality and behavior. It is conceivable that some such individuals have personality strengths that allow them to secure some benefit from appropriate types of psychotherapy whereas for others the prognosis is realistically dim. For example, Budman and Gurman (1988) state that some individuals with personality (or character) disorders can be helped if the therapist selects a particular focus such as a personal loss or an exacerbation of an interpersonal conflict as the central concern of therapy and not the character disorder. At the same time, however, they do emphasize that "the characterologically impaired patient will be seen for many courses of treatment over many years" (Budman & Gurman, 1988, p. 215).

Thus, as is true of other issues in the field of psychotherapy, there are differing views as to who may profit from brief psychotherapy. My own view is a fairly liberal one. As I have stated in a previous book:

> With the exception of the very seriously disturbed individuals mentioned earlier, brief therapy can be considered for most patients who are in touch with reality, are experiencing some discomfort, and have made the effort to seek help for their difficulties. Several of the psychodynamic approaches to brief therapy emphasize that there should be a focal problem or specific focus for the therapy. Although the theoretical rationale for this is that in brief or time-limited therapy only a limited goal is possible, I would concur that brief therapy should be focused therapy. In fact all psychotherapy should be focused therapy and focused on the problems of the patient. . . .The therapist, of course, has to evaluate the significance of what occurs in psychotherapy and guide the therapeutic process accordingly. However, the problems a patient has are not completely separate and disconnected. Rather, they are interrelated manifestations of less than adequate adjustment in one human being, and in one sense the therapist is dealing with one problem—the problem that a particular individual is having in his or her life situation at a particular time. (Garfield, 1989, p. 14)

Other workers in the field have also expressed comparable views. Wolberg (1965), for example, who edited one of the earlier books on brief therapy, stated that, "The best strategy, in my opinion, is to assume that every patient, irrespective of diagnosis, will respond to short-term treatment unless he proves himself refractory to it" (p. 140). It was also Wolberg's view that if the patient does not respond to brief therapy, the therapist can resort to longer term therapy. A somewhat similar view was expressed by Harris, Kalis, and Freeman (1964). Although they did not view brief therapy as a definitive treatment for all patients, they felt it was at least a worthwhile intake procedure for most patients, and that it enabled a large number to actually reach a desirable level of functioning in a very short time. In the nonsuccessful cases, it was seen as providing potentially useful information for any additional therapy that was provided.

There appears to be a shared belief in the statements made by Wolberg (1965) and Harris et al. (1964) that if the brief therapy is not successful, a try at long-term therapy will produce the desired results. Although therapists may have this belief, it does not have any really substantive empirical support. As will be discussed in a later chapter, there is literally little systematic research on long-term psychotherapy. Most of the research on outcome is based on studies of brief psychotherapy. Budman and Gurman (1983) also pointed out that "to assume that a particular patient has failed at brief therapy because of a poor response to a trial of such treatment and now has no alternative other than long-term therapy fails to take into account a variety of other alternatives" (p. 287). A change of therapists, the type of treatment, and the between visits intervals are some of the alternatives that they mention.

Apart from theoretical differences concerning who may profit from brief psychotherapy, the appropriate goals and relative efficacy of such therapy, and what are the important foci of brief therapy, there are also external variables that influence both the process and length of psychotherapy. Among these are the patients, themselves, and third-party payers. The latter include governmental agencies, insurance companies and Health Maintenance Organizations (HMOs) who set up certain guide lines and restrictions concerning psychotherapy (Newman & Bricklin, 1991). In fact, when time limits or session limits are prescribed by such agencies, the therapist, if he or she accepts the case, must operate within those limits or be able to convince the agency that additional sessions are warranted. The large increase in the number of psychotherapists in recent years and the lack of unlimited funds for mental health services have essentially forced a number of therapists to participate in HMOs or otherwise to accommodate to such restrictions (Austad & Berman, 1991). Many of them have also stated that under such conditions they have learned how to conduct brief psychotherapy and as a result have become more eclectic in their therapeutic work.

We should also keep in mind that therapy clients also have something to say about the length of their therapy, and many of them will make their own decisions about abbreviating therapy without even discussing this with us. As we noted earlier, most clients want their therapy to be brief, and surveys of the average or median length of therapy have repeatedly shown that outpatient therapy is brief (Garfield, 1994). Furthermore, the requirement on the part of many health plans for co-payments by the client after a certain number of sessions may also motivate some clients to keep their therapy brief. In a one-year follow-up study of 138 patients with prepaid mental health insurance and 283 patients with fee-for-service insurance, an annual mean of 6.1 treatment sessions was secured (Blackwell, Gutmann, & Gutmann, 1988). Over three-quarters of the patients completed therapy within 8 sessions and, interestingly, the two groups did not differ in the amount of treatment received. There are some patients who are high users of outpatient mental health services. In an analysis of data secured in a national survey of individuals who made mental health outpatient visits in 1980, it was found that 9.4 percent made 25 or more visits (Taube, Goldman, Burns, & Kessler, 1988). These visits accounted for 50 percent of the mental health visits and expenditures. One-third of these high users of mental health services were judged to be highly disabled and to have multiple medical disorders. The total group, however, was quite heterogeneous.

For individuals who have been trained in long-term psychodynamic therapy that has emphasized uncovering repressed conflicts and attempting character or personality change, engaging in a more focused type of brief psychotherapy is not easily done. Nevertheless, such a transition has had to be made by a least some psychotherapists and consequently a fair amount of on-the-job training has occurred. There have also been other negative aspects of the gradual growth of managed health care in the United States such as smaller fees and reviews of one's work by various kinds of reviewers. Although one cannot condone the negative aspects of what is now taking place in our health care system, and more changes can be anticipated, such features are not intrinsic features of brief psychotherapy, and brief psychotherapy should not be evaluated in terms of them. Brief psychotherapy has led to a view of the therapeutic process that differs from traditional views, but one that has many positive attributes that we have already mentioned. It can be mentioned again that brief therapy does not cure all ills and that at least some of the clients may seek additional help in the future when they are faced with new stresses in their lives. There is nothing inherently bad about this, particularly if the new contact is brief and the client is able to profit from this experience. I can recall two former clients of mine who called me for an appointment several years after I had seen them for brief therapy. I saw each of them for one session that centered around a new problem. The one session sufficed and, as far as I could tell, met their needs.

Thus, it is evident that psychotherapists need to be flexible in their views of the psychotherapeutic process and of the therapeutic needs of their clients. Not all of them require long-term therapy, some show significant progress in relatively few sessions, and some may have to contact the therapist for quite brief sessions at later times as the need arises.

REFERENCES

Alexander, F. (1944). The brief psychotherapy council and its outlook. *Psychosomatic medicine, proceedings of the second brief psychotherapy council.* Chicago: Institute for Psychoanalysis, 1–4.

Alexander, F., & French, T. M. (1946). *Psychoanalytic therapy. Principles and application.* New York: Ronald Press.

Austad, C. S., & Berman, W. H. (Eds.). (1991). *Psychotherapy in managed health care: The optimal use of time and resources.* Washington, DC: American Psychological Association.

Avnet, H. H. (1965). How effective is short-term therapy? In L. R. Wolberg (Ed.), *Short-term psychotherapy.* New York: Grune & Stratton.

Ballint, M., Ornstein, P. H., & Ballint, E. (1972). *Focal psychotherapy.* London: Tavistock Publications.

Beck, A. T., Rush, A. J., Shaw, B. F., & Emery, G. (1979). *Cognitive therapy of depression: A treatment manual.* New York: Guilford.

Bellak, L., & Small, L. (1965). *Emergency psychotherapy and brief psychotherapy.* New York: Grune & Stratton.

Bergin, A. E., & Lambert, M. J. (1978). The evaluation of therapeutic outcomes. In S. L. Garfield & A. E. Bergin (Eds.), *Handbook of psychotherapy and behavior change* (2nd ed.) (pp. 139–189). New York: Wiley.

Blackwell, B., Gutmann, M., & Gutmann, L. (1988). Case review and quantity of outpatient care. *American Journal of Psychiatry, 145,* 1003–1006.

Budman, S. H., & Gurman, A. S. (1983). The practice of brief therapy. *Professional Psychology: Research and practice, 14,* 277–292.

Budman, S. H., & Gurman, A. S. (1988). *Theory and practice of brief therapy.* New York: Guilford.

Davanloo, H. (1978). *Basic principles and techniques in short-term dynamic psychotherapy.* New York: Spectrum.

Elkin, I., Parloff, M. B., Hadley, S. W., & Autry, J. H. (1985). NIMH Treatment of Depression Collaborative Research Program: Background and research plan. *Archives of General Psychiatry, 42,* 305–316.

Ferenczi, S., & Rank, O. (1925). *The development of psychoanalysis.* New York: Nervous and Mental Disease Monograph, No. 40.

Freud, S. (1950). Analysis terminable and interminable. In *Collected papers,* Vol. V (pp. 316–357). London: The Hogarth Press and the Institute of Psycho-Analysis.

Frohman, B. S. (1948). *Brief psychotherapy.* Philadelphia: Lea and Febiger.

Garfield, S. L. (1957). *Introductory clinical psychology.* New York: Macmillan.

Garfield, S. L. (1989). *The practice of brief psychotherapy.* New York: Pergamon.

Garfield, S. L. (1994). Research on client variables in psychotherapy. In A. E. Bergin & S. L. Garfield (Eds.), *Handbook of psychotherapy and behavior change* (4th ed.) (pp. 190–228). New York: Wiley.

Harris, M. R., Kalis, B., & Freeman, E. (1963). Precipitating stress: An approach to brief therapy. *American Journal of Psychotherapy, 17,* 465–471.

Harris, M. R., Kalis, B. L., & Freeman, E. H. (1964). An approach to short-term psychotherapy. *Mind, 2,* 198–206.

Herzberg, A. (1946). *Active psychotherapy.* New York: Grune & Stratton.

Hollon, S. D., & Beck, A. T. (1994). Cognitive and cognitive-behavioral therapies. In A. E. Bergin & S. L. Garfield (Eds.), *Handbook of psychotherapy and behavior change* (4th ed.) (pp. 428–466). New York: Wiley.

Klerman, G. L., Weissman, M. M., Rounsaville, B. J., & Chevron, E. S. (1984). *Interpersonal psychotherapy of depression* (IPT). New York: Basic Books.

Kalis, B. L., Freeman, E. H., & Harris, M. R. (1964). Influence of previous help-seeking experiences on applications for psychotherapy. *Mental Hygiene, 48,* 267–272.

Koss, M. P., & Butcher, J. (1986). Research on brief psychotherapy. In S. L. Garfield & A. E. Bergin (Eds.), *Handbook of psychotherapy and behavior change* (3rd ed.) (pp. 627–670). New York: Wiley.

Lewinsohn, P. M., & Hoberman, H. M. (1982). Behavioral and cognitive approaches. In E. S. Paykel (Ed.), *Handbook of affective disorders.* Edinburgh: Churchill Livingstone.

Luborsky, L. (1984). *Principles of psychoanalytic psychotherapy: A manual for supportive-expressive treatment.* New York: Basic Books.

Malan, D. H. (1963). *A study of brief psychotherapy.* New York: Plenum.

Malan, D. H. (1976). *Toward the validation of dynamic psychotherapy.* New York: Plenum.

Mann, J. (1973). *Time-limited psychotherapy.* Cambridge, MA: Harvard University Press.

Newman, R., & Bricklin, P. M. (1991). Parameters of managed mental health care: Legal, ethical, and professional guidelines. *Professional Psychology: Research and practice, 22,* 26–35.

Schmideberg, M. (1958). Values and goals in psychotherapy. *The Psychiatric Quarterly, 32,* 233–265.

Sifneos, P. E. (1965). Seven-years experience with short-term dynamic psychotherapy. *Proceedings of the 6th International Congress of Psychotherapy,* Selected Lectures (pp. 127–135). London 1964, Basel/New York: S. Karger.

Sifneos, P. E. (1981). Short-term anxiety provoking psychotherapy: Its history, technique, outcome, and instruction. In S. H. Budman (Ed.), *Forms of brief therapy* (pp. 45–81). New York: Guilford.

Strupp, H. H., & Binder, J. L. (1984). *Psychotherapy in a new key. A guide to time-limited dynamic psychotherapy.* New York: Basic Books.

Taube, C. A., Goldman, H. H., Burns, B. J., & Kessler, L. G. (1988). High users of outpatient mental health services: I. Definition and characteristics. *American Journal of Psychiatry, 145,* 19–24.

Wolberg, L. R. (Ed.). (1965). *Short-term psychotherapy.* New York: Grune & Stratton.

CHAPTER 12

Research in Psychotherapy

Although most psychotherapists are primarily interested in practice and have much less interest in research, these two aspects of psychotherapy should not be viewed as inherently antagonistic to each other. In the preceding chapters, references have been made to a number of research findings and to the importance of such research for psychotherapy practice. However, although no one would seriously deny that scientific research has contributed greatly to the expansion of knowledge and to a marked increase in our material well-being, there are some who would argue that science and scientific procedures are applicable only to certain kinds of problems and pursuits. The methods of science have clearly paved the way for significant advances in the physical sciences, and more recently, in the biological sciences. However, according to some observers, when we get into the social sciences and particularly to the problems of human adjustment and the human psyche, these methods are inappropriate and unsuitable. Furthermore, a number of psychotherapists believe that psychotherapy as practiced is an art, and that it involves such difficult to grasp human qualities as intuition and sensitivity, which are beyond the methods of science. While there is some truth to such assertions, they appear to be overly extreme and, in some instances, reflect biases against the attempt to utilize more systematic empirical procedures for appraising the processes and outcomes of psychotherapy. Although psychotherapy is a complex process, there is no sound reason that research investigations should not be undertaken. Actually, as noted, considerable research has been carried out and considerable progress has been made in our ability to conduct research which is meaningful and clinically relevant.

Because of the demands made by governmental and other agencies in recent years for evidence demonstrating the efficacy of psychotherapy, there has been an increased interest in research on psychotherapy. Research that demonstrates the effectiveness of psychotherapy is gladly accepted even by those therapists who are critical of conducting research on psychotherapy. In the following chapter, we shall review some of the important research that has attempted to evaluate psychotherapy outcome. However, before doing so, it is worthwhile to review some of the basic considerations pertaining to research on psychotherapy.

BASIC CONSIDERATIONS IN
PSYCHOTHERAPY RESEARCH

If research on psychotherapy is to be of any real value it must pay attention to the basic canons of research design, as well as taking into consideration the unique characteristics and requirements of the psychotherapeutic situation. When one examines the latter, it seems clear that attention will have to be devoted to the variables that are deemed important to the psychotherapeutic process, as well as to any possible influencing or contaminating variables that might influence this process. That is, we must consider all of the variables that presumably may influence the course of therapy, but we must also *not* overlook extra-therapy variables which might play some role in influencing outcome.

The basic variables hypothesized to be important in psychotherapy can be categorized in a number of ways, but in general they derive their reputed significance from one or the other participant in psychotherapy and in the possible interaction effects between these two. Thus, we can speak of client or patient variables as one class of variables which have obvious importance for outcome in psychotherapy, and a previous chapter dealt in some detail with this group of variables. Included here were such client variables or attributes as age, sex, educational level, social class status, degree of disturbance, type of disturbance, expectations about therapy, motivation, suggestibility, and the like. Conceivably, any aspect of the client which could influence outcome in psychotherapy would be a variable of importance with reference to research. Furthermore, since client variables presumably affect the possible outcome of psychotherapy, they are of critical importance for two types of research investigations. One is comparative studies of the relative effectiveness of two or more types of psychotherapy. If two very different groups of clients are assigned to different types of therapy respectively, we will not be able to draw any valid conclusions concerning the relative effectiveness of the two types of therapy. Any differences obtained could be due to differences in the two samples of clients and not to the differences in the therapies. Also, if no differences are secured, one cannot rule out the possibility that client differences in the two samples have influenced the outcome obtained and that other results might have been secured if the samples of clients were matched or comparable in most important respects. Consequently, in comparative studies of outcome, the research investigator has to make some effort to insure the comparability of his groups of subjects and to guard against bias in the selection of subjects. He can do this by matching subjects on essential attributes before assigning them to the respective treatment or control groups, or by insuring complete randomization in the allocation of subjects to the treatment groups. Such procedures are a means of reducing possible bias or selectivity in assigning clients to the different types of treatment and to increase the probability that whatever differences are secured can be presumed to be the result of the independent or manipulated variable, that is, the type of treatment.

Client or patient variables are also the central variables in research which attempts to discover what patient attributes may be predictive of outcome in psychotherapy, or more specifically, what kind of patients or clinical problems will respond best to specific kinds of treatment. This is clearly an important kind of research in psychotherapy, for it attempts to discover what types of interventions may be most effective with particular kinds of problems.

It is important that in research planning the investigator pay adequate attention to those variables that are of some potential significance and not just to those that are easily appraised and secured. For example, in trying to select two comparable groups of subjects, the investigator may try to equate them mainly on variables on which he has information but which may not be crucial ones, and fail to pay attention to variables which are of greater importance. Thus, he may equate his groups on the basis of age, sex, and marital status, but not on degree of disturbance, willingness to undergo treatment, and similar variables. To the extent that the former group of attributes may not be critical ones for the study being undertaken, the matching of groups is really a sort of window dressing that actually does not handle the problem adequately.

The critical problems in evaluating client variables are the selection of the variables which presumably are related significantly to outcome and, also, the adequate appraisal of these variables. One of the serious problems here is that so many of the client variables hypothesized to be of potential significance for psychotherapy are not couched in operational terms. They tend to be personality variables or other hypothesized constructs that are poorly defined, are viewed in different ways by different therapists, and that are difficult to measure or evaluate. A concept conceivably may pertain potentially to an attribute of possible importance, but if it cannot be operationalized in some way or adequately appraised, it will have little actual value since it cannot be reliably evaluated. Thus, such constructs as ego-strength, motivation for therapy, anxiety, and the like, present real problems for research. Different measures of the same construct frequently show modest or low correlations with each other and one is not really sure what each is actually measuring. In the final analysis, our methods of appraising the variables we are interested in investigating have to be reliable and valid ones. If they are not, then the research investigation is seriously weakened. To the extent that many of the research investigations conducted by behavior therapists have utilized behavioral criteria of outcome which have some degree of reliability and validity, their research is not as much influenced by this type of problem. However, to the extent that other client variables may also be involved in influencing outcome, such considerations pertain to behavioral therapies as well.

Another problem concerns the generalizability of the results secured in the research project. Any research investigation of psychotherapy utilizes a finite number of clients or subjects. The number and type of clients studied are of some importance for the kinds of conclusions and generalizations to be drawn from the particular study. If the number of clients is relatively small, one has to be particularly cautious in drawing conclusion since sample size affects reliability. The type of sample also has to be considered. If one has a very mixed group of patients, the results may not be applicable to many other patient populations, or if the sample is very selective, the results again may be limited only to a comparable group of patients and not apply to others. A great deal of the earlier research in psychotherapy was carried on with mixed or heterogeneous samples of subjects from a particular clinic or hospital setting with the implication that the results were meaningful for all other clinic and hospital settings, an inference that was frequently found wanting. Usually, such samples covered the psychiatric waterfront with the traditional exclusion of brain damaged and mentally retarded patients. Since not all clinical settings secured the same kind of patients in exactly the same kind of mix, comparability of results was hampered. A better strategy is to try to do research on samples of patients who have a similar type of problem. In this way, variability in research samples will be lessened and more reliable results can be secured.

There is another aspect of this problem that has received some attention and discussion. This also pertains to the matter of generalizability and refers primarily to research studies carried out with college student volunteers. Although some of these studies have been clearly referred to as analogue studies, that is, experimental demonstrations of operations presumed to be analogous to those occurring in actual psychotherapy, others have not made such a distinction and have treated their studies as studies of psychotherapy. A number of studies of behavior therapy, in particular, but of other therapies as well, have utilized student volunteers. The issue here is, are college student volunteers who are recruited for such research studies by means of advertising or for meeting course requirements to be considered comparable to patients who seek out treatment for supposedly comparable complaints (Marks, 1978)? If the two groups of subjects are in fact different, are the results of the one applicable to the other? Unless the results secured with students or other types of volunteers are cross-validated on some sample of actual patients with comparable complaints, the results are probably best viewed as preliminary and tentative, for it is not uncommon for more negative results to be secured with clinical patients.

In a review of 14 studies that compared solicited and nonsolicited patient groups that were treated in clinical settings the authors commented as follows, "Although the existing data suggest that treatment response may also be similar across these groups, these data are too limited to permit conclusions regarding generalizability of treatment efficacy findings based on solicited patient samples" (Krupnick, Shea, & Elkin, 1986, p. 68). Because of the variability among the studies surveyed, the authors concluded that "studies using solicited patients . . . must be interpreted with caution" (p. 77).

It is a perfectly reasonable procedure to try out new techniques on student volunteers in a more controlled laboratory type of setting, but before these results can be considered to have wider application, they would have to be cross-validated on a clinically appropriate sample. Otherwise, one would be safest in generalizing the results obtained only to a like sample of student volunteers. In all research, however, the greater the specificity of the client variables appraised, the greater the probability of securing reliable results.

Besides the variables ascribed to the client, the possible variables associated with the therapist are also important in psychotherapy research. Those that have tended to receive the most emphasis have been personal attributes of the therapist and his length of experience in psychotherapy. Although, as noted in a previous chapter, many desirable personal qualities have been deemed important for the psychotherapist, comparatively little research has been conducted on such variables, and of the research that has been done, much of it has produced conflicting and at times disappointing results (Beutler, Machado, & Neufeldt, 1994; Parloff, Waskow, & Wolfe, 1978). Although a few studies have shown some relationship between the experience of the therapist and outcome, the overall results are relatively modest at best and leave a large amount of the variance unaccounted for (Auerbach & Johnson, 1977).

The most promising research on therapist attributes appeared to be the research conducted by the client-centered therapists on the fundamental variables of empathy, warmth, and genuineness (Truax & Carkhuff, 1967). However, as noted in Chapter 4, subsequent research and appraisal has failed to support this earlier promise.

Thus, although it seems most likely that the qualities of the therapist are of some importance in psychotherapy, and this is a view held by most clinicians, the research to identify these qualities has not yet produced truly definitive findings. In actuality most of the research on psychotherapy has focused on type of therapy or techniques of therapy. However, a few studies have been reported that indicate that certain therapist attributes or patterns of relating to clients are of potential importance in the progress of psychotherapy (Lambert, 1989). In the study of encounter groups by Lieberman, Yalom, and Miles (1973), for example, strongly confrontative therapist behaviors appeared to be related to the number of casualties produced. In a

study comparing three different treatments, marked differences were secured in outcome among the therapists studied (Luborsky, McLellan, Woody,
O'Brien, & Auerbach, 1985). These differences occurred both within and
between treatments. Comparable differences were reported by Orlinsky and
Howard (1980) who studied 23 therapists. Thus, some therapists secured positive results with most of their cases whereas some were successful with 50
percent or less of their cases. Lambert (1989), in particular, has called attention to the potential importance of the therapist for both process and outcome in psychotherapy and the need for further research. It can be mentioned
also that in several studies, patients generally mention attributes of the
therapist when asked what features of psychotherapy accounted for their
improvement.

Consequently, although our techniques and rationales for appraising therapist variables are limited and leave much to be desired, any systematic research will have to make some attempt at studying potential variables of this
type. Otherwise, we continue the uniformity myth that all therapists are
equal and interchangeable and we will have to settle for "average" results.
Comparable studies of diagnosticians have shown that there is tremendous
variability in the accuracy of different clinicians (Garfield, 1983a). Whereas
the average of a group of clinicians shows them to be little better than chance
in their diagnostic acumen, some clinicians are decidedly accurate while others seem to be completely off the mark. Similar studies of psychotherapists
would be extremely helpful, particularly if some intensive studies were then
pursued to study those who were most effective so that our knowledge of the
attributes and behaviors that contribute to desired outcome could be ascertained. More recently, the use of therapy manuals to insure the integrity of
the treatments being evaluated, has tended to minimize therapist differences
in the research. This, however, raises some other issues (Garfield, 1992)
which will be discussed in the following chapter.

One other point that has been commented upon by some research critics
also can be mentioned. A fair number of studies of psychotherapy have tended
to use psychotherapists in training. Such individuals tend to be more readily
available or more easily induced to participate in research investigations. To
the extent that these individuals are not yet fully trained and proficient psychotherapists, how much confidence can we place in the results secured, and
how far can we generalize from the findings obtained? If training and experience make some difference in the quality of the psychotherapy performed,
then it would seem most prudent to generalize only to situations where comparable therapists are employed. If one is conducting research on the possible effectiveness of psychotherapy, it seems reasonable to use experienced
and capable therapists. On the other hand, to the extent that a significant
percentage of clients in clinical settings are being serviced by therapists in
training, research on the effectiveness of such therapy can be considered of

possible practical value. The kinds of generalizations made would, of course, differ for the two different situations.

In addition to considering therapist and client variables, ideally, research should also consider the possible interaction between these two sets of variables. Since one therapist may conceivably be more effective with certain kinds of clients and some clients may work better in therapy with certain types of therapists than others, attention should be paid to these possible interaction effects. This calls for a more complex research design and may explain why few studies of this kind have been attempted. However, in spite of its difficulties, attention will have to be paid to problems of this kind, and such matters will have to be considered in appraising the possible variables influencing outcome in psychotherapy (Berzins, 1977; Beutler, Machado, & Neufeldt, 1994).

A final item of importance in psychotherapy research concerns outcome variables and the methods of evaluating outcome. Outcome in psychotherapy refers to the changes that are secured by means of the therapeutic intervention and constitutes a measure of its effectiveness. As a consequence, criteria of outcome are of decided importance for both research and practice in psychotherapy. Research in psychotherapy which is not intimately linked with criteria of outcome is ultimately of limited value, and the importance of any research on the effectiveness of psychotherapy is thus very much influenced by the quality of the criteria of outcome used. Let us, therefore examine some of the criteria of outcome which have been used in such research.

Probably, the most frequently used criterion of outcome in psychotherapy generally has been the judgment of improvement provided by the therapist. Because the therapist is available and can offer some judgment concerning the outcome of psychotherapy, such evaluations can be readily secured, and this most likely accounts for the frequency with which this type of evaluation has been used. As a result, various types of rating scales have been used in research to ascertain the therapist's evaluation of outcome. In defense of this procedure, it is usually stated that the therapist is the one who has been most intimately involved with the patient and is in the best position to make a firsthand appraisal of outcome. Although this statement is at least partially correct and appears to have some face validity, there are some limitations in relying on therapists' judgments as the sole or primary criterion of outcome. In the first place, the therapist is not a completely objective observer or rater. To the extent that he has been an involved participant in the psychotherapy which is being evaluated, he cannot be presumed to make a completely unbiased evaluation, no matter how well he knows the patient. In addition, different therapists may judge their effectiveness in idiosyncratic ways. Some may be overly optimistic, while others may be too severe in their judgments.

Finally, to the extent that therapists' ratings are global ratings of outcome made only at the end of therapy, there are other potential limitations to be considered. One is that the therapist has to compare the client's condition at the end of therapy to what it supposedly was when the client began therapy. Not only may the therapist's recollection be faulty, but the overall level of the client's integration and adjustment may tend to influence the therapist's evaluation accordingly. That is, a client who was only mildly disturbed to begin with may be seen as very much improved at the end of therapy because he is functioning at a relatively high level at the end of therapy, even though the changes secured are modest. Also, global rating scales of improvement may be poorly defined and lacking in terms of clear operational definitions of the categories used. For these reasons, therapists' ratings of outcome may leave much to be desired and should not be relied upon as a sole criterion of outcome.

The ratings of outcome by patients who have undergone psychotherapy also have been frequently used as criteria of outcome, and appear to have somewhat similar limitations as measures of outcome as the ratings secured from therapists. The patient should be in a good position to evaluate what changes he or she has undergone, but, again, there are problems of subjectivity, perception, attitudes toward the therapist and the need also to justify one's expenditure of time and money. Nevertheless, because the patient is a central participant in psychotherapy and is usually agreeable to providing some ratings, such evaluations have been widely used.

In a number of studies, both therapist and client ratings have been secured and the findings are interesting. Although the total percentage of those judged to be improved is quite similar in the two sets of ratings secured, the correlation between the two sets of ratings tends to be rather modest. In one study, for example, where such ratings were obtained, both sets of ratings indicated that about 70 percent of the clients were considered to be "improved." However, the correlation between the ratings was 0.44 (Garfield, Prager, & Bergin, 1971). Other studies have reported even lower correlations. In the study by Sloane, Staples, Cristol, Yorkston, and Whipple (1975), a correlation of 0.21 was secured between the ratings of patients and therapists, whereas a nonsignificant correlation of 0.10 was reported for these two sets of ratios by Horenstein, Houston, and Holmes (1973). With such low agreement between the ratings of the two groups of participants in psychotherapy, the meaningfulness of these criteria of outcome leave something to be desired.

Besides these kinds of outcome ratings, the ratings of supervisors, significant others, and independent judges have also been used in psychotherapy research. Although supervisors' ratings may also be open to similar kinds of criticism as those already mentioned, in at least one study their ratings were less positive than those provided by either the therapists or the clients (Garfield, Prager, & Bergin, 1971). The ratings by such significant others as parents, spouses, close friends, and employers, would also appear to be of potential value in evaluating psychotherapy. However, similar problems seem to be evident with the use of such ratings as well. The ratings of parents of children with specific behavioral problems were reported to be overly positive as compared with other criteria in two well controlled studies (Patterson, 1971). Ratings by employers or work supervisors might be of value in some cases, but securing such data could be viewed as an invasion of the client's privacy and as a threat to the confidentiality of the therapeutic contacts. Certainly, many clients might not want their employers to know that they had received psychotherapy. On the other hand, ratings made by independent trained observers on the basis of interviews or tapes of therapy sessions can be checked for reliability and be of some utility in appraising outcome. Among all the various ratings obtainable, they would at least appear to be the ones open to the least subjective bias. The fact that therapists and clients perceive outcome somewhat differently in a sizeable number of cases is an interesting finding which is worthy of further investigation in its own right.

Besides ratings and judgments of overall outcome which suffer from the fact that they tend to be made mainly at the end of therapy, other types of ratings can be secured which are potentially of greater value. Instead of a global judgment of improvement, attention can be focused on specific complaints or problems presented at the intake or initial session with the patient and which can be evaluated again at the end of therapy without reference to the initial ratings. These have several advantages. They focus on specific problems and behaviors instead of a global measure of improvement, and they are based on judgments or ratings made at the beginning and end of therapy.

In addition to ratings, a variety of psychological tests and questionnaires have also been used to appraise outcome in psychotherapy. Such estimates of progress in therapy are no better than the tests upon which they are based. To the extent that well standardized tests are used, comparisons between comparable studies are possible if the tests are appropriate to the outcomes sought by means of therapy. If the tests used are lacking in validity or otherwise inappropriate for the types of outcome to be anticipated, then such instruments probably will provide very little useful data.

The use of tests thus does not provide any simple or ready-made solutions for evaluating outcome in psychotherapy. The tests must have some demonstrated reliability and validity for the particular variables they are supposed to measure, and the hypothesized variables must also be directly relevant for the desired therapeutic outcome. It is a relatively easy matter to use a popular test or battery of tests, but the tests should be appropriate to the types of problems presented by the client. Many so-called general tests of personality may not be the most appropriate instruments to use unless an overall personality change is the goal of therapy. Within limits, the changes sought by means of therapy should determine the kinds of measures used.

One of the problems evident in psychotherapy research is the wide variety of tests and questionnaires used in such research. In a review of 348 outcome studies discussed by Lambert and Hill (1994), for example, a total of 1,430 different outcome measures were noted. This has led to real difficulties in comparing and evaluating the results of different studies. Tests that purport to measure the same or similar variables frequently show disappointingly low correspondence between them. As a result, it has been extremely difficult to draw definitive conclusions from the diverse and conflicting results secured. If comparability of results are to be obtained, it would be desirable to have research investigators utilize the same standardized tests. However, this would only be feasible if comparable groups of patients with similar treatment goals were being studied. Since patients may have variable problems, standard tests may not be completely applicable and other outcome measures would also have to be used.

Still another type of outcome criterion used is a measure of the actual behavioral change sought by means of psychotherapy. This type of measure of outcome has understandably been utilized most frequently by behavior therapists. Since they tend to focus their work on behavior and to conceptualize the patient's problems in behavioral terms, it follows naturally that evaluation of outcome would be primarily concerned with behavioral change. There are several positive features of this type of emphasis. Behavioral change is important in most cases and therefore, should be included in most appraisals of outcome. This has not been the case in a large number of instances, and has been a weakness in previous research. Furthermore, behavior is observable and thus can be appraised in a reasonably objective manner.

Strupp and Hadley (1977) also offered some suggestions concerning the evaluation of outcome which deserve mention here. They discussed the lack of congruence among different appraisals of outcome, but instead of questioning the value of such evaluations on this basis, have stated that each evaluation perspective is of some importance. For example, although patients and therapists may evaluate the outcome of therapy differently, they are evaluating it from their different perspectives or vantage points and both perspectives need to be considered in evaluating outcome. They also believe other perspectives need to be considered as well. Consequently, they offered a tripartite scheme of evaluation. In essence, three vantage points for evaluation of therapy are suggested: (1) Society; (2) The individual client; and, (3) That of the mental health professional. Society is concerned with social roles and mores, and thus the focus here would be on the observation of behavior in terms of social expectations and criteria. From the individual client's viewpoint, the important criteria of outcome would involve subjective perceptions and feelings of self-esteem and well-being. The criteria of professional mental health personnel would depend on observations of behavior, psychological tests, and clinical judgments as mediated by some theoretical view of personality structure and overall personal functioning and integration. While there is some overlap among these criteria, they do represent different vantage points and frames of reference.

Although the scheme proposed by Strupp and Hadley points up one important aspect of the problems encountered in appraising therapeutic outcome, it does not provide a complete solution to these problems. If the three modes of evaluation are discrepant, what kinds of judgment concerning the effectiveness of psychotherapy can be made? Are all three types of evaluations to be considered as valid? According to Strupp and Hadley, a truly adequate and comprehensive appraisal is possible only if the three types of data are evaluated and integrated—but who will perform the integration? Presumably, an independent and objective fourth party would be called for. However, if this person is a professional mental health worker, one component of the tripartite arrangement may appear to be overweighted. In any event, the tripartite scheme of evaluation is an interesting one which does call into question the limitations of relying on a single source for data on outcome. Research which attempted to investigate, systematically, the bases for the differences among different sources of outcome evaluation would appear to be of potential worth.

There are, thus, a number of basic considerations pertaining to the client, to the therapist, and to the criteria of outcome that have to be considered in research on outcome in psychotherapy. Deficiencies in any aspect will of necessity affect the value of the results secured. Consequently, the serious student of psychotherapy must not only try to keep abreast of the research which is done in his field, but he must also be able to evaluate the merits and limitations of the research studies that he reads. This stricture holds for all aspects of psychotherapy research and not just those that have been discussed thus far.

CONTROLLED AND UNCONTROLLED RESEARCH

In addition to variation in the variables already mentioned, research in the area of psychotherapy has demonstrated diversity in other aspects as well. Some reports of research have tended to be rather well designed and controlled studies modeled after the more traditional approaches in scientific research. The dependent variables, or outcome criteria, are clearly specified and the independent variables, or therapeutic conditions, are manipulated in a clearly designated manner. However, the laboratory experiment is only one type of research model, and because it is a very difficult one to follow in most clinical situations, many other types of research studies have been carried out in the field of psychotherapy.

One of the most common types of reports on outcome in psychotherapy is a simple evaluative report on a certain number of patients who have received treatment in a clinical setting over a given period of time. In some instances, the report is of a retrospective study of a sample of patients who have been treated in the past, and the investigator simply goes through the closed case files in the clinic and tabulates the final evaluations or comments noted in the files by the various therapists who have treated the patients in the period studied. As shown in one early investigation of this type, such reports have many deficiencies (Garfield & Kurz, 1952). Among other things, many records tend to be incomplete, some of the information is inadequate, there is considerable variability among therapists in how they evaluate outcome and in how they record it, and the outcome is based on the therapist's global judgment made at the end of therapy. In the study referred to above, a large number of therapists did not provide any final appraisal of outcome, and in those cases where evaluations were recorded in the case files, a variety of descriptions and terminology was used so that it was extremely difficult to equate these judgments. Consequently, although such an investigation may be of some value to the clinical facility in showing a need for more systematic appraisal, it is of little value in telling us anything about the effectiveness of psychotherapy.

In other instances, somewhat better prospective clinical investigations have been carried out in that the study has been designed in advance and patients as well as therapists may be asked for evaluations of outcome based on rating scales devised for the study. Although this type of study has certain improvements over the previous one, it, too, has limitations. The judgments of outcome tend to be global and poorly defined, and, usually, the information about client variables also leaves a great deal to be desired. Because of this, some investigators have attempted to improve this particular approach to research by adding more objective and comprehensive measures of outcome, usually some standard tests and questionnaires. This type of research, while an improvement still allows us only very limited kinds of conclusions. It may tell us something about the rate of estimated improvement in a group of usually heterogeneous clients who have undergone psychotherapy with a particular sample of therapists in a specific clinical setting at a given time. If these results are generally seen as positive, they may be viewed as affirming the effectiveness of the psychotherapy being carried out in that clinical setting or even of the effectiveness of psychotherapy more generally. However, such conclusions are basically not tenable in the absence of some sort of control group. Without adequate controls, one cannot draw any cause-and-effect relationships with any reasonable degree of confidence.

The matter of adequately controlled studies is an important one in all research and is certainly so in the case of research on psychotherapy. If one is to draw certain inferences or conclusions about the effect of one variable on another, one must be able to control all other variables which may be operating in the situation at hand and which could also have some influence on the second or dependent variable. For example, if someone is studying the effect of noise level on performance but fails to control for other variables such as temperature which might also influence performance, the results which are secured may be contaminated by the influence of the uncontrolled variable. In the possible study of outcome in psychotherapy mentioned in the previous paragraph, a result may be obtained to the effect that 68 percent of the patients who received psychotherapy are judged to have shown some improvement. However, we cannot convincingly state that this result is due to psychotherapy unless we have ruled out the possibility that other factors may also have played a role in the improvement secured. One of the more obvious considerations here is what would have occurred if this same group of patients had not secured psychotherapy but had simply been left alone. Over a similar period of time, would they also have shown a comparable percentage of improvement or would the percentage of improvement have been less or more? Unless we have data on this question or have some other reasonable basis for making judgments, we are unable to provide any adequate answer to this type of question. Consequently, our ability to draw conclusions about the effectiveness of therapy is thereby limited. The matter of controlling for possible extraneous influences on psychotherapy outcome is thus of some significance, and it is for such reasons that a control group is usually required in research evaluating outcome.

Research in psychotherapy, therefore, has increasingly made use of some type of control group. One obvious kind is to have an untreated control group—that is, a group of clients considered to be comparable to the group receiving psychotherapy, but which receives no treatment. Both groups receive the same evaluation procedures, and whatever differences are secured are presumed to be due to the effects of treatment. Although this procedure seems to be an adequate one, it has become difficult to apply with our increased concern about the use of human subjects in research. If the therapy being evaluated takes a long period of time, it is extremely difficult to secure and retain a control group, and more importantly, there are ethical, as well as practical considerations involved, for no ethical practitioner would want to withhold therapy for a long period from patients who are seriously disturbed and in need of treatment (Garfield, 1987). Where the length of treatment is relatively short, this is not as serious a problem but provisions need to be made for any special requests or emergency needs of control subjects.

In addition, there are also difficulties in getting a control group that is comparable to the treatment group or in securing randomly selected groups for the research investigation. If a large number of the initially selected control group patients refuse to wait, and seek treatment elsewhere, it is not always possible to replace them in kind, and such attrition raises questions about the representativeness of those patients who are content to wait for treatment and constitute the control group.

A variant of the no-treatment control group is the wait-list control group. In this design, when patients are seen initially, they are told there is a waiting list for assignment to therapy but that they will be called as soon as an opening occurs, and they are promised that they will be given therapy. In the study by Sloane and coworkers (1975), the patients were told that they would definitely be assigned to therapy within four months at the latest since this was the period of therapy evaluated.

Although a no-treatment or wait-list control group adds considerably to the value of a study attempting to appraise outcome in psychotherapy, this type of research design also has been criticized by some as not being completely satisfactory (Paul, 1967). This criticism is concerned essentially with the variables that are presumed to be of significance in affecting change. For example, if a research study indicates that significantly greater changes are secured by means of psychotherapy than is the case with no treatment, are the results really attributable to the stated psychotherapeutic procedures or are they attributable to some other possible variables? Could it be that instead of the hypothesized variables in psychotherapy producing the change secured, it is simply having an opportunity to talk to someone that is responsible for the obtained improvement? This point of view appears to derive largely from work in the area of pharmacology on the so-called placebo effect (Shapiro & Morris, 1978). As discussed in an earlier chapter, in testing drugs it has been found that some individuals will respond positively to any type of medication or pill, even if it contains ingredients which are physiologically inert. That is, the mere taking of a pill seems to have a therapeutic effect, regardless of what the pill contains. Thus, in research on new drugs, the experimental drug is usually compared with a placebo which resembles it in appearance and also tastes as much as possible like it. If similar results are secured from the two pills, even if they are very positive, the effects of the experimental medication are judged to be due to the placebo effect rather than to the specific medication. Only if the "real" drug produces a decidedly superior result as compared with the placebo will it be judged to be an effective pharmacological agent.

Because of this, some psychotherapy researchers made use of what was termed an "attention-placebo" group. One of the difficulties in using an attention-placebo group beyond the ethical concerns involved, was in making the attention-placebo procedures believable and realistic. In order to have an effective control group of this kind, the rationale and procedures devised for the research investigation must have credibility, but at the same time, must not utilize procedures which are part of the psychotherapy being investigated. It is not easy to design such procedures and many of those that were devised, varied greatly in their comparability and utility (Garfield, 1983b).

There would appear to be little question that well-designed and controlled studies can contribute much more valuable information to our knowledge of psychotherapy than can uncontrolled studies. Research that is worth doing is worth doing well. However, there are many other kinds of research which are not primarily involved with the effectiveness of psychotherapy and which do not necessarily require the use of complicated control groups. Among these are studies of prognosis in psychotherapy, the matching of therapist and patient, premature termination, the significance of structure or therapist activity in therapy, and the like. Each of these types of studies has different concerns, but the matter of a controlled study in terms of controlling significant variables is just as important here as in the use of control groups in the study of outcome. No matter what one is studying, one needs to control for the influence of chance or extraneous variables if he or she is interested in how a specific variable or variables affect some criterion variable. If there is no control over such influences, it is difficult to conclude that a particular cause is responsible for the results secured. It is only when we can draw conclusions with at least some degree of confidence that we can advance our knowledge.

STATISTICAL AND CLINICAL CONSIDERATIONS

Another matter worth discussing here pertains to various statistical and clinical considerations regarding the significance of the results obtained through research. No attempt will be made here to discuss the intricacies of research design and statistical analysis since good reference sources are available elsewhere (Kazdin, 1994). Rather, some points of importance for the psychotherapist who follows the literature in his field will be discussed.

Statistics and statistical analyses are important aids in research. They help us to understand the data and results that have been obtained in research investigations and they allow us to make various appraisals and comparisons between different sets of results. There is one area, however, in which their value is sometimes misinterpreted or incorrectly appraised. This has to do with various statistical measures used to determine the significance of the findings secured in a particular study. For example, if two groups of subjects are compared statistically after treatment on the basis of the differences secured, a test of significance is used and the results are reported as reaching a certain level of significance. In contemporary research the 0.05 and 0.01 levels of statistical significance are commonly used. When a finding is reported to be significant at the 0.05 level, this denotes that the result obtained could have been secured by chance about 5 percent of the time. Thus, the interpretation is made that because a chance occurrence of this type is very unlikely, the results are considered to be significant—that is, not due to chance. This is the value of such statistical tests of significance, for they allow you to make some judgment about the probability that the findings obtained are simply chance fluctuations. The size of the groups, their variability, and the

actual differences obtained will all influence the resulting level of significance. However, such measures only tell you part of what may be important
to the professional clinician. They tell one about *statistical* significance, but
not about *clinical* significance.

If an investigator has large samples of subjects, a small difference may
actually turn out to be statistically significant, that is, not due to chance.
However, the difference may be so small that it is of little practical value.
It may suffice for some purposes, but be inadequate for clinical purposes.
In order to make a decision or judgment for practical purposes, other kinds
of criteria have to be employed. Basically, the issue is not merely whether
a finding is statistically significant, but also how much of the variance between the variables studied is accounted for by the findings secured. For
example, let us assume that we are comparing two types of treatments and
that treatment A is found to be significantly better statistically than treatment B. When we go beyond the test of significance and examine the actual results obtained, however, we discover that the patients receiving
treatment B show a slight decrease in status, whereas those receiving treatment A have improved a small amount. While the difference between the
two groups is statistically significant, the actual gain shown by the patients receiving treatment A is so small that it appears to be of relatively
little clinical value. Or, it may be that upon examining the results carefully, we note that only 15 percent of the patients receiving treatment A actually show what might be termed significant clinical improvement and it
is this small group which appears to account for the significant findings secured. Although this latter finding might be important in terms of seeking
out possible predictive variables for positive response to treatment A, the
overall findings would tend to indicate that this treatment has only limited value for most patients.

Some actual reports in the literature can also be cited to illustrate the point
made previously. In one study which examined possible correlates of premature termination from psychotherapy, it was found that age was significantly
related to such early termination (Sullivan, Miller, & Smelser, 1958). However, the age difference between the terminators and remainers was only two
years and it would be very difficult to apply this finding in any constructive
way. In other words, the actual difference is so small that it is of little clinical utility. In another study evaluating the effectiveness of implosive therapy,
a significant degree of improvement was reported (Levis & Carrera, 1967).
However, an analysis of the scores on the MMPI, one of the criteria used,
showed that the mean score on the schizophrenia scale was reduced by nine
points in the desired direction, from a mean of 83.5 to a mean of 74.1. The
final score obtained was still indicative of serious pathology even though there
was a *statistically* significant degree of improvement. Clinical judgments of

improvement would also be important in deciding how significant this degree of improvement really was.

Thus, statistical significance, while an important and necessary require-ment in research on psychotherapy, is not necessarily sufficient in reaching clinical judgments about the effectiveness of particular approaches and pro-cedures in psychotherapy. One must also examine the data provided by the investigator in order to appraise the extent of the changes secured. For this reason, it is important that the research report contain adequate and suffi-cient data in order that the reader can evaluate and interpret the findings presented. The presentation of data is extremely important, and this is an ob-vious advantage which systematically reported research has over narrative accounts or clinical reports. The investigations which have been discussed above did present sufficient data so that the reader could evaluate critically the research reported.

It should be clear that the author is not criticizing the use of statistics in research on psychotherapy since statistical procedures are essential research tools and provide us with significant information. What is being discussed and evaluated here is the meaning of statistically significant results as com-pared with the possible clinical significance of the results secured. Like any other tools, statistics may be inappropriately applied and misused. However, they make a valuable contribution when used intelligently and appropriately. It is the author's practice to disregard findings that lack statistical signifi-cance even though a number of investigators sometimes try to make much of "trends" in their findings which have failed to reach an acceptable level of sig-nificance, but which appear to be in the desired direction. In other words, sta-tistical significance is a necessary but not necessarily sufficient condition for judging the practical significance of a set of research results. One must also determine how much of the variance is accounted for by the particular findings at hand before one can make a more reasoned judgment. For exam-ple, the correlation between height and intelligence has usually been reported as being somewhere in the neighborhood of 0.15. Large samples of subjects have been studied and the finding is significant statistically and thus a reli-able one. If future large scale samples are tested one can expect that the re-sults will not vary too much from 0.15. However, this finding accounts for only about 2 percent of the variance, and thus, height is not considered a very good predictor of intelligence.

It is unfortunate that sometimes essential data for evaluating the results of a study are not included in the published report. However, in most cases it is possible to make some appraisal of the data presented and to reach at least some tentative conclusions about the utility of the research reported. Mean or average scores are not always informative and one should scan the distri-bution of scores if they are available, as well as the percentage of cases which attain certain scores or levels of improvement. In this way, the reader may get a better and more concrete picture of what has taken place. Two groups with comparable means may have very different distributions and this finding may be of some value. For example, in one instance practically all of the patients may show modest gains, whereas in another instance, a certain number may show very large gains although the majority of the patients show little or no gain at all. In the latter instance, it is possible that the particular approach may be very effective with certain kinds of patients, or that a small number of therapists were particularly effective and accounted for most of the overall change that was secured.

Before concluding this section, it is important to mention one other aspect of psychotherapy research that has clear clinical relevance. Here I refer to the issue of adequate follow-up research after treatment completion. In essence, how lasting are the effects of psychotherapy? Securing data to answer this question adequately is a difficult and complicated task.

As already indicated, conducting clinically important and scientifically adequate research on psychotherapy is a complex undertaking. Securing the necessary number of subjects who meet our research criteria, using qualified psychotherapists, avoiding significant attrition from both patients and therapists, utilizing adequate measures of outcome, carrying out appropriate statistical analyses, and preparing clear accounts of the research project at the completion of treatment require considerable time and effort from those conducting the research project. However, despite the effort involved, such reports tell us only about the efficacy of therapy at the end of treatment. To provide answers on how long treatment outcomes will last, a follow-up study is required and new problems then are encountered. Therapists and investigators may move during this interval as well as subjects. It may be difficult to maintain contact with subjects and to have them complete outcome measures. Adequate funding may also be difficult to secure since the longer a research study lasts, the more expensive it becomes. The length of the post-treatment follow-up is also of some importance. There is no absolute time period that has been set down from on high. One or two months is too short, and several years may be too long for most studies. The type of problem evaluated would influence the length of follow-up.

Although I believe most individuals would endorse the importance of follow-up studies, differences of opinion do exist. In one review of a number of follow-up studies with an average follow-up period of about seven months, the results were generally stable and follow-up studies were not considered required for most studies (Nicholson & Berman, 1983). However, the more recent results of the NIMH Treatment of Depression Collaborative Research Program tell a different story (Shea et al., 1992). Clearly, individual clinical judgment is required in making an appropriate decision.

SOME GENERAL OBSERVATIONS ON RESEARCH IN PSYCHOTHERAPY

Although we have made considerable progress in research methodology and in our knowledge of psychotherapy as a result of research conducted since the previous edition of this book was published, this does not mean that there is no need for continued research. There is still too much deference toward individuals who speak with authority and conviction and people are still swayed by those who make glowing promises and claim to have the key to the promised land. It sometimes seems as if it is sufficient merely to be told that a particular approach is very effective. Too infrequently are research data requested to support a particular claim or pronouncement. Apparently psychotherapists, like other lesser humans, also believe what they want to believe, rather than manifesting a desire for evidence, although probably a majority of psychotherapists have received some scientific and research training.

I would like to propose the view that every professional psychotherapist has some responsibility to contribute in some way to the advancement of our knowledge of the field. For some practitioners this may take the form of participating as a therapist in some kind of clinical or research investigation or in contributing some of his work with patients to a broader cooperative research project. Not everyone is capable of devising or directing a research project on psychotherapy. This involves a great deal of time and expertise. However, most psychotherapists can contribute in various ways. Another simple procedure is to try to objectify one's own work and to make one's own case files more systematic. Instead of just writing narrative notes in the file, the psychotherapist could at least use a simple rating scale and strive to make as objective ratings as possible at the beginning and end of therapy. If it serves no other purpose, it may at least help the therapist to be more concerned with the outcomes he or she secures in psychotherapy and with the need for evaluation. More systematic record keeping may also allow the psychotherapist to be more readily able to profit from his/her past experience with certain types of cases and to formulate hypotheses which later might be tested by means of more systematic investigation. Furthermore, if individual clinicians get into the habit of trying to be more objective and systematic in the evaluation of their own work, they are more likely to be agreeable to participating in a research project carried out in their own center or to collaborate in other ways.

It is certainly understandable that many psychotherapists are reluctant to carry out research or to participate in research projects carried out by others (Bednar & Shapiro, 1970). There is a natural concern about exposing oneself to others and there also appears to be some suspicion of researchers on the part of clinicians. It is as if the latter believe that the former are out to expose or discredit their work. It is also true that the demands placed upon clinicians to fill out forms or to adhere to certain research protocols are sometimes time-consuming and difficult, and there is no particular reward for the person who cooperates. In fact, he may even be shown to be an ineffective therapist! For such reasons, it is understandable that many practicing therapists may not be particularly eager to participate in research projects.

There are also some other reasons given by therapists for not participating in research investigations which do not appear as valid as the reason given above. Some believe that the extra demands placed on the patient for taking tests or completing forms interferes with the process of psychotherapy. Some therapists have even been opposed to taping their therapy sessions for reasons such as this. However, in many instances such complaints do not appear to be fully justified, but, instead, reflect either a defensiveness on the part of the therapist or a negative view of research. A large number of studies have been carried out without any apparent negative effects on the patients and tape recordings of therapy sessions today are standard procedures in most training and clinical centers. In fact, even videotaping of families appears to have no real interfering effect on the interactions that occur between the family members.

If research is to take place in a clinical setting, it is important that the research investigators consider the demands they are making on the clinical staff and the potential threat they constitute, and plan accordingly. They should meet with those who are being asked to participate and give them some general understanding of the proposed project and its importance for the field of psychotherapy. Although certain aspects of the research may have to remain secret in order not to bias the results to be obtained, some general orientation to the project and its overall rationale should be provided. It is desirable that discussions be held with the staff so that ambiguities can be clarified and their own doubts and misgivings be explored and answered. It is also desirable to ask them for suggestions so that they feel more like professional collaborators instead of people who are being used or exploited. It is also extremely important to emphasize and to guarantee the complete confidentiality of the project so that the work of any individual staff member remains completely anonymous, and even the identity of the clinic withheld if this seems to be reasonable. It is also a sound procedure to provide the participants with a report of the overall results secured since they can be presumed to have more than a passing interest in the results secured and deserve such personal consideration.

It is indeed unfortunate that a number of professional psychotherapists have a rather negative view of the value of research on psychotherapy. There are some who adhere strongly to the view that psychotherapy is a distinctly personal affair and that the research is a contrived and quantitative affair which can never get at the essence of the process and, consequently, is of little value. Such individuals are not swayed or influenced in any manner by research data and, perhaps, research will have no effect on their work as psychotherapists. Most psychotherapists, however, probably would not fall into this category. A number of these, nevertheless, would state that much of the research which has been done is of little direct value or relevance for them. There is some justification for this view since a number of studies in the past have used college students or volunteers as subjects, have used quite brief periods of therapy, have employed students in training as therapists, and have utilized certain measures of outcome which may not be of direct clinical concern. To the extent that these limitations exist, the criticisms made of research are justified. However, such criticisms do not apply to all research studies, and the level of research has increased noticeably in more recent times. Recent reviews of research provide evidence of the utility of research findings, as well as indicating the lacks in our current knowledge (Bergin & Garfield, 1994).

Many psychotherapists also appear to over react to the possible difficulties of doing research and, consequently, come to feel that research is too complicated for them. It is important to recognize that there are many types and levels of research possible, and that they may serve different purposes. Certain kinds of systematic data collection, for example, may be of real practical value for a specific clinical setting or provide a basis for more refined research investigations. Most clinical settings are potential sources of data, and more systematic procedures for securing and recording data would allow for many types of clinical research investigations. Such types of information as actuarial data on the patients seen, the number of sessions missed, the average length of treatment, average time on the waiting list, the relationship of certain variables to early termination or to measures of outcome, patterns of performance of individual therapists, and many more could be secured in most clinical settings with the proper planning, interest and just a little extra effort. Certainly, the advances in computer technology make such tasks relatively simple operations. Furthermore, although many of these types of analyses may not be seen as conclusive research or as work which merits its publication, they can provide information which is of real value to the clinical facility in appraising the work of the center and in identifying problems which have not received adequate attention previously.

The type of clinical research just described may also be a step toward planning a more rigorous type of investigation which might have implications beyond the particular setting involved. For example, if an analysis of accumulated data revealed a possible relationship between time on the waiting list and the refusal of psychotherapy, a study could be planned and initiated in which new patients were randomly assigned either to the waiting list or to immediate therapy and the results analyzed. This would be a more definitive test of the hypothesis in question. Other comparable kinds of studies might also be undertaken, depending upon the types of data secured or the particular interests of certain members of the staff. Such research should be seen as a regular and important part of the clinic's functions, for in the long run, such investigations may help in the identification of clinical problems and in the improvement of clinical services and procedures.

Research should not be viewed as some esoteric or ethereal activity which is engaged in by others and which is far removed from the realities of professional existence. On the contrary, it can be of potentially great practical value and definitely can be carried out in many clinical settings. It need not and should not necessarily be divorced from ongoing clinical activities. In fact, the more directly research is performed on clinical problems of a practical nature, the more directly relevant may be the results secured. Research and the evaluation of clinical services are essential if we are to move beyond the existing state of practice and to make our procedures more effective and more efficient.

There are, thus, many aspects to research on psychotherapy and many kinds of research that can be done. Even single case studies can be studied in a systematic manner and offer leads and information of potential value (Barlow & Hersen, 1984; Kazdin, 1992; Lazarus & Davison, 1971). Some research can be done in a relatively straightforward and simple manner while other types may have to be carried out with complex designs and statistical analyses. At the same time, for reasons already discussed, not all research is of equal value. The psychotherapist must be able to evaluate critically the research reports he scrutinizes and when he is in doubt concerning certain procedures or results, he should consult with others who may be more knowledgeable about such matters. When planning a research project, it may be wise to get expert consultation. However, when discussing such matters with so-called experts, the clinical investigator should be sure that he understands what is being suggested and not let his project become so modified that it is no longer the project he was interested in doing. With proper discussion, the final project should be a better plan for investigating the problem which he is interested in pursuing. As is true of other endeavors, what is worth doing is worth doing well, and poor research will only provide poor answers.

REFERENCES

Auerbach, A. H., & Johnson, M. (1977). Research on the therapist level of experience. In A. S. Gurman & A. M. Razin (Eds.), *Effective psychotherapy: A handbook of research*. Oxford: Pergamon.

Barlow, D. H., & Hersen, M. (1984). *Single-case experimental designs: Strategies for studying behavior change* (2nd ed.). Elmsford, NY: Pergamon.

Bednar, R. L., & Shapiro, J. G. (1970). Professional research commitment: A symptom or a syndrome. *Journal of Consulting and Clinical Psychology, 34*, 323–326.

Bergin, A. E., & Garfield, S. L. (Eds.) (1994). *Handbook of psychotherapy and behavior change* (4th ed.). New York: Wiley.

Berzins, J. I. (1977). Therapist-patient matching. In A. S. Gurman & A. M. Razin (Eds.), *Effective psychotherapy. A handbook of research* (pp. 222–251). Oxford: Pergamon.

Beutler, L. E., Machado, P. P. P., & Neufeldt, S. A. (1994). Therapist variables. In A. E. Bergin & S. L. Garfield (Eds.), *Handbook of psychotherapy and behavior change* (4th ed.) (pp. 229–269). New York: Wiley.

Garfield, S. L. (1983a). *Clinical psychology. The study of personality and behavior* (2nd ed.). Hawthorne, NY: Aldine.

Garfield, S. L. (1983b). Commentary. Does psychotherapy work? Yes, no, maybe? *The Behavioral and Brain Sciences, 6,* 292–293.

Garfield, S. L. (1987). Ethical issues in research on psychotherapy. *Counseling and Values, 31,* 115–125.

Garfield, S. L. (1992). Major issues in psychotherapy research. In D. K. Freedheim (Ed.), *History of psychotherapy: A century of change* (pp. 335–359). Washington, DC: American Psychological Association.

Garfield, S. L., & Kurz, M. (1952). Evaluation of treatment and related procedures in 1216 cases referred to a mental hygiene clinic. *Psychiatric Quarterly, 26,* 414–424.

Garfield, S. L., Prager, R. A., & Bergin, A. E. (1971). Evaluating outcome in psychotherapy: A hardy perennial. *Journal of Consulting and Clinical Psychology, 37,* 320–322.

Horenstein, D., Houston, B., & Holmes, D. (1973). Clients', therapists', and judges' evaluations of psychotherapy. *Journal of Counseling Psychology, 20,* 149–153.

Kazdin, A. E. (1992). *Research design in clinical psychology* (2nd ed.). Boston: Allyn & Bacon.

Kazdin, A. E. (1994). Methodology, design, and evaluation in psychotherapy research. In A. E. Bergin & S. L. Garfield (Eds.), *Handbook of psychotherapy and behavior change* (4th ed.) (pp. 19–71). New York: Wiley.

Krupnick, J., Shea, T., & Elkin, I. (1986). Generalizability of treatment studies utilizing solicited patients. *Journal of Consulting and Clinical Psychology, 54,* 68–78.

Lambert, M. J. (1989). The individual therapist's contribution to psychotherapy process and outcome. *Clinical Psychology Review, 9,* 469–485.

Lambert, M. J., & Hill, C. E. (1994). Assessing psychotherapy outcomes and processes. In A. E. Bergin & S. L. Garfield (Eds.), *Handbook of psychotherapy and behavior change* (4th ed.) (pp. 72–113). New York: Wiley.

Lazarus, A. A., & Davison, G. C. (1971). Clinical innovation in research and practice. In A. E. Bergin and S. L. Garfield (Eds.), *Handbook of psychotherapy and behavior change* (pp. 196–213). New York: Wiley.

Levis, D. J., & Carrera, R. (1967). Effects of ten hours of implosive therapy in the treatment of outpatients: A preliminary report. *Journal of Abnormal Psychology, 72,* 504–508.

Lieberman, M. A., Yalom, I. E., & Miles, M. B. (1973). *Encounter groups: First facts.* New York: Basic Books.

Luborsky, L., McLellan, A. T., Woody, G. E., O'Brien, C. P., & Auerbach, A. (1985). Therapist success and its determinants. *Archives of General Psychiatry, 42,* 602–611.

Marks, I. (1978). Behavioral psychotherapy of adult neurosis. In S. L. Garfield & A. E. Bergin (Eds.), *Handbook of psychotherapy and behavior change* (2nd ed.) (pp. 493–547). New York: Wiley.

Nicholson, R. A., & Berman, J. S. (1983). Is follow-up necessary in evaluating psychotherapy? *Psychological Bulletin, 93,* 555–565.

Orlinsky, D. E., & Howard, K. I. (1980). Gender and psychotherapeutic outcome. In A. M. Brodsky & R. T. Hare-Mustin (Eds.), *Women and psychotherapy* (pp. 3–34). New York: Guilford.

Parloff, M. B., Waskow, I. E., & Wolfe, B. E. (1978). Research on therapist variables in relation to process and outcome. In S. L. Garfield & A. E. Bergin (Eds.), *Handbook of psychotherapy and behavior change* (2nd ed.) (pp. 233–282). New York: Wiley.

Patterson, G. R. (1971). Behavioral intervention procedures in the classroom and in the home. In A. E. Bergin & S. L. Garfield (Eds.), *Handbook of psychotherapy and behavior change* (pp. 751–775). New York: Wiley.

Paul, G. L. (1967). Insight versus desensitization in psychotherapy two years after termination. *Journal of Consulting Psychology, 31,* 333–348.

Shapiro, A. K., & Morris, L. A. (1978). Placebo effects in medical and psychological therapies. In S. L. Garfield & A. E. Bergin (Eds.), *Handbook of psychotherapy and behavior change* (2nd ed.) (pp. 369–410). New York: Wiley.

Shapiro, M. B. (1966). The single case in clinical-psychological research. *Journal of Genetic Psychology, 76,* 3–23.

Shea, M. T., Elkin, I., Imber, S. D., Sotsky, S. M., Watkins, J. T., Collins, J. F., Pilkonis, P. A., Beckham, E., Glass, D. R., Dolan, R. T., & Parloff, M. B. (1992). Course of depressive symptoms over follow-up. Findings from the National Institute of Mental Health Treatment of Depression Collaborative Research Program. *Archives of General Psychiatry, 49,* 782–787.

Sloane, R. B., Staples, F. R., Cristol, A. H., Yorkston, N. J., & Whipple, K. (1975). *Psychotherapy versus behavior therapy.* Cambridge: Harvard University Press.

Strupp, H. H., & Hadley, S. W. (1977). A tripartite model of mental health and therapeutic outcomes: With special reference to negative effects in psychotherapy. *American Psychologist, 32,* 187–196.

Sullivan, P. L., Miller, C., & Smelser, W. (1958). Factors in length of stay and progress in psychotherapy. *Journal of Consulting Psychology, 22,* 1–9.

Truax, C. B., & Carkhuff, R. R. (1967). *Toward effective counseling and psychotherapy.* Chicago: Aldine.

CHAPTER 13

Evaluating the Effectiveness of Psychotherapy

In the previous chapter we have discussed some of the important considerations in conducting research on psychotherapy. In this chapter, our primary focus will be on research that has attempted to evaluate the effectiveness of psychotherapy—an important goal of research on psychotherapy.

During the first half of the present century there was relatively little research conducted on evaluating the outcome of psychotherapy and there was relatively little concern about this matter. In 1952, however, the British psychologist, Hans Eysenck published his critical appraisal of 24 studies and concluded that there was no evidence to support the effectiveness of psychotherapy. Needless to say, this article and its strong negative conclusion was not received by psychotherapists with any degree of enthusiasm. Whether or not Eysenck's critique acted as a catalyst, in the following 40 plus years a considerable amount of research has been produced. However, the controversy about the effectiveness of psychotherapy has not fully subsided. In the remainder of this chapter, we shall review some of the major research studies and reviews concerned with psychotherapy's effectiveness and with the increased concerns expressed for demonstrating its effectiveness.

IMPORTANT EARLIER STUDIES AND REVIEWS OF THE EFFECTIVENESS OF PSYCHOTHERAPY

As already indicated, there were a number of critical rebuttals to the negative review of the effectiveness of psychotherapy by Eysenck (1952). These responses pointed to a number of problems in Eysenck's review which were noted in the previous edition of this book (Garfield, 1980). Undaunted by such criticisms, Eysenck (1961) extended his evaluations of psychotherapy with an analysis of additional studies and devoted greater attention to the results of more recent studies which used control groups. His conclusions this time were even somewhat stronger than those presented earlier, although he did have a kind word for behavior therapy:

> With the single exception of the psychotherapeutic methods based on learn-
> ing theory, results of published research with military and civilian neurotics,
> and with both adults and children, suggest that the therapeutic effects of psy-
> chotherapy are small or non-existent, and do not in any demonstrable way
> add to the non-specific effects of routine medical treatment, or to such events
> as occur in the patients' everyday experience. (Eysenck, 1961, p. 720)

This evaluation was updated and published along with comments from a
number of knowledgeable people in the field who represented diverse views
(Eysenck, 1965, 1966). Again, there were a number of critical comments
from psychotherapists who stated that Eysenck had overstated and biased
his case, although others agreed that Eysenck's presentation had merit. Although it sometimes appeared as if Eysenck were single-handedly taking on
the field of psychotherapy, in these later critiques he had assembled a large
amount of research data to support his views. Although some of his analyses and conclusions could be fairly contested, in a real sense he hurled a
challenge to his critics to present data to support their views.

The next really significant response to Eysenck's appraisal came from
Bergin's (1971) extensive review of the outcome literature, although the volume by Meltzoff and Kornreich (1970) also contained an extensive review
of outcome studies and reached more positive conclusions that those secured
by Eysenck. Bergin was critical of Eysenck's interpretation of data reported
by the Berlin Psychoanalytic Institute and of the high spontaneous remission
rate posited by Eysenck. Although both Eysenck and Bergin reported almost identical improvement rates for the eclectic psychotherapies, 64 percent and 65 percent respectively, the interpretations of the other data
mentioned led to very different conclusions. Undoubtedly, the inadequacy of
the data evaluated at the time was in part responsible for the differing interpretations made.

Two other reviews and an important study can also be mentioned here.
Luborsky, Singer, and Luborsky (1975) compared the effectiveness of different kinds of psychotherapy based on studies that had included some type
of control group. The latter varied for the 33 studies evaluated and included
"no psychotherapy," "a wait-group," "minimal psychotherapy," or just hospital care without psychotherapy. In the overall comparison or "box score," 20
of the 33 studies, about 61 percent, showed psychotherapy to be significantly
more effective than the control condition, in 13 of the studies there were no
differences between psychotherapy and controls, and in none of the studies
was the control group more effective than the psychotherapy group. These results were generally supported in the comprehensive review by Bergin and
Lambert (1978). The latter critically reviewed important studies and reviews
but only a very brief reference will be made to it here. They concurred that
of the therapies evaluated, the results achieved were superior to the various

control conditions. They also noted the relatively few differences secured between the therapies evaluated, the growing trend for eclecticism, and concluded with a discussion of measurement issues and recommendations for future research on assessing outcome in psychotherapy.

One of the best known studies conducted during this period was that conducted by Sloane, Staples, Cristol, Yorkston, and Whipple (1975) and various references to this study have been made previously in the present book. Noteworthy in this study comparing brief psychoanalytically oriented therapy and behavior therapy were the following:

1. Very experienced and well-known therapists were used.
2. The appraisal of outcome was focused on the three major complaints of the patients.
3. The patients, selected from a regular outpatient population, were deemed appropriate for short-term psychotherapy (4 months duration).
4. A wait-list control group was used.
5. Random assignment of patients were made to treatment and control groups.
6. Independent assessors, blind to type of treatment assessed patients before and after therapy.
7. A list "of stipulative definitions of each treatment was drawn up" (p. 81) and approved by the participants.
8. Tape recordings of the fifth therapy session were made to evaluate the in-therapy behavior of therapist and patients.

Although criticized by some behavior therapists because the behavior therapists in the study were not restricted to just one technique (e.g., systematic desensitization), the study was highly regarded by most reviewers and acknowledged with an award by the Society for Psychotherapy Research. As noted earlier, both therapies did significantly better than the control group on the main complaints evaluated and there was no difference between them. The authors emphasized that client evaluations at the end of therapy generally indicated that the effectiveness of therapy "was due to factors common to both therapies rather than to any particular theoretical orientation or techniques" (Sloane et al., 1975, p. 207).

Thus, by the late 1970s, there were several relatively more sophisticated appraisals of the effectiveness of psychotherapy and they tended to agree on two major findings:

1. Psychotherapy was more effective than no therapy.
2. Few differences were secured among the forms of psychotherapy evaluated.

Although such findings and conclusions were well received by most workers in the field, there were still individuals, both within the field and outside, who still raised questions about the efficacy of psychotherapy (Garfield, 1981, 1983). Let us now turn our attention to the more recent developments in the field.

META-ANALYSIS AND CONCERNS ABOUT THE EFFECTIVENESS OF PSYCHOTHERAPY

Reference has been made to several well-known reviews of the research literature on outcome in psychotherapy. In such reviews, one or more individuals attempt to survey the existing studies and then to make some appraisal of the studies selected. In some instances, certain criteria may be used to select the studies to be evaluated. Regardless of how the research literature was surveyed and appraised, the final review and evaluation was determined by the individual reviewers, and different reviewers might view the same study somewhat differently. This may explain some of the conflicting views expressed about the effectiveness of psychotherapy. However, a procedure was introduced in the late 1970s that was considered to reduce the subjectivity of previous reviews of the effectiveness of psychotherapy. This more systematic procedure was meta-analysis. Although meta-analysis was an important innovation, it has not completely lessened the controversy surrounding issues of effectiveness.

Basically, meta-analysis is a procedure for combining or synthesizing in a systematic manner the results of a number of studies dealing with a specific problem:

> The claimed value for this procedure is that it allows one to analyze studies statistically in a manner comparable to the analysis performed on subjects in an individual study, although studies usually are not selected randomly. In this way, the idiosyncratic, subjective judgments and values of the individual reviewer are apparently minimized.
>
> In essence, once the . . . reviewer has stated clearly the criteria for inclusion of studies, comparisons of the average difference in outcome between treated and control groups are obtained, and expressed in some standard manner. Thus, the data from individual studies can be combined. (Garfield, 1984, p. 297)

The difference between treatments or between treatments and control groups is expressed in standard deviation units as an "effect size." The latter frequently is the mean difference between treated and control subjects divided by the standard deviation of the control subjects or of the pooled sample of both groups. The effect size thus provides a quantitative estimate of the degree of change. Thus, if an effect size of 0.70 is secured favoring the treatment group, one can say that the average person who received therapy is better off than 76 percent of the control group. Cohen (1984) has also classified an effect size of 0.5 as medium and an effect size of 0.8 as large, information that also helps one to interpret effect size. However, expertise in meta-analysis is not the objective of this section nor is the writer really qualified to provide this. Rather, a brief introduction intended to facilitate an understanding of the use of meta-analysis in psychotherapy research is offered here since most reviews of psychotherapy outcome are now reported in this fashion.

The first meta-analysis of this type was published in 1977 and was based on an analysis of 375 studies (Smith & Glass, 1977). This was then followed by a more comprehensive appraisal of 475 studies by Smith, Glass, and Miller in 1980—the largest review of studies on the effectiveness of psychotherapy ever published. In brief, as probably already known to many readers, psychotherapy was judged to be clearly effective. The obtained effect size was 0.85, indicating that 80 percent of the groups receiving psychotherapy exceeded the means of the respective control groups. Needless to say, the findings reported by Smith, Glass, and Miller (1980) were very well received by psychotherapists who viewed them as vindicating their own views. There were also individuals who were critical of the two meta-analyses by Smith and colleagues, prominently among the former were Eysenck (1978) and Rachman and Wilson (1980). Rachman and Wilson's own review, *The Effects of Psychological Therapy* (2nd ed.), also published in 1980, reached quite different conclusions than did Smith et al. (1980). In addition to finding no support for psychoanalysis, they reported only limited data to support the effectiveness of psychotherapy. Behavior therapies, however, were found to be superior to the other therapies.

The lack of complete agreement in interpreting the research results on psychotherapy outcome, despite the positive results reported, has persisted over the years. Some of the criticisms made of many of the research reviews are that many poor studies have been included, that the criteria for inclusion of studies were not clearly spelled out, that many worthwhile studies were excluded, and that many varied types of subject samples were used. For example, the Smith et al. (1980) meta-analysis was criticized for including studies that varied greatly in quality. Additional criticisms were that many essentially non-clinical samples were used, the average age of the subjects was about 23 years, certain problems such as phobias were over-represented, and many of the therapists were relatively inexperienced.

Smith et al. (1980) and also Glass and Kliegl (1983) responded to such criticisms. Among other responses, they pointed out that it is not necessary to discard studies arbitrarily since they can be variously categorized and the influence of potential variables can be evaluated systematically. Various examples were provided in support of their views. For example, few differences were secured in comparing published and unpublished studies and in the results reported for experienced and inexperienced therapists. In fact, one of the distinctive advantages claimed for meta-analysis is that it is possible to discover how a number of substantive issues (type of psychotherapy) or methodological issues (nature of outcome measures) relate to the type of outcome secured (Cohen, 1984).

Thus, although there have been critics of meta-analysis, it has become the currently most accepted method for conducting reviews of research. However, before proceeding to discuss the most recent research, it is desirable to make a brief mention of the social climate surrounding psychotherapy in the 1970s and 1980s, sometimes referred to as the "age of accountability." Several critical books and articles about psychotherapy were published during this time. Such books as Tennov's (1975) *Psychotherapy: The Hazardous Cure* and Masson's (1988) *Against Therapy: Emotional Tyranny and the Myth of Psychological Healing* as well as Gross' (1978) book, *The Psychological Society: A Critical Analysis of Psychiatry, Psychotherapy, Psychoanalysis, and the Psychological Revolution* were all highly critical of psychotherapy. Furthermore, these critical accounts were accompanied by demands from funding sources and legislators for evidence of the effectiveness of psychotherapy. In the February 1, 1980, issue of *Science* an article entitled "Psychotherapy Works, But for Whom?" (Marshall, 1980) characterized the situation as follows:

> The field's most insistent critic at the moment is Congress, which has begun to demand hard clinical proof of psychotherapy's accomplishments before agreeing to finance it under Medicare (*Science*, 4 January). This demand and other demands from within the field for standardization of research have put new stress on attempts to demonstrate that psychotherapy really works. (p. 506)

As a result of such developments, research evaluating the efficacy of psychotherapy was no longer to be viewed as of interest only to researchers, but was of basic importance for the practice of psychotherapy. Some large scale research studies exemplifying the latest advances in research design were arranged and supported by the National Institute of Mental Health (NIMH) and a number of meta-analyses were completed. We shall now turn our attention to one large scale study and to reviews of other recent findings.

THE NATIONAL INSTITUTE OF MENTAL HEALTH (NIMH) TREATMENT OF DEPRESSION COLLABORATIVE RESEARCH PROGRAM

The NIMH collaborative study had a number of desirable features that had been lacking or deficient in most previous research. First of all, a considerable amount of planning and consultation with experts in various related fields led finally to a more carefully designed study. One motivating factor was the need to try a collaborative study of psychotherapy using several different research centers which would all adhere to a common research design. Such a procedure provides a potentially larger sample of subjects and guards against any particular bias on the part of a specific setting. Another reason was to respond to the "increasing demands for 'accountability' from consumers, third-party payers, and policymakers" (Elkin, 1994, p. 114).

Other positive aspects were to focus on one disorder, depression; to compare two forms of psychotherapy that had secured positive results and for which training manuals were available; to use a variety of tested outcome measures; to have a central center for data analysis; to select qualified psychiatrists and clinical psychologists as therapists in the study; to have the training and supervision of the therapists conducted by experts in the designated therapies; and to have some type of adequate control condition. As might be evident, there were no completed studies that were really comparable to the proposed study when it was first being discussed in late 1977. The study was actually begun in a pilot-training phase in 1980 and then continued through 1986. A more complete description of the planning and preparation for the collaborative study is published elsewhere (Elkin, Parloff, Hadley, & Autry, 1985).

The two psychotherapies chosen were cognitive-behavioral therapy (CBT) (Beck, Rush, Shaw, & Emery, 1979) and interpersonal therapy (Klerman, Weissman, Rounsaville, & Chevron, 1984). Selecting an appropriate control group, however, was a more difficult task. Since there was no existing psychotherapy that could be considered an adequate control, it was decided to use the widely studied antidepressant drug, imipramine hydrochloride, as a standard reference condition. It was also decided to use a pill-placebo plus clinical management condition as a control. Because of ethical concerns, discussed in the previous chapter, the clinical management condition included not only management of the medication and side effects but also included support and encouragement. Thus, it was more than just a pill-placebo. Subjects were seen weekly by a psychiatrist and if required, could be removed from the study and appropriate treatment provided.

On the basis of applications for participation in the program, three sites were selected for funding and three other sites were selected for training therapists. The University of Pittsburgh Western Psychiatric Center, the

University of Oklahoma Medical School, and the George Washington University Medical Center were the collaborating research sites selected. Each of them was to provide 20 patients for each of the four research groups who met strict diagnostic selection criteria. The patients consisted of nonbipolar, nonpsychotic depressed outpatients who met the Research Diagnostic Criteria (Spitzer, Endicott, & Robins, 1970) for such disorder and who attained at least a score of 14 on a modified 17-item Hamilton Rating Scale for Depression (Hamilton, 1960, 1967).

In addition to measures of depression and overall functioning, some specific measures related to the individual treatments also were included. Measures of social adjustment and dysfunctional attitudes aimed at appraising features emphasized by interpersonal therapy and cognitive-behavioral therapy respectively were added to the list of outcome measures.

The material presented will suffice as a brief description of the collaborative study. Let us now look at some of the major findings of the study at the end of the 16 weeks of treatment and at the 18 month follow-up period. A total of 239 patients entered treatment and 155, who received at least 12 sessions and at least 15 weeks of treatment, were termed "completers." Other analyses were made of those who received at least 4 sessions and of the total group of 239 patients who entered treatment. We shall mention mainly the results of the completers. More detailed results and summaries are available elsewhere (Elkin, 1994; Elkin et al., 1989; Shea et al., 1992).

A significant reduction in depressive symptomatology and improvement in general functioning over the course of treatment was noted for patients in all four groups. "There was consistent ordering of treatments at termination, with imipramine plus clinical management generally doing best, placebo plus clinical management worst, and the two psychotherapies in between but generally closer to imipramine plus clinical management. . . . On mean scores, however, there were few significant differences in effectiveness among the four treatments in the primary analyses. Secondary analyses, in which patients were dichotomized on initial level of severity of depressive symptoms and impairment of functioning, helped to explain the relative lack of significant findings in the primary analyses. Significant differences among treatments were present only for the subgroup of patients who were more severely depressed and functionally impaired; here there was some evidence of the effectiveness of interpersonal psychotherapy with these patients and strong evidence of the effectiveness of imipramine plus clinical management" (Elkin et al., 1989, p. 971). For the less severely depressed, however, no significant differences among treatments were secured, including the placebo plus clinical management control. Using a score of 6 or less on the Hamilton Rating Scale for Depression as a predefined level of recovery the results secured were quite positive, ranging from 51 percent to 57 percent for the three main treatments and 29 percent for the placebo plus clinical management condition.

Of particular interest was the lack of significant differences secured for the two forms of psychotherapy despite their different theoretical emphases and the specific manualized training received by the two groups of therapists. Not only were there no significant differences between the two psychotherapies on the general measures of depression and overall functioning, but there were few differences on the special measures of social adjustment and dysfunctional attitudes. Consistent with the views presented in the present book, the authors of the report of outcome in the collaborative study stated that "The general lack of differences between the two psychotherapies suggests once again the importance of common factors in different types of psychologically mediated treatment" (Elkin et al., 1989, p. 979).

The data analysis for the follow-up period differs in several ways from the post-treatment analysis just described and were considered "secondary and exploratory as the primary hypotheses . . . concerned outcome in the short-term phase" (Shea et al., 1992, p. 784). Statistical analyses focused mainly on the original sample that entered treatment. The results can be summarized very briefly. Defining recovery as manifesting eight weeks of minimal or no symptoms following the end of treatment, the percentage of recovered patients who remained well during the follow-up period was relatively small and did not differ significantly among the four treatments: "30% (14/46) for those in the cognitive behavior therapy group, 26% (14/53) for those in the interpersonal group, 19% (9/48) for those in the imipramine plus CM group, and 20% (10/51) for those in the placebo plus CM group" (Shea et al., 1992, p. 782). Among those who were considered recovered at the end of treatment on the basis of the Hamilton Rating Scale, the percentage of each group who relapsed with a major depressive disorder ranged from 39 percent to 56 percent, although the number of cases evaluated at follow-up was relatively small ranging from 12 in the placebo group to 25 in the interpersonal therapy group.

As is evident from the material presented, the follow-up results are somewhat discouraging, especially when compared to the positive results secured at the end of treatment. "There were no significant differences among any of the treatment conditions in terms of the proportion of the original sample who recovered and remained well" (Shea et al., 1992, p. 786). Two important conclusions offered by these investigators were:

What is clear from our findings is that 16 weeks of these particular treatments is insufficient treatment to achieve full recovery and lasting remission for most outpatients with MDD (Major depressive disorder). This finding is similar to that of other studies. (p. 786)

The increasing evidence for high rates of relapse and chronicity in patients with depression argues for continued research directed at improving strategies for initial and maintenance treatment. (p. 787)

There are a number of comments that can be made about the collaborative study and I will offer some at the end of this chapter. However, a few brief comments can be made here. The complexity of adequately designed and conducted research on psychotherapy is certainly illustrated in this study as is the importance of adequate follow-up in such research. It should be pointed out also that as the follow-up increases in length, the number of subjects that are available for appraisal diminishes, even with a relatively large sample. Conclusive answers to important issues also cannot be expected from any individual study. It seems reasonable to conclude that one's expectations about outcome in psychotherapy have to be realistic and consider the nature of the problem treated. Clinical depression tends to have a higher rate of relapse or recurrence than many other disorders although good follow-up results have been reported in studies of elderly depressives (Gallagher-Thompson, Hanley-Peterson, & Thompson, 1990). Although one should avoid making a patient dependent on psychotherapy or on a specific therapist, the providing of maintenance or booster sessions when indicated appears to be worthwhile.

SOME CURRENT TRENDS

Discussions about the value of meta-analysis and the effectiveness of psychotherapy still occur. Matt (1989), for example, discussed decision rules for selecting effect sizes in meta-analysis and illustrated the problem by using a random sample of 25 studies from the report by Smith, Glass, and Miller (1980). He identified many more effect sizes and they were about half the size of those reported by Smith et al. (1980). The problem, according to Matt (1989), "arises from the fact that studies . . . often have designs with several time points, treatment groups, or control groups. Hence, many different effect sizes can be computed and different estimates of treatment effectiveness might be obtained" (p. 106).

On the other hand, in a recent appraisal of a large number of meta-analytic reviews, Lipsey and Wilson (1993) reach a clearly positive conclusion about the results obtained. They evaluated 302 meta-analyses of psychological, educational, and behavioral treatments. On separate analyses of 19 general psychotherapy meta-analyses and 23 such reports on cognitive behavioral/behavioral modification meta-analyses, the overall results were generally positive. The median effect sizes for the two groups computed by the writers were respectively 0.72 and 0.62. Although lower than the effect size of 0.85 secured by Smith et al. (1980), they are still clearly positive.

Lipsey and Wilson (1993) discuss some of the problems and issues that have been raised concerning meta-analysis, but reach a firm and positive conclusion." We thus believe that a strongly favorable conclusion about the efficacy of well developed psychological treatment is justified by the results of meta-analytic investigation." (Lipsey & Wilson, 1993, p. 1200).

Recently also, Lambert and Bergin (1994) in their comprehensive review of the research on the effectiveness of psychotherapy summarize the results of 48 meta-analytic reviews of psychotherapy outcome, a number of which were also included in the review by Lipsey and Wilson (1993). Their appraisal is also positive:

Despite some residual difficulties in interpreting results, the overall findings that psychological treatments are in general effective cannot be 'explained away' by reference to methodological weaknesses in the data reviewed or to the reviewing methods. An overwhelming number of controlled studies reveal a positive therapeutic effect when compared with no treatment; and very few reviewers disagree with this basic overall observation." (Lambert & Bergin, 1994, p. 149)

At least a few observations can be made of the current situation with reference to research on the effectiveness of psychotherapy. At present a considerable amount of such research has been completed and the results published. The number of meta-analyses reviewing this body of research has increased noticeably since the first such meta-analysis was published by Smith and Glass (1977). Some controversies about methodological issues in the preparation of meta-analytic reviews continues and some continue to question their real value. Besides such methodological critics there still are individuals who continue to question the efficacy of psychotherapy including our old friend, Hans Eysenck (1992). However, with the available research data that generally tends to support the value of the therapies evaluated, there is little question that today psychotherapy is viewed positively as a treatment for a variety of psychological problems. This is not to proclaim it as a panacea for all psychological disorders. For individuals with mild to moderate problems, psychotherapy may well be the treatment of choice. For more seriously disturbed individuals, medication or medication combined with psychotherapy may be more efficacious. As with any clinical problem, wise professional judgment is required in decision making.

NEGATIVE EFFECTS IN PSYCHOTHERAPY

A final topic pertaining to the issue of the effectiveness of psychotherapy concerns possible negative effects in psychotherapy. We know that not everyone who undergoes psychotherapy achieves a positive outcome. Some show no improvement and some may even appear worse at the end of treatment. Bergin (1971), in an early review of studies with possible indications of what he termed deterioration, estimated that deterioration occurs in about five to ten percent of cases seen in psychotherapy. However, in a later review it was stated that the range of deterioration among studies is so large that no precise estimate can be given (Lambert, Bergin, & Collins, 1977). In their review of the research on marital and family therapy, Gurman and Kniskern (1978) also indicated a probable deterioration rate of five to ten percent. These estimates would suggest then that a small but clinically important portion of those who undergo psychotherapy show some sort of negative outcome. Nevertheless, there is some question about what types of negative outcomes are secured, the seriousness of such outcomes, and their incidence.

Because of such concerns, the 48 studies previously cited by Lambert, Bergin, and Collins (1977) were evaluated critically in a review by Strupp, Hadley, and Gomes-Schwartz (1977). They stated that many, if not most, of the studies reviewed had serious deficiencies and that it was not possible to draw any hard and fast conclusions concerning the frequency of negative effects and the determination of such effects. However, they stated "This is not to suggest that negative effects in psychotherapy do not occur, but that interpretations based on the reported findings must be carefully qualified" (Strupp et al., 1977, p. 28).

A similar view was expressed by Mays and Franks (1985). These authors were critical of the views expressed by Bergin (1971) and by Lambert, Bergin, and Collins (1977) as pointing to therapy and/or the therapist as the main causal factors in producing negatives effects. "Other potential sources of influence upon negative outcome, especially patient characteristics and extra therapeutic events, have been inadequately explored, largely because, by definition, these factors cannot produce negative effects" (Mays & Franks, 1985, p. 4).

The most recent discussion of the research and issues pertaining to negative effects related to psychotherapy is contained in the review of research on the effectiveness of psychotherapy by Lambert and Bergin (1994). It is clear in their review that negative effects may have different causal agents. They state:

> Although negative effects are difficult if not impossible to study in an experimentally controlled way, research more than suggests that some patients are worse as a result of psychotherapy. This does not mean that all worsening is therapy produced. Some cases may be on a progressive decline that no therapist effort can stop. The extent or rate of such negative change or of "spontaneous" deterioration in untreated groups has never been determined,

so there is no baseline from which to judge deterioration rates in treated groups. The alternative is to observe negative change in experiments using treated versus control conditions and to study the specific connections between therapy processes and patient responses. (p. 176)

These authors then go on to discuss and review research on client and technique interaction effects, therapist factors, differential effects across various modalities of therapy (e.g., group, marital), and type of therapy. It seems reasonably clear that patient diagnosis and degree of disturbance do have some relationship to negative outcome, "especially when they are combined with therapeutic techniques that are aimed at breaking down, challenging or undermining habitual coping strategies or defenses" (Lambert & Bergin, 1994, p. 176). There are a moderate number of studies that indicate that the more seriously disturbed patients such as borderline personality disorders and psychotics not only have poorer prognoses but are more likely to show negative effects or deterioration when exposed to more confrontative therapies. Although the research on therapist effects are rather limited, therapists who lack empathy, are strongly challenging, and who push for quick or dramatic results also appear more likely to secure negative outcomes. Even professional mental health workers have experienced some negative effects from their own therapy (Strupp, 1984). The best way to avoid negative effects, therefore, would be to evaluate very carefully the patients for therapy and to be as skillful and empathic as possible in adapting therapy to the problems and needs of the patient.

SOME CONCLUDING COMMENTS

A relatively large amount of research on the effectiveness of psychotherapy has been referred to in this chapter, although a detailed analysis was not attempted. Individuals interested in the latter can consult the appropriate references and the most recent edition of the *Handbook of Psychotherapy and Behavior Change* (Bergin & Garfield, 1994). However, what has been presented should illustrate the important developments that have taken place, the major over-all findings, and some of the major problems and issues pertaining to research on outcome in psychotherapy. A few specific points can be discussed in a bit more detail before we conclude this chapter.

It seems evident that the quality of research has improved and its importance more generally recognized. For example, in the Clinical Practice Guidelines for Depression published by the Agency for Health Care Policy and Research of the U.S. Public Health Service (Depression Guideline Panel, 1993), the recommendations for practice are based to a considerable extent on the available research. At the same time, truly final or definitive decisions have to be held in check since not all problems have been overcome. For example, the NIMH collaborative study of depression was a large scale, expensive study that took over a decade before the final results were published. Nevertheless, only two forms of psychotherapy were evaluated and there were essentially no significant differences between the two supposedly different psychotherapies—a puzzling but rather consistent finding over the years. To attempt to evaluate all of the hundreds of different forms of psychotherapy in truly adequate studies would not only require centuries but might bankrupt our national treasury!

I would also like to comment on one other aspect of current research and here I refer to the use of therapy manuals. The primary reason for using manuals is to insure treatment integrity. If the therapy has not been carried out according to the designated procedures and "rules" for that specific form of therapy, then supposedly valid conclusions cannot be obtained. In essence, by using manuals, researchers are attempting to reduce differences among therapists and to emphasize the type of therapy. However, this raises an issue about external validity. In other words, do such research findings have relevance for the actual therapy that is performed by most psychotherapists in their clinical settings? Most therapists, it would appear, perform in their own individual way and with no particular conformity to a therapy manual. Consequently, research based on the use of therapy manuals may have limited direct relevance for clinical practice. This is indeed an intriguing issue for studies have shown both considerable differences in outcome among therapists (Lambert, 1989; Luborsky et al., 1986; Luborsky, McLellan, Woody, O'Brien, & Auerbach, 1985) and reduced variability as a result of using manuals (Crits-Christoph et al., 1991). Although it has been stated that therapy differences may be due in part, at least, to therapist differences, and therefore manuals are required to reduce these differences (Crits-Christoph & Mintz, 1991), as noted previously, even with the use of training manuals, no marked differences have been secured between the therapies compared. The attempt to minimize therapist differences also raises other issues. Is adherence to a manual the same thing as therapeutic competence? Is the therapeutic approach more important than the overall therapeutic skill of specific therapists or should a competent therapist vary his approach for specific patients?

As is evident from such questions, research has not settled all issues pertaining to psychotherapy. The effectiveness of psychotherapy has received some clear support, but research issues remain concerning the factors that lead to successful outcome. However, research on such matters have shown a definite increase in the past decade (Orlinsky, Grawe, & Parks, 1994).

REFERENCES

Beck, A. T., Rush, A. J., Shaw, B. F., & Emery, G. (1979). *Cognitive therapy of depression. A treatment manual.* New York: Guilford.

Bergin, A. E. (1971). The evaluation of therapeutic outcomes. In A. E. Bergin & S. L. Garfield (Eds.), *Handbook of psychotherapy and behavior change: An empirical analysis* (pp. 299–344). New York: Wiley.

Bergin, A. E., & Garfield, S. L. (Eds.) (1994). *Handbook of psychotherapy and behavior change* (4th ed.). New York: Wiley.

Bergin, A. E., & Lambert, M. J. (1978). The evaluation of therapeutic outcomes. In S. L. Garfield & A. E. Bergin (Eds.), *Handbook of psychotherapy and behavior change* (2nd ed.) (pp. 139–189). New York: Wiley.

Cohen, J. (1984). The benefits of meta-analysis. In J. B. W. Williams & R. L. Spitzer (Eds.), *Psychotherapy research: Where are we and where should we go?* (pp. 332–339). New York: Guilford.

Crits-Christoph, P., Baranackie, K., Kurcias, J. S., Beck, A. T., Carroll, K., Perry, K., Luborsky, L., McLellan, A. T., Woody, G. E., Thompson, L., Gallagher, D., & Zitrin, C. (1991). Meta-analysis of therapist effects in psychotherapy outcome studies. *Psychotherapy Research, 1,* 81–91.

Crits-Christoph, P., & Mintz, J. (1991). Implications of therapist effects for the design and analysis of comparative studies of psychotherapies. *Journal of Consulting and Clinical Psychology, 59,* 20–26.

Depression Guideline Panel. (April, 1993). *Depression in Primary Care:* Vol. 2. Treatment of major depression. Clinical practice guideline, No. 5. Rockville, MD: U.S. Department of Health and Human Services, Public Health Service, Agency for Health Care Policy and Research. AHCPR Publication No. 93–0551.

Elkin, I. (1994). The NIMH treatment of depression collaborative research program: Where we began and where we are. In A. E. Bergin & S. L. Garfield (Eds.), *Handbook of psychotherapy and behavior change* (4th ed.) (pp. 114–139).

Elkin, I., Parloff, M. B., Hadley, S. W., & Autry, J. H. (1985). NIMH treatment of depression collaborative research program. *Archives of General Psychiatry, 42,* 305–316.

Elkin, I., Shea, M. T., Watkins, J. T., Imber, S. D., Stotsky, S. M., Collins, J. F., Glass, D. R., Pilkonis, P. A., Leber, W. R., Docherty, J. P., Fiester, S. J., & Parloff, M. B. (1989). National Institute of Mental Health Treatment of Depression Collaborative Research Program. General effectiveness of treatment. *Archives of General Psychiatry, 46,* 971–982.

Eysenck, H. J. (1952). The effects of psychotherapy: An evaluation. *Journal of Consulting Psychology, 16,* 319–324.

Eysenck, H. J. (1961). The effects of psychotherapy. In H. J. Eysenck (Ed.), *Handbook of Abnormal Psychology* (pp. 697–725), New York: Basic Books.

Eysenck, H. J. (1965). The effects of psychotherapy. *International Journal of Psychiatry, 1,* 97–178.

Eysenck, H. J. (1966). *The effects of psychotherapy.* New York: International Science Press.

Eysenck, H. J. (1978). An exercise in mega-silliness. *American Psychologist, 33,* 517.

Eysenck, H. J. (1992). The outcome problem in psychotherapy. In W. Dryden & C. Feltham (Eds.), *Psychotherapy and its discontents* (pp. 100–124). London: Open University Press.

Gallagher-Thompson, D., Hanley-Peterson, P., & Thompson, L. W. (1990). Maintenance of gains versus relapse following brief psychotherapy for depression. *Journal of Consulting and Clinical Psychology, 58,* 371–374.

Garfield, S. L. (1980). *Psychotherapy: An eclectic approach.* New York: Wiley.

Garfield, S. L. (1981). Psychotherapy. A 40-year appraisal. *American Psychologist, 36,* 174–183.

Garfield, S. L. (1983). Effectiveness of psychotherapy: The perennial controversy. *Professional Psychology: Research and Practice, 14,* 35–43.

Garfield, S. L. (1984). Psychotherapy: Efficacy, generality, and specificity. In J. B. W. Williams & R. L. Spitzer (Eds.), *Psychotherapy research. Where are we and where should we go* (pp. 295–308). New York: Guilford.

Glass, G. V., & Kliegl, R. M. (1983). An apology for research integration in the study of psychotherapy. *Journal of Consulting and Clinical Psychology, 51,* 28–41.

Gross, M. L. (1978). *The psychological society: A critical analysis of psychiatry, psychotherapy, psychoanalysis, and the psychological revolution.* New York: Random House.

Gurman, A. S., & Kniskern, D. P. (1978). Research on marital and family therapy. In S. L. Garfield & A. E. Bergin (Eds.), *Handbook of psychotherapy and behavior change* (2nd ed.) (pp. 817–901). New York: Wiley.

Hamilton, M. A. (1960). A rating scale for depression. *Journal of Neurology, Neurosurgery, and Psychiatry, 23,* 56–62.

Hamilton, M. A. (1967). Development of a rating scale for primary depressive illness. *British Journal of Social and Clinical Psychology, 6,* 278–296.

Klerman, G. L., Weissman, M. M., Rounsaville, B. J., & Chevron, E. S. (1984). *Interpersonal therapy of depression (I.P.T.).* New York: Basic Books.

Lambert, M. J. (1989). The individual therapist's contribution to psychotherapy process and outcome. *Clinical Psychology Review, 9,* 469–485.

Lambert, M. J., & Bergin, A. E. (1994). The effectiveness of psychotherapy. In A. E. Bergin & S. L. Garfield (Eds.), *Handbook of psychotherapy and behavior change* (4th ed.) (pp. 143–189). New York: Wiley.

Lambert, M. J., Bergin, A., & Collins, J. L. (1977). Therapist-induced deterioration in psychotherapy. In A. Gurman & A. Razin (Eds.), *Effective psychotherapy. A handbook of research* (pp. 452–481). New York: Pergamon.

Lipsey, M. W., & Wilson, D. B. (1993). The efficacy of psychological, educational, and behavioral treatment. Confirmation from meta-analysis. *American Psychologist, 48,* 1181–1209.

Luborsky, L., Crits-Christoph, P., McLellan, A. T., Woody, G., Piper, W., Liberman, B., Imber, S., & Pilkonis, P. (1986). Do therapists vary much in their success? Findings from four outcome studies. *American Journal of Orthopsychiatry, 56*, 501–512.

Luborsky, L., McLellan, A. T., Woody, G. E., O'Brien, C. P., & Auerbach, A. (1985). Therapist success and its determinants. *Archives of General Psychiatry, 42*, 602–611.

Luborsky, L., Singer, B., & Luborsky, L. (1975). Comparative studies of psychotherapies. *Archives of General Psychiatry, 32*, 995–1008.

Marshall, E. (1980). Psychotherapy works, but for whom? *Science, 207*, 506–508.

Masson, J. M. (1988). *Against therapy: Emotional tyranny and the myth of psychological healing.* New York: Atheneum.

Matt, G. E. (1989). Decision rules for selecting effect sizes in meta-analysis: A review and reanalysis of psychotherapy outcome studies. *Psychological Bulletin, 105*, 106–115.

Mays, D. T., & Franks, C. M. (1985). *Negative outcome in psychotherapy and what to do about it.* New York: Springer.

Meltzoff, J., & Kornreich, M. (1970). *Research in psychotherapy.* New York: Atherton Press.

Orlinsky, D. E., Grawe, K., & Parks, B. K. (1994). Process and outcome in psychotherapy—Noch einmal. In A. E. Bergin & S. L. Garfield (Eds.), *Handbook of psychotherapy and behavior change* (4th ed.) (pp. 270–376). New York: Wiley.

Rachman, S. J., & Wilson, G. T. (1980). *The effects of psychological therapy* (2nd ed.). New York: Pergamon.

Shea, M. T., Elkin, I., Imber, S. D., Stotsky, S. M., Watkins, J. T., Collins, J. F., Pilkonis, P. A., Beckham, E., Glass, D. R., Dolan, R. T., & Parloff, M. B. (1992). Course of depressive symptoms over followup. Findings from the National Institute of Mental Health Treatment of Depression Collaborative Research Program. *Archives of General Psychiatry, 49*, 732–787.

Sloane, R. B., Staples, F. R., Cristol, A. H., Yorkston, N. J., & Whipple, K. (1975). *Psychotherapy versus behavior therapy.* Cambridge, MA: Harvard University Press.

Smith, M. L., & Glass, G. V. (1977). Meta-analysis of psychotherapy outcome studies. *American Psychologist, 32*, 752–760.

Smith, M. L., Glass, G. V., & Miller, T. L. (1980). *The benefits of psychotherapy.* Baltimore: The Johns Hopkins University Press.

Spitzer, R. L., Endicott, J., & Robins, E. (1978). Research diagnostic criteria: Rationale and reliability. *Archives of General Psychiatry, 35*, 773–782.

Strupp, H. H. (1984). Psychotherapy research: Reflections on my career and the state of the art. *Journal of Social and Clinical Psychology, 2*, 3–24.

Strupp, H. H., Hadley, S. W., & Gomes-Schwartz, B. (1977). *Psychotherapy for better or worse: An analysis of the problem of negative effects.* New York: Jason Arsonson.

Tennov, D. (1975). *Psychotherapy: The hazardous cure.* New York: Abelard-Schuman (Thomas Y. Crowell).

CHAPTER 14

Psychotherapy: A Concluding Note

In the preceding pages, the author has attempted to present his views of psychotherapy. As a practitioner, teacher and, at times, research worker in the field of psychotherapy for 50 years, my views have been influenced by my own experience, the observations of others, and by serious attempts to keep up with the vast literature in this field. Although not all readers will necessarily agree with my observations and formulations, they may agree that the field has not been static. In the decade and a half since the publication of the first edition of this book, a number of developments have occurred. As noted in the previous pages, the influence and popularity of some traditional approaches such as psychoanalysis have continued to decline, whereas the acceptance and popularity of cognitive-behavioral approaches has increased. This potential trend was actually described in the concluding comments of the first edition as follows:

> Another development noted previously which also appears to offer promise is the appearance of cognitive behavior therapy (Mahoney & Arnkoff, 1978). Although a quite recent development, it has been represented by a number of different therapeutic approaches and procedures, and although all of them may not turn out to be particularly effective, this development may represent a significant change in what many saw as a somewhat parochial school of psychotherapy, behavior therapy. This enlargement and flexibility of orientation manifested within a relatively short period of time by followers of a young and vigorous approach to psychotherapy and behavior change is an unusual and potentially important development. Whether or not it really portends a beginning realization of the limitations of a single approach and the possible rapprochement of some of the different emphases in psychotherapy remains to be seen. However, it is a step in this direction and, therefore, a very welcome development. Furthermore, many of the individuals involved in this development are very able, active and energetic researchers, and one can anticipate continued contributions from them in the future. (Garfield, 1980, p. 290)

It is always satisfying to have made a correct decision!

The popularity of an eclectic approach with a decreased commitment to a single theoretical orientation has also continued. A new development in this area has been the attempt to develop a more systematic integration of two or more different approaches. Although this is a recent and difficult undertaking, it represents a clear recognition of the need to broaden one's approach to psychotherapy and to use procedures and techniques that appear useful for particular patients, regardless of the approach that has produced them (Norcross & Goldfried, 1992; Stricker & Gold, 1993). Although there is a danger that the movement for integration in psychotherapy may produce as many integrated forms of psychotherapy as there currently are of different psychotherapeutic orientations, the rationale for integration is a sound one. Such an emphasis has long been favored by the present author.

> Clearly, individualizing psychotherapy to meet the needs of a particular client appears to be a necessary and sound procedure, and one which requires the use of techniques and procedures which are not limited to any one school of thought. While considerable work is required to enable us to know which procedures will work best with what types of individuals and problems, a recognition and acceptance of such a view is a step in the right direction. (Garfield, 1980, p. 290)

Another very important development is the clear recognition that most of the psychotherapy now conducted in the United States, at least, is brief psychotherapy. Although brief psychotherapy has had advocates for a period of over 70 years, it is only in the last 30 years that brief psychotherapy has achieved real recognition and acceptance. Whereas the dominant psychoanalytic model of therapy emphasized long-term psychotherapy, research on the actual length of most of the psychotherapy conducted clearly indicated the relative brevity of such therapy. Also, in more recent yeas, the reimbursement patterns of third-party payers and related practices have strongly favored brief psychotherapy.

In the previous two chapters, we discussed the important developments pertaining to research on psychotherapy. There has been a significant increase in the amount of research published on psychotherapy in the past 15 to 20 years. In the past 5 years, seven new journals concerned with psychotherapy and psychotherapy research have come into being, attesting to the popularity of both psychotherapy and research.

In previous chapters, we have also discussed the increased quality of psychotherapy research and the problems and difficulties in conducting such research. Not only is research on psychotherapy a complex undertaking that involves the proper selection of research subjects, trained and competent therapists, and adequate measures of psychotherapy process and outcome, but it also requires trained investigators, considerable financial resources, and time. As noted in our discussion of the NIMH Treatment of Depression Collaborative Research Program, it required over a decade to plan and carry out a study of two forms of psychotherapy. Although this study clearly represented the "state of the art" of psychotherapy research, it could only deal with a small segment of the problems that need research in the area of psychotherapy.

The use of meta-analysis has provided a more objective procedure for reviewing research findings, although it is not without its critics. A large number of meta-analytic reviews have been conducted and generally the results tend to be positive for psychotherapy. The more recent trend is to evaluate treatments for specific problems or disorders. There remains a need for continued systematic and well-controlled studies, particularly studies of what in-therapy variables produce or contribute to positive outcome. The matching of client, therapist, and therapy variables has also been emphasized as a potentially important area of future research to increase therapeutic outcome (Beutler, 1991). Interest in more systematic process research on psychotherapy has increased recently and represents a new frontier for expanding our knowledge of the interactions that take place in therapy and their role in therapeutic outcome. Such research is complicated and will not be done overnight (Garfield, 1990).

The current emphasis on health costs and accountability will require more evidence of therapeutic outcome and efficiency on the part of clinics, Health Maintenance Organizations, group practices, and the individual practitioner. Attention will be paid to the number of sessions required, sessions missed, and the type of outcome secured. Thus, all individuals and groups involved in providing psychotherapeutic services not only need to devise and keep adequate records of their patient sessions for such purposes, but adequate therapy notes and tape recordings can provide potentially valuable feedback to the individual therapists. Hopefully, we can learn from our mistakes.

SOME REMAINING ISSUES

Although psychotherapy has become increasingly accepted by both governmental agencies and the population at large, some important issues remain. We have commented previously on the tremendous growth and proliferation of theories and approaches to psychotherapy that have caused some concern about what psychotherapy really is. Although there has been a greater acknowledgment of common factors among the psychotherapies and attempts at integration, considerable diversity exists. Although diversity per se is not necessarily bad, the existence of so many "universal" therapies (good for all ills) does raise some skepticism about the current stage of development in psychotherapy. The more recent appearance of therapies developed for specific disorders is an opposite trend and raises questions about future practice and training.

Until recently, a form of psychotherapy was considered to be applicable to many different psychological disorders and individuals were trained primarily in terms of one orientation. Now, however, we have specific manuals developed for treatment for depression, anxiety disorders, eating disorders, and the like. To meet society's needs for psychological services, shall we train future therapists to be generalists or specialists? If specialists, how many specialties could an individual master? Could individual practitioners survive specializing only in one particular disorder? At present, if you examine the listings in the yellow pages of telephone directories, you will discover that a number of psychotherapists claim expertise in treating children and adults, in conducting individual and group therapy, as well as treating a variety of disorders and addictions.

Who should provide psychotherapeutic services and how should such individuals be trained? This is a complex issue. Because of the way psychotherapy has evolved, there is no recognized profession of psychotherapy that sets up and regulates the standards and qualifications for its practice. Instead we have a number of separate recognized professions, as well as other groups, which engage in some type of psychotherapeutic practice. Professional standards, training requirements, and codes of ethics are regulated by the separate professions, and psychotherapy constitutes just one of the activities of the established professions. In spite of some past attempts to consider the formation of a separate profession of psychotherapy (Kubie, 1954, 1971; Holt, 1971), little progress toward this objective was attained, for reasons already discussed. Thus, varying standards and requirements for the practice of psychotherapy can be expected to continue for at least the near future.

Progress in the identification of the necessary personal requisites of psychotherapists for effective psychotherapy will also depend on renewed research attempts to relate such attributes to positive outcome in psychotherapy. We must move beyond merely listing the ideal characteristics of the psychotherapist to studying what kind of personal qualities and interactions are positively related to outcome. Furthermore, successful completion of training programs that include psychotherapy as an important part of the program should be based on clear demonstrations of skill and successful outcome measured in some objective manner. Anything less than this leads primarily to the perpetuation of the supervisor's biases and a certification of adequacy that is based on criteria other than psychotherapeutic competence. There will also have to be a clearer recognition by all of the established professions that include psychotherapy as one of their main functions that individuals who do not demonstrate a clear competence in psychotherapy must not be graduated or certified as possessing these skills. This objective will not be easy to accomplish because each of the professions is made up of skills and knowledge besides those pertaining to psychotherapy. Consequently, an individual who is bright and otherwise capable, will usually not be held back because of inadequate or deficient skills in psychotherapy. The hope is that such individuals will engage in other professional functions and not in psychotherapy, but this does not always follow and there are no current procedures for handling such a problem. However, a problem it certainly is, and each of the recognized mental health professions has an obligation to the public at large to do something about it.

Questions can also be asked about the training provided by the established professions currently involved in the practice of psychotherapy. Although attempts to set up an ideal training program for a distinctive profession of psychotherapy have not been successful, are the programs currently provided by departments of psychiatry, and psychology, or by schools of social work and nursing actually the best and quickest ways to provide qualified psychotherapists? Each established profession will strongly defend the type of training it provides. However, psychotherapists may not necessarily have to go through current professional programs to become competent therapists. The experimental program devised by Margaret Rioch and her collaborators at the National Institute for Mental Health to train college-educated "middle-age" housewives to become psychotherapists is one source of data (Rioch, 1967; Rioch, Elkes, & Flint, 1965). These rather highly selected housewives received the equivalent of one year of intensive training in psychotherapy, spread over a two-year period and became the most intensively studied and evaluated group of psychotherapists ever. In terms of a variety of criteria, they preformed at least as well as the average professional psychotherapist, even as judged by professional colleagues. In fact, even psychiatrists rated them as performing as well as the average psychologist or social worker, although not quite as well as the average psychiatrist! The study by Strupp and Hadley (1979) of professional therapists and untrained college professors sought out by students showed surprisingly little difference in outcome between the two groups of therapists. Such findings do raise some questions about the significance of current training models and the kind of therapist variables that are important in psychotherapy.

To the extent that individuals with certain personal qualities, but less than full professional qualifications, can perform satisfactorily as psychotherapists, serious questions can be raised concerning the current modes of training and entry into the practice of psychotherapy. Although such concerns were voiced in the previous edition, there has been no clear response to them. At some future point, perhaps, this issue will be considered and responded to appropriately. In clinical settings where adequate supervision from competent and experienced psychotherapists is available, there should be no real difficulty in utilizing nonprofessional therapists who have received some training and have been screened as being potentially capable therapists. The real problem is one of maintaining adequate standards so that the individual's performance as a psychotherapist is adequately evaluated in terms of suitable outcome criteria, a requirement that applies to professional psychotherapists as well. With the increased emphasis on accountability, this may occur in the future. As noted earlier, there has been an increasing demand for evidence that programs and attempts at treatment are really effective and deserving of continued support. Are programs for delinquents, alcoholics, drug addicts, and the like actually effective in meeting their stated aims? Do treatment programs for disturbed children help in preventing later adjustment problems? Although progress has been made in the collection of data concerning treatment outcome, more can be done. Data on length of stay, missed appointments, early termination, outcome in terms of standard measures, and data on individual therapists are merely examples of the types of important information that can be obtained. Such data provide opportunities for self-appraisal for both clinical settings and individual therapists.

CONCLUDING COMMENTS

Psychotherapy has developed from a number of different sources over a period of years and has gradually come to be recognized as a group of procedures and practices devised to help people with a variety of problems encountered in their daily lives. At different times, it has been practiced in different ways and under different auspices. A variety of individuals and professions have offered psychotherapeutic services in a variety of social and cultural contexts ranging from priests, shamans, and witch doctors to physicians, psychologists, psychoanalysts, trainers, and even "quacks" (Frank, 1973; Kiev, 1964). It would appear that people have had a need to confide in others, to talk over problems, to receive advice and suggestions, and even to adhere to certain rituals or modes of treatment. Not only during the comparative present, but even in more remote periods of time, there were different schools of psychotherapy, although they were not so designated and they differed from those of the present day. Most of these forms of therapy also claimed to be effective and the successful healing procedures were passed on to a group of loyal devotees and disciples.

It seems likely that a number of these earlier "psychotherapeutic" systems utilized some of the same common and even some of the specific factors that appear to be operative in most current psychotherapies (Frank, 1973; Torrey, 1972). Later psychotherapies have followed in the path of some of these earlier forerunners, although they have cloaked their procedures with different formulations. To be sure, there have been some new and unique procedures developed, and there is currently more awareness of the possible factors operating in psychotherapy, as well as more sophisticated evaluations of the effectiveness of psychotherapy. Although what have been termed "placebo effects" (Shapiro & Morris, 1978) may have played an important role in the results secured by most of the psychotherapies, we are much more aware of such effects at present, and in comparison with other older forms of therapy, we need not be overly apologetic or beset by feelings of inadequacy. As point out by Shapiro and Morris a few years ago (1978), "Since almost all medications until recently were placebos, the history of medical treatment can be characterized as the history of the placebo effect" (p. 370). They also point out that "Patients took almost every known organic and inorganic substance—crocodile dung, teeth of swine, hooves of asses, spermatic fluid of frogs, eunuch fat, fly specks, lozenges of dried vipers, powder of precious stones, bricks, furs, feathers, hair, human perspiration, oil of ants, earthworms, wolves, spiders, moss scraped from the skull of a victim of violent death, and so on. Throughout medical history patients were purged, puked, poisoned, punctured, cut, cupped, blistered, bled, leached, heated, frozen, sweated, and shocked" (Shapiro & Morris, 1978, p. 370). While one can, perhaps, draw some partial analogy to certain aspects of psychotherapy, on the whole, psychotherapists have used less fearsome methods of treatment. It should also be pointed out that with the increase in scientific knowledge and the improvement in medical training resulting from medical schools becoming affiliated with universities, medicine has shown remarkable progress in the past 60 years or so, and as a profession can be justly proud of its achievements.

Psychotherapy, in spite of some of its current manifestations, has also shown significant progress in recent years and has the potential for even more important advances in the years ahead. The investigative spirit is strong, the hold on the field of traditional approaches has diminished, and there has been a trend for both experimentation and an open eclecticism that is conducive to change and possible progress.

We have adequate research sophistication at present to develop research projects that can provide answers to many of our questions. There is also a greater awareness than ever before of the possible factors which may be operative in facilitating change by means of psychotherapy. Coupled with this, there is also a clearer recognition of our social responsibility for providing as efficient and effective psychotherapeutic services as possible. Thus, while our current knowledge and our current procedures are modest in comparison to what we would ideally prefer, we have made progress and we have a reasonable basis for optimism in the future. If psychotherapists can accept the fact that our knowledge is relative and that we must not only anticipate change, but actively seek it in order to improve our level of practice, then progress will be secured more readily and with less apprehension and concern. In the final analysis, the society we serve and the individuals we seek to help will be the recipients of our efforts to face reality squarely and to improve the work that we do.

REFERENCES

Beutler, L. E. (1991). Have all won and must all have prizes? Revisiting Luborsky et al.'s verdict. *Journal of Consulting and Clinical Psychology, 92,* 226–232.

Frank, J. D. (1973). *Persuasion and healing* (2nd ed.). Baltimore: The Johns Hopkins Press.

Garfield, S. L. (1980). *Psychotherapy: An eclectic approach.* New York: Wiley.

Garfield, S. L. (1990). Issues and methods in psychotherapy process research. *Journal of Consulting and Clinical Psychology, 58,* 273–280.

Holt, R. R. (Ed.) (1971). *New horizon for psychotherapy.* New York: International Universities Press.

Kiev, A. (1964). *Magic, faith, and healing. Studies in primitive psychiatry today.* New York: Free Press.

Kubie, L. S. (1955). The pros and cons of a new profession: A doctorate in medical psychology. In M. Harrower (Ed.), *Medical and psychological teamwork in the case of the chronically ill.* Springfield, IL: Thomas.

Kubie, L. S. (1971). A doctorate in psychotherapy. The reasons for a new profession. In R. R. Holt (Ed.), *New horizon for psychotherapy. Autonomy as a profession* (pp. 11–36). New York: International Universities Press.

Mahoney, M. J., & Arnkoff, D. B. (1978). Cognitive and self-control therapies. In S. L. Garfield and A. E. Bergin (Eds.), *Handbook of psychotherapy and behavior change* (2nd ed.) (pp. 689–722). New York: Wiley.

Norcross, J. C., & Goldfried, M. R. (Eds.) (1992). *Handbook of integrative psychotherapy.* New York: Basic Books.

Rioch, M. J. (1967). Pilot projects in training mental health counselors. In E. L. Cowen, E. A. Gardner, & M. Zax (Eds.), *Emergent approaches to mental health problems* (pp. 110–127). New York: Appleton-Century-Crofts.

Rioch, M. J., Elkes, C., & Flint, A. A. (1965). *National Institute of Mental Health project in training mental health counselors.* Washington, DC: U.S. Department of H.E.W. Public Health Service Publication No. 1254.

Shapiro, A. K., & Morris, L. A. (1978). Placebo effects in medical and psychological therapies. In S. L. Garfield & A. E. Bergin (Eds.), *Handbook of psychotherapy and behavior change* (2nd ed.) (pp. 369–410). New York: Wiley.

Stricker, G., & Gold, J. R. (1993). *Comprehensive handbook of psychotherapy integration.* New York: Plenum.

Strupp, H. H., & Hadley, S. W. (1979). Specific vs. nonspecific factors in psychotherapy. A controlled study of outcome. *Archives of General Psychiatry, 36,* 1125–1136.

Torrey, E. F. (1972). What western psychotherapists can learn from witch doctors. *American Journal of Orthopsychiatry, 42,* 69–76.

Author Index

Subject Index

ABA design, 103
Affect in psychotherapy, 31, 206–208, 209
Age of accountability, 233
Age of client/patient:
  and continuation in therapy, 46
  and outcome in psychotherapy, 53
Analogue studies, 236
Analytically oriented therapy, *see*
  Psychoanalytic therapy
Anxiety, treatment of client/patient, 139,
  167, 204, 210, 217
Appraisal of client/patient, 26, 27, 51
Assertiveness training, 28, 141, 170
Attention-placebo control group, 246
Attitude, of therapist, 78, 84, 85, 153, 227
Availability of psychotherapeutic services,
  11–14
Aversive conditioning, 212, 213

Behavior:
  as a criterion of change, 26, 205
  observation of, 26, 136, 158, 159
  as a variable in psychotherapy, 26,
    208–210
Behavioral change, 205, 206
Behavioral observation, 136
Behavior therapy, 26–28, 205, 206,
  211–214
  cognitive factors, 28, 29
  contribution, 27, 28, 215–216
  description, 26, 211–214
  emphases, 26, 27, 205, 206
  evaluation, 27, 213, 214
  operant emphases, 102–104
  systematic desensitization, 27, 28,
    108–110
Brief psychotherapy, 221–230, 275
  cognitive-behavioral approach, 225
  diversity, 222–225
  focused approach, 226
  interpersonal psychotherapy, 225

managed care, 199, 229, 230, 276
psychodynamic types, 222, 224
suitability for client-patients, 223, 227
training manuals, 263, 277

Cancellation of therapy appointments, 46,
  161, 162
Catharsis, 100–102, 136, 157
Change, *see* Effectiveness of therapy
Client-centered therapy, 23–25
  research, 24
  techniques, 24, 25
  therapeutic conditions, 24, 133
Client/patient, 10–11, 39–60
  acceptance for psychotherapy, 41–44
  acceptance of psychotherapy, 42, 43, 148
  age, 46, 53
  appraisal of, 51, 53, 59, 148–150, 161
  change, 51, 52, 205, 206, 239–243
  characteristics and outcome, 10, 51–60
  communication, 66, 131, 156, 158, 161,
    176
  compliance, 48, 59, 164
  congruence with therapist, 50, 59
  continuation in psychotherapy, 44–51
  degree of disturbance, 40, 53, 54, 55
  demographic variables of, 43, 44
  dependency, 84, 85, 190, 197
  diagnosis, 47, 139
  ego strength or weakness, 53, 54
  expectations, 48–50, 56, 57, 149, 150
  improvement, 51, 52, 59
  intelligence, 56
  likability, 58
  motivation, 10, 50, 57, 59, 195
  negative outcome, 167–269
  perceptions, 51, 78, 137
  persistance, 48
  personality attributes, 47, 48, 53, 54,
    157, 180, 235
  preferences for therapy, 58

Training, 6–9
  and professional disciplines, 6–9, 67, 68
  of therapist, 6–9, 67, 68–70
  variations, 6–9
Transference,
  problems, 19, 99, 202
  relationship, 18, 19, 82, 190

Understanding and insights, 95–99, 135, 136
Uniformity myths, 3, 238

Values:
  and outcome in psychotherapy, 17, 26, 28, 242, 243
  client/patient-therapist similarity, 43, 44, 46, 49, 50
  influence of therapist, 78, 81, 82, 85
Ventilation and emotional expression, 100–102, 206–208

Warmth, 24, 66
Working through, 20